The Longman Companion to
Renaissance Europe 1390–1530

Longman Companions to History

General Editors: Chris Cook and John Stevenson

Now available

The Longman Companion to

Renaissance Europe
1390–1530

Stella Fletcher

LONGMAN

An imprint of PEARSON EDUCATION

Harlow, England · London · New York · Reading, Massachusetts · San Francisco · Toronto · Don Mills, Ontario · Sydney
Tokyo · Singapore · Hong Kong · Seoul · Taipei · Cape Town · Madrid · Mexico City · Amsterdam · Munich · Paris · Milan

Pearson Education Limited
Edinburgh Gate,
Harlow, Essex CM20 2JE, United Kingdom
and Associated Companies throughout the world.

Visit our world wide web site at
http://www.pearsoned-ema.com

© Pearson Education Limited 2000

First published 2000

ISBN 0–582–29881–4 CSD
ISBN 0–582–29882–2 PPR

British Library Cataloguing in Publication Data

A catalogue entry for this title is available from the British Library

Library of Congress Cataloging-in-Publication Data

Fletcher, Stella.
    The Longman companion to Renaissance Europe, 1390–1530 / Stella
Fletcher.
        p.   cm. — (Longman companions to history)
    Includes bibliographical references and index.
    ISBN 0–582–29881–4. — ISBN 0–582–29882–2 (pbk.)
    1. Renaissance.   2. Europe—History—15th century.   3. Europe—
History—1492–1648.   I. Title.   II. Series.
D203.F58   1999
940.2′1—dc21   99–12941
                                                                                    CIP

Set by 35 in 9½/12pt New Baskerville
Produced by Addison Wesley Longman Singapore (Pte) Ltd.
Printed in Singapore

Contents

List of illustrations

List of genealogical tables

Preface

This *Companion* is designed to be of use to a wide range of students who find themselves under the inter-disciplinary umbrella of Renaissance studies, whether their primary interest lies in history, literature, art history or elsewhere. It is hoped that it will answer straightforward questions of the 'who', 'what', 'where' and 'when' variety. The format does not lend itself, however, to answering 'why' questions, though it is fervently hoped that students of the period will assimilate the raw material provided here and be encouraged to devise questions of their own. If they make connections between the various disciplines represented in this volume, then it will have served its purpose.

The format of the *Companion* has been determined by both the primary and secondary sources available for pre-Reformation Europe. While modern history provides the scholar with a great variety and a great quantity of information that is easily adapted to this type of study, sources for the period labelled, for convenience, 'Renaissance' are considerably less uniform and have survived much more patchily. Thus the secondary literature available in English presents the student with a uneven impression of Europe, in which some regions or topics are covered in immense detail – many aspects of the history of fifteenth-century Florence provide cases in point – while others receive only cursory attention. To some extent these strengths and weaknesses are reflected in the material presented here, though an attempt has been made to create a geographical balance as well as an inter-disciplinary one.

It has not proved possible to create a comprehensive picture of even the western half of Europe during a long fifteenth century, let alone the East. Topics have been selected for the ease with which they suit the format of a work of reference. Thus there are some obvious lacunae in the realm of social history, including gender and domestic life, which have received considerable scholarly attention in recent years. Each of the topics which were finally selected was analysed with a view to deciding on the most immediately useful way of presenting the information. Thus a chronological approach seemed appropriate for some and a biographical approach for others. Biographical material has not been placed in a discrete section, because there was a danger that it would overwhelm and unbalance the volume: a reflection of that much-celebrated Renaissance individualism? Readers should therefore make full use of the index, in which the principal reference to an individual appears in bold type. Similarly, there is no general glossary of terms, though particular glossaries are provided where appropriate.

The period 1390 to 1530 was chosen for a combination of cultural and political reasons, commencing as it did with the arrival in Florence of the Greek scholar Manuel Chrysoloras in 1397 and the development of civic humanism shortly afterwards, and concluding with the Sack of Rome in 1527 and the death of Pope Clement VII in 1534. These choices may be considered an Italianate indulgence, though it is hoped that the material covered in this volume provides a reasonably balanced coverage of the political and cultural life of western Europe.

Though the term 'Renaissance' has been employed here as shorthand for 'late medieval and early modern' or 'fifteenth- and sixteenth-century', it is nevertheless fitting to say something about its significance, for this explains the cultural emphasis not only of this volume but also of the abundance of literature generated by the word itself. The term 'Renaissance' (literally 'rebirth'), employed by the nineteenth-century French historian Jules Michelet with reference to the history of his own country, but thereafter inextricably associated with the history of late medieval and early modern Italy thanks to Jacob Burckhardt's seminal *Civilisation of the Renaissance in Italy* (1860), is as evocative as it is nebulous. What was reborn, revived, resurrected? Essentially knowledge of, and enthusiasm for, Greek and Latin literature. The heroes of ancient Greece and Rome lived once more, in the minds, manuscripts and, later, printed books of men of letters. From that root stemmed multi-faceted and interconnected interests in the classical past, its history, personalities, philosophy and ethics, politics, poetry and visual arts. For some, Cicero became the ultimate arbiter of life in civilised society. If Plautus wrote a particular kind of drama, then that was drama to be emulated. In the visual arts, knowledge of classical sculpture was essential to Michelangelo's figures, sculpted and painted; if the ancients emphasised solidity of muscle then he did too, rejecting sinewy, pared-away Gothic. In Rome this obsession was inevitably exceptionally strong, since the Romans lived among or even within the ruins of the ancient civilisation. Yet, in spite of their knowledge of the classical world, devotees rarely deviated from allegiance to Christianity. For the purposes of the present exercise, though, 'Renaissance' is being used to refer to the period of time in which this cultural phenomenon was experienced and any student of the period ought to be able to appreciate the flexibility of the term.

The existence of Rosemary O'Day's *Longman Companion to the Tudor Age* and the more recent *Longman Companion to the European Reformation, c. 1500–1618* by Mark Greengrass means that the politics and culture of early Tudor England, as well as the convulsions of the Reformation, can be dealt with in cursory fashion here. It is, on the other hand, a serious distortion to divide Renaissance from Reformation in so brutal a manner, a fact which all students of the period should be urged to remember. Two other dangerous distortions are, however, avoided, the first being that of the traditionally over-emphasised divide between late medieval and early modern. It is highly improbable that anyone woke on 1 January (or 1 March or 15 March, depending on the preferred calendar) 1501 and declared himself to be an early modern man. Second, in reaction to the privileging of English history in syllabuses at all levels, many of the distinctive preoccupations of fifteenth- and sixteenth-century English historians find no place in this volume. Instead, emphasis is placed rather on connections, political, ecclesiastical and cultural, between England and its neighbours, both insular and continental.

In the preparation of a volume which attempts to balance so many disciplines, advice was sought about what students might require from it and how their requirements might be met. I am, in consequence, grateful to Francis Ames-Lewis, Michael Hicks, Robert Knecht and Shayne Mitchell for the readiness with which they shared their expertise, but particularly to Michael Mallett for commenting in detail on a earlier version of the text. Encouragement and practical assistance was also provided by Chris Aldous, Elaine Anderson, Brenda and Frank Fletcher, Colin Haydon and Colin Jones. Commissioning Editor Hilary Shaw and General Editor John Stevenson repeatedly quelled the anxieties of a novice author.

Stella Fletcher
October 1998

Written with Warwick students in mind

1   Chronology of public events, 1378–1534

The emphasis in this general chronology is on politics and inter-state relations. Intellectual life, the visual arts and extra-European exploration are among the themes treated chronologically elsewhere in this volume.

1378
8 Apr.: Election of Bartolomeo Prignano as Urban VI.
June–Aug.: Revolt of the Ciompi: Florentine wool workers reacted to the economic impact of war with the papacy (War of the Eight Saints) and demanded their own guilds, which they enjoyed for a short while.
9 Aug.: French cardinals at Anagni declared Urban's election invalid.
20 Sept.: Election of Robert of Geneva as antipope Clement VII by rebel cardinals at Fondi created a papal schism.
29 Nov.: Death of Holy Roman Emperor Charles IV.

1381
June–July: Peasants' Revolt in England.
Aug.: Conclusion of the three-year War of Chioggia against Genoa left Venice as the dominant naval power in the Mediterranean.

1384
Florentine conquest of Arezzo.
20 Aug.: Death of Geert Groote, founder of the quasi-monastic Brethren of the Common Life at Deventer and the spiritual revival known as the *Devotio moderna* (modern devotion), with both of which Erasmus was later associated.
31 Dec.: Death of Oxford philosopher and theologian John Wycliffe, whose attacks on ecclesiastical authority and the doctrine of transubstantiation were condemned by the Church, but inspired English Lollards and Bohemian Hussites.

1385
Ottoman conquest of Sofia.
14 Aug.: Portuguese victory at the battle of Aljubarrota ensured their independence from Castile.

1386

18 Feb.: Marriage of Władysław Jagiełło of Lithuania, who converted from paganism to Christianity, and Jadwiga of Poland resulted in the creation of a united Poland–Lithuania, though formal union did not occur until 1401.

May: Giangaleazzo Visconti's coup against his uncle Bernabò, lord of Milan, secured him the entire Visconti inheritance.

1387

War between the khan of the Golden Horde and the Mongol ruler Timur (Tamerlane, d. 1405) until 1396.

9 Apr.: Ottoman conquest of Salonica, the second largest city of what remained of the Byzantine empire.

1388

19 Aug.: Scots defeated the English at the battle of Otterburn.

27 Aug.: Ottomans defeated at Ploshnik by Bosnians allied with Serbia and Bulgaria.

1389

Feb.: Building on Scandinavian fears of German dominance in the region, Margrete of Denmark conquered Sweden and thereby engineered the union of the crowns of Denmark, Norway and Sweden, embodied in the 1397 Union of Kalmar.

15 June: Sultan Murâd I assassinated on the morning of the first battle of Kosovo, in which the Serbians and their allies were massacred, a victory which confirmed Ottoman rule in the Balkans while leaving Constantinople even more isolated.

15 Oct.: Death of the Roman pope Urban VI.

2 Nov.: election of Pietro Tomacelli as Boniface IX.

1390

For four months from **Apr.**, John VII Palaeologos reigned as Byzantine emperor in defiance of his grandfather John V, but with the support of Sultan Bâyezîd. Florentine acquisition of Montepulciano. Outbreak of war between republican Florence and Gian Galeazzo Visconti's Milan, the latter being in expansionist mode; Hans Baron (d. 1988) interpreted this conflict, which lasted until 1402, as a war for the defence of liberty against a tyrannical regime, a Florentine David versus a Milanese Goliath.

1392

League of Bologna formed by Florence, Padua, Ferrara, Mantua and Bologna in an attempt to halt Milanese expansion.

5 Aug.: Charles VI of France suffered his first bout of mental incapacity, after which his uncle Philip the Bold, duke of Burgundy, became the dominant figure in French political life until 1400, when civil war erupted between rival noble factions.

1393
Danubian Bulgaria annexed by the Ottomans.

1394
Sept.: Beginning of the Ottoman land blockade of Constantinople which lasted until 1402, but which Venetians were able to break by sea.
16 Sept.: Death of the Avignonese antipope Clement VII.
28 Sept.: Election of Pedro de Luna as Benedict XIII, the second anti-pope at Avignon.

1395
Gian Galeazzo Visconti of Milan purchased the title of duke from Emperor Wenceslas.

1396
9 Mar.: Twenty-eight years' truce signed at Leulinghen between England and France, under which no further hostilities occurred until 1403, and Charles VI's daughter Isabel married Richard II of England.
25 Sept.: Battle of Nicopolis in Bulgaria, in which the Christian forces of Sigismund of Hungary, Venice and France were led by John the Fearless, future duke of Burgundy, to a decisive defeat at Ottoman hands; Burgundian leadership and financing of this 'crusade of Nicopolis' increased the international standing of these semi-detached French dukes; Sigismund escaped unscathed.
25 Oct.: Charles VI of France became overlord of Genoa until 1409.

1397
20 July: Union of Kalmar formally united the crowns of Denmark, Norway and Sweden.
1 Oct.: Giovanni di Bicci de' Medici transferred his main banking office from Rome to Florence, thereby founding the Medici Bank as generally understood.

1398
French obedience to the Avignonese antipope withdrawn, leaving the kingdom with allegiance to neither claimant until 1403.
Sept.: Henry Bolingbroke, duke of Hereford, and Thomas Mowbray, duke of Norfolk banished by Richard II as a result of a dispute between them.

1399
5 Aug.: Lithuanians defeated by Mongols at the River Vorskla.
29-30 Sept.: Deposition of Richard II and Bolingbroke's succession as Henry IV of England.

10 Dec.: After fighting through the Ottoman blockade of Constantinople, Jean le Meignre, the 'worthy' Marshal Boucicaut (1365–1421), began the return journey to the West, joined by the Byzantine emperor Manuel II Palaeologus; Manuel's nephew and co-emperor John VII was left in command in Constantinople.

1400

In the course of continued Milanese expansion, Perugia accepted Gian Galeazzo Visconti as its *signore*. Beginning of a campaign by Louis, duke of Orléans, to acquire greater power in France, taking advantage of Charles VI's periodic mental incapacity.

14 Feb.: Richard II murdered at Berkeley Castle.

Apr.: Manuel II's arrival in Venice, from where he travelled to Milan, reaching Paris by June and London in Sept., seeking support for beleaguered Byzantium.

21 Aug.: Disputed election of Rupert of the Palatinate to replace Emperor Wenceslas; the votes came from the three ecclesiastical electors and Rupert himself in a move opposed by the other three imperial electors.

From Sept.: The Welsh under Owain Glyn Dŵr repeatedly revolted against English rule until 1410.

Oct.: Paolo Guinigi effectively became *signore* of otherwise republican Lucca.

1401

18 Jan.: Formal union of Poland and Lithuania under a single crown.

Sept.: The army of Rupert of the Palatinate, king of the Romans and uncrowned Holy Roman Emperor, descended into Italy in traditional imperial fashion, only to be repulsed by a Milanese victory near Brescia (21 Oct.) and retreat back over the mountains in Apr. 1402.

1402

26 June: Significant Milanese victory over Florence at Casalecchio, leading to the submission of Bologna to Gian Galeazzo Visconti and the effective encirclement of Florence by Milanese forces.

28 July: Timur's decisive defeat of Ottoman forces at Ankara meant a reprieve for blockaded Constantinople and prevented the Turks renewing their European advance for some years; there followed a power struggle among sons of Sultan Bâyezîd I until 1413.

3 Sept.: Death of Gian Galeazzo Visconti meant the relief of Florence.

1403

28 May: France returned to the obedience of Benedict XIII in Avignon, a sign of Philip the Bold's loss of control over policy.

9 June: Manuel II returned to Constantinople.

July–Aug.: Rebellion in England by the Percy earl of Northumberland and his allies.

21 July: Percys defeated at the battle of Shrewsbury by Henry IV; Northumberland's son, Henry Percy, called 'Hotspur', was killed in this encounter.

Nov.: Resumption of war between England and France.

1404

Apr.: Venetian conquest of Vicenza, previously held by the Della Scala of Verona.

27 Apr.: Death of Philip the Bold at Hal, near Brussels, left Louis, duke of Orléans, as the dominant force in French government.

1 Oct.: Death of the Roman pontiff Boniface IX.

17 Oct.: Election of Cosimo de' Migliorati as Innocent VII.

1405

June: Venetian conquest of Verona.

14 Sept.: League of Marbach united princes and Free Imperial Cities against Rupert of the Palatinate.

19 Nov.: Venetian conquest of Padua, previously held by the Carrara family, after a siege of more than a year.

1406

30 Mar.: James I of Scotland taken prisoner and held in England until 1424.

9 Oct.: Florentine conquest of Pisa, the city having previously been held by Louis of Orléans.

6 Nov.: Death of the Roman pope Innocent VII.

30 Nov.: Election of the Venetian Angelo Correr as Gregory XII.

25 Dec.: Accession of Juan II of Castile, a minor, sparked off a period of instability in which his mother, Catalina of Lancaster, and paternal uncle, Fernando, were joint but mutually hostile regents; Muhammad VII of Granada took this opportunity to invade Castile.

1407

23 Nov.: Louis, duke of Orléans, assassinated in Paris by supporters of John the Fearless, duke of Burgundy.

1408

Rebellion in Liège against Burgundian rule.

21 Apr.: Rome occupied by Ladislas of Durazzo, king of Naples.

May: French neutrality again declared in the papal schism debate.

29 June: Thirteen cardinals, from Rome and Avignon, summoned a General Council at Pisa to resolve the schism; Benedict XIII left Avignon and retired to his native Aragon.

1409

Death of Martí of Sicily and Sardinia resulted in the rule of those islands by the kings of Aragon. Rule over Genoa passed from France to Teodoro da Monferrato. War between Florence and Naples until 1414.
18 Jan.: Czech 'nation' granted control of the University of Prague, leading to it becoming a Hussite stronghold.
Mar.: Opening of the General Council of the Church at Pisa.
5 June: Council of Pisa deposed both Gregory XII and Benedict XIII.
26 June: Election by the Council of Pisa of the Cretan Petros Philargis, archbishop of Milan, as Alexander V.

1410

League of French princes, headed by Bernard, count of Armagnac, formed to counter the ambitions of John the Fearless, duke of Burgundy, thereby fuelling civil war between Armagnacs (Orléanists) and Burgundians. Capture of Antequera from Granada after a five-month siege by the Castilian regent Fernando (thereafter known as 'Ferdinand of Antequera') was an important Christian victory in the ongoing *reconquista*.
9 Mar.: Alexander V published an anti-Wycliffite Bull aimed at Jan Hus, who advocated some of the Englishman's heretical opinions.
3 May: Death of the Pisan pope Alexander V.
17 May: Election of Baldassare Cossa as antipope John XXIII in succession to Alexander.
18 May: Death of Rupert of the Palatinate.
19 May: Victory in a naval battle led to Louis II, duke of Anjou, temporarily occupying the throne of Naples, though he was soon forced out by Ladislas of Durazzo, who had been crowned king in 1390.
31 May: Death of Martí I created a succession crisis in Aragon, his son having predeceased him in 1409.
15 July: Battle of Tannenberg (Grünwald), in which the Teutonic Knights were defeated by Polish forces, thereby heralding a decline in their fortunes.
20 Sept.: Sigismund, king of Hungary, elected Holy Roman Emperor.
1 Oct.: Election of Jost of Moravia to the same post created a schism in the Empire.

1411

Constantinople again besieged by Ottomans.
18 Jan.: Death of Jost of Moravia ended the imperial schism.
1 Feb.: First peace of Toruń (Thorn) resulted in territorial losses for the Teutonic Order.
Feb.: Hus excommunicated.
19 May: Battle of Roccasecca, a victory over Ladislas of Durazzo by a papal–Florentine–Angevin alliance; addition of Cortona to the expanding Florentine state, the city having been held by Ladislas since 1409.

21 July: Re-election of Sigismund of Luxemburg as Holy Roman Emperor focused attention on the continuing papal schism.
Oct.: Peace agreed between Castile and Portugal.

1412
16 May: Assassination of Giovanni Maria Visconti, duke of Milan.
June: Occupation of Rome by Ladislas of Durazzo caused John XXIII to flee to Florence.
24 June: By the Compromise of Caspe the throne of Aragon was offered to the Castilian prince Ferdinand of Antequera, who thereafter ruled as king of Aragon and regent of Castile until his death in 1416; this measure was an important step along the road to the ultimate unification of Aragon and Castile.

1413
Deposition of Heinrich von Plauen, High Master of the Teutonic Knights, after his unsuccessful attempts to reform their order.
23 May: Anglo-Burgundian alliance.
5 July: A battle near Sofia confirmed Mehmet I as victor in the Ottoman internecine power struggle.
30 Oct.: Emperor Sigismund initiated a proposal for a General Council at Constance to solve the papal schism.

1414
In England, Lollard revolts led by Sir John Oldcastle were decisively quashed.
6 Aug.: Death of Ladislas of Durazzo, thereby ending his dream of creating an Italian kingdom.
5 Nov.: Opening of the Council of Constance, in session until 1418.

1415
Feb.: Council of Constance instructed all three papal claimants to resign.
20 Mar.: Flight of John XXIII from Constance, but he was soon caught.
29 May: Deposition of John XXIII at Constance ended the confusion created by the Council of Pisa.
4 July: Reluctant abdication of Gregory XII.
6 July: Jan Hus burned for heresy at Constance, where he had gone under an imperial safe-conduct to defend his orthodoxy.
11 Aug.: Invasion of France by Henry V of England.
22 Sept.: Fall of the strategically important port of Harfleur in Normandy to the English.
25 Oct.: Battle of Agincourt, south of Calais, a remarkable English victory, late in the campaigning season, against vastly superior French numbers; the English were not in a position to build on this success and merely returned home, though not without important prisoners including Charles, duke of Orléans, and Marshal Boucicaut.

1416

Jan.: Benedict XIII, at Peñiscola in Aragon, lost the support of Ferdinand of Antequera, a decision which precipitated the end of the papal schism.
1 May: Emperor Sigismund, allied with the Iberian monarchs, arrived in England on a peace mission which also took him to France, with the aim of uniting the Christian powers to counter the Ottoman threat.
29 May: In a war lasting until 1419, the Ottoman fleet was defeated at Gallipoli by Venetian naval forces under Pietro Loredan.
30 May: Hussite Jerome of Prague burned as a heretic at Constance.
15 Aug.: Treaty of Canterbury between Henry V and Emperor Sigismund.
Sept.: Anglo-French truce.
Oct.: Secret Anglo-Burgundian alliance formed.

1417

12 Jan.: Rouen, capital of Normandy, taken by Burgundians.
26 July: Benedict XIII deposed by the Council of Constance, as he had been at Pisa eight years earlier.
Aug.–Sept.: Many towns around Paris fell to Burgundian forces.
8 Sept.: English capture of Caen in Normandy.
9 Oct.: Decree *Frequens* called for regular General Councils of the Church.
18 Oct.: Death of Angelo Correr, formerly Gregory XII.
11 Nov.: Election of Oddone Colonna, a member of the powerful Roman baronial family, as Martin V effectively healed the schism.

1418

War between Venice and Hungary until 1420, from which the former emerged with territorial gains in Friuli and Istria.
16 Mar.: Coutances taken by the English.
22 Apr.: Conclusion of the Council of Constance.
Late May: Burgundian troops took control of Paris and, with it, of Charles VI.
28 May: Meaux fell to the Dauphin Charles (the future Charles VII).
June: Bernard, count of Armagnac, killed, after which the dauphin became leader of the Armagnac faction.
24 June: Constitution of the Hanseatic League agreed by cities engaged in Baltic trade.
21 July: Compiègne fell to the dauphin.
19 Sept.: Publication of the treaty of Saint-Maur-des-Fossés between the dauphin and John the Fearless, duke of Burgundy.
Oct.: Papal court in residence at Mantua until Feb. 1419, after which it moved to Florence.
30 Dec.: Tours taken by the dauphin.

1419

Ottoman war with Hungary.
19 Jan.: Rouen fell to the English.

30 May–30 June: Negotiations between Henry V, the dauphin and Burgundians at Melun, but no general agreement reached.

29 July: Peace of Melun agreed between the dauphin and the Burgundians.

13 July: Pontoise fell to the English.

30 July: Acts of violence marked the beginning of the Hussite Revolt in Bohemia, where a state of war existed until 1433.

10 Sept.: Supposed parley between Dauphinists and Burgundians on the bridge at Montereau, south-east of Paris, was the opportunity for the dauphin's supporters to assassinate John the Fearless, in consequence of which Philip the Good became the third Valois duke of Burgundy; Philip soon allied with Henry V against the dauphin.

22 Nov.: Death of John XXIII, whose body was placed in a magnificent tomb in the Florentine Baptistery at the expense of Cosimo de' Medici.

2 Dec.: Anglo-Burgundian alliance.

1420

Emperor Sigismund crowned king of Bohemia, but rapidly driven from Prague by Hussite rebels led by Jan Žižka; between 1420 and 1436 the Hussites refused to recognise Sigismund as their king; as early as 1420, though, divisions grew among the Hussites between extreme Taborites and moderate Calixtines. Venice extended her *terraferma* possessions by acquiring Belluno and Feltre.

Feb.: Martin V reached agreed terms with the *condottiere* Braccio da Montone (Fortebraccio), who controlled much of central Italy and was therefore a key to the papacy returning to Rome.

21 May: Treaty of Troyes, by the terms of which Henry V of England married Catherine, daughter of Charles VI, and was acknowledged as her father's regent and heir, while the dauphin was disinherited.

July: The four Articles of Prague defined Hussite beliefs on freedom of preaching, communion in both kinds (Utraquism) for the laity, an end to the Church's secular powers and the punishment of serious sins committed by clerics.

Aug.: Arrival in the kingdom of Naples of Alfonso 'the Magnanimous', king of Aragon and Sicily, adopted as heir to Giovanna II, last of the so-called first Neopolitan House of Anjou; between 1420 and 1434 Louis III, duke of Anjou, campaigned for the Angevin cause in Naples.

Sept.: Martin V entered Rome.

1421

Renewed dynastic conflict in the Ottoman empire followed the death of Sultan Mehmet I. Philip the Good acquired Namur by purchase. Florentine purchase of Livorno on the Tuscan coast.

22 May: The dauphin ended Henry V's run of military success with victory at the battle of Baugé in Anjou.

2 Nov.: Filippo Maria Visconti of Milan conquered Genoa.

1422
Territorial war between Florence and Milan until 1426.

2 June–6 Sept.: Constantinople once more besieged by the Ottomans, but resisted due to the city's strong defences and the weakness of the Ottoman navy.

31 Aug.: Death of Henry V left his brother John, duke of Bedford (d. 1435), as English regent in France while another brother, Humphrey, duke of Gloucester (d. 1447) and their uncle Cardinal Henry Beaufort (d. 1447) were the infant Henry VI's chief councillors in England.

21 Oct.: Death of Charles VI resulted in the ten-month-old Henry VI being king of both England and France by the terms of the treaty of Troyes, though this was disputed by Charles VII, the former dauphin and *roi de Bourges*, so called from his power base in the southern half of the kingdom.

1423
Salonica ceded to Venice by its Byzantine rulers, the city thereafter becoming the focus of war between Venice and the Ottomans until 1430. Loss of the Morea to the Ottomans.

Apr.: Opening of the General Council of Pavia–Siena in compliance with *Frequens*.

23 May: Death of Benedict XIII.

10 June: Election of the Catalan Gil Sanchez Muñoz as Clement VIII, in succession to Benedict.

1 July: Louis III of Anjou adopted as heir to the throne of Naples by Giovanna II.

Nov.: John VIII Palaeologus left Constantinople to seek support for Byzantium in Venice, Milan and Hungary.

1424
22 Feb.: Peace treaty between the Ottomans and Byzantium took pressure off Constantinople, while attention was still fixed on the Venetian defence of Salonica.

7 Mar.: Dissolution of the Council of Pavia–Siena.

2 June: Battle of Aquila, a victory by Francesco Sforza for Giovanna of Naples over Alfonso's commander Braccio da Montone, who died three days later.

July: Milanese military dominance over Florence confirmed by victory in the battle of Zaganara in the Romagna.

17 Aug.: Defeat of Charles VII by the English, led by John, duke of Bedford, at the battle of Verneuil completed the English conquest of Normandy.

11 Oct.: Death of Jan Žižka, leader of the Taborite Hussites.

Oct.: Until Nov. 1425, Humphrey, duke of Gloucester, was engaged in military ventures in Hainault in support of his wife Jacqueline of Bavaria's claim, which were threatened by Philip of Burgundy.

1 Nov.: John VIII returned to Constantinople having failed to secure support for Byzantium in Latin Christendom.

1425
Rise of Procopius the Bald as a Hussite leader in Bohemia. An obscure cleric called Bernard Garnier took the name Benedict XIV in a French reaction against the Spanish antipope Clement VIII.
4 Dec.: Alliance between Florence and Venice led to a sequence of wars between Venice and Milan for territorial domination of northern Italy.

1426
20 Nov.: Capture of Milanese-held Brescia for Venice by Francesco Bussone, count of Carmagnola.

1427
Institution of the Florentine *catasto*, a means-test for property taxation. Escalation of conflict in the Balkans between Ottomans and Hungarians. Cardinal Henry Beaufort's ineffective crusade against the Hussites.
11 Oct.: Battle of Maclodio, a victory over Carlo Malatesta for Milan by the Venetian forces of Carmagnola, with the consequence that Bergamo passed into Venetian hands.

1428
26 May: Treaty of Ferrara agreed peace between Florence, Venice and Milan, Brescia and Bergamo being ceded to Venice by Milan.
3 July: By the treaty of Delft Philip the Good reinforced his claim to Hainault, Holland, Freisland and Zeeland; it was to counter this claim that Philip's cousin Jacqueline, countess of Bavaria, had married Humphrey, duke of Gloucester.
12 Oct.: English troops began to besiege the strategically important city of Orléans.

1429
20 Feb.: Death of Giovanni di Bicci de' Medici, leaving his son Cosimo as head of the family and its business interests.
23 Feb.: The teenage girl known as Jeanne d'Arc (hereafter Joan of Arc) from Domrémy, near the French border with Lorraine, prompted by heavenly voices to save the French cause, identified Charles VII among a crowd of courtiers at Chinon – this was regarded as a positive omen; although her subsequent career was not militarily important, her presence was crucial to the raising of French morale.
29 Apr.: Entry of Joan of Arc into Orléans.
8 May: Relief of Orléans from the besieging Anglo-Burgundian forces, who retreated.
18 June: Joan's victory over the English, under the command of John Talbot, earl of Shrewsbury, and Sir John Fastolf, at Patay, west of Orléans.

17 July: Charles VII crowned at Reims with Joan at his side: the climax of her career.

26 July: Resignation of the Spanish antipope Clement VIII.

Nov.: Florentine declaration of war on Lucca, the small neighbouring Tuscan republic which Florence had long sought to conquer; Lucca received support from Milan in a conflict which lasted until Apr. 1433.

1430

Philip the Good acquired Brabant and Limburg upon the death of their ruler, Philip of Saint Pol.

10 Jan.: Philip announced the foundation of the Order of the Golden Fleece, membership of which came to act as a focus for supporters of the Valois dukes of Burgundy against French kings.

29 Mar.: Ottoman capture and sack of Salonica after the seven-year Venetian occupation of the city.

23 May: Joan of Arc captured by Burgundians at Compiègne.

1431

Republic of Genoa controlled by Milan until 1435.

9 Jan.: Joan of Arc's trial by pro-Burgundian French clergy opened at Rouen, capital of English-ruled Normandy.

20 Feb.: Death of Martin V.

3 Mar.: Election of the Venetian patrician Gabriele Condulmer as Eugenius IV.

30 May: Joan of Arc burned as a relapsed heretic.

23 July: Opening of the General Council of the Church at Basel, again in compliance with *Frequens*.

Aug.: Cardinal Giuliano Cesarini's crusade against the Bohemian Hussites defeated on the battlefield at Tauss.

16 Dec.: Coronation in Paris of the ten-year-old Henry VI of England as king of France.

18 Dec.: Eugenius IV attempted to dissolve the Council of Basel, but its members abided by the spirit of Constance and it remained in session until 1449, but was in schism from 1437.

1432

5 May: Execution of the *condottiere* Carmagnola for treason against the Venetian state; he had previously been employed by Milan and maintained strong contacts there, regardless of his contract (*condotta*) with Milan's Venetian enemies.

1 June: Battle of S. Romano, west of Empoli, in which the forces of Niccolò da Tolentino and Micheletto Attendolo for Florence bettered the Sienese allies of Milan led by Niccolò Piccinino, an encounter later depicted by Paolo Uccello (see p. 212).

1433

Confusion over the possession of Hainault was resolved when Jacqueline of Bavaria abdicated in favour of Philip of Burgundy.

28 Jan.: Florentine victory against the Lucchese at Collodi, between Lucca and Montecatini.

26 Apr.: Conclusion of the war between Florence and Lucca and a temporary peace signed by participants in the Lombard wars.

31 May: Emperor Sigismund crowned at Rome.

7 Sept.: In Florence, Rinaldo degli Albizzi and his faction had leading members of the Medici family arrested, accusing them of inciting the disastrous war with Lucca; the Medici were exiled to Ancona, Fano, Padua, Rimini, Rome and Venice; exile was a common feature of faction-ridden Italian politics.

30 Nov.: Reconciliation at Prague between moderate Hussites and representatives of the Council of Basel.

15 Dec.: By the Bull *Dudum sacrum* Eugenius revoked his 1431 decision about the Council.

1434

Increased Ottoman aggression in the Balkans countered Hungarian influence in the region.

29 May: Short-lived republican revolution in Rome led to the flight (4 June) of Eugenius IV to Florence.

30 May: Defeat by Catholics and moderate Hussites of Taborite extremists led by Procopius the Bald at Lipany, east of Prague.

28 Aug.: Important victory by Piccinino for Milan over Gattamelata and Niccolò da Tolentino for Venice at Castel Bolognese, between Imola and Faenza.

29 Sept.: Cosimo de' Medici recalled to Florence following the appointment in Aug. of a Signoria weighted in his favour; opponents of the Medici, including the Strozzi and Albizzi, were exiled or received alternative penalties.

9 Oct.: Cosimo arrived at Florence.

Oct.: Cardinal Giovanni Vitelleschi imposed papal authority in Rome, as he did throughout the Patrimony of the Church in subsequent years.

Dec.: Treaty between Emperor Sigismund and France precipitated the former's declaration of war on Burgundy, but this came to little.

1435

2 Feb.: Death of Giovanna II of Naples, bequeathing her kingdom to René of Anjou, who had succeeded to the claim of Louis III upon the latter's death three months earlier; however, within weeks Alfonso of Aragon entered the city of Naples as king.

4 Aug.: Battle of Ponza, off Gaeta, a naval confrontation in which a Catalan fleet was defeated by the Genoese, themselves then subject to

Milan; Alfonso of Aragon was captured but came to an agreement with Filippo Maria Visconti.

5 Aug.: Congress of Arras opened as tripartite negotiations between England, France and Burgundy, but the English delegation left on 6 Sept.

15 Sept.: Death of John, duke of Bedford, English regent in France.

21 Sept.: Treaty of Arras marked the apparent reconciliation of Charles VII and Philip the Good, though the French were primarily interested in detaching the Burgundians from their English alliance; France ceded territory to Burgundy, including the controversial 'Somme towns', Saint-Quentin, Corbie, Amiens, Abbeville, Doullens, Saint-Riquier, Crèvecoeur, Arleux and Mortagne.

1436

Anglo-Flemish war launched by Humphrey of Gloucester. Genoa rebelled against Milanese rule.

21 Jan.: Alfonso of Aragon and Naples placed his brother Joan (Juan) in control of Iberian policy, leaving himself free to concentrate on his Italian interests.

13 Apr.: Paris abandoned by the English and recovered by the forces of Charles VII.

5 July: Compacts of Prague agreed between Hussites and the Council of Basel, by which the Bohemians were received back into the Church.

23 Aug.: Emperor Sigismund's return to Prague after sixteen years in which rebels had kept him out.

1437

Flemish revolt against the monetary policies of Philip the Good. Cardinal Vitelleschi's invasion of Naples on behalf of Eugenius IV, the kingdom's nominal overlord, and of the Angevin claim.

21 Feb.: James I of Scotland assassinated at Perth by a disaffected subject.

18 Sept.: Dissolution of the Council of Basel by Eugenius.

Nov.: Byzantine emperor John VIII and Patriarch Joseph II, leading a party which included the young Bessarion, bishop of Nicaea, the Platonist Gemistos Plethon and anti-unionist Markus Eugenikos, left Constantinople for the ecumenical Council at Ferrara, though partisans of the Council at Basel urged them to go there instead.

12 Nov.: Entry of Charles VII into Paris.

9 Dec.: Death of Emperor Sigismund.

1438

Trade war between Holland and the Hanseatic League until 1441.

8 Jan.: Opening of the ecumenical Council of Ferrara.

24 Jan.: Schismatic Council of Basel suspended Eugenius IV from office, but was powerless to enforce this decision.

8 Feb.: John VIII Palaeologus and his party arrived at Venice, from where he proceeded to Ferrara for the Council, arriving 1 Mar.

18 Mar.: Election of Albert, Sigismund's son-in-law, as Holy Roman Emperor, the first Habsburg to hold that office.

From Apr. until June 1442: René of Anjou in Italy, campaigning for acknowledgement of his claims to the kingdom of Naples and assisted by Francesco Sforza, son of the *condottiere* Muzio Attendolo.

7 July: French clergy meeting at Bourges enacted the Pragmatic Sanction to defend Gallican liberties and limit papal authority, particularly with regard to appointments to vacant benefices.

From July until 1440: Piccinino's siege of Venetian-held Brescia for Milan, while the Venetian captain, Gattamelata, made a remarkable retreat through the Alpine foothills.

1439

Erik of Pomerania, king of Denmark, Norway, Sweden, deposed and exiled.

10 Jan.: Ecumenical Council transferred from Ferrara to Florence due to plague and the threatening presence of Piccinino, who invaded the Veronese and Vicentino between Mar. and May.

25 June: Eugenius IV formally deposed by the schismatic Council of Basel.

5 July: Reunion of the Eastern and Western churches proclaimed in Florence but later rejected by the Orthodox hierarchy in Constantinople.

Sept.: Meeting of the French Estates General at Orléans.

19 Oct.: Greek delegation left Florence for the journey home.

27 Oct.: Death from plague of Emperor Albert, then on campaign against the Turks.

5 Nov.: Election by Council of Basel of Amédée VIII of Savoy as Felix V.

1440

Rhodes besieged by Egyptian Mamluks until 1444. Ottoman conquest of Serbia checked by their failure to take Belgrade, which encouraged George Castriotes (known as Scanderbeg or Iskender Beg), Hungarians and others. Eugenius IV called for crusade.

1 Feb.: John VIII Palaeologus arrived at Constantinople.

2 Feb.: Election of Frederick of Styria as Holy Roman Emperor.

Feb.–July: French revolt known as the Praguerie (the name deriving from the centre of Hussite rebellion), in which senior nobles, led by the duke of Bourbon and including the Dauphin Louis (the future Louis XI) and duke of Brittany, took arms against Charles VII; Philip of Burgundy was also implicated; revolt suppressed by the king.

19 Mar.: Arrest of Cardinal Vitelleschi by order of Eugenius on the grounds that he was becoming too powerful and was thought to be over-ambitious.

2 Apr.: Death of Cardinal Vitelleschi.

14 June: Siege of Brescia relieved by Francesco Sforza for Venice, after defeating Piccinino's Milanese army.

29 June: Battle of Anghiari, near Arezzo, in which Piccinino, for Milan and with Florentine anti-Medicean exiles, was defeated by papal–Florentine forces commanded by Francesco Sforza; this battle was later celebrated pictorially by Leonardo, but caricatured by Machiavelli in arguments against the employment of mercenaries.

9 Nov.: Thanks to the intervention of Philip the Good, Charles, duke of Orléans, the noted poet, was released from captivity in England, where he had been held since being captured at Agincourt in 1415.

1441

János Hunyadi, *voyvode* of Transylvania, checked the otherwise steady Ottoman advance through the Balkans, doing so again in 1442. English driven out of the Seine valley by their French adversaries.

10–11 Feb.: Extravagantly celebrated marriage of Jacopo, son of Venetian doge Francesco Foscari, to Lucrezia Contarini, one of the acts by which this doge appeared to behave in the manner of a non-Venetian prince.

21 Feb.: Ravenna seized by Venice from the papal vicar Ostasio da Polenta.

21–31 Aug.: *Condottiere* Francesco Sforza and Bianca Maria Visconti, illegitimate daughter of and heir to the duke of Milan, married near Cremona.

10 Dec.: Publication of the peace of Cavriana between Venice and Milan, confirming the River Adda as the boundary between them and acknowledging Venetian possession of Ravenna.

1442

Spring: General Council meeting at Florence transferred to Rome, after which little business was transacted.

2 June: Alfonso V entered the city of Naples, which had been besieged since November 1441; René of Anjou's cause was thereby lost, though Eugenius IV later (20 Sept.) invested him with the kingdom, which was a papal fief.

From June: French recovered some Gascon lands from the English.

30 Nov.: Milanese–papal–Neapolitan alliance against Florence and Venice signalled the pope's rejection of René, who had returned to France in Oct.

1443

From June: Crusade launched by Władysław of Poland, János Hunyadi and the Serbian despot George Brankovič. Anti-Turkish resistance in northern Albania continued to be led by Scanderbeg, who was friendly with Hunyadi and supported by Alfonso of Naples, but who was regarded as a threat and an annoyance by Venice.

6 July: Eugenius IV formally invested Alfonso with the kingdom of Naples.

28 Sept.: Eugenius returned to Rome after ten years in exile.

Nov.: Philip of Burgundy acquired Luxemburg by peaceful conquest, though he was already heir to his aunt, Elizabeth of Görlitz.

3 Nov.: At the battle of Nisch, near Sofia, crusaders defeated Ottoman forces.

1444

28 May: Truce agreed at Tours between the English and French, under the terms of which Henry VI was betrothed to Marguerite (hereafter Margaret), daughter of René of Anjou; negotiations were led on the English side by William de la Pole, duke of Suffolk.

12 June: Ten-year truce agreed at Edirne near Constantinople between Christians and Ottomans, by which an independent despotate was restored in Serbia and the Hungarians undertook to keep to their side of the Danube.

10 Nov.: Battle of Varna on the Bulgarian Black Sea coast, where Hungarian crusaders and their allies were heavily outnumbered by Turks and suffered a serious defeat which ultimately sealed the fate of Byzantium in 1453.

1445

19 May: Victory for Álvaro de Luna, Constable of Castile, and the future Enrique IV at Olmedo over an Aragonese force, which had invaded Castile in reaction to Luna's control of government.

1446

28 Sept.: In the battle of Casalmaggiore, near Cremona, Venetians under Micheletto Attendolo, cousin of Francesco Sforza, were victorious against Milanese forces.

29 Dec.: Alliance between Charles VII of France and Filippo Maria Visconti of Milan.

1447

Jan.–Feb.: In view of Venetian expansion in northern Italy, Charles VII of France sought to strengthen his position in that region, but his intervention in Genoa failed.

18 Feb.: Humphrey, duke of Gloucester, arrested for treason at Bury St Edmunds, where he died a few days later, probably of natural causes.

23 Feb.: Death of Eugenius IV.

6 Mar.: Election of the humanist Tommaso Parentucelli as Nicholas V.

19 Mar.: With Venetian forces close to Milan itself, an agreement was made between Filippo Maria Visconti and his son-in-law Francesco Sforza.

11 Apr.: Death of Cardinal Henry Beaufort left power in England in the hands of Henry VI's favourites.

13 Aug.: Death of Filippo Maria Visconti, after which the Ambrosian Republic was proclaimed in Milan.
30 Aug.: Sforza allied with the Ambrosian Republic.
16 Oct.: Battle of Bosco Marengo, south of Alessandria, at which Bartolomeo Colleoni and Astorre Manfredi for Milan defeated French forces allied with Venice.

1448

János Hunyadi campaigning in Serbia.
17 Feb.: Concordat of Vienna between the papacy and Frederick, King of the Romans, defused the power of nationalism in the German church; this had been preceded in 1447 by the Concordat of Nuremberg between the papacy and the imperial electors.
11 Mar.: England surrendered Maine by the treaty of Lavardin, which extended the Anglo-French truce until Apr. 1450.
July: Remnants of the Council of Basel moved to Lausanne.
19 July: Battle of Caravaggio, a victory for Francesco Sforza's Milanese over the Venetians commanded by Micheletto Attendolo.
17–19 Oct.: Ottoman victory in the second battle of Kosovo was part of their campaign against Scanderbeg; Hunyadi escaped.
18 Oct.: Treaty of Rivoltella between Venice and Sforza, the republic acknowledging the latter's lordship of Milan.

1449

24 Mar.: English raid on Fougères breached the Anglo-French truce and led to the French invasion of Normandy.
7 Apr.: Abdication of antipope Felix V.
25 Apr.: Council of Lausanne (formerly of Basel) finally dissolved itself.
10 Sept.: Fall of Rouen to French forces.
24 Sept.: Venice and republican Milan allied against Florence and confirmed their respective territorial holdings.
24 Nov.: Port of Harfleur fell to the French.
27 Dec.: Francesco Sforza laid siege to Milan.

1450

Jubilee year witnessed multitudes of pilgrims in Rome. Sultan Murâd campaigning in Serbia.
25 Feb.: Milanese invitation to Francesco Sforza to assume power marked the end of their republican experiment.
26 Mar.: Sforza invested as duke of Milan, a position he held with financial support from Cosimo de' Medici, who engineered friendly relations between their respective states after decades of conflict and suspicion.
2 May: Death at sea of the duke of Suffolk, following his impeachment as a result of English defeats in France. Further French victories over the English, including the fall of Avranches in May and that of Caen on

24 June, led to the complete French recovery of Normandy, though England yet retained Gascony and Calais.

Summer: Rebellions in southern England associated with Jack Cade, Captain of Kent.

Aug.: Richard, duke of York, returned to England from Ireland to lead opposition to alleged royal misgovernment.

1451

28 Apr.: Defensive league agreed between Venice, Naples, Savoy and Monferrato.

30 July: Alliance between Florence and Milan against Venice, which was widely regarded as a threat to neighbouring powers due to her acquisition of a *terraferma* empire at their expense.

Aug.: Serious French attempt to reconquer Gascony.

10 Sept.: Ottoman peace with Venice.

20 Nov.: Ottoman peace with Hungary renewed.

Winter: Beginning of insurrection in prosperous Ghent against the rule of Philip the Good, though conflict over tax had existed since 1447.

1452

Year of military preparations for the final Ottoman assault on Constantinople.

16 Mar.: Emperor Frederick III crowned in Rome, the last imperial coronation there.

26 Oct.: Papal legate Cardinal Isidore of Kiev arrived in Constantinople as a gesture of support from Latin Christendom, after which Catholic and Orthodox liturgies were celebrated in S. Sophia in accordance with the Union agreed at Florence in 1439 (12 Dec.).

31 Oct.: Opening of war between Venice, Milan and their allies, which eventually ended in stalemate in 1454.

1453

Early Jan.: Stefano Porcari's failed republican conspiracy in Rome, leading to the rapid arrest and execution of its leader.

6 Apr.–29 May: Seige and fall of Constantinople to the Ottoman Turks, led by Sultan Mehmet II, known as 'the Conqueror' from this time on.

29 May: The last Byzantine emperor, Constantine XI, died in the final assault; Ottoman capital transferred from Edirne (Adrianople) to Constantinople.

3 June: Following his arrest in Apr., Constable of Castile, Álvaro de Luna, executed at Valladolid by order of Juan II, having effectively ruled Castile since 1431.

June–Oct.: Second French expedition to Gascony.

17 July: John Talbot, earl of Shrewsbury, defeated at Castillon, a landmark in the English loss of Gascony.

10 Aug.: Henry VI 'lost his wits' for the first time, three days before the birth of Edward, prince of Wales.

From Aug.: René of Anjou undertook a fresh Italian campaign, no more successful than earlier initiatives.

20 Oct.: Fall of Bordeaux marked the end of the Hundred Years War, the English having lost all their French possessions except Calais and the Channel Islands.

1454

Polish aggression initiated the Thirteen Years War with the Teutonic Knights, which lasted until 1476 and included the surrender of the Knights' headquarters at Marienburg and their retreat into German-speaking lands.

17 Feb.: Philip the Good's exceptionally extravagant Feast of the Pheasant at Lille, committing Burgundy to a crusade.

27 Mar.: Beginning of Richard, duke of York's first Protectorate in England, brought to an end when Henry VI 'recovered his wits' nine months later.

9 Apr.: Peace of Lodi, a settlement between Venice and Milan; Venice lost no *terraferma* possessions.

18 Apr.: Ottoman peace with Venice.

30 Aug.: Defensive league signed between Venice, Milan and Florence, to which Alfonso of Aragon and Naples and Nicholas V adhered early in 1455: thus the five major Italian powers were bound by a twenty-five-year mutual non-aggression pact.

Nov.: The Polish Charters of Nieszawa introduced significant constitutional changes.

1455

26 Jan.–25 Feb.: Peace of Lodi ratified by Alfonso of Naples and Nicholas V, thereby establishing the 'Lega Italica', which was important for the deceptive notion that the powers were balanced, and that the Italian states were at peace with each other until the French invasion of 1494. Confirmation of Francesco Sforza's ducal title by Emperor Frederick III contributed to the sense of a new era in Italy.

24 Mar.: Death of Nicholas V.

8 Apr.: Election of the Catalan Alonso de Borja as Calixtus III.

22 May: First battle of St Albans, a brief affray which marked the beginning of the Wars of the Roses, was a victory for Richard, duke of York, with his associates the Neville earls of Salisbury and Warwick, and saw the death of the royal favourite, Edmund Beaufort, duke of Somerset.

Late June: Scanderbeg's defeat at Berat.

5 Oct.: Moldavia formally subject to Ottoman control.

19 Nov.: Richard of York's second Protectorate, until Mar. 1456.

1456
Ottoman conquest of Athens.
May–June: Official rehabilitation of Joan of Arc, overturning the verdict of 1431 and following enquiries undertaken in 1450 and 1452.
22 July: Ottomans failed to take Belgrade after a three-week siege, the defence being led by János Hunyadi after inspirational preaching by the Franciscan Giovanni da Capistrano, who had previously been a notable preacher against the Hussites.
11 Aug: Hunyadi's death from plague, to which Giovanni da Capistrano also succumbed (23 Oct.).
31 Aug.: After nine years' experience as ruler of Dauphiné and of poor relations with his father Charles VII, Dauphin Louis, the future Louis XI, fled to the court of Philip of Burgundy.

1457
1 Nov.: Death of Francesco Foscari, less than a week after being deposed as Venetian doge.
23 Dec.: Scanderbeg, 'Soldier of Christ', appointed captain-general by Calixtus III for a crusade against the Ottomans.

1458
French overlordship of Genoa until 1464, after having been under French protection since 1456 on account of an Aragonese naval attack.
24 Jan.: Matthias Corvinus, son of János Hunyadi, elected king of Hungary.
2 Mar.: George of Poděbrady, a moderate Hussite noble who favoured *rapprochement* with Rome, elected king of Bohemia.
6 Aug.: Death of Calixtus III.
19 Aug.: Election of Sienese humanist Enea Silvio Piccolomini as Pius II, the central feature of whose pontificate was the renewed call for a crusade.

1459
Turks overran Serbia. Campaign by the Angevin duke of Calabria, son of René of Anjou, to recover Naples for his father, until 1463.
1 June: Congress of Mantua opened by Pius II, but delegates were so slow to arrive that the first sitting was not possible until 26 Sept., after which diplomatic disputes prevented progress towards a crusade being achieved.
23 Sept.: Indecisive battle at Blore Heath, Shropshire, between followers of Margaret of Anjou and those of the earl of Salisbury.
12–13 Oct.: Battle of Ludford, also in Shropshire, a Lancastrian victory after which Richard, duke of York, retreated to Ireland and Richard Neville, earl of Warwick, to Calais.

1460
Baronial rebellion against King Ferrante I of Naples, until 1464.
19 Jan.: Pius II left Mantua in disappointment, issuing at this time the Bull *Execrabilis*, which forbade appeals to General Councils.

May: Final Ottoman conquest of the despotate of the Morea, including Mistra, home of Gemistos Plethon.

26 June: Invasion of England by the earls of March (future Edward IV), Warwick and Salisbury.

10 July: Battle of Northampton, in which Lancastrian commanders were killed and Henry VI was captured by Yorkists, leading Richard of York to assert his own claim to the crown.

3 Aug.: Accidental death of James II of Scotland at the siege of Roxburgh, an extension of the English civil war in which James supported the Lancastrian cause.

2 Dec.: Carlos of Viana arrested at Lérida by his father Joan II of Aragon after negotiating with Enrique IV of Castile for the hand of the latter's half-sister Isabella; an armed rising in Catalonia supported Carlos, who had already been disinherited in 1455.

25 Dec.: Sigismondo Malatesta of Rimini excommunicated by Pius for alleged irreligion and immorality, to which Malatesta reacted with violence.

30 Dec.: Battle of Wakefield, in which the Yorkists defeated Margaret of Anjou but Richard of York was killed.

1461

2 Feb.: Battle of Mortimer's Cross, near Wigmore, a Yorkist victory over Welsh Lancastrians.

17 Feb.: Second battle of St Albans, a victory for the Lancastrians of Margaret of Anjou.

25 Feb.: Joan II of Aragon freed his son Carlos of Viana under pressure.

4 Mar.: Edward IV proclaimed king of England.

29 Mar. (Palm Sunday): overwhelming Yorkist victory at Towton, near York, after which Henry VI and Margaret retreated into Scotland.

21 June: Capitulation of Villafranca secured victory for rebellious Catalans over Joan II, with Carlos of Viana named as their lieutenant-general.

c. **15 Aug.**: Final fall of the empire of Trebizond to the Ottomans.

23 Sept.: Death of Carlos of Viana.

27 Nov.: Louis XI's temporary revocation of the Pragmatic Sanction of Bourges, which he abolished permanently in 1467, after restoring it in 1464.

1462

Catalan civil war until 1472, in which cities and nobles sided against the king in defence of their privileges, while the Church tended to support him.

12 Apr.: Treaty of Olite between France and Aragon ensured that Joan II's daughter Leonor and her husband Gaston de Foix succeeded to the throne of Navarre.

May: Alum, a mineral essential to cloth manufacture, discovered at Tolfa, near Civitavecchia in the Papal States; the significance of this was that other sources were in Ottoman-controlled Asia Minor, so the papacy could be sure of finding markets.

3 May: Treaty of Sauveterre between France and Aragon promised mutual armed assistance.

9 May: Treaty of Bayonne, also between France and Aragon, transferred Cerdagne (Cerdaña) and Rousillon (Rosellón) to French control at a time when Joan II of Aragon did not even control any Catalan territory.

28 June: By the treaty of Tours, Louis XI promised to assist Margaret of Anjou with the recovery of the English throne for the Lancastrians.

By end June: Bosnia an Ottoman province, putting increased pressure on Venice.

18 Aug.: Victory at Troia for Ferrante over his rebellious barons and the duke of Calabria, the king's son and heir.

25 Oct.: Margaret of Anjou at Bamborough, Northumberland, but had retreated into Scotland by Nov.

1463

Philip the Good returned the Somme towns and county of Ponthieu to France, all having been ceded to him by the treaty of Arras in 1435; this move was deeply resented by Philip's heir Charles, count of Charolais, whose hostility to Louis XI became a major ingredient in international relations. French occupation of the counties of Rousillon and Cerdagne, disputed with the Crown of Aragon.

June: Ottoman conquest of Bosnia, its last king, Stjepan Tomasevič, dying in the process.

28 July: Venice declared war on the Turks, this *grande guerra* lasting until 1479.

Sept.: Alliance between Venice and Hungary.

Dec.: Accord agreed between Louis XI and Francesco Sforza, whereby the latter was granted overlordship of Genoa and Savoy.

1464

Feb.: Francesco Sforza occupied Savoy and entered Genoa in Mar.

1 May: Edward IV thwarted Richard Neville's plans for a marriage between the king and Louis XI's sister-in-law Bona of Savoy by secretly marrying the widow Elizabeth Woodville.

1 Aug.: Death of Cosimo de' Medici, *pater patriae* (father of the people) of Florence.

15 Aug.: Death at Ancona of Pius II after over-optimistically awaiting the arrival there of crusading forces.

30 Aug.: Election of the Venetian Pietro Barbo as Paul II.

28 Sept.: Noble manifesto published at Burgos, detailing their complaints against Enrique IV and demanding the dismissal of his favourite Beltrán de la Cueva, marked the beginning of civil war in Castile.

25 Oct.: Enrique IV acknowledged his half-brother Alfonso as heir, in accordance with noble demands.

1465

Rebellion of Liège against Burgundian rule, until 1468. Ottoman siege of Kroia, the Albanian capital.

3 June: Enrique IV's effigy deposed by nobles at Ávila who crowned Alfonso in his stead.

Mar.–Oct.: War of the Public Weal (*bien public*) in France, in which many nobles, including the dukes of Brittany, Anjou and Bourbon and the king's brother Charles de France, and led by Philip of Burgundy, united against Louis XI, who had dismissed his father's ministers and reacted against his policies.

15–16 July: Inconclusive battle of Montlhéry, south of Paris, between Burgundians and royal forces, in the presence of Louis XI and Charles, count of Charolais, the future Charles the Bold.

5 Oct.: French civil war ended by the treaty of Conflans.

1466

8 Mar.: Death of Francesco Sforza, duke of Milan.

19 Oct.: Second peace of Toruń (Thorn) marked the end of the Thirteen Years War, in which Poland acquired much of Prussia and the Grand Master of the Teutonic Knights nominally accepted Polish overlordship.

Dec.: Scanderbeg feted in Rome.

1467

15 June: Death of Philip the Good brought about the succession of Charles the Bold as duke of Burgundy, known in Italy as the 'great duke of the West'.

1468

17 Jan.: Scanderbeg died from fever after further campaigns against Ottoman forces in 1466 and 1467.

16 Feb.: Anglo-Burgundian marriage treaty agreed in Brussels, under the terms of which Charles the Bold married, as his third wife, Edward IV's sister Margaret of York on 3 July; this was part of various anti-French diplomatic moves by Edward, which further alienated Richard Neville from his king.

Late Feb.: Arrest of Pomponio Leto's Roman Academicians by order of Paul II, who suspected them of pagan practices and feared that they sought to assassinate him; Bartolomeo Sacchi, known as il Platina, was among those imprisoned in Castel Sant'Angelo.

5 July: Death of Infante Alfonso of Castile.

10 July: Caterina Cornaro of Venice married by proxy to Jacques II of Lusignan, king of Cyprus.

19 Sept.: Agreement at Toros de Guisando whereby Isabella of Castile was recognised as heir to the throne of her half-brother Enrique IV, in preference to Juana 'la Beltraneja', alleged daughter of Beltrán de la Cueva.
9–14 Oct.: Meeting at Péronne between Louis XI and Charles the Bold following military activity in that border region; effectively held prisoner, Louis conceded to Burgundian demands, agreeing to uphold previous treaties.
30 Oct.: Burgundian troops entered the rebel city of Liège, which had previously been backed by Louis XI; buoyed by these developments, England declared war on France.

1469

Turkish raids into Friuli, regularly repeated during each campaigning season in the 1470s. Matthias Corvinus of Hungary proclaimed himself king of Bohemia, but a majority of the Bohemian Estates countered by electing the Jagiełłonian prince Vladislav II in 1471.
26 July: Battle of Edgecote, near Banbury, a focus for widespread rebellion in England, after which Edward IV was briefly captured by Richard Neville, earl of Warwick; an alliance between Warwick and the king's brother, George, duke of Clarence (d. 1478), was confirmed by the marriage of Clarence with Warwick's daughter Isabel.
18 Oct.: Marriage of Isabella of Castile and Ferdinand of Aragon at Valladolid, a surprise move by Isabella, who had not previously met the groom, designed to out-manoeuvre her opponents; Enrique disinherited Isabella as a result, restored Juana as heir and promised the latter in marriage to Afonso V of Portugal.
2 Dec.: Death of Piero de' Medici, his son Lorenzo assuming the mantle of Florence's first citizen at the request of the Medicean faction.

1470

12 Mar.: Battle of 'Lose-Cote Field', near Stamford, in which rebels supporting Warwick and Clarence were routed.
Apr.: Having failed to secure noble support for their rebellion, Warwick and Clarence fled to France.
12 July: Venetian loss of Negroponte (modern Euboea) to Sultan Mehmet, a defeat which focused Venetian minds on the seriousness of the Turkish threat to the republic's sea empire.
July: Alliance between Venice, Milan and Florence renewed.
2 Oct.: Following Warwick's invasion of England, Edward IV fled to the Low Countries, leading to the Readeption of Henry VI (recrowned 13 Oct.) until 1471, a puppet ruler in the hands of Warwick and Clarence.

1471

Anti-Ottoman alliance between Turcoman ruler Uzun Hasan of Akkoyunlu in eastern Anatolia, Venice, Jacques II of Cyprus and Knights of St John.

Jan.: Inconclusive military campaign by Charles the Bold against France.

14 Mar.: Edward IV landed at Ravenspur, Yorkshire, to reclaim his crown.

14 Apr. (Easter Sunday): Battle of Barnet, a decisive Yorkist victory in which the earl of Warwick was killed.

4 May: Battle of Tewkesbury, Yorkist victory over Margaret of Anjou, in which Edward, prince of Wales, son of Henry VI, was killed.

21 May: Edward IV entered London, Henry VI dying in the Tower the same night.

26 July: Death of Paul II.

9 Aug.: Election of the Savonese Francesco della Rovere as Sixtus IV.

Oct.: Siege of Barcelona, which fell to Joan II in 1472, marking the end of the civil war in Aragon.

1472

Scottish annexation of the Orkney and Shetland Islands, following a marriage alliance with Norway.

30 Apr.: Florence declared war against Volterra, where alum deposits had been found; as papal bankers, the Medici had an interest in Tolfa alum prices so sought to fix those at Volterra; Lorenzo de' Medici persuaded the Florentine Signoria to crush the Volterran protest, which was done with a violent sack of the hill-town in mid-June.

May: Papal fleet sent against the Turks, but disputes with Venetian and Neapolitan allies rendered it ineffective. Marriage of Sixtus IV's nephew Girolamo Riario with Galeazzo Maria Sforza's illegitimate daughter Caterina (c. 1462–1509).

1 June: Marriage by proxy of Ivan III of Muscovy with Zoë Palaeologus of the former Byzantine ruling dynasty.

14 July: Caterina Cornaro 'adopted' by the Venetian Republic, giving Venice a 'dynastic' interest in the kingdom of Cyprus.

11 Sept.: Anglo-Breton treaty of Chateaugiron prepared the ground for an English invasion of France, but the Bretons' nerve did not hold.

Oct.: Turks reached the River Isonzo and Udine.

16 Oct.: By the Capitulation of Pedralbes Joan II of Aragon confirmed Catalan privileges, a major issue in the civil war of the previous decade.

18 Nov.: Death of Cardinal Bessarion at Ravenna.

1473

1 Feb.: Joan II of Aragon entered Perpignan, in the disputed county of Rousillon, while Louis XI was distracted in the north, though it fell to France again in 1475.

22 Mar.: Anglo-French truce agreed.

June: Sixtus IV's purchase of Imola from Galeazzo Maria Sforza for his nephew Girolamo Riario.

11 Aug.: Sultan Mehmet defeated Uzun Hasan at the battle of Baskent on the Euphrates.

26 Oct.: Anglo-Scottish alliance agreed.

Dec.: Charles the Bold's ordinance of Thionville established a Burgundian parlement at Mechelen (Malines), a significant sign of the duke's independence from both Louis XI and the Parlement of Paris.

1474

Year-long siege and heroic resistance of the stategically important Venetian Adriatic port of Scutari.

Before July: The Pazzi became papal bankers in place of the Medici, whose political power in Florence was regarded with deep suspicion in Rome.

25 July: Treaty of London by which Edward IV and Charles the Bold agreed on a joint invasion of France.

July–Oct.: Neuss, near Cologne, besieged by Charles the Bold, as part of his ambition to recreate a 'middle kingdom' between France and Germany.

4 Oct.: Death of the marquis of Villena, a power behind the cause of Juana 'la Beltraneja', assisted Isabella of Castile in her claim to the throne.

26 Oct.: Louis XI persuaded the Swiss cantons to declare war on Charles the Bold.

2 Nov.: An implicitly anti-papal league concluded between Milan, Florence and Venice.

11 Dec.: Death of Enrique IV of Castile.

13 Dec.: Coronation of Isabella at Segovia.

27 Dec.: Cardinal Mendoza and other members of his influential family swore to support Isabella, thereby determining her ultimate victory.

1475

Jubilee year. Genoese possessions in the Crimea lost to the Ottomans.

15 Jan.: By the Concord of Segovia, Ferdinand of Aragon was given powers in Castile equal to those enjoyed by Isabella; the right of female succession was also secured; Isabella received corresponding powers in Aragon in 1481, though female succession did not apply there.

30 May: Betrothal of Afonso V of Portugal to Juana of Castile, after which they were proclaimed joint rulers of Castile.

May–June: Final Franco-Burgundian conflict before the dismemberment of Valois Burgundy; French military successes were not pressed home.

July–Aug.: In alliance with Burgundy, Edward IV invaded France but was bought off by Louis XI in the treaty of Picquigny (29 Aug.).

13 Sept.: Treaty of Soleuvre marked a truce between France and Burgundy.

From Sept.: Charles the Bold's successful campaigns against René of Anjou's duchy of Lorraine, part of his plan to recreate a 'middle kingdom'; this threatened Swiss independence, resulting in Swiss attacks on Charles from late summer.

29 Nov.: Truce of Neuchâtel between Charles and the Swiss.

30 Nov.: Charles entered Nancy, marking his annexation of the duchy of Lorraine, from which a coalition of imperial cities sought to drive him.

1476

Fresh Turkish incursions into Friuli, besides an Ottoman campaign against Matthias Corvinus of Hungary.

Late Jan.: Burgos surrendered to Isabella.

1 Mar.: Battle of Toro, the single most significant military victory for the Isabellines over Juana's Portuguese supporters.

2 Mar.: Battle of Grandson, near Lake Neuchâtel, from which Charles the Bold's Burgundians fled, a victory for the Swiss and their allies.

Apr.: Cortes of Madrigal used by Ferdinand and Isabella as a demonstration of support for their regime after the defeat of the Portuguese; it also founded the Santa Hermandad to unify local *hermandades* (brotherhoods) to act as a police force.

22 June: Burgundian army routed at battle of Murten (Morat), thereby freeing Savoy from the threat of Burgundian domination.

22 Dec.: Marriage of Matthias Corvinus of Hungary with the daughter of Ferrante of Naples paralleled a renewal of cultural contacts between Hungary and Italy.

26 Dec.: Assassination of Galeazzo Maria Sforza, duke of Milan, who was succeeded by his eight-year-old son with his widow Bona of Savoy as regent and Cicco Simonetta as chief adviser, though Ludovico il Moro engineered the fall of Simonetta and himself headed the Milanese government from 1479.

1477

5 Jan.: Charles the Bold killed in battle against the Swiss Confederation at Nancy, which left a power vacuum in western Europe and gave Louis XI the opportunity to annex the duchy of Burgundy while René of Anjou was restored to his duchy of Lorraine.

Feb.: Congress at Ghent became the first regular meeting of the States General of the Netherlands when Mary of Burgundy granted it a charter known as the Great Privilege.

June: George, duke of Clarence, arrested for high treason, his fall partly precipitated by being considered a prospective consort for the heiress Mary of Burgundy.

19 Aug.: Betrothal of Maximilian of Habsburg and Mary of Burgundy, which contributed to the eventual creation of their grandson Charles V's vast personal empire.

1478

Venetian city of Scutari in Dalmatia besieged again by Ottomans.

6 Jan.: Death of Uzun Hasan, Christendom's eastern ally against the Ottomans.

8 Feb.: Sixtus IV and Ferrante of Naples allied against Florence, Milan and Venice.

18 Feb.: Execution of the duke of Clarence in the Tower of London.

26 Apr. (Easter Sunday): Pazzi Conspiracy in Florence, in which Giuliano de' Medici was killed, while his brother Lorenzo survived this assassination attempt in the Duomo; Lorenzo had the Pazzi family and their accomplices killed or exiled and the papal nephew Cardinal Raffaele Riario was imprisoned, thereby creating a diplomatic crisis in which Florence was placed under papal interdict (i.e. excommunicated).

17 May: Sixtus, Naples and Siena united in an anti-Florentine league with a view to driving the Medici from Florence.

15 June: Kroia surrendered to the Turks after a lengthy siege.

30 June: Succession to the thrones of Aragon and Castile was supposedly ensured by the birth of the Infante Juan.

June–Aug.: Successful Genoese rebellion against Milanese rule, though the city remained internally unstable.

From July until 1480: Pazzi War, in which Venice and Milan supported Florence, and Ferrante of Naples backed the papacy.

9 Oct.: France abandoned her previous commitment to Portugal to make a peace with Castile which held until 1494.

1 Nov.: Sixtus responded to Ferdinand and Isabella's request for a specifically Castilian Inquisition by granting them power to appoint their own Inquisitors to seek out lapsed Jewish *conversos*.

7 Dec.: Peace of Olomouc (Olmütz) between Matthias of Hungary and Vladislav of Bohemia divided Bohemia between them.

1479

19 Jan.: Ferdinand II became king of Aragon following the death of his father Joan II, thus creating the impression of Ferdinand and Isabella as king and queen of a far from united 'Spain'.

25 Jan.: Venice made peace with the Turks, negotiated by Giovanni Dario, builder of the Ca' Dario in Venice, the terms including Venetian loss of Scutari and other territories but preservation of her Black Sea and other trade at the heavy price of an annual indemnity of 10,000 ducats.

7 Aug.: Battle of Guinegate, in which Maximilian of Austria was victorious over the French.

4 Sept.: Four interrelated treaties signed at Alcaçovas, by which Portugal gave up all claims to the throne of Castile, while Castile acknowledged Portugal's possession of African and Atlantic conquests, including the Canary Islands.

18 Dec.: Lorenzo de' Medici arrived in Naples to induce Ferrante to break the deadlock of the Pazzi War and make peace; he remained there until Mar. 1480.

1480

Grand Master Pierre d'Aubusson led the Hospitaller defence of Rhodes against Ottoman attack.

Jan.: At the Cortes of Toledo it was decided both that Valladolid would be the administrative centre of Castile, even while the monarchs themselves remained itinerant, and that *corregidores* were to be employed as the Crown's main administrative and judicial agents in the localities.

25 Mar.: An alliance between Florence and Naples concluded in Naples by Lorenzo de' Medici marked the effective conclusion of the Pazzi War; Milan joined this alliance four months later.

16 Apr.: Counter-alliance formed between Venice and the papacy for mutual defence.

10 July: Death of René of Anjou.

11 Aug.: After military landings in late July, Otranto in the kingdom of Naples was captured by an Ottoman invasion force led by Gedik Ahmed Pasha; 12,000 of the city's 20,000 inhabitants were killed, including all the males; this episode caused consternation throughout Italy.

4 Sept.: Girolamo Riario and Caterina Sforza invested with the papal vicariate of Forlì in the Romagna.

13 Dec.: Florence absolved by Sixtus for crimes committed during the Pazzi crisis.

1481

3 May: Death of Sultan Mehmed II led to conflict between his sons Bâyezîd II and Djem.

11 Sept.: Ottoman forces surrendered at Otranto, thanks to the combined military initiative of Naples, the papacy, Aragon and Portugal; contemporaries were quick to note Venetian reluctance to involve themselves in this crisis.

1482

12 Feb.: Ferdinand and Isabella announced the resumption of war between Castile and Muslim Granada, a campaign which ultimately led to the fall of the city of Granada in 1492.

Mar.: Meeting at Basel which claimed unconvincingly to be a General Council of the Church.

2 May: Opening of the War of Ferrara, as a result of Venetian territorial ambitions; Venice's alliance with the papacy and Ferrara's with Naples gave the conflict wider geographical significance, with Neapolitan armies surrounding Rome.

22 July: James III of Scotland seized by rebel lords and imprisoned at Edinburgh; his brother, the duke of Albany, was briefly installed by Richard, duke of Gloucester, as an English puppet.

23 July: Roberto Malatesta finally relieved Rome.

July: Ottoman prince Djem fled from his brother Bâyezîd to the Hospitallers at Rhodes; Djem was moved to Savoy and France later in year.

Aug.: Richard of Gloucester's acquisition of Berwick confirmed his military reputation.

21 Aug.: Battle of Campomorto, Malatesta's victory for the papacy over Neapolitan forces.

10 Sept.: Deaths of the *condottieri* Roberto Malatesta at Rome and Federico da Montefeltro at Ferrara.

12 Dec.: Disillusioned by his Venetian allies, Sixtus made peace with Naples, Milan, Florence and Ferrara, thereby isolating Venice.

23 Dec.: Peace of Arras divided Burgundian domains between France and the Empire after the death of Mary of Burgundy (27 Mar.); the widower Maximilian of Habsburg received Franche Comté, Luxemburg and the Low Countries.

1483

Inquisition extended from Castile to Aragon, in spite of papal opposition and the fact that Aragon did not have a serious *converso* problem; it was essentially a unifying measure.

Feb.: Anti-Venetian Congress of Cremona determined war strategy.

9 Apr.: Death of Edward IV of England.

30 Apr.: Anthony Woodville, earl Rivers, and other members of Edward V's Woodville entourage arrested by Richard of Gloucester.

24 May: Venice placed under papal interdict for failing to make peace with Ferrara and its allies.

26 June: Usurpation of Richard III; Edward V and his brother Richard, duke of York, probably murdered in the Tower of London.

30 Aug.: Death of Louis XI brought about the regency of his daughter Anne and her husband Pierre de Beaujeu.

Oct.–Nov.: Rebellion by Henry Stafford, duke of Buckingham, Richard III's erstwhile lieutenant.

1484

15 Jan.: French Estates General meeting at Tours opened with a speech by Chancellor Guillaume de Rochefort condemning the shedding of royal infants' blood in England in contrast to French loyalty to their youthful king Charles VIII; it met until 7 Mar.

May: Venetian naval forces captured Gallipoli and other Apulian ports.

Summer: Stalemate in the War of Ferrara broken by Ludovico Sforza opening negotiations with Venice.

7 Aug.: Peace of Bagnolo confirmed Venetian possession of Polesine.

12 Aug.: Death of Sixtus IV.

29 Aug.: Election of Sixtus's fellow Ligurian Giovanni Battista Cibo as Innocent VIII.

1485

Ferdinand of Aragon gained a protectorate over Navarre.

22 May: Vienna captured by Matthias Corvinus after a siege.

Summer: Outbreak of the Barons' War in Naples, where nobles resented autocratic government and allied themsleves with the papacy against King Ferrante, who in turn enjoyed the diplomatic support of Milan, Florence and Hungary.

July–Aug.: Synod of Sens debated reform of the French church.

7 Aug.: Henry Tudor landed near Milford Haven, with support from the Beaujeu regime in France.

22 Aug.: Battle of Bosworth, in which Richard III killed, resulting in the advent of the Tudor dynasty in England.

2 Nov.: Peace of Bourges between Charles VIII and rebel nobles brought to an end the *Guerre folle* (Mad war), a revolt by French nobles led by Louis, duke of Orléans, against the government of regent Anne de Beaujeu.

1486

Publication of *Malleus maleficarum* (*Hammer of the witches*) at papal request initiated widespread hysteria, especially in Germany, where the problem of witchcraft was thought to be particularly acute.

18 Jan.: Marriage of Henry VII and Elizabeth of York united the Houses of Lancaster and York.

16 Feb.: Maximilian of Habsburg elected King of the Romans.

22 Apr.: Sentencia de Guadalupe, by which Ferdinand of Aragon abolished the 'six evil customs', freeing peasants in the Crown of Aragon from their lords, in exchange for payment to Crown.

June: Brief surprise attack on northern France by Maximilian of Habsburg.

17 July: Ferrante agreed to pay annual tribute to the pope, a hitherto disputed matter.

9–10 Aug.: Peace treaty between Innocent VIII and Ferrante, but terms were soon broken by the king.

1487

Austrian invasion of Venetian territory repulsed by the *condottiere* Roberto da Sanseverino.

Mar.: Agreement between Charles VIII and rebel Breton nobles as a prelude to Franco-Breton hostilities which began in May.

24 May: Lambert Simnel, claiming to be the earl of Warwick, son of the attainted duke of Clarence, crowned king of England in Dublin.

16 June: Simnel's supporters defeated at the battle of Stoke.

1488

Foundation of the Swabian League by imperial princes, knights and cities to support Emperor Frederick III against the aggression of the Swiss and the Wittelsbachs of Bavaria. Renewed Milanese control over Genoa until 1499.

20 Jan.: Marriage of Innocent VIII's son Franceschetto Cibo with Lorenzo de' Medici's daughter Maddalena.

14 Apr.: Assassination of Girolamo Riario at Forlì by Romagnole nobles left his widow Caterina Sforza to defend his states against aggressors.

11 June: Assassination of James III of Scotland after a rebellion by lowland nobles who used his heir, the future James IV, as their figurehead.

28 July: Important French victory over the Bretons at Saint-Aubin-du-Cormier.

20 Aug.: Franco-Breton peace signed at Le Verger.

9 Sept.: Death of François II of Brittany, succeeded by his daughter, Duchess Anne, who was betrothed to Maximilian of Habsburg in order to try to prevent French annexation of the duchy.

11 Dec.: In spite of alliances with Maxilimian and Ferdinand of Aragon, Brittany was overwhelmed by French forces, who eventually forced a truce in Oct. 1490.

1489

14 Feb.: Anglo-Breton treaty of Redon provided for the defence of Brittany against the invading French.

26 Feb.: Caterino Cornaro, mother of the last Lusignan king of Cyprus, abdicated, later ceding the island to her native Venice (1 June).

9 Mar.: Lorenzo de' Medici achieved his fervent ambition of having his son Giovanni (the future Leo X), then thirteen, made a cardinal.

13 Mar.: Arrival in Rome of Djem, a bargaining tool in Christian negotiations with the Ottomans.

17 Mar.: Anglo-Spanish treaty of Medina del Campo included arrangements for the marriage of Arthur, prince of Wales, and Catalina (Catherine of Aragon), youngest daughter of Ferdinand and Isabella.

20 June: Caterina Cornaro compensated by Venice with the Veneto hilltown of Asolo.

22 July: Peace of Frankfurt between Maximilian and France, with agreement over Brittany among the terms.

1490

Savonarola invited to Florence to deliver Lenten sermons.

4 Apr. (Palm Sunday): Charles VIII entered the Breton capital, Nantes, thereby intensifying the conflict between France and Brittany.

6 Apr.: Sudden death of Matthias Corvinus of Hungary at the height of his power; Maximilian claimed the throne of Hungary.

11 Apr. (Easter Sunday): Infanta Isabel, daughter of Ferdinand and Isabella, married by proxy to the Portuguese crown prince, but he died July 1491.
30 Nov.: Ottoman embassy in Rome.

1491

Apr.: City of Granada besieged after a sequence of Castilian military successes in the 1480s.
July: Girolamo Savonarola elected prior of the Florentine Dominican convent of S. Marco.
Mid-June: Anne of Brittany forced to capitulate to French invaders and consent to marriage with Charles VIII.
Oct.: Henry VII's invasion of France leading to a siege of Boulogne.
Nov.: In Ireland, Perkin Warbeck claimed to be Edward IV's son, Richard, duke of York.
7 Nov.: Peace of Bratislava (Pressburg) ended war in Hungary and marked Maximilian's recognition of King Ulászló's right to the throne.
6 Dec.: Their previous attachments broken, Anne of Brittany and Charles VIII married at Langeais, signalling the loss of Breton independence.

1492

2 Jan.: Granada finally fell to besieging Castilian forces, igniting tremendous national self-confidence among the victors.
31 Mar.: Edict ordering the expulsion of Jews from the Spanish kingdoms within four months; 120–150,000 Jews are estimated to have left Spain, but this act of 'pious cruelty' was generally approved by Christian powers, and their compatriot Alexander VI granted Ferdinand and Isabella the title of 'Catholic Kings' in 1494.
8 Apr.: Death of Lorenzo de' Medici at his villa at Careggi, near Florence, Giovanni Pico and Savonarola having been among his last visitors.
3 June: Dynastic alliance between Naples and the papacy.
25 July: Death of Innocent VIII.
11 Aug.: Election of the Catalan Rodrigo Borgia as Alexander VI.
3 Nov.: By the treaty of Étaples, Charles VIII agreed not to support English rebels and restored Henry VII's pension, leaving himself free for Italian ambitions.

1493

19 Jan.: Treaty of Barcelona renewed the alliance between France and Spain, Roussillon and Cerdagne being returned to the latter in fulfilment of a vow made by Louis XI, while Ferdinand broke with his Neapolitan relatives.
25 Apr.: Holy League formed between the papacy, Milan, Venice, Mantua and Ferrara.

23 May: Treaty of Senlis between Maximilian and Charles VIII, by which France recognised imperial control over Luxemburg and the Low Countries.
19 Aug.: Death of Emperor Frederick III, paving the way for the election of his son Maximilian.

1494
Year in which the 'calamities of Italy' began with Charles VIII's invasion. Treaty of peace and marriage between Russia and Lithuania prevented further Tartar attacks on Moscow, and Ivan III was accepted as sovereign 'of All Russia'.
25 Jan.: Death of Ferrante of Naples initiated a power struggle in Italy.
5 Sept.: Charles VIII in Turin.
22 Oct.: Mysterious death of Gian Galeazzo II Maria Sforza, duke of Milan, brought about formal rule by his uncle Ludovico 'il Moro', after a period in which Ludovico had effectively held power.
30 Oct.: Florentine fortresses yielded to Charles by Piero de' Medici.
5 Nov.: Savonarola among the Florentine envoys who met Charles at Pisa.
9 Nov.: Pisa revolted against Florentine rule, leading to French control over this city until 1509; Florence also lost control of Livorno and other subject cities; the crisis in Florence witnessed the flight of Piero de' Medici, the exile of the Medici family, whose property was confiscated, and the collapse of the Medici Bank, after years of decline due to economic trends and poor management.
17 Nov.: Charles's entry into Florence.
31 Dec.: Charles's entry into Rome.

1495
21 Jan.: Alfonso II of Naples abdicated in favour of his son Ferrante and fled to Sicily.
2 Feb.: Submission of Naples to the invading French.
19 Feb.: French forces entered Naples, followed by Charles himself three days later.
25 Feb.: Death at Naples of the fugitive Ottoman prince Djem, who had been handed over to Charles by Alexander VI in 1494.
Mar.: The 'Great Captain' Gonzalvo Fernándoz de Córdoba (1453–1515) attacked French garrisons in Naples by order of Ferdinand of Aragon as king of Sicily and in support of Ferdinand's Neapolitan cousins.
31 Mar.: Holy League signed in Venice between the papacy, Ferdinand of Aragon, Emperor Maximilian, Milan, Florence and Venice.
12 May: Charles VIII crowned in Naples.
6 July: Battle of Fornovo, near Parma, the first major confrontation of the Italian Wars and a victory for Franco-Swiss forces, commanded by Charles and Gaston de Foix, over Italians, led by Gian Francesco Gonzaga.

July: French armies retired from Italy.

21 July: Savonarola summoned to Rome in connection with his attacks on papal worldliness and corruption.

9 Oct.: Franco-Milanese treaty of Vercelli returned Novara to Milan as the price of Ludovico Sforza's support for Charles.

1496

Polish-Hungarian alliance formed.

17 Feb.: Ferrante II restored to the throne of Naples.

Sept.: Scottish military incursion into England.

1 Oct.: Anglo-Spanish treaty renewed marriage negotiations.

7 Oct.: Ferrante II of Naples succeeded by his uncle Federico, who was recognised by Venice but opposed by his kinsman Ferdinand of Aragon.

21 Oct.: Marriage of Philip the Fair, son of Emperor Maximilian and Mary of Burgundy, with Infanta Juana, daughter of Ferdinand and Isabella.

1497

War between Ottomans and Poles until 1499, in which the Poles did not acquit themselves well. Beginning of Pandolfo Petrucci's fifteen-year 'tyranny' in Siena. Annulment of 1492 marriage between Lucrezia Borgia, daughter of Alexander VI and Vanozza Catanei, and Giovanni Sforza of Pesaro freed her for marriage in 1498 with Alfonso, duke of Bisceglie, illegitimate son of Alfonso II of Naples.

2 Apr.: Marriage of the Infante Juan with Margaret (hereafter Margaret of Austria), daughter of Emperor Maximilian and Mary of Burgundy.

13 May: Savonarola excommunicated.

14 June: The murder of Alexander VI's son Juan, duke of Gandia, whose body was found in the Tiber, so shocked the pope that he initiated an ecclesiastical reform programme.

4 Oct.: Death of the Infante Juan, heir to crowns of Aragon and Castile, the succession passing to his sister Isabel, wife of Manoel I of Portugal.

5 Oct.: Surrender of Perkin Warbeck, who was executed two years later.

1498

Cesare Borgia, son of Alexander VI and Vanozza Catanei and a cardinal since 1493, returned to the secular life.

11 Feb.: Savonarola preached on the invalidity of his own excommunication.

7 Apr.: Death of Charles VIII.

22 May: Ecclesiastical and Florentine secular authorities agreed on the condemnation of Savonarola.

23 May: Burning of Savonarola in the Piazza della Signoria, Florence.

23 Aug.: Death of Isabel, queen of Portugal, heir to the crowns of Aragon and Castile; her sister Maria married the widowed King Manoel in 1500.

17 Dec.: Marriage of Louis XII with Louis XI's daughter Jeanne de France annulled, enabling the king to marry Charles VIII's widow, Anne of Brittany, thereby retaining French control over her duchy.

1499

First Revolt of the Alpujarras, Muslim rebellion in Granada, after which Cardinal Cisneros instituted a policy of forced conversion to Christianity or expulsion from the kingdom. French control over Genoa until 1512.

8 Jan.: Louis XII and Anne of Brittany married at Nantes.

9 Feb.: Franco-Venetian alliance agreed, by which Venice acquired some Milanese territory.

18 July: First French troops arrived in Milanese territory in pursuit of Louis' claims to the duchy as duke of Orléans and great-grandson of Gian Galeazzo Visconti (d. 1402), whose daughter Valentina married Louis, duke of Orléans, in 1389.

12 Aug.: Naval battle of Navarino (Zonchio), off the Morea, a clear Ottoman victory in their 1499–1503 war with Venice.

2 Sept.: Ludovico Sforza fled to the imperial court while the city of Milan submitted to the French invaders without a fight.

22 Sept.: Emperor Maximilian confirmed Swiss independence in the peace of Basel after the Swiss Confederation proved victorious in their war with the Swabian League.

6 Oct.: Arrival of Louis XII in Milan.

12 Dec.: Cesare Borgia wrested Imola from Caterina Sforza, widow of Girolamo Riario, one of the first moves in his carving out of a Romagnole state for himself.

1500

Jubilee year. Hungary declared war on the Turks.

12 Jan.: Cesare Borgia captured Forlì after a stout defence by Caterina Sforza.

25 Jan.: Following the return of Ludovico Sforza to his duchy, the French withdrew from the city of Milan.

10 Apr.: Ludovico taken prisoner by the French at Novara, after which he spent his last years in France, leaving Louis XII in control of the duchy of Milan.

20 July: Death of Miguel, infant heir to the crowns of Aragon, Castile and Portugal, grandson of Ferdinand and Isabella.

Oct.: Pandolfo Malatesta of Rimini and Giovanni Sforza of Pesaro fled before Cesare Borgia's invading forces.

11 Nov.: Treaty of Granada between Aragon and France partitioned the kingdom of Naples.

1501

25 Apr.: Manfredi city of Faenza fell to Cesare Borgia; added to the cities secured earlier, this created the duchy of the Romagna, with which Alexander VI invested his son.

May: Holy League created, consisting of the papacy, Hungary and Venice.

Early July: French forces reached the kingdom of Naples; simultaneously, Gonzalvo de Córdoba, acting for Ferdinand of Aragon, was also sent to Naples with a military force, precipitating an extensive period of Franco-Spanish conflict for possession of the kingdom.

July: Cesare Borgia secured control of the duchy of Piombino from Jacopo d'Appiano.

4 Aug.: French army entered the city of Naples, causing King Federico to capitulate, flee to France and never return to his kingdom.

Aug.: One-year-old Charles of Ghent, son of Philip the Fair and Juana of Castile, betrothed to Louis XII's two-year-old daughter Claude of France.

1502

All unconverted Moors ordered to leave Castile.

24 Jan.: Anglo-Scottish treaty of 'perpetual' peace arranged the marriage Henry VII's daughter Margaret with James IV.

1 Mar.: Fall of Taranto to Gonzalvo de Córdoba.

2 Apr.: Death of Arthur, prince of Wales, after only six months of unconsummated marriage with Catherine of Aragon.

Summer: Louis XII returned to Italy, where his presence inspired a revival in French military fortunes.

21 June: Cesare Borgia's invasion of Urbino, from which Duke Guidobaldo da Montefeltro fled; Borgia went on to capture Camerino from the papal vicar Giulio Cesare da Varano.

22 Sept.: Piero Soderini (1452–1522), friend of Machiavelli, elected Florentine Gonfaloniere di Giustizia for life, in an attempt to create greater stability in government.

Oct.: Revolt plotted at Magione, near Lake Trasimeno, by some erstwhile followers of Cesare Borgia, who in turn tricked them and exacted bloody revenge at Fano (Dec.).

1503

28 Apr.: Battle of Cerignola in Apulia, the first major confrontation between French and Spanish arms in Italy, an easy victory for the Spanish led by Gonzalvo de Córdoba (the 'Great Captain') aided by the Colonna family; this victory was the key to the fall of Naples on 16 May.

Mid-July: The Great Captain entered Naples unopposed by the French.

8 Aug.: Marriage of James IV of Scotland and Margaret Tudor paved way for the ultimate Union of the Crowns (1603).

10 Aug.: Peace signed between Venice, Hungary and the Ottomans.

18 Aug.: Death of Alexander VI.

22 Sept.: Election of Francesco Todeschini-Piccolomini as Pius III.
18 Oct.: Death of Pius III.
1 Nov.: Election of Giuliano della Rovere, nephew of Sixtus IV, as Julius II, which his arch-rival Cesare Borgia had been unable to prevent due to illness; Borgia refused to hand over his Romagnole possessions to the new pope, was duly imprisoned, escaped and fled to his wife Charlotte d'Albret's homeland of Navarre.
29 Dec.: Battle of Garigliano, near Gaeta, a clear victory for Spanish forces over the already retreating French of Francesco Gonzaga.

1504
31 Mar.: Treaty of Lyon, by which France acknowledged the Spanish as lawful possessors of the kingdom of Naples.
22 Sept.: First treaty of Blois between Louis XII, Maximilian and Philip the Fair prepared the ground for what became the League of Cambrai against Venice, which Ferdinand was invited to join; at this stage a marriage between Charles of Ghent and Claude of France was still a possibility.
26 Nov.: Death of Isabella of Castile at Medina del Campo, having written a will excluding Juana and Philip from the Castilian succession and in favour of her grandson Charles of Ghent, upon him attaining twenty years of age.

1505
Spanish capture of Mers-el-Kebir.
7 Apr.: In accordance with the first treaty of Blois, Maximilian conferred Milan upon Louis XII, making him also protector of Genoa.
12 Oct.: Second treaty of Blois, between Ferdinand and Louis, arranged the former's marriage to Germaine de Foix, Louis's niece.
24 Nov.: Treaty of Salamanca, whereby Castile was to be jointly ruled by Ferdinand, Philip and Juana, but this proved unworkable.

1506
Popular revolt in Genoa against French rule.
9 Feb.: Treaty of Windsor between England and Philip the Fair countered the second treaty of Blois.
18 Mar.: Fifty-three-year-old Ferdinand of Aragon married seventeen-year old Germaine de Foix.
26 Apr.: Juana and Philip arrived in Castile, after a journey from the Low Countries via England.
30 Apr.: Anglo-Burgundian treaty signed.
21 May: Betrothal of Claude of France to François, count of Angoulême (the future Francis I), overriding the earlier commitment to Charles of Ghent and reflecting the changed balance of power in western Europe, with Philip claiming the throne of Castile.

13 Sept.: Julius II entered Perugia following its surrender by the Baglioni family.

25 Sept.: Death of Philip left his grief-stricken widow mentally incapable of exercising power.

11 Nov.: Julius's entry into Bologna, from which the ruling Bentivoglio family was expelled; the most striking episode in this pope's imposition of papal authority over the Papal States.

1507

Brussels became the capital of the Low Countries; Margaret of Austria, widow of both Infante Juan and Philibert of Savoy, governor of the Netherlands until 1515.

12 Mar.: Death in Spain of Cesare Borgia.

Apr.: Louis XII's suppression of a Genoese revolt and annexation of the republic by France.

21 Dec.: Betrothal of Mary, daughter of Henry VII of England, to Charles of Ghent.

1508

Feb.: Venetian territory invaded from Austria by imperial forces, which were soon defeated by Venetians under Bartolomeo d'Alviano and Niccolò Orsini, count of Pitigliano, at the battle of Pieve di Cadore in Friuli.

10 Dec.: League of Cambrai formed between Emperor Maximilian (for whom negotiations were led by Margaret of Austria), Louis XII, Ferdinand of Aragon and pope Julius II; under the cover of a crusade against the Turks, the signatories bound themselves to reverse a century of Venetian *terraferma* expansion, with Milan and surrounding territories being provisionally allocated to Louis, and the Veneto and Friuli to Maximilian, while Julius claimed Ravenna and certain Romagnole towns; Ferdinand made a bid for Otranto, and other claims were made by Mantua and Ferrara; Venice was placed under an interdict.

1509

13 Apr.: League of Cambrai declared war on Venice, Louis XII returning to Italy three days later.

3 May: Birth of a very short-lived son to Ferdinand and Germaine de Foix did nothing to alter the Spanish succession problem.

May: Oran captured by Spaniards led by Cardinal Cisneros.

14 May: Battle of Agnadello (Ghiardadda), east of Milan near the River Adda, in which a Venetian army led by the count of Pitigliano and Bartolomeo d'Alviano was decisively defeated by the French, representing the League of Cambrai; Venice lost all her *terraferma* possessions with the exception of Treviso; in the face of this French threat Caterina Cornaro's court at Asolo dispersed.

8 June: Restoration of Florentine rule over Pisa.

11 June: Marriage of the new English king Henry VIII with his brother's widow, Catherine of Aragon.

15–30 Sept.: Padua besieged by French and imperial troops.

1510

Spanish subjection of Algiers until 1511.

24 Feb.: Having distanced himself from the League of Cambrai and being mindful of the importance of Venetian sea power for a projected crusade, Julius II lifted the interdict placed on Venice in 1508; following this papal defection there were months of fighting around Ferrara between French and papal contingents; in return for his neutrality, Ferdinand was invested with Naples by Julius.

1511

Martin Luther in Rome, in the winter of 1510/11. Spanish capture of Tripoli. With support from Maximilian and Louis XII, five rebel cardinals called for a General Council of the Church to meet at Pisa in autumn 1511, with a view to deposing the pope; Julius reacted by calling his own Council for Apr. 1512.

23 May: *Condottiere* Gian Giacomo Trivulzio entered Bologna, where the Bentivoglio family was restored to power.

4 Oct.: Holy League formed between Julius, Ferdinand of Aragon and Venice in opposition to France, which had become too powerful in northern Italy; this league lasted until 1513.

13 Nov.: England joined the Holy League, promising an invasion of Picardy.

16 Nov.: Ferdinand affirmed his commitment to Julius's proposed Lateran Council while condemning Louis XII as an enemy of the Church.

1512

Russo-Polish war until 1522.

Jan.: Venice recovered Brescia and Bergamo.

11 Apr. (Easter Sunday): Battle of Ravenna, a victory for the French led by Gaston de Foix, duke of Nemours, himself a casualty in the battle, over the forces of the Spanish-led Holy League led by Ramón de Cardona, viceroy of Naples.

25 Apr.: Sultan Bâyezîd forced to abdicate.

3 May: Opening of Fifth Lateran Council.

6 May: A Swiss army descended into Italy in concert with Venice, contributing to the French retreat from the peninsula in June.

July: Southern half of Navarre siezed by Ferdinand from its king Jean d'Albret and incorporated into the kingdom of Castile.

12 July: Franco-Scottish alliance of 1492 renewed.

29/30 Aug.: Sack of Prato by Ramón de Cardona for the allied powers of the papacy, Ferdinand and Venice.

1 Sept.: Fall of Piero Soderini and reform of the Florentine constitution paved the way for the return of the Medici, with support from the Holy League.

Nov.: Maximilian joined the Holy League.

Dec.: Massimiliano Sforza, son of Ludovico il Moro, installed as duke of Milan at the expense of the French.

1513

20/21 Feb.: Death of Julius II.

9 Mar.: Election of Giovanni de' Medici as Leo X.

16 Mar.: Renewal of the anti-English alliance between France and Scotland, in the same month as France allied with Venice.

5 Apr.: Holy League between Maximilian, England, the papacy and Ferdinand agreed at Mechelen (Malines), where Margaret of Austria held court.

May: French forces of Louis de La Trémoïlle returned to Italy, coming into conflict with the Swiss in Lombardy.

6 June: Battle of Novara, in which French troops bound for Milan, from where they intended to oust Maximilian, were defeated by the emperor's Swiss allies.

Late June: An English army arrived in France.

16 Aug.: French disgraced themselves in the so-called battle of the Spurs, near Thérouanne, fleeing from the invading English.

Sept.: Swiss laid siege to Dijon.

9 Sept.: Battle of Flodden Field, near Berwick, in which James IV and the 'flower' of the Scottish nobility were killed; war with the English fulfilled the Scots' obligation to their French allies.

17 Oct.: Treaty of Lille created a triple alliance of England, the Empire and the Spanish kingdoms to contain France, this being the central aim of Ferdinand's foreign policy.

1514

Jan.: Louis XII recognised the Fifth Lateran Council.

18 May: Marriage of Louis's daughter Claude with the heir to the French throne François, count of Angoulême.

7 Aug.: Anglo-French peace treaty signed at Saint-Germain-en-Laye, including the arrangement of a marriage between the recently widowed fifty-three-year-old Louis XII and Henry VIII's eighteen-year-old sister Mary, which was duly celebrated at Abbeville (9 Oct.).

1515

1 Jan.: Death of Louis XII and succession of François, count of Angoulême, as Francis I.

24 Mar.: Treaty of Paris arranged the marriage of Charles of Ghent and Renée of France, daughter of Louis XII.

5 Apr.: Anglo-French treaty of London, by which Francis consented to honour his predecessor's debts to Henry VIII.

15 July: The king's mother, Louise of Savoy, created regent in France as Francis prepared for his first Italian expedition.

13–14 Sept.: Battle of Marignano, near Milan, in which Francis, with Venetian troops under the captaincy of Gian Giacomo Trivulzio, defeated a papal-Milanese army, including Swiss infantry; this led to the renewed French occupation of Milan from 11 Oct., and subsequently of Genoa, until 1522; the reputation of Swiss soldiery was thereby tarnished.

7 Nov.: Treaty of Geneva between France and the Swiss Confederation.

11–15 Dec.: Meeting at Bologna between Francis and Leo X for negotiations leading to the Concordat of Bologna, which rendered the Pragmatic Sanction of Bourges obsolete and arranged for the king's appointments to senior benefices to be merely confirmed by the pope, while the latter could again draw annates from France.

1516

23 Jan.: Death of Ferdinand of Aragon, leaving Aragon to his grandson Charles of Ghent, while Cisneros led the government of Castile.

Mar.: In an anti-French move, Emperor Maximilian invaded Italy to restore the Sforza in Milan, but soon retreated.

13 Aug.: Franco-Spanish treaty of Noyon isolated England, while Francis renounced his dynastic claims to Naples.

18 Aug.: Concordat of Bologna ratified by Leo X, though not registered by the Parlement of Paris until 22 Mar. 1518.

8 Nov.: Death of Cisneros left Adrian of Utrecht, Charles's former tutor, as the leading political figure in Spain.

29 Nov.: Perpetual peace of Fribourg between Francis and the Swiss, the latter undertaking not to serve the enemies of France.

4 Dec.: Truce of Brussels, by which Charles of Ghent (now Carlos I of Aragon and Castile) agreed to French control over Milan.

1517

Ottoman conquest of Egypt. War in Italy over Leo X's appointment of his kinsman Lorenzo de' Medici as duke of Urbino, ousting Julius II's nephew Francesco Maria I della Rovere.

11 Mar.: Treaty of Cambrai between Francis I, Emperor Maximilian and Charles of Spain.

16 Mar.: Closing of Fifth Lateran Council.

Apr.: Conspiracy against Leo X by Cardinal Alfonso Petrucci and others came to light.

26 Aug.: New Franco-Scottish alliance.

Sept.: Arrival of Charles in Spain to claim his maternal inheritance, but his Flemish advisers, such as Guillaume de Croy, *seigneur* de Chièvres (1458–1521), were detested by Spain's political class.

31 Oct.: Luther's ninety-five theses posted at Wittenberg, provoked by Johann Tetzel's sale of indulgences, the proceeds of which were directed towards the rebuilding of St Peter's basilica, Rome.

1518
Margaret of Austria re-appointed regent of the Netherlands, a post she held until her death in 1530.
July: Imperial-Venetian truce.
5 Oct.: Cardinal Wolsey's treaty of London made 'universal' peace between France, England, the Empire, the papacy, Spain and many lesser states.
12 Oct.: At Augsburg, Luther refused to recant before Cardinal Cajetan.

1519
Beginning of the Zwinglian reformation in Zürich. City of Valencia in revolt due to famine and in reaction to the policies of the viceroy Diego Hurtado de Mendoza; this revolt is known as the *Germanía* and it continued until 1523.
Jan.: Cortes of Aragon recognised Charles as king, in preference to his brother Ferdinand, who had been groomed for the post by their maternal grandfather Ferdinand.
12 Jan.: Death of Emperor Maximilian.
26 June: Francis I withdrew his candidature for the imperial election after Leo X ceased to support him.
28 June: Unanimous election at Frankfurt of Charles of Spain, head of the House of Habsburg, as Emperor Charles V.

1520
Cortes of Castile, meeting at Corunna, sought to raise taxes to finance Charles's imperial venture.
From Feb.: Castilian cities began to revolt against this; Revolt of the Comuneros began in Toledo and spread to Segovia, Zamora, Toro, Madrid, Guadalajara, Alcalá, Soria, Ávila, Cuenca, Burgos, Salamanca, León, Murcia, Mula and Alicante.
20 May: Charles sailed from Corunna to accept the imperial office.
7–23 June: Meeting between Francis I and Henry VIII at the 'Field of the Cloth of Gold' at Guînes marked an entente between France and England, though Wolsey was also involved in negotiations with Charles about mutual Anglo-imperial defence.
15 June: Leo X excommunicated Luther in the Bull *Exsurge Domine*.
June–Oct.: Luther wrote three treatises in which his beliefs were expounded: *Address to the Christian nobility of the German nation, The Babylonish captivity of the Church, On Christian freedom*.
30 Sept.: Accession of Süleymân, known as 'the Magnificent', to the Ottoman sultanate.

23 Oct.: Charles V crowned King of the Romans at Aachen.

31 Oct.: Castilian regents declared war on *comunero* cities.

10 Dec.: Luther publicly burned *Exsurge Domine* at Wittenberg.

1521

3 Jan.: *Exsurge Domine* confirmed by the Bull *Decit Romanum Pontificem*, by which Luther and his followers were excommunicated.

17 Jan.–25 May: Imperial Diet met at Worms, at which the papal case against Luther was presented by Girolamo Aleandro.

18 Apr.: Appearing at the Diet, Luther made his famous declaration: 'Here I stand; I can do no other; God help me; amen.'

23 Apr.: Battle of Villalar, between Valladolid and Tordesillas, at which *comunero* rebels were defeated; their leader, Juan Padilla, was executed at Valladolid the next day; Charles's rule over Spain was largely peaceful thereafter.

12 May: Diet concluded by passing the Edict of Worms, denouncing the Lutheran heresy and outlawing Lutherans.

28 Apr.: Charles V surrendered his Austrian inheritance to his brother Ferdinand.

8 May: Papal-imperial alliance agreed, leading to conflict between the papacy and France.

July onwards: international peace conference at Calais, chaired by Wolsey and attended by Gattinara for Charles and Cardinal Antoine Duprat for Francis, but this was thwarted by military activities.

20 Aug.: Imperial invasion of northern France.

25 Aug.: Secret Anglo-imperial treaty of Bruges, negotiated by Charles and Wolsey, created an alliance in the event of war with France.

29 Aug.: Ottoman conquest of Belgrade.

26 Oct.: Leo conferred the title *Defensor fidei* (Defender of the Faith) on Henry VIII of England.

19 Nov.: Milan captured by the French and their allies, the Sforza being reinstated there until 1524.

1 Dec.: Death of Leo X.

1522

German Knights' War between pro- and anti-Lutheran factions, until 1523.

9 Jan.: Election of Adrian of Utrecht, Charles V's former tutor and principal councillor in Spain, as Adrian VI.

27 Apr.: Battle of Bicocca near Milan, a victory for the Spanish, led by the marquis of Pescara and Prospero Colonna, over French and Swiss forces allied with those of Giovanni 'delle Bande Nere' de' Medici.

29 May: English declaration of war on France in accordance with the terms of the 1521 Anglo-imperial alliance.

30 May: Capitulation of Genoa and its sack by Spanish troops reduced French possessions in northern Italy to fortresses at Milan and Cremona.
19 June: Although negotiated in 1521, the anti-French treaty of Windsor was signed during Charles V's English visit, after which he returned to Spain.
July–Oct.: English invasion of France.
17 Nov.: Opening of the imperial Diet at Nuremberg.
21 Dec.: Ottoman conquest of Rhodes; the fugitive Hospitallers were eventually granted Malta as their base by Charles in 1530.

1523
29 July: Peace agreed at Worms between Charles V, Venice and Milan.
6 Aug.: Sequestration of lands disputed by Charles, duke of Bourbon and Constable of France, and queen dowager Louise of Savoy; this precipitated Bourbon's treasonous plan to invade France with imperial and English aid while Francis was preoccupied in Italy; Bourbon fled to Charles when the plot was disovered.
12 Aug.: Louise of Savoy again appointed regent in France, while Francis prepared for another Italian expedition.
Aug.–Sept.: English invasion of Picardy, in spite of Wolsey's peace efforts.
14 Sept.: Death of Adrian VI.
19 Nov.: Election of Giulio de' Medici as Clement VII.

1524
1 July: Bourbon's invasion of Provence, leading to a brief siege of Marseille in Aug., had been heralded by a new anti-French treaty between Charles V and Henry VIII in May.
From summer (until spring 1526): various rebellions in central and southern Germany collectively known as the Peasants' War, combined elements of traditional revolts with new Lutheran spiritual fervour.
Sept.: Erasmus's *Discourse on free will* attacked the central tenets of Lutheranism.
17 Oct.: Louise of Savoy made regent of France for the third time, prior to her son's Italian campaign.
25 Dec.: Luther replied to Erasmus with *The will in bondage.*

1525
Headquarters of the Teutonic Knights moved further westwards, from Königsberg to Mergentheim, matching their territorial losses, in the same year that Albrecht von Hohenzollern, the Grand Master, was the first of the German princes to turn Lutheran.
24 Feb.: Capture of Francis I at the battle of Pavia by imperialist troops commanded by Bourbon and Charles de Lannoy, viceroy of Naples; this battle destroyed French hopes in Italy.
13 June: Luther's marriage with the former nun Katharina von Bora.

11 Aug.: Captive Francis arrived in Madrid, where he was detained for over a year, causing great loss of morale in France; during his absence the Paris Parlement accused the Crown of being responsible for the spread of heresy through royal patronage of ecclesiastical reformers and humanists.

30 Aug.: Anglo-French treaty of the More, Hertfordshire, negotiated by Wolsey, securing English support for the campaign to release Francis.

Nov.: Francis's mock abdication in favour of his elder son, François.

1526

14 Jan.: Franco-imperial treaty of Madrid, the terms of which included Francis giving up his claims to Milan and Naples, pardoning Bourbon, and a marriage alliance between Francis, a widower since 1524, and Charles V's sister Eleanor; French concessions were the price of Francis's freedom, but his subsequent failure to ratify the treaty rendered it void.

17 Mar.: Release of Francis, in exchange for which his two young sons, the Dauphin François and Henri, duke of Orléans, were held as hostages in Spain.

2 May: German Lutheran princes formed the League of Torgau.

22 May: League of Cognac united France, the papacy, England, Milan, Florence and Venice against the Empire.

June: First Diet of Speyer, at which delegates were instructed by Charles V to enforce the Edict of Worms, but this appeal was rejected on account of the emperor's war with the papacy.

27 Aug.: Diet ruled that princes should determine ecclesiastical affairs in their own lands: 'Cuius regio eius religio'.

29 Aug.: Battle of Mohács, near the Danube in southern Hungary, a significant victory for the armies of Sultan Süleymân, meant the collapse of Jagiełłon rule in Hungary and Bohemia; Louis II of Hungary and Bohemia was killed in this encounter and succeeded by his brother-in-law Ferdinand of Habsburg, but the latter's claim was contested by János Zápolya, *voyvode* of Transylvania.

1527

30 Apr.: Anglo-French treaty of Westminster planned for war against Charles V unless their terms were met by the imperialists.

6 May: Imperial troops entered and sacked Rome after a siege, during which Clement VII took refuge in Castel Sant'Angelo.

May: News of the Sack of Rome meant the inevitable overthrow of the Medici in Florence; this led to the establishment of the last Florentine Republic, which survived until 1530 and was of a distinctly Savonarolan stamp; another consequence of the Sack of Rome was that France made territorial acquisitions in northern Italy, including Genoa.

17 May: Opening of the tribunal investigating the validity of Henry VIII's marriage to Catherine of Aragon.

June: Clement agreed to become the virtual prisoner of the imperialists.

22 June: Henry VIII told Catherine they had been living in sin for eighteen years.

Aug.: French conquest of Lombardy with the exception of Milan itself.

18 Aug.: Wolsey's Anglo-French treaty of Amiens, by which Henry VIII's daughter Mary was promised in marriage to Francis's son Henri, duke of Orléans.

1528

22 Jan.: Declaration of war on the emperor by France and England, because Charles still held captive Francis's sons.

Feb.: French invasion of the kingdom of Naples by an army from Lombardy.

9 Feb.: As in the 1490s, Christ was declared 'sole and true lord and king' of Florence.

10 Aug.: Reacting to French determination to keep Genoa and Savona under French control, the Genoese naval *condottiere* Andrea Doria (1466/68–1560) defected from the French to the imperial side.

12 Sept.: Genoa thus gained independence from France with Doria's help.

Dec.: Clement VII escaped from Rome to Orvieto.

1529

21 Feb.: Opening of the second imperial Diet at Speyer, notable for marking the end of toleration for Lutherans in Catholic states, thereby turning the former into 'Protestants'.

Apr.: Revolt in Lyon known as the Grande Rebeine, the most obvious sign of widespread poverty in France.

18 June: Opening of the legatine court at Blackfriars to try the marriage of Henry VIII and Catherine of Aragon.

21 June: Imperial victory over the French at Landriano, near Genoa.

29 June: Treaty of Barcelona signed between Clement VII and Charles V, the terms of which included the restoration of Clement's Medici kinsmen to Florence, absolution for the Sack of Rome and the promise of an imperial coronation.

16 July: Henry VIII's divorce case revoked to Rome in the wake of agreement between pope and emperor, the latter being Catherine of Aragon's nephew; an unlikely means to the king's desired objective.

3 Aug.: Peace of Cambrai (*Paix des Dames*), negotiated by Louise of Savoy and Margaret of Austria, Charles V's aunt and governor in the Netherlands; a humiliating deal for France, according to which Francis gave up his Italian and other territorial claims in return for the recovery of his sons for payment of a ransom; the Sforza were also reinstated in Milan until 1535, when the duchy became Spanish Habsburg territory.

8 Sept.: Sultan Süleymân captured Buda.

26 Sept.–16 Oct.: Vienna besieged by Ottoman forces.

25 Oct.: Thomas More appointed English lord chancellor in succession to Cardinal Wolsey, whose failure to secure the royal annulment led to his downfall the following year.

Oct. Florence beseiged by an imperial army until Aug. 1530.

1530

24 Feb.: Charles V crowned emperor by Clement VII at Bologna.

5 June: Death at Innsbruck of Gattinara, who was succeeded as imperial chancellor by Nicolas Perrenot de Granvelle, who specialised in Nether-landish and German affairs, while Francisco de Los Cobos was Charles's principal minister in Spain.

25 June: Confession of Augsburg drawn up by Luther and Philipp Melanchthon and presented to Charles at the imperial Diet.

12 Aug.: Medici returned to Florence after the fall of the Last Republic; Alessandro de' Medici became the first duke of Florence.

23 Sept.: Religious autonomy of German princes denied by the Recess of Augsburg.

4 Nov.: Wolsey's arrest for treason.

24 Nov.: Death of Wolsey.

1531

27 Feb.: League of Schmalkalden concluded between certain German Protestant princes opposed to the Recess of Augsburg, other states join-ing in subsequent years.

1532

Annexation of Brittany by Francis I.

16 May: Resignation of Thomas More as lord chancellor, due to his conflict of conscience about Henry VIII's claim to supremacy over the Church in England.

1533

28 Oct.: Marriage of the future Henri II of France with Clement VII's niece Caterina (Catherine) de' Medici.

1534

25 July: Death of Clement VII.

18 Oct.: Affaire des Placades, an attempt by French evangelicals to force Francis I off the confessional fence; this backfired when the king promptly arrested the leading reformers, the young Calvin being among those who thereupon fled from Paris.

2   Popes

2.1   Popes and antipopes

Pontificate	Papal title	Name	Year and place of birth; date of death if not in office
1370–78	**Gregory XI**	Pierre Roger de Beaufort	1329, near Limoges
1378–89	**Urban VI**	Bartolomeo Prignano	*c.* 1318, Naples
1389–1404	**Boniface IX**	Pietro Tomacelli	*c.* 1350, Naples
1404–6	**Innocent VII**	Cosimo de' Migliorati	*c.* 1336, Sulmona, Abruzzi
1406–15	**Gregory XII**	Angelo Correr	*c.* 1325, Venice; d. 1417
1417–31	**Martin V**	Oddone Colonna	*c.* 1368, Genazzano, near Rome
1431–47	**Eugenius IV**	Gabriele Condulmer	*c.* 1383, Venice
1447–55	**Nicholas V**	Tommaso Parentucelli	1397, Sarzana, Liguria
1455–58	**Calixtus III**	Alfonso de Borja (Borgia)	1378, Játiva, Valencia
1458–64	**Pius II**	Enea Silvio Piccolomini	1405, Corsignano (the future Pienza), S. of Siena
1464–71	**Paul II**	Pietro Barbo	1417, Venice
1471–84	**Sixtus IV**	Francesco della Rovere	1414, Celle, near Savona
1484–92	**Innocent VIII**	Giovanni Battista Cibo	1432, Genoa
1492–1503	**Alexander VI**	Rodrigo Borgia	1431, Játiva, Valencia
1503	**Pius III**	Francesco Todeschini-Piccolomini	1439, Siena

Pontificate	Papal title	Name	Year and place of birth; date of death if not in office
1503–13	**Julius II**	Giuliano della Rovere	1443, Albissola, near Savona
1513–21	**Leo X**	Giovanni de' Medici	1475, Florence
1521–23	**Adrian VI**	Adrian Florisz Dedel	1459, Utrecht
1523–34	**Clement VII**	Giulio de' Medici	1468, Florence

Antipopes at Avignon

1378–94	**Clement VII**	Robert of Savoy	1342, Geneva
1394–1415	**Benedict XIII**	Pedro de Luna	c. 1328, Illueca, Aragon

Spanish successor to Benedict XIII:

1423–29	**Clement VIII**	Gil Sanchez Muñoz	c. 1360, Teruel; d. 1446

French successor to Benedict XIII in reaction to Clement VIII:

1425–30	**Benedict XIV**	Bernard Garnier	dates of birth and death unknown

With Clement VIII and Benedict XIV the Spanish and French schismatic lines fizzled out ingloriously.

Antipopes at Pisa

1409–10	**Alexander V**	Petros Philargis	c. 1339, Crete
1410–15	**John XXIII**	Baldassare Cossa	Naples; d. 1419

Alexander's title is regarded as legitimate, but John's is not.

Antipope at Basel

1439–49	**Felix V**	Amadeus VIII, duke of Savoy	1383, Savoy

2.2 Profiles of Renaissance popes

Adrian VI 1521–23 (Adrian Florisz Dedel, Adrian of Utrecht)
Education: Zwolle and Deventer with the Brethren of the Common Life; University of Louvain (doctorate in theology, 1491), where he was rector (1491–1501), and chancellor from 1497.

Experience prior to papal election: As a successful teacher he was appointed tutor to the future Charles V in 1507, becoming his councillor in 1512 and councillor to Margaret of Austria, regent of the Netherlands, in 1515. Made a cardinal in 1517 at Charles's request. Moved to Spain when Charles succeeded to the crown of Aragon. Inquisitor of Aragon from 1516 and of Castile from 1518, in succession to Cardinal Cisneros. Did not attend the conclave that elected him as a compromise candidate and as the last non-Italian pope before John Paul II in 1978.

Political role as pope: Tried to mediate between Francis I and Charles V in order to unite Habsburgs and Valois in a common Christian cause. With the loss of Belgrade (1521) and the fall of Rhodes (1522), Adrian threatened excommunications to restore the unity of Christendom, but that merely caused a breach with France. In 1523 he joined Charles V, Henry VIII and Venice in an anti-French league. In Rome he undertook ecclesiastical reforms but his frugal tastes were not popular with the citizens.

Nepotism: None.

Cultural patronage: Limited interest in humanistic culture.

Alexander VI 1492–1503 (Rodrigo Borgia)
Education: University of Bologna.
Experience prior to papal election: Nephew of Calixtus III, who made him a cardinal (1456), vice-chancellor of the Church (1457) and the holder of numerous benefices, to which he added during his long Roman career, thereby gaining immense wealth. In the conclave of 1492 Borgia promised the office of vice-chancellor to the Milanese Cardinal Ascanio Maria Sforza (d. 1505) in order to counter the papal ambitions of Giuliano della Rovere, a tactic not atypical at that time but which contributed to Borgia's negative reputation.

Political role as pope: Alexander's Spanish origins emerged in his political generosity to Ferdinand of Aragon and Isabella of Castile as their states asserted new-found strength in both Europe and the New World. It was Alexander who fixed the line of demarcation between Spanish and Portuguese hemispheres of influence in the process of discovery and conquest. The infamous Borgia reputation owed a good deal to Italian xenophobia. Enmity with Ferrante of Naples meant that Alexander did not initially oppose Charles VIII's invasion of Italy in 1494, but the pope later joined the anti-French coalition and opposed Louis XII's 1499 invasion of Milan. Following the death in 1497 of Juan, duke of Gandia, Alexander's eldest son by Vanozza Catanei, the pope made genuine attempts to reform the Curia. Savonarola's denunciation of luxury and corruption in the Vatican were well founded.

Nepotism: Of the eighteen Spanish cardinals created by Alexander ten were his kinsmen, one of those ten being his son Cesare (d. 1507). After the

death of the duke of Gandia, Cesare renounced the cardinalate (1498) in order to pursue the family's secular ambitions, which were also forwarded by the marriages of the pope's daughter Lucrezia and other lay members of the dynasty.
Cultural patronage: Borgia Apartments in the Vatican decorated by Pinturicchio.

Calixtus III 1455–58 (Alfonso de Borja or Borgia)
Education: University of Lerida.
Experience prior to papal election: Taught at the University of Lerida and owed his rise to the support of antipope Benedict XIII and the royal house of Aragon; bishop of Valencia and cardinal (1444).
Political role as pope: Made genuine if ultimately futile appeals for the Christian powers to reconquer Constantinople, though the crusaders were notably victorious at Belgrade in 1456.
Nepotism: Notable for the promotion of his fellow Iberians and enriching of his family, including his nephew Rodrigo Lanzol-Borja or Borgia, the future Alexander VI.
Cultural patronage: Indifference to classical scholarship resulted in negative publicity from humanists.

Clement VII 1523–34 (Giulio de' Medici)
Education: Humanist type, before canon law at the University of Pisa.
Experience prior to papal election: On the expulsion of the Medici from Florence (1494), this illegitimate son of Giuliano di Piero (d. 1478) went into exile until 1512. Created cardinal and archbishop of Florence (1513) by his cousin Leo X with responsibility for ruling that city on behalf of the Medici dynasty.
Political role as pope: While earlier popes had operated on an essentially Italian stage, Clement's manifold problems appeared to be on an altogether larger scale. Italy was dominated by foreign powers, with papal actions determined by the relative strengths of the French and imperialists in the peninsula. The 1527 Sack of Rome by imperialist troops forced the pope to take refuge in Castel Sant'Angelo, after which he was essentially a pawn of Charles V. Clement also proved unequal to the Lutheran challenge in Germany and to the English schism.
Nepotism: Created some Florentine cardinals, but was not excessively indulgent. Engineered the dynastic marriage of Caterina (Catherine) de' Medici to Henri, duke of Orléans, the future Henri II of France.
Cultural patronage: Michelangelo worked for him in Florence, Antonio da Sangallo, Giulio Romano, Raphael, Sebastiano del Piombo and others in Rome.

Eugenius IV 1431–47 (Gabriele Condulmer)
Education: University of Padua.

Experience prior to papal election: A Venetian patrician who came to prominence thanks to the patronage of his uncle Gregory XII; cardinal (1408).
Political role as pope: Like Martin V, Eugenius upheld papal primacy against conciliarism, but the tenacity with which he did so resulted in the Council of Basel electing Amadeus VIII of Savoy as antipope Felix V. Unlike Martin, Eugenius was not a Roman; he could not control the city and was forced into exile in Florence, where he took up residence at S. Maria Novella between 1433 and 1443, with significant implications for the Medici as papal bankers and for the employment of Florentine humanists in the papal chancery. Attempts to assert control over the Papal States were led by Cardinal Vitelleschi (d. 1440). The ecumenical Council of Ferrara-Florence was the diplomatic high point of this pontificate; reconciliation between the Latin and Greek churches proved to be illusory though the cultural spin-offs were of monumental importance.
Nepotism: Promoted his kinsmen Francesco Condulmer and Pietro Barbo, the future Paul II, to the Sacred College, in addition to the Greek Bessarion, who came to identify himself as Venetian by adoption.
Cultural patronage: Patron of many leading artists including Donatello and Fra Angelico, and humanists Poggio Bracciolini and Flavio Biondo.

Innocent VIII 1484–92 (Giovanni Battista Cibo or Cibò)
Education: Universities of Padua and Rome.
Experience prior to papal election: Bishop of Savona (1469) and of Molfetta (1472); cardinal (1473).
Political role as pope: Elected thanks to the influence of Cardinal Giuliano della Rovere (the future Julius II), who remained the power behind the papal throne throughout this pontificate. While relations with Florence and Venice improved, Italian problems centred on Naples and King Ferrante's refusal to pay tribute to Rome. War broke out between Naples and the papacy as well as between King Ferrante and the Neapolitan barons.
Nepotism: His nephew Lorenzo Cibo was made a cardinal and his son, Franceschetto, was married to Lorenzo de' Medici's daughter Maddalena.
Cultural patronage: Not a notable patron, the cultural high point of his pontificate being the employment of Mantegna to decorate the Vatican Belvedere.

Julius II 1503–13 (Giuliano della Rovere)
Education: with Franciscans at Perugia.
Experience prior to papal election: Cardinal (1471), legate to Umbria (1474), bishop of Avignon (1474), legate to France (1480–82), all of which and more he owed to his uncle Sixtus IV. Further benefices were accumulated during Innocent VIII's pontificate, bringing the total to one archbishopric and eight bishoprics. After a period as the power behind Innocent VIII, the 1492 election of his great rival Rodrigo Borgia as

Alexander VI forced Della Rovere first to Ostia and then into voluntary exile in France, where he actively supported Charles VIII's plans to invade Italy.

Political role as pope: Julius's greatest impact was in the Papal States, where he personally imposed his authority as his predecessors had failed to do. He recovered territory which been appropriated by Venice or had formed Cesare Borgia's Romagnole duchy, drove the Baglioni family from Perugia and the Bentivoglio from Bologna (1506). The States of the Church also benefited from monetary reform and sound administration. In inter-state relations, he joined the anti-Venetian League of Cambrai and placed Venice under interdict (1509), making peace with the republic the following year. He supported the 1512 return of the Medici to Florence. French military withdrawal from Italy enabled Julius to present himself as the peninsula's liberator. Louis XII contributed an ecclesiastical dimension to Franco-papal hostility by backing the Council of Pisa, which Julius trumped by calling the Fifth Lateran Council and displaying a genuine commitment to reform (see 12.5).

Nepotism: Three further members of this extensive clerical dynasty were added to the Sacred College: not excessive by the standards of his predecessors.

Cultural patronage: Renaissance culture, typified by Michelangelo (Julius's tomb, Sistine Chapel), Bramante (St Peter's basilica) and Raphael (Vatican Stanze), is generally associated with Rome from this pontificate onwards, though the pope's worldly preoccupations alienated Erasmus, who responded with the *Julius exclusus*, written soon after the pope's death.

Leo X 1513–21 (Giovanni de' Medici)

Education: Latin with Angelo Poliziano, Greek with Demetrius Chalcondyles and music with Heinrich Isaac; canon law at the University of Pisa.

Experience prior to papal election: A cardinal at thirteen (1489), due to his father Lorenzo de' Medici's alliance with Innocent VIII. Went into exile from Florence in 1494 along with other members of the family, visiting Bologna, Venice, Germany, Flanders and Rome, their return to Florence coming shortly before his election to the papacy.

Political role as pope: After the bellicose Julius, Leo was greeted as a doctor (*medicus*) who would heal the ills of Italy and of the Church. The Fifth Lateran Council did indeed continue to meet, Henry VIII of England was accorded the title 'Defender of the Faith', and Franco-papal relations improved when the Concordat of Bologna (1516) finally abolished the contentious Pragmatic Sanction of Bourges. To counter this, Leo's confiscation of the duchy of Urbino (1516) from Francesco Maria I della Rovere to confer it on his nephew Lorenzo precipitated a war, while Cardinal Alfonso Petrucci and others were found guilty of conspiring to kill the pope (1517).

Nepotism: Promoted a number of Mediceans to the cardinalate, but the only actual Medici was his cousin Giulio, the future Clement VII.

Cultural patronage: In Florence he repurchased most of the Medici library from the Dominican convent of S. Marco (1508–9). Leonine Rome witnessed something of a golden age as writers, scholars, artists and musicians benefited from the pope's enlightened patronage of both letters and the visual arts. Erasmus acquired Leo's patronage of the *Novum Instrumentum* (see 15.2).

Martin V 1417–31 (Oddone Colonna)

Experience prior to papal election: Roman patrician from one of the city's most powerful families; cardinal (1405); elected at the Council of Constance, thereby marking the end of the papal schism which had divided western Christendom between the obediences of at least two popes.

Political role as pope: With the return of the papacy to Rome, Martin's priorities were to regain control over the Papal States and to assert papal privileges against the conciliar movement which had just witnessed its finest hour at Constance. In accordance with the decree *Frequens* (see 12.5), Martin summoned a short-lived council at Pavia and Siena (1423–24) but died before the Council of Basel met. A crusade against the Bohemian Hussites failed.

Nepotism: In keeping with the spirit of Constance, Martin appointed cardinals from diverse geographical origins, with only one member of the Colonna family raised to the cardinalate, though they were favoured in other respects.

Cultural patronage: Martin initiated building and restoration programmes in Rome which created a pattern for his successors to follow, as did his employment of humanists such as Poggio Bracciolini. Cardinals Giuliano Cesarini (d. 1444) and Giordano Orsini (d. 1439) were also active patrons of learning during Martin's pontificate.

Nicholas V 1447–55 (Tommaso Parentucelli)

Education: University of Bologna.

Experience prior to papal election: A humanist scholar befriended by Palla Strozzi and Cosimo de' Medici, and employed in the household of Cardinal Niccolò Albergati (d. 1443); cardinal (1446).

Political role as pope: The schismatic threat of the Council of Basel faded away with most of the remaining conciliarists being won over to Rome, where the republican Stefano Porcari's January 1453 republican conspiracy was somewhat ironic in the light of this pope's own humanist interests. Crusading initiatives proved fruitless in spite of the fall of Constantinople in 1453.

Nepotism: Promoted his half-brother Filippo Calandrini to the Sacred College but was otherwise even-handed with his favours.

Cultural patronage: An active humanist who strengthened the connection between the papacy and the New Learning. Made his own translations from Greek and patronised Greek scholars including Bessarion, together with Italian humanists such as Poggio Bracciolini, Leonardo Bruni, Francesco Filelfo, Giannozzo Manetti (1396–1459) and Lorenzo Valla. Founded the Vatican library. Undertook ambitious town planning in Rome, including the reconstruction of the Capitol and initial attempts to rebuild St Peter's basilica, which had fallen into a state of considerable decay: Jubilee pilgrims in 1450 contributed funds for these projects. Fra Angelico, Leon Battista Alberti and Benozzo Gozzoli also received this pope's patronage.

Paul II 1464–71 (Pietro Barbo)
Education: Studied with George of Trebizond among others.
Experience prior to papal election: Venetian patrician who owed his rise to the patronage of his uncle Eugenius IV. Bishop of Cervia (1440), cardinal (1440), bishop of Vicenza (1451) and of Padua (1459).
Political role as pope: The ongoing campaign to regain or maintain control over the Papal States continued with the defeat of the rebellious counts of Anguillara and a war between Paul and Roberto Malatesta of Rimini (1469). Elsewhere, papal representatives continued to intervene in Bohemia, with attempts to try George of Poděbrady for heresy from 1465.
Nepotism: His kinsmen Marco Barbo (d. 1491), Giovanni Michiel (d. 1503) and Giovanni Battista Zen (d. 1501) were all made cardinals.
Cultural patronage: Paul's cultural commitments have been the subject of controversy, arising from his arrest of Pomponio Leto and the Roman Academicians in 1468 and Platina's literary responses on behalf of the humanists charged with anti-papal conspiracy. Defence of Paul as a cultural patron comes in the form of his magnificent Palazzo di S. Marco (now the Palazzo Venezia), Rome, which housed his collections of bronzes, cameos and gems, many of which were acquired by Lorenzo de' Medici after the pope's death.

Pius II 1458–64 (Enea Silvio Piccolomini)
Education: University of Siena.
Experience prior to papal election: From a prominent Sienese family; secretary to Cardinals Domenico Capranica (d. 1458) and Niccolò Albergati and to the Basel antipope Felix V. He undertook diplomatic missions on behalf of the Council of Basel, but thereafter entered imperial service, was crowned poet laureate by Emperor Frederick III (1442) and finally made his peace with Rome, taking holy orders in 1446. Bishop of Trieste (1447), and of Siena (1450), cardinal (1456).
Political role as pope: In office, Pius reacted against his own previous worldliness and his support for the schismatics of Basel, being as zealous

as any other Renaissance pope for the cause of papal primacy. In 1462 the revocation of the Pragmatic Sanction of Bourges was a victory for the papacy *vis-à-vis* the French crown. Nicholas Krebs/Nicholas of Cusa (1401–64) led papal negotiations with German princes while relations between Rome and the Bohemian Hussites thawed. The 1459 Congress of Mantua was designed to coordinate a crusade but the Christian powers deserted Pius, who died at Ancona while waiting for their forces to assemble. In the Papal States Pius asserted his authority against the rebellious papal vicar Sigismondo Malatesta of Rimini.

Nepotism: Adopted Francesco Todeschini, who added 'Piccolomini' to his name and was elected pope in 1503. The Piccolomini family became first among equals in republican Siena.

Cultural patronage: Of less significance than his own literary works, which were numerous and varied, including *Commentarii concilii basiliensis* (1440, a history of the Council of Basel which he later disclaimed), *De liberorum educatione* (1450, on educational theory), *Artis rhetoricae praecepta* (1456, on rhetoric, a common humanist subject), *Germania* (1457; other works of historical geography being devoted to Europe and Asia), *Historia Friderici III* (pre-1458), *Historia bohemica* (1458). In addition, he wrote biography and poetry, but is best known for the autobiographical memoirs, *Commentaries*, written while he held the papal office. The ennobling of his birthplace, Corsignano, near Montepulciano, as the papal residence Pienza provides an enduring architectural monument to the Sienese pope.

Pius III 1503 (Francesco Todeschini-Piccolomini)
Education: University of Perugia.
Experience prior to papal election: Nephew of Pius II, whose family name he added to his own. Bishop of Siena and cardinal (1460); legate to Germany.
Political role as pope: After a heavily contested election, Pius reigned for just twenty-seven days.
Nepotism: None.
Cultural patronage: Prior to his election, Cardinal Todeschini-Piccolomini was a significant patron of literary culture.

Sixtus IV 1471–84 (Francesco della Rovere)
Education: University of Padua.
Experience prior to papal election: Franciscan theologian who taught at the universities of Padua, Bologna, Pavia, Siena, Florence and Perugia; cardinal (1467).
Political role as pope: Initial plans for uniting western Christendom in a crusade were thwarted by disputes among the secular powers, after which bout of idealism Sixtus became fully embroiled in Italian inter-state politics, ranging from dynastic alliances with Naples and the Sforza of Milan, to war in alliance with Naples against Florence (the 1478–79

Pazzi War) in the aftermath of the anti-Medicean Pazzi Conspiracy, with Venice against Naples (1482–83) and finally against Venice (1483–84, but together known as the War of Ferrara). Meanwhile, conflicts between Rome's baronial families were played out in miniature in the Sacred College, as were those of the Italian states.

Nepotism: Nephews Pietro Riario (d. 1474) and Giuliano della Rovere (the future Julius II) were the first two of six Sistine *nipoti* raised to the cardinalate, the others being Cristoforo della Rovere (d. 1478), Girolamo Basso della Rovere (d. 1507), Raffaele Riario (d. 1521) and Domenico della Rovere (d. 1501). Girolamo Riario (d. 1488), brother of Pietro, was the pope's principal secular adviser.

Cultural patronage: Best remembered for the building and initial decoration of the Sistine Chapel, he also refounded the Vatican library, appointing Platina as librarian.

3 Holy Roman Empire

3.1 Emperors of the Houses of Luxemburg (to 1400, 1410–37), Wittelsbach (1400–10) and Habsburg (from 1437)

Dates of election rather than coronation are given in the first column, since a number of years could elapse between the two. Prior to coronation the title King of the Romans, rather than Holy Roman Emperor, properly applied.

1378–1400 **Wenceslas** of Luxemburg: b. 1361, son of Emperor Charles IV. *Other titles*: duke of Luxemburg (1411–12), king Vaclav IV of Bohemia (1378–1419). Deposed 1399 by imperial electors, including Ruprecht III Wittelsbach, Elector Palatine of the Rhine. d. 1419. m. (1) Joanna of Wittelsbach, (2) Sofie of Wittelsbach.

1400–10 **Rupert** of Wittelsbach: b. 1352, son of Ruprecht II of the Palatinate. Uncrowned 'anti-king' in opposition to the weak rulership of Wenceslas. *Other title*: Ruprecht III, Elector Palatine of the Rhine (1398–1410).

1410–11 **Jost** of Moravia (Jossus): b. 1351, cousin of Wenceslas. *Other title*: margrave of Brandenburg. Rival of Sigismund for the imperial crown.

1410–37 **Sigismund** of Luxemburg: b. 1368, son of Emperor Charles IV; brother of Emperor Wenceslas; cousin of Jost. *Other titles*: margrave of Brandenburg (1378–1417), king of Hungary (1397–1437) and of Bohemia (1419–37). m. (1) Maria (d. 1392), daughter of Louis the Great of Hungary, (2) Barbara (d. 1451), daughter of Hermann, count of Cilli. Provided the initiative behind the General Council of the Church at Constance (1414–18) to break the deadlock of the papal schism, and also attempted to negotiate peace after Henry V of England renewed war with France.

1437–39 **Albert II** of Habsburg: b. 1397, son of Albrecht IV of Austria; son-in-law of Sigismund. *Other titles*: duke of Austria (1404–39), king of Hungary (1437–39) and king of Bohemia (1438–39), the last two by virtue of his marriage. m. Elizabeth of Luxemburg (1409–c.1442), daughter and heiress of

Emperor Sigismund. Died before he could be crowned as emperor and before the birth of his son and heir, Ladislas Posthumous.

1440–93   **Frederick III** of Habsburg: b. 1415, son of Ernst of Habsburg; cousin of Albert II. *Other titles*: archduke of Austria (1457–93), duke of Styria, Carinthia and Carniola, which duly passed to Maximilian I and Charles V. m. Leonor, daughter of Duarte I of Portugal. Succession to Sigismund's vast domains was complicated by the posthumous birth of Ladislas (1440), son of Albert II and Elizabeth of Luxemburg, to whom the kingdoms of Bohemia and Hungary passed.

1493–1519   **Maximilian I** of Habsburg: b. 1459, son of Frederick III. *Other title*: archduke of Austria (1493–1519). m. (1) Mary (1457–82), duchess of Burgundy, daughter of Charles the Bold, (2) Bianca Maria (1472–1510), daughter of Galeazzo Maria Sforza of Milan. While yet King of the Romans, Maximilian's first marriage made him a figure of considerable importance in western European diplomacy, a position he maintained and which he enjoyed as his imperial predecessors had not. A significant patron of literature, music and the visual arts, Maximilian was a man of letters in his own right. His imperial councillors included Willibald Pirckheimer (1470–1530) of Nuremburg, an Italian-educated friend of Dürer and correspondent of Erasmus, who made a number of translations from Greek to Latin and was one of Germany's most significant cultural patrons.

1519–56   **Charles V** of Habsburg: b. 1500, son of Philip the Fair and Juana of Castile; grandson of Maximilian I. *Other titles*: archduke of Austria (1519–22), king of Aragon and Castile (1516–56); also received the accumulated Burgundian inheritance of his paternal grandmother Mary of Burgundy. Abdicated as emperor 1556. d. 1558. m. Isabella (1503–39), daughter of Manoel I of Portugal. Charles's manifold commitments meant that councillors and advisers became particularly vital to the government of his vast and widely spread territories. Of first importance were the imperial chancellors, Mercurino Arborio de Gattinara (1465–1530) and Nicolas Perrenot de Granvelle (1486–1550) (see 3.7). Like his grandfather, Maximilian, Charles favoured men of letters, including his secretary Alfonso de Valdes (c. 1490–1532) (see 15.5). In addition to Willibald Pirckheimer, his imperial councillors included Erasmus (see 15.5) and Konrad Peutinger (1465–1547) of Augsburg, another Italian-educated friend of Dürer.

3.2   Imperial electors

Imperial elections were regulated by the Golden Bull (1356) of Emperor Charles IV (d. 1378). Listed in the order in which they cast their votes, the seven members of the electoral college were:

1. Archbishop of Trier
2. Archbishop of Cologne
3. King of Bohemia
4. Count Palatine of the Rhine
5. Duke of Saxony-Wittenberg
6. Margrave of Brandenburg
7. Archbishop of Mainz

3.3   Secular principalities of the Empire

In theory, the Empire included the duchies of Milan and Savoy, together with the other Italian states north of papal territory, but with the conspicuous exception of the republic of Venice. Those Italian states are not listed here.

Kingdom	Bohemia		
Archduchy	Austria		
Landgraviate	Hesse		
Margraviates	Ansbach	Bayreuth	Moravia
	Baden	Brandenburg	
Principality	Anhalt		
Duchies	Bar	Gelders	Sagan
	Bavaria	Jülich	Saxony
	Brabant	Lorraine	Silesia
	Brunswick	Luxemburg	Styria
	Carinthia	Mecklenburg	Württemberg
	Carniola	Pomerania	
Counties	Burgundy (N.B. not *duchy*, which was French)		
	E. Friesland	Lippe	Ravensburg
	Fürstenberg	Mark	Ruppin
	Hainault	Nassau	Tyrol
	Holland	Oldenburg	Zeeland
	Hoya	Palatinate	Zweibrücken

3.4   Ecclesiastical States in the Empire

Archbishoprics	Bremen	Magdeburg	Salzburg
	Cologne	Mainz	Trier

Bishoprics	Augsburg	Hildersheim	Regensburg/Ratisbon
	Bamberg	Lausanne	Schwerin
	Basel	Liège	Seckau
	Brixen	Lübeck	Speyer
	Cambrai	Meissen	Strasbourg
	Chiemsee	Merseburg	Toul
	Chur	Metz	Trento
	Constance	Minden	Utrecht
	Eichstatt	Münster	Verden
	Freising	Naumburg	Verdun
	Geneva	Osnabrück	Worms
	Gurk	Paderborn	Würzburg
	Halberstadt	Passau	
	Havelberg	Ratzeburg	

3.5   Free Imperial Cities

These owed their allegiance directly to the Holy Roman Emperor without obligations to any intermediate prince. They were also exempt from imperial taxation.

Aachen	Hamburg	Reutlingen
Augsburg	Heilbronn	Ritzebüttel
Besançon	Isny	Rothenburg
Bremen	Kaufbeuren	Rottweil
Colmar	Lindau	Schlettstadt
Cologne	Lübeck	Schweinfurt
Constance	Memmingen	Speyer
Dortmund	Metz	Strassbourg
Esslingen	Mülhausen (Alsace)	Toul
Frankfurt-am-Main	Mühlhausen	Ulm
Gelnhausen	(Thuringia)	Wangen
Giengen	Nordhausen	Weil
Gmüund	Nördlingen	Weissenburg (Alsace)
Goslar	Nuremberg	Weissenburg (Bavaria)
Haganau	Ravensburg	Wetzlar
Hall	Regensburg/Ratisbon	Worms

3.6   Swiss Confederation, *c.* 1500

Abbey of Angelberg	Basel	Glarus
Abbey of St Gallen	Berne	Greyerz
(St Gall)	Fribourg	Lucerne
Appenzell	Gersau	League of God's House

League of the Ten	Schaffhausen	Upper Valais
Jurisdictions	Schwyz	Uri
Nidwalden	Solothurn	Zug
Obwalden	Upper/Grey League	Zürich

Swiss independence from the Empire was recognised by the peace of Basel, 1499.

3.7 Imperial chancellors

Mercurino Arborio de Gattinara (1465–1530) Savoyard lawyer who studied under the humanist and political theorist Claude de Seyssel (*c.* 1450–1520), received his doctorate from Turin (1493) and entered the service of Margaret of Austria, regent of the Netherlands, as a result of her brief marriage to Philibert of Savoy (1501–4). While in her employ he played an important part in the formation of the anti-Venetian League of Cambrai (1508). Chancellor of the future Charles V from 1518, following the death of Jean Le Sauvage (1455–1518), who had himself been chancellor of Burgundy from 1515 and of Castile from 1516. As Grand Chancellor, Gattinara negotiated with his English and French counterparts, the cardinals Thomas Wolsey and Antoine Duprat, at Calais between August and December 1521. He reorganised Spanish governmental administration, had a genuine interest in letters and erudition, and was made a cardinal in 1529.

Nicolas Perrenot de Granvelle (1486–1550) From Ornans in Franche-Comté and educated at the university of Dôle, where he met the imperial chancellor Gattinara, who proved to be the key to the younger man's success. Public office in Dôle preceded service with Margaret of Austria, regent of the Netherlands. He succeeded Gattinara as Grand Chancellor (1530) but specialised in Netherlandish and German affairs, while Francisco de Los Cobos (1477–1547) dealt with Spain; by contrast, Gattinara had been responsible for all these regions.

4   Heads of states and dynasties

In most cases the date of death is given in the first column. Variations appear in the cases of kings and princes who were deposed or who abdicated. Assassinations are noted as such.

The anglicising of names has been restricted to only the most familiar of cases, such as Francis I of France and Ferdinand II of Aragon. The spellings given in bold are those adopted throughout this volume, but some alternatives are also provided, local or anglicised as appropriate.

Spouses have been included if the dynastic links were of importance or if the individuals concerned were of political or cultural significance in their own right.

4.1   Anjou: French royal dukes

1384–1417   **Louis II**: b. 1377, son of Louis I, duke of Anjou, king of Naples. *Other titles*: count of Maine and Provence; crowned king of Naples 1389. m. Yolande, daughter of Joan I of Aragon.

1417–34   **Louis III**: b. 1403, son of Louis II. *Other titles*: duke of Touraine, count of Maine and Provence, titular king of Naples.

1434–80   **René I** ('Good King René'): b. 1409, son of Louis II and brother of Louis III. *Other titles*: duke of Bar, duke of Lorraine (by marriage) and Touraine, count of Maine and Provence, king of Naples (1435–42) and titular king of Jerusalem. m. (1) Isabel (d. 1452), daughter of Charles, duke of Lorraine, (2) Jeanne de Laval (d. 1498). Unsuccessful claimant to regal titles, cultural patron, reputed artist in his own right, and founder of the Order of the Crescent.

1480–81   **Charles II**: b. 1436, nephew of René. *Other title*: count of Provence. After his death the duchy was incorporated into the kingdom of France.

4.2   Aragon (Aragon, Catalonia and Valencia): kings of the Houses of Trastámara and Habsburg

1387-95   **Joan I** (Cast.: Juan): b. 1350, son of Pedro IV. m. (1) Leonor of Aragon, (2) Beatriz of Portugal.

1395-1410   **Martí I**: Son of Pedro IV and brother of Joan I. *Other title*: Martí II of Sicily, from 1409. m. (1) Maria de Luna (d. 1407), (2) Margarita de Pardes (d. 1451).

1410-12   Interregnum: resolved by Compromise of Caspe, whereby Castilian prince Ferdinand of Antequera appointed king.

1412-16   **Ferdinand I** of Antequera (Cast.: Fernando; Cat.: Ferran): b. 1380, son of Juan I of Castile and Leonor of Aragon. m. Leonor of Albuquerque (1374-1435).

1416-58   **Alfonso V** ('the Magnanimous'): b. 1396, son of Ferdinand I. *Other title*: Alfonso I of Naples (1442-58); after 1442 Alfonso prioritised Naples over Aragon, leaving his brother Joan to rule the latter. m. Maria (d. 1458), daughter of Enrique III of Castile.

1458-79   **Joan II** (Cast.: Juan): b. 1398, son of Ferran I and brother of Alfonso V. *Other title*: King Juan of Navarre, by virtue of his first marriage. This reign saw Aragon sink into protracted civil war. m. (1) Blanche (1385-1441), daughter of Charles III of Navarre, (2) Juana Enríquez of Castile. Blanche had previously been married to Martí of Aragon, king of Sicily (d. 1404). By Joan II she was mother of Carlos of Viana.

1479-1516   **Ferdinand II** ('the Catholic'; Cast.: Fernando; Cat.: Ferran): b. 1452, son of Joan II and Juana Enríquez. *Other titles*: Fernando V of Castile, by virtue of his first marriage; king of Naples (from 1503) and of Navarre (from 1512). m. (1) Isabella I, queen of Castile, (2) Germaine de Foix (1488-1537), daughter of Jean Gaston de Foix and Marie of Orléans, great-granddaughter of Joan II of Aragon and Blanche of Navarre. Their son Juan d. 1509. Castilian matters invariably took priority over those of Aragon during the joint reign of the Catholic Kings, which suited Ferdinand's subjects, who enjoyed greater freedom *vis-à-vis* the crown than did their Castilian neighbours.

1516-56   **Carlos I** (Emperor Charles V): b. 1500, son of Juana, queen of Castile, and Philip the Fair (Felipe I); grandson of Ferdinand II. *Other titles*: archduke of Austria (1519-22), king of Castile (1516-56), Holy Roman Emperor (1519-56). m. Isabella (1503-39), daughter of Manoel I of Portugal. Abdicated as king of Aragon 1556. d. 1558.

4.3 Bohemia: elected kings

1378–1419 **Wenceslas IV** of Luxemburg (Czech: Vaclav): b. 1361, son of Emperor Charles IV. *Other titles*: duke of Luxemburg (1411– 12), Holy Roman Emperor (1378–1400). m. (1) Johanna of Wittelsbach, (2) Sophie of Wittelsbach.

1419–37 **Sigismund** of Luxemburg: b. 1368, brother of Vaclav IV. *Other titles*: margrave of Brandenburg (1378–1417), king of Hungary (1397–1437) by virtue of his first marriage, Holy Roman Emperor (1410–37). m. (1) Maria (d. 1392), daughter of Louis the Great of Hungary, (2) Barbara (d. 1451), daughter of Hermann, count of Cilli. Sigismund was crowned king of Bohemia but was immediately driven from Prague by Hussite rebels, leaving Bohemia without effective royal government from 1420 to 1436.

1437–39 **Albert** of Habsburg: b. 1397, son of Albrecht IV of Austria. *Other titles*: duke of Austria (1404–39), king of Hungary (1437–39) by virtue of his wife, Holy Roman Emperor (1438– 39). m. Elizabeth of Luxemburg (1409–c. 1442), daughter and heiress of Emperor Sigismund.

1440–57 **Ladislas V** ('Posthumous'; Czech: Vladislav): b. 1440, son of Albert. *Other titles*: archduke of Austria (1440–57), king of Hungary (1444–57). Born four months after the death of his father. m. Madeleine, daughter of Charles VII of France. She married secondly Gaston de Foix, prince of Viana. Although the Bohemian Estates recognised the infant Ladislas as their king, the effective ruler of Bohemia was the moderate Hussite George of Poděbrady (1420–71).

1457–71 **George of Poděbrady** (Czech: Jiri z Poděbrad): b. 1420, governor of Bohemia for Ladislas V and elected by the Estates as his successor. Tried to unite Bohemia's Catholics and Utraquists. His rule was threatened by Mátyás Hunyadi who invaded Moravia as an agent of the papacy and was proclaimed king of Bohemia.

1469–78 **Matthias Corvinus** (Hung.: Mátyás Hunyadi): b. 1440, son of János Hunyadi (d. 1456). Ruled in Bohemia in opposition to George of Poděbrady. *Other title*: king of Hungary (1458–90). m. Katharina, daughter of George of Poděbrady, (2) Beatrice d'Aragona (1457–1508), daughter of Ferrante I of Naples.

1471–1516 **Vladislav II**: b. 1456, son of Kazimierz IV of Poland and nephew of Ladislas Posthumous. *Other title*: king of Hungary (1490–1526). m. (1) Beatrice d'Aragona, his predecessor's widow, but marriage annulled 1500, (2) Anne de Foix (d. 1506).

1516–26   **Louis II**: b. 1506, son of Vladislav II. *Other title*: King Lajos II of Hungary (1516–26). Killed at the battle of Mohács. m. Maria (1505–58), daughter of Philip the Fair and Juana of Castile, and sister of Emperor Charles V. As a widow, Mary of Hungary, as she is known, served her brother as governor of the Netherlands from 1530.

1526–64   **Ferdinand I** of Habsburg: b. 1503, son of Philip the Fair and Juana of Castile. *Other titles*: archduke of Austria (1521–64), king of Hungary (1526–64) and Holy Roman Emperor (1556–64). m. Anne (1503–47), daughter of Vladislav II of Hungary.

4.4   Bourbon: French royal dukes

1356–1410   **Louis II**: b. 1337, son of Pierre I.

1410–34   **Jean I**: b. 1380, son of Louis II.

1434–56   **Charles I**: b. 1401, son of Jean I. m. Agnès (*c.* 1410–76), daughter of John the Fearless, duke of Burgundy.

1456–88   **Jean II**: b. 1426, son of Charles I. m. Jeanne, daughter of Charles VII of France.

1488   **Charles II**: b. *c.* 1434, brother of Jean II. Cardinal-archbishop of Lyon.

1488–1503   **Pierre II**: b. 1438, brother of Charles II. *Other title*: lord of Beaujeu. m. Anne de France (1461–1522), daughter of Louis XI. With his wife, joint regent of France (1483–91).

1503–21   **Suzanne**: b. 1491, daughter of Pierre II.

1503–27   **Charles III**: b. 1490, son of Gilbert, count of Montpensier. Husband of Suzanne. Constable of France and traitor to the same.

4.5   Brandenburg: margraves and electors of the House of Hohenzollern

1417–40   **Friedrich I**: b. 1371, governor of Brandenburg from 1411 for Emperor Sigismund who was margrave (1378–1417).

1440   **Johann** (John 'the Alchemist'): b. 1406, son of Friedrich I. Deposed. d. 1464.

1440–70   **Friedrich II**: b. 1413, son of Friedrich I. Abdicated. d. 1471.

1470–86   **Albrecht III Achilles**: b. 1414, brother of Friedrich II. Patron of Dürer, Grünewald and Cranach. Abdicated. d. 1499.

1486–99   **Johann Cicero**: b.1455, son of Albrecht III Achilles.

1499–1535   **Joachim I Nestor**: b. 1484, son of Johann Cicero.

4.6   Brittany: dukes of the House of Montfort

1365–99   **Jean IV**: b. 1339.
1399–1442 **Jean V**: b. 1389, son of Jean IV.
1442–50   **François I**: b. 1414, son of Jean V.
1450–57   **Pierre II**: b. 1418, brother of François I.
1457–58   **Artur III** (Arthur of Richemont): b. 1393. Uncle of Pierre II. Constable of France (1425–58). m. Margaret (1393–1442), daughter of John the Fearless, duke of Burgundy.
1458–88   **François II**: b. 1435, nephew of Artur III. m. Marguerite de Foix.
1488–1514 **Anne**: b. 1477, daughter of François II. Duchy incorporated into the kingdom of France, as a result of Anne's marriages to Charles VIII (1491) and Louis XII (1499).

4.7   Burgundy: dukes of the House of Valois

1363–1404 **Philip** ('the Bold', Philippe *le hardi*): b. 1342, son of Jean II of France. m. Margaret (1349–1405), daughter of Louis de Mâle, count of Flanders. Most powerful French magnate during the reign of Charles VI.
1404–19   **John** ('the Fearless', Jean *sans peur*): b. 1371, son of Philip the Bold. m. Margaret, daughter of Albrecht I, duke of Bavaria. Head of the Burgundian faction in the French civil war with the Orléanists/Armagnacs.
1419–67   **Philip** ('the Good', Philippe *le bon*): b. 1396, son of John the Fearless. m. (1) Michelle (d. 1422), daughter of Charles VI of France, (2) Bonne of Artois (1395–1425), (3) Isabel (1397–1471), daughter of João I of Portugal. Philip's numerous illegitimate children included Antoine, known as the 'Grand Bastard' of Burgundy.
1467–77   **Charles** ('the Bold' or 'the Rash', Charles *le téméraire*): b. 1433, son of Philip the Good and Isabel of Portugal. Count of Charolais before succeeding his father as duke of Burgundy. m. (1) Catherine (1428–46), daughter of Charles VII of France, (2) Isabel (d. 1465), daughter of Charles I, duke of Bourbon, (3) Margaret (1446–1503), sister of Edward IV of England.
1477–82   **Mary** (Marie): b. 1457, daughter of Charles the Bold and Isabelle de Bourbon. Ruled with her husband Maximilian I, archduke of Austria and Holy Roman Emperor.
1482   Duchy (but not county of Burgundy and Mary's other imperial territories) incorporated into the kingdom of France.

4.8   Byzantium: emperors of the House of Palaeologus

1390–91   **John V**: b. 1332, son of Andronicus III. Also ruled 1341–76, 1379.

1391–1425   **Manuel II**: b. 1350, son of John V. While Manuel travelled in western Europe from 1399, his nephew and co-emperor John VII (d. 1408) ruled in his absence.

1425–48   **John VIII**: b. 1390, son of Manuel II.

1448–53   **Constantine XI**: b. 1403, brother of John VIII. Killed at the fall of Constantinople to the Ottomans.

4.9   Castile and León: kings of the Houses of Trastámara and Habsburg

1390–1406   **Enrique III**: b. 1379, son of Juan I and Leonor of Aragon. m. Catalina of Lancaster (d. 1420), daughter of John of Gaunt, duke of Lancaster and son of Edward III of England, and Constanza of Castile.

1406–54   **Juan II**: b. 1405, son of Enrique III. m. (1) Maria, daughter of Ferran I of Aragon, (2) Isabel of Portugal.

1454–74   **Enrique IV**: b. 1425, son of Juan II and Maria of Aragon. m. (1) Blanca of Navarre, daughter of Joan II of Aragon; marriage annulled 1453, (2) Juana of Portugal. His daughter by Juana was known as Juana 'la Beltraneja' (1462–1530), being the presumed offspring of a liaison between Queen Juana and the king's favourite Beltrán de la Cueva.

1474–1504   **Isabella I** ('the Catholic'; Cast.: Isabel): b. 1451, daughter of Juan II and Isabel of Portugal; half-sister of Enrique IV. Ruled jointly with her husband Fernando V of Castile (Ferdinand II of Aragon); together they were regarded as king and queen of *Spain*, but did not use that title. During Isabella's reign the monarchs succeeded in reimposing royal authority on the kingdom after a period of civil war and invasion by Portugal.

1504–16   **Juana** (*la loca*, 'the Mad'): b. 1479, daughter of Isabella I and Ferdinand of Aragon. Ruled jointly with her husband Felipe (Philip) I 'the Fair', son of Emperor Maximilian I and Mary of Burgundy. Following Philip's death in 1506 and the worsening of Juana's already fragile mental condition, Ferdinand returned as regent of Castile (1507–16), succeeded in that capacity by Cardinal Francisco Jiménez de Cisneros (1436–1517), the Observant Franciscan who had been confessor to Isabella, Franciscan provincial in

Castile (1494), archbishop of Toledo and primate of Spain (1495), head of the regency council which governed Castile after the death of Philip the Fair, cardinal and grand inquisitor of Aragon and Castile.

1516–56   **Carlos I** (Emperor Charles V): b. 1500, son of Juana and Felipe I. *Other titles*: king of Aragon (1516–56), archduke of Austria (1519–22), Holy Roman Emperor (1519–56). m. Isabella (1503–39), daughter of Manoel I of Portugal. Time spent in Spain: September 1517–May 1520, July 1522–July 1529, April 1533–April 1535, December 1536–early 1538, July 1538–November 1539, November 1541–May 1543, September 1556 onwards. Abdicated as king of Castile 1556, retiring to the Hieronymite monastery at Yuste. d. 1558.

4.10   Cyprus: kings of the House of Lusignan

1399–1432   **Jannus**: b. 1374, son of Jacques I.

1432–58   **Jean II**: b. 1414, son of Jannus. m. Elena Palaeologus.

1458–64   **Charlotte**: b. 1436, daughter of Jean. Deposed by her illegitimate half-brother Jacques II. d. 1487.

1464–73   **Jacques II**: b. 1440, illegitimate son of Jean II. m. Caterina (1454–1510), daughter of Venetian patrician Marco Cornaro (or Corner).

1473   **Jacques III**: b. 1473, son of Jacques II. Cyprus was then under Venetian protection with his mother, Caterina, as regent. d. 1474.

1474–89   **Caterina Cornaro** (Corner): b. 1454, mother of Jacques III. Cyprus was under Venetian protection until the republic forced Caterina's abdication and incorporated the island into the Venetian sea empire (1489).

4.11   Denmark (with Norway): elected kings

Iceland ruled from Denmark.

1376–87   **Olaf III**: b. 1370, son of Haakon VI of Norway. *Other title*: Olaf IV of Norway (1380–87).

1387–1412   **Margrete** (Margaret): b. 1353, daughter of Valdemar Atterdag of Denmark; wife of Haakon VI and mother of Olaf III. Regent of Denmark (from 1367), of Norway (from 1380) and of Sweden (from 1389). Union of Kalmar (1397) formally united the crowns of Denmark, Norway and Sweden.

1412–39   **Erik VII** of Pomerania: b. 1382, great-nephew of Margrete; cousin of Emperor Sigismund. *Other titles:* duke of the Upper Palatinate, king of Norway (from 1412) and Sweden (from 1397), but deposed in all three kingdoms because he failed to obey a decree of 1436 which stipulated that he should divide his time equally between them. m. Philippa (1394– *c.* 1430), daughter of Henry IV of England. d. 1459.

1439–48   **Kristoffer III**: b. 1416, nephew of Erik VII. *Other titles:* duke of the Upper Palatinate, king of Norway. m. Dorothea of Brandenburg.

1448–81   **Kristian I**: b. 1426. *Other titles:* count of Oldenburg, king of Norway (from 1483), of Sweden (1459–65, but forced to resign). First king of the House of Oldenburg. Married his predecessor's widow.

1481–1513   **Hans**: b. 1455, son of Kristian I. *Other title:* king of Norway.

1513–23   **Kristian II**: b. 1481, son of Hans. *Other title:* king of Norway. m. Isabella (1501–25), daughter of Philip the Fair and Juana of Castile; sister of Emperor Charles V. Deposed. d. 1559.

1523–33   **Frederick I**: b. 1471, son of Kristian I; elected in succession to his nephew Kristian II.

4.12   England: kings of the Houses of Plantagenet, Lancaster, York and Tudor

1377–99   **Richard II**: b. 1367, son of Edward, the Black Prince, grandson of Edward III. m. (1) Anne of Bohemia (1366–94), daughter of Emperor Charles IV, (2) Isabelle (1387–1409), daughter of Charles VI of France. Deposed. d. 1400.

1399–1413   **Henry IV** Bolingbroke: b. 1367, son of John of Gaunt, duke of Lancaster; grandson of Edward III. First king of the House of Lancaster. m. (1) Mary Bohun (1369–94), (2) Joan (1370–1437), daughter of Charles II of Navarre.

1413–22   **Henry V**: b. 1387, son of Henry IV and Mary Bohun. m. Catherine (1401–37), daughter of Charles VI of France. She married Owain Tudor as her second husband; their son was Edmund Tudor, earl of Richmond, father of Henry Tudor/Henry VII. Renowned as the victor at the battle of Agincourt (1415) after he renewed the Anglo-French war.

1422–61   **Henry VI**: b. 1421, son of Henry V. m. Marguerite (Margaret of Anjou, 1430–82), daughter of René, duke of Anjou. Deposed 1461. Restored 1470–71. d. 1471.

1461–83   **Edward IV**: b. 1442, son of Richard, duke of York (d. 1460) and Cecily Neville (d. 1495). First king of the House of York.

m. Elizabeth (1437–92), daughter of Richard Woodville, Earl Rivers, and Jacquetta of Luxemburg (1416–c. 1472), widow of John, duke of Bedford, Henry V's brother.

1470–71   Readeption of Henry VI.

1483   **Edward V**: b. 1470, son of Edward IV.

1483–85   **Richard III**: b. 1452, brother of Edward IV. m. Anne (1456–85), daughter of Richard Neville, earl of Warwick; widow of Edward (1453–71), prince of Wales, son of Henry VI.

1485–1509   **Henry VII**: b. 1457, son of Edmund Tudor, earl of Richmond, and Margaret Beaufort (1443–1509), daughter of John Beaufort, duke of Somerset; great-great-granddaughter of Edward III. First king of the House of Tudor. m. Elizabeth of York (1466–1503), daughter of Edward IV.

1509–47   **Henry VIII**: b. 1491, son of Henry VII. m. (1) Catalina (Catherine, 1485–1536), daughter of Ferdinand of Aragon and Isabella of Castile; widow of Arthur (1486–1502), prince of Wales, Henry VIII's elder brother. Their daughter Mary (1516–58) reigned between 1553 and 1558. Henry contracted five other marriages.

4.13   Ferrara: *signori*, marquises (from 1393) and dukes (from 1471) of the House of Este

1388–93   **Alberto**: b. 1347, brother of Niccolò II.

1393–1441   **Niccolò III**: b. 1383, son of Alberto. m. (1) Gigliola da Carrara of Padua, (2) Parisina Malatesta of Rimini, (3) Ricciarda da Saluzzo. Acknowledged many illegitimate offspring.

1441–50   **Leonello**: b. 1407, illegitimate son of Niccolò III. m. (1) Margherita Gonzaga of Mantua (d. 1435), (2) Maria d'Aragona (d. 1444).

1450–71   **Borso**: b. 1413, illegitimate son of Niccolò III. Duke of Modena and Reggio from 1452, first duke of Ferrara from 1471. Unmarried.

1471–1505   **Ercole I**: b. 1431, son of Niccolò III and Ricciarda da Saluzzo. m. Eleonora d'Aragona (d. 1493), daughter of Ferrante I of Naples.

1505–34   **Alfonso I**: b. 1476, son of Ercole I. m. (1) Anna (1473–97), daughter of Galeazzo Maria Sforza, duke of Milan, (2) Lucrezia Borgia (1480–1519), daughter of Pope Alexander VI and Vanozza Catanei. Lucrezia had previously been married to (1) Giovanni Sforza of Pesaro, and (2) Alfonso, duke of Bisceglie, illegitimate son of Ferrante I of Naples, but gained a positive reputation as duchess of Ferrara.

4.14   Florence: heads of the Medici family, later dukes of Florence (from 1537) and grand dukes of Tuscany (from 1569)

The Medici were merely private citizens in republican Florence, their eventual rise to noble status being facilitated by the two Medici popes. This list gives heads of the principal (Cafaggiolo) branch of the family. The dates in the first column relate to their headship of the family.

-1429   **Giovanni di Bicci**: b. 1360, son of Averardo de' Medici, known as Bicci. d. 1363. m. Piccarda de' Bueri (1368–1433). Founded the family's banking fortune.

1429–64   **Cosimo** (*il vecchio*, 'the elder'; *Pater patriae*, 'father of his country'): b. 1389, son of Giovanni di Bicci. m. Contessina Bardi (d. 1473) of Florence. Successful banker and entrepreneur; mafia-style 'boss' of the Medici faction in Florentine politics who also changed the course of Florentine foreign policy from hostility to alliance with Milan. One of the greatest patrons of Renaissance culture through his sponsorship of Brunelleschi, Donatello, Ficino and others.

1464–69   **Piero** (*il gottoso*, 'the gouty'): b. 1416, son of Cosimo. m. Lucrezia Tornabuoni (1425–82) of Florence.

1469–92   **Lorenzo** (*il magnifico*, 'the magnificent'): b. 1449, son of Piero. m. Clarice Orsini (1450–88), daughter of Giacomo Orsini of Rome. Led Medici interests in Florentine politics and represented Florence, officially and unofficially, in inter-state diplomacy. A notable poet in his own right, while diminishing returns from banking and commercial interests rendered him more an arbiter of cultural taste and beneficial influence than a patron on the scale of his grandfather. Prior to his murder by the Pazzi conspirators, Lorenzo's brother Giuliano (1453–78) was also a notable figure. *Magnifico* was a title accorded to distinguished non-nobles and its use was by no means confined to Lorenzo.

1492–94   **Piero**: b. 1471, son of Lorenzo. m. Alfonsina Orsini (1472–1520), daughter of Roberto Orsini of Rome. d. 1503.

1494–1512   Medici exiled from Florence.

1512–13   **Giovanni** (Pope Leo X): b. 1475, son of Lorenzo 'il magnifico'. Cardinal (1489); pope (1513–21) (see 2.2).

1513   **Giuliano**: b. 1479, son of Lorenzo. *Title*: duke of Nemours. d. 1516. m. Filiberta (1498–1524), daughter of Philibert II, duke of Savoy.

1513–19   **Lorenzo**: b. 1492, son of Piero; grandson of Lorenzo *il magnifico*. *Title*: duke of Urbino. m. Madeleine de la Tour d'Auvergne (1501–19), cousin of Francis I. Their daughter Caterina (1519–89) became queen of France.

1519–34 **Giulio** (Pope Clement VII): b. 1478, illegitimate son of Giuliano (d. 1478). Cardinal (1513); pope (1523–34) (see 2.2).

1523–27 **Ippolito**: b. 1511, illegitimate son of Giuliano, duke of Nemours. Cardinal (1529). Together with his second cousin, Alessandro, he represented the Medici family in Florence while Clement VII remained head of the dynasty. d. 1535.
Alessandro: b. 1511, illegitimate son of Lorenzo, duke of Urbino. Together with his second cousin, Ippolito, represented the Medici family in Florence while Clement VII remained head of the dynasty. m. Margaret of Parma (1522–86), illegitimate daughter of Emperor Charles V. d. 1537.

1527–30 Medici exiled from Florence.

1530–37 **Alessandro**: First duke of Florence (1537): details as above.

1537–74 **Cosimo I**: b. 1519, son of the *condottiere* Giovanni 'delle Bande Nere' de' Medici (1498–1526, great-great-great-grandson of Giovanni di Bicci) and Maria Salviati (1499–1543), granddaughter of Lorenzo *il magnifico*. *Titles*: duke of Florence (1537–69), grand duke of Tuscany (1569–74). m. (1) Eleonora of Toledo (1522–62), (2) Camilla Martelli (1545–90).

4.15   France: kings of the House of Valois

1380–1422 **Charles VI** (*le bien-amé*): b. 1368, son of Charles V and Jeanne de Bourbon (d. 1377). m. Isabel (known as Isabeau, 1370–1435) of Bavaria. Royal government broke down during his bouts of mental incapacity, paving the way for civil war and the English invasion.

1422–61 **Charles VII** (*roi de Bourges, le victorieux*): b. 1403, son of Charles VI. m. Marie (d. 1463), daughter of Louis II, duke of Anjou. Dauphin from 1417, after the deaths of his elder brothers; regent for insane father from 1418. His soubriquets refer respectively to the period of English occupation, when Charles was based at Bourges, and to the eventual defeat of the English.

1461–83 **Louis XI**: b. 1423, son of Charles VII. m. (1) Margaret (1425–45), daughter of James I of Scotland, (2) Charlotte (1439–83), daughter of Louis, count of Savoy. By 'harvesting' royal duchies as they came vacant, Louis bequeathed his son a considerably reunified kingdom.

1483–98   **Charles VIII** (*l'affable*): b. 1470, son of Louis XI and Char-
           lotte of Savoy. m. Anne (1477–1514), duchess of Brittany.
           1483–91: regency of Anne (1461–1522) and Pierre (1438–
           1503) de Beaujeu, duke of Bourbon, daughter and son-in-
           law of Louis XI. Notable as the king who invaded Italy in
           1498, in pursuit of his claim to the Neapolitan throne. His
           four children predeceased him.

1498–1515 **Louis XII** (*le père du peuple*): b. 1462, son of Charles (1391–
           1465), duke of Orléans and Marie de Clèves (d. 1487). *Previ-
           ous title*: duke of Orléans (see 4.25). Claimed and invaded
           the duchy of Milan (1499). m. (1) Jeanne de France (1464–
           1505), daughter of Louis XI; marriage dissolved, (2) Anne
           of Brittany, widow of Charles VIII, (3) Mary Tudor (1496–
           1533), daughter of Henry VII of England.

1515–47   **Francis I** (François): b. 1494, son of Charles (1458–95),
           count of Angoulême, and Louise (1476–1531), daughter of
           Philibert I of Savoy. m. (1) Claude de France (1499–1524),
           daughter of Louis XII and Anne of Brittany, (2) Eleanor of
           Austria (1498–1558), daughter of Philip the Fair and Juana
           of Castile; sister of Emperor Charles V. Francis was prede-
           ceased by his son François (d. 1536), so succeeded by his
           second son, Henri.

4.16   Granada: Nasrid kings

1391–92   **Yusuf II**: Son of Muhammad V.
1392–1408 **Muhammad VII**: Son of Yusuf II.
1408–17   **Yusuf III**: Brother of Muhammad VII.
1417–19   **Muhammad VIII**: Son of Yusuf III. First reign. Overthrown
           by a cousin due to his youth.
1419–27   **Muhammad IX**: Cousin of Muhammad VII and Yusuf III.
           First reign. Forced into exile.
1427–29   **Muhammad VIII**: Second reign: personal details as above.
           Executed when Muhammad IX returned from exile.
1429–45   **Muhammad IX**: Second reign: personal details as above.
1431–32   **Yusuf IV**: Grandson of Muhammad VI; distant cousin of
           Muhammad IX. His claim to the throne supported by Castile
           when Muhammad IX refused to pay tribute. Assassinated.
1445–47   **Muhammad X**: Nephew of Muhammad VIII. Reign inter-
           rupted by that of Yusuf V.
1445–46   **Yusuf V**: Nephew of Muhammad VII and Yusuf III. First reign.
1447–53   **Muhammad IX**: Third reign: personal details as above. Con-
           sented to Muhammad XI as co-ruler. Yusuf V claimed the
           throne again in 1450.

1448–54   **Muhammad XI**: Son of Muhammad VIII. Ousted after death of co-ruler, Muhammad IX.

1454–64   **Sa'd**: Grandson of Yusuf II, nephew of Muhammad VII and Yusuf III. Reign interrupted by that of Yusuf V.

1462–63   **Yusuf V**: Personal details as above.

1464–82   **Abu-l-Hasan 'Ali**: Son of Sa'd. First reign.

1482   **Muhammad XII**: Son of Abu-l-Hasan 'Ali. First reign. d. 1487. Known to Christian adversaries as Boabdil.

1482–85   **Abu-l-Hasan 'Ali**: Second reign: personal details as above. Overthrown by his brother al-Zagal.

1486–92   **Muhammad XII**: Second reign, lasting until the fall of the city of Granada to the Christian forces of Ferdinand and Isabella.

4.17   Holy Roman Empire: emperors of the Houses of Luxemburg (to 1400), Wittelsbach and (from 1437) Habsburg

See 3.1.

4.18   Hungary: elected kings

1397–1437   **Sigismund** of Luxemburg: b. 1368, son of Emperor Charles IV; king of Hungary by virtue of his first wife. *Other titles*: margrave of Brandenburg (1378–1417), king of Bohemia (1419–37), Holy Roman Emperor (1410–37). m. (1) Maria (d. 1392), daughter of Louis the Great of Hungary, (2) Barbara (d. 1451), daughter of Hermann, count of Cilli.

1437–39   **Albert** of Habsburg: b. 1397, son of Albrecht IV of Austria; son-in-law of Sigismund. *Other titles*: duke of Austria (1404–39), Holy Roman Emperor (1437–39), king of Bohemia (1438–39). m. Elizabeth of Luxemburg, daughter of Emperor Sigismund.

1440–44   **Ulászló I** (Ladislas): b. 1424, son of Władysław II Jagiełło of Lithuania and Jadwiga of Poland; grandson of Emperor Sigismund and Maria of Hungary. *Other title*: King Władysław III of Poland (1434–44). Killed at the battle of Varna.

1444–57   **Ladislas** ('Posthumous') (Hung. László): b. 1440, son of Emperor Albert. *Other titles*: archduke of Austria (1440–57), King Vladislav of Bohemia (1440–57). Born four months after the death of his father. m. Madeleine, daughter of Charles VII of France. She married secondly Gaston de Foix, prince of Viana. János Hunyadi (1407/9–56), *voyvode* of

Transylvania, acted as his regent in Hungary (1444–53) and led the Christian forces to victory at Belgrade (1456).

1458–90   **Matthias Corvinus** (Hung.: Mátyás Hunyadi): b. 1440, son of János Hunyadi. m. (1) Katharina, daughter of George of Poděbrady, (2) Beatrice d'Aragona (1457–1508), daughter of Ferrante I of Naples. A strong king who offered the region some stability and ruled over a short-lived 'empire' (1485–90) consisting of Bohemia, Hungary, Austria, part of Styria, Silesia, Moravia and Transylvania. His capital, Buda, was a major cultural centre. 'Corvinus' derives from the Hunyadi family emblem, the raven.

1490–1516   **Ulászló II** (Ladislas): b. 1456, son of Kazimierz IV of Poland; nephew of Ladislas Posthumous. *Other title*: King Vladislav II of Bohemia (1471–16). m. (1) Beatrice d'Aragona, his predecessor's widow, but marriage annulled 1500, (2) Anne de Foix (d. 1506).

1516–26   **Louis II** (Hung.: Lajos): b. 1506, son of Ulászló. *Other title*: king of Bohemia (1516–26). Killed at the battle of Mohács. m. Maria (1505–58), daughter of Philip the Fair and Juana of Castile; sister of Emperor Charles V. As a widow, Mary of Hungary, as she is known, served her brother as governor of the Netherlands from 1530.

1527   Disputed election between János Zápolya (1487–1540) *voyvode* of Transylvania, and Ferdinand of Habsburg (1503–64), king of Bohemia (1526–64) and Holy Roman Emperor (1556–64).

4.19   Mantua: marquises (from 1433), then dukes (from 1530) of the House of Gonzaga

1382–1407   **Francesco I**: b. 1363, son of Ludovico I. m. (1) Agnese Visconti of Milan, (2) Margherita Malatesta of Rimini.

1407–44   **Gian Francesco I**: b. 1395, son of Francesco I. m. Paola Malatesta of Rimini (d. 1453).

1444–78   **Ludovico III**: b. 1414, son of Gian Francesco I. m. Barbara of Brandenburg (1422–81), niece of Emperor Sigismund.

1478–84   **Federico I**: b. 1441, son of Ludovico III. m. Margherita (d. 1479), daughter of Albrecht III, duke of Bavaria.

1484–1519   **Gian Francesco II**: b. 1466, son of Federico I. m. Isabella d'Este (1474–1539), daughter of Ercole d'Este, duke of Ferrara.

1519–40   **Federico II**: b. 1500, son of Gian Francesco II. m. (1) Maria Palaeologus, (2) her sister Margherita.

4.20   Milan: dukes (from 1395) of the Houses of Visconti (to 1447) and Sforza (from 1450)

1378–1402   **Gian Galeazzo**: b. 1351, son of Galeazzo II. m. (1) Isabelle de Valois (d. 1372), daughter of Jean II of France, (2) Caterina, daughter of Gian Galeazzo's uncle Bernabò Visconti.

1402–12   **Giovanni Maria**: b. 1389, son of Gian Galeazzo. m. Antonia Malatesta. Assassinated.

1412–47   **Filippo Maria**: b. 1392, brother of Giovanni Maria. m. (1) Beatrice of Tenda (d. 1418), widow of the *condottiere* Facino Cane, (2) Marie (d. 1469), daughter of Amadeus VII, count of Savoy.

1447–50   Ambrosian Republic.

1450–66   **Francesco Sforza**: b. 1401, son of Muzio Attendolo, the *condottiere* known as 'Sforza'. m. (1) Polissena Ruffo of Montalto (d. 1427), (2)? Caldora, (3) Bianca Maria Visconti (1424–68), illegitimate daughter of Filippo Maria by Agnese del Maino.

1466–76   **Galeazzo Maria**: b. 1444, son of Francesco. m. Bona (*c.* 1450–1505), daughter of Louis, duke of Savoy.

1476–94   **Gian Galeazzo II Maria**: b. 1469, son of Galeazzo Maria. Regents for this young duke were his mother, Bona of Savoy, until 1480, and his uncle Ludovico *il moro* thereafter. m. Isabella d'Aragona (1472–1524), daughter of Alfonso II of Naples and Ippolita Sforza.

1494–99   **Ludovico Maria** *il moro*: b. 1452, son of Galeazzo Maria. Effectively ruler of Milan continuously from 1480, due to the youth of his nephew Gian Galeazzo. m. Beatrice d'Este (1475–97), daughter of Ercole I d'Este of Ferrara. Ablest of Francesco Sforza'a sons. d. 1508.

1499–1500   French occupation of Milan.

1500   **Ludovico** *il moro*: Second rule, February–April: personal details as above.

1500–12   French occupation of Milan.

1512–15   **Massimiliano**: b. 1491, son of Ludovico *il moro*. Exiled 1515. d. 1530.

1515–21   French occupation of Milan.

1521–24   **Francesco II Maria**: b. 1495, son of Ludovico *il moro*. Abdicated under French pressure. d. 1535.

1524–25   French occupation of Milan.

1525–29   Imperial occupation of Milan.

1529–35   **Francesco II Maria**: Second rule, but as an imperial vassal: personal details as above.

1535   Milan became an imperial possession.

4.21   Muscovy: grand dukes

1389–1425   **Vasili I** (Basil): b. 1371, son of Dmitri Donskoi.
1425–62   **Vasili II** (Basil): b. 1415, son of Vasili I. Rule briefly inter-
             rupted (1432, 1434) by Yuri IV (d. 1434), son of Dmitri
             Donskoi.
1462–1505   **Ivan III** (the Great): b. 1440, son of Basil II. m. Zoë (1448–
             c. 1503), daughter of Thomas Palaeologus, despot of the
             Morea; changed her name to Sophia upon marriage.
1505–33   **Vasili III** (Basil): b. 1479, son of Ivan III.

4.22   Naples: kings of the Houses of Anjou (to 1442) and Aragon

1389–99   **Louis II** of Anjou: b. 1377, expelled by Ladislas of Durazzo.
             d. 1417.
1399–1414   **Ladislas** of Durazzo: b. 1377, son of Charles III of Durazzo.
             Ladislas had also ruled Naples 1386–90.
1414–35   **Giovanna II** of Anjou-Durazzo: b. 1373, sister of Ladislas.
             Having no children, Giovanna adopted first Alfonso V,
             king of Aragon and Sicily, as her heir, before revoking that
             decision in favour of René of Anjou.
1435–42   **René** of Anjou: b. 1409, son of Louis II, duke of Anjou.
             Other titles: count of Maine and Provence, duke of Anjou, Bar,
             Lorraine and Touraine, titular king of Jerusalem. Expelled
             from Naples. d. 1480.
1442–58   **Alfonso I** ('the Magnanimous'): b. 1385, son of Ferdinand I
             of Aragon. *Other title*: king of Aragon (1416–58). Following
             the conquest of Naples, Alfonso based himself in Italy, leav-
             ing his brother Joan to rule Aragon in his stead. m. Maria
             (d. 1458), daughter of Enrique III of Castile.
1458–94   **Ferrante I** (Ferdinando): b. 1423, illegitimate son of
             Alfonso I. m. (1) Isabella di Chiaramonte (d. 1465), (2)
             Juana (d. 1517), illegitimate daughter of Joan II of Aragon.
             Neapolitan barons revolted against his tyrannical rule.
1494–95   **Alfonso II**: b. 1448, son of Ferrante I. m. Ippolita (1442–
             88), daughter of Francesco Sforza of Milan. Previously duke
             of Calabria. Abdicated and fled. d. 1495.
1495   **Ferrante II** (Ferrantino, Ferdinando): b. 1469, son of Alfonso
             II. Deposed. m. Giovanna, daughter of Ferrante I. d. 1496.
1495   French occupation.
1495–96   **Ferrante II**: Second reign: personal details as above.
1496–1501   **Federico**: b. 1452, son of Ferrante I; uncle of Ferdinand II.
             Abdicated. d. 1504.

1501-3   French occupation.
1504   Beginning of rule by Spanish viceroys which lasted until
          1713.

4.23 Navarre: kings of the Houses of Evreux, Aragon (from 1425) and Foix (from 1479)

1387-1425 **Charles III** ('the Noble'): b. 1361, son of Charles II. Essentially a French noble. m. Leonor of Castile.
1425-41   **Blanche** (Blanca): b. 1385, daughter of Charles III. m. (1) Martí I of Aragon, king of Sicily, (2) Joan II of Aragon.
1441-46   **Carlos** (Charles of Viana): b. 1421, son of Blanche and Joan II of Aragon, to whose crown he was also heir. Although the legitimate king, Carlos was repeatedly imprisoned or exiled by his father. d. 1461.
1446-79   **Joan** (Cast.: Juan): b. 1398, son of Ferdinand I of Aragon; husband of Blanche. *Other title*: Joan II of Aragon.
1479   **Leonor**: daughter of Joan II of Aragon and Blanche of Navarre. m. Gaston IV, count of Foix (d. 1472).
1479-83   **François-Phébus**: b. 1467, son of Gaston de Foix, prince of Viana, and Madeleine, daughter of Charles VII of France; grandson of Leonor. *Other title*: count of Foix.
1483-1512 **Catherine**: b. 1468, daughter of Gaston de Foix, prince of Viana; sister of François-Phébus. *Other title*: countess of Foix. m. Jean d'Albret. d. 1517.
1512   Most of the kingdom was occupied by Ferdinand of Aragon and absorbed into that of Castile, leaving the Albret family as rulers of the smaller, French-speaking portion. Charlotte d'Albret (1482-1514), sister-in-law of Catherine, was married to Cesare Borgia in 1499. Catherine's son Henri II d'Albret married Marguerite of Angoulême (1492-1549), sister of Francis I of France, making her queen of Navarre.

4.24 Norway: kings

See 4.11.

4.25 Orléans: French royal dukes

1392-1407 **Louis I**: b. 1372, son of Charles V of France and Jeanne de Bourbon. *Other title*: duke of Luxemburg (1402-7) after deposition of Jost of Moravia. Assassinated by Burgundian opponents in the French civil war. m. Valentina (d. 1408), daughter of Gian Galeazzo Visconti, duke of Milan.

1407–65	**Charles**: b. 1394, son of Louis I. Senior commander at the battle of Agincourt (1415); prisoner of war in England after Agincourt; notable poet. m. (1) Isabel (d. 1409), daughter of Charles VI of France and widow of Richard II of England, (2) Bonne (1401–*c*. 1416), daughter of Bernard VII, count of Armagnac, leader of Orléanist/Armagnac faction in the French civil war, (3) Marie de Clèves (1427–87). Charles's illegitimate son Jean, count of Dunois, was an important military captain in the war with England and an associate of Joan of Arc.
1465–	**Louis II**: b. 1462, son of Charles and Marie de Clèves. *Other title*: Louis XII of France (1498–1515), in which capacity he pursued the Orléanist claim to the duchy of Milan, as a result of his grandfather's marriage with Valentina Visconti. m. Jeanne de France (1464–1505), daughter of Louis XI, but the marriage was dissolved when he became king, enabling him to marry (2) Anne of Brittany (1477–1514).
1498	Duchy united with the kingdom of France.

4.26   Ottoman Empire: sultans

1389–1403	**Bâyezîd I**: b. 1347, son of Murâd I.
1403–11	**Süleymân Çelebi**: Son of Bâyezîd I.
1411–13	**Mûsâ Çelebi**: Brother of Süleymân.
1413–21	**Mehmed I**: b. 1387, son of Bâyezîd I.
1421–22	**Mustafa**: Son of Bâyezîd I.
1422–23	**Mustafa Küçük**: Son of Mehmed I.
1421–44	**Murâd II**: b. 1404, son of Mehmed I. First reign. d. 1451.
1444–46	**Mehmed II**: b. 1430, son of Murâd II. First reign. d. 1481.
1446–51	**Murâd II**: Second reign: personal details as above.
1451–81	**Mehmed II** ('the Conqueror'): Second reign: personal details as above. Name by which he is known relates to the Ottoman conquest of Constantinople in 1453.
1481–1512	**Bâyezîd II**: b. 1447, son of Mehmet II.
1512–20	**Selîm I**: b. 1467, son of Bâyezîd II.
1520–66	**Süleymân I**: b. 1496, son of Selîm I.

4.27   Palatinate of the Rhine: electors of the House of Wittelsbach

A branch of the Wittelsbach dynasty also ruled the duchy of Bavaria.

1390–98	**Ruprecht II**: b. 1325.
1398–1410	**Ruprecht III** (Rupert): b. 1352, son of Ruprecht II. *Other title*: uncrowned claimant to the imperial title.

1410–36	**Ludwig III**: b. 1378, son of Ruprecht III.
1436–49	**Ludwig IV**: b. 1424, son of Ludwig III.
1449–76	**Friedrich I** ('the Victorious'): b. 1425, brother of Ludwig IV.
1476–1508	**Philipp**: b. 1448, son of Ludwig IV.
1508–44	**Ludwig V**: b. 1478, son of Philipp.

4.28 Poland–Lithuania: elected kings of the House of Jagiełło (from 1386)

1384–99	**Jadwiga** (Hedwig): b. 1374, daughter of Louis the Great, king of Poland and Hungary. See also 12.8. m. Władysław II Jagiełło of Lithuania.
1385/86 –1434	**Władysław II** Jagiełło: b. 1351. Consort of Jadwiga. *Other titles*: grand duke of Lithuania (1377–81, 1382–1401), supreme duke of Lithuania (1401–34). m. (1) Jadwiga of Poland, thereby creating the united kingdom of Poland–Lithuania, (2) Sophia of Holszany.
1434–44	**Władysław III**: b. 1424, son of Władysław II and Jadwiga. *Other title*: King Ulászló I of Hungary (1440–44). Killed at the battle of Varna.
1444–47	Interregnum.
1447–92	**Kazimierz IV** (Casimir): b. 1427, son of Władysław III. *Other title*: grand duke of Lithuania. m. Elizabeth, daughter of Emperor Albert II and Elizabeth of Luxemburg, so granddaughter of Emperor Sigismund.
1492–1501	**Jan Olbracht**: b. 1450, son of Kazimierz IV.
1501–6	**Alexander**: b. 1461, brother of Jan Olbracht. m. Elena, daughter of Ivan III of Muscovy.
1506–48	**Zygmunt I** ('the Old'): b. 1467, son of Kazimierz IV, brother of Alexander. m. (1) Barbara, daughter of Stephan Zápolya, (2) Bona, daughter of Gian Galeazzo II Sforza of Milan.

4.29 Portugal: kings of the Houses of Avis (to 1495) and Braganza

1383–1433	**João I** ('Master of Avis'): b. 1358, illegitimate son of Pedro I. m. Philippa of Lancaster (1360–1415), daughter of John of Gaunt and Blanche of Lancaster. Their sons included 'Henry the Navigator'.
1433–38	**Duarte I**: b. 1391, son of João I. m. Leonor, daughter of Ferdinand I of Aragon.
1438–81	**Afonso V** ('the African'): b. 1432, son of Duarte I.
1481–95	**João II** ('the Perfect'): b. 1455, son of Afonso V.

1495–1521   **Manoel I** ('the Fortunate'): b. 1469, cousin of João II. m. (1) Isabel (1470–98), eldest daughter of Ferdinand of Aragon and Isabella of Castile, previously wife of Manoel's elder brother Afonso, (2) María (1482–1517), daughter of Ferdinand of Aragon and Isabella of Castile, (3) Eleanor (1498–1558), daughter of Philip the Fair and Juana of Castile.

1521–57   **João III**: b. 1502, son of Manoel I and Maria of Aragon and Castile.

4.30   Savoy–Piedmont: counts and (from 1416) dukes

1383–91   **Amadeus VII** (Amédée): b. 1360, son of Amadeus VI.

1391–1451   **Amadeus VIII** (Amédée): b. 1383, son of Amadeus VII. *Other title*: antipope Felix V (1439–49) and afterwards a cardinal. This career change was facilitated by the death of his wife, Marie (1386–1428), daughter of Philip the Bold, duke of Burgundy.

1451–65   **Louis**: b. 1402, son of Amadeus VIII. m. Anne de Lusignan (d. 1462), daughter of Jean II of Cyprus.

1465–72   **Amadeus IX** (Amédée): b. 1435, son of Louis. m. Yolande (1434–78), daughter of Charles VII of France.

1472–82   **Philibert I**: b. 1464, son of Amadeus IX.

1482–90   **Charles I**: b. 1468, brother of Philibert I. m. Blanche of Monferrato, who acted as regent for their son Charles II.

1490–96   **Charles II**: b. 1489, son of Charles I.

1496–97   **Philippe II**: b. 1438, great-uncle of Charles II.

1497–1504   **Philibert II**: b. 1480, son of Philippe II. m. Margaret of Austria (1480–1530), daughter of Emperor Maximilian and first married to Infante Juan of Aragon and Castile. As regent of the Netherlands, Margaret's court at Mechelen (Malines) was a major centre of patronage for artists and men of letters. It was also where Charles V and his sisters were brought up by their aunt. As duchess of Savoy she was patron of the mausoleum at Brou (see 20.3, pp. 231–2).

1504–53   **Charles III**: b. 1486, brother of Philibert II.

4.31   Saxony: dukes and (from 1423) electors of the House of Wettin

1381–1428   **Friedrich I** (Frederick 'the Warlike'): b. 1370

1428–64   **Friedrich II**: b. 1412, son of Friedrich I.

1464–86   **Ernst**: b. 1441, son of Friedrich II. Joint ruler with his brother Albrecht.

1464–1500   **Albrecht III**: b. 1443, son of Friedrich II. Joint ruler with his
             brother Ernst and, later, with his nephew Friedrich.

1486–1525   **Friedrich III** (Frederick 'the Wise'): b. 1463, son of Ernst.
             Founder of the University of Wittenberg and protector of
             Martin Luther.

1525–32   **Johann** (John 'the Constant'): b. 1469, brother of Friedrich.

4.32   Scotland: kings of the House of Stuart

1390–1406   **Robert III**: b. 1337, son of Robert II. m. Annabella
             Drummond (d. 1401).

1406–37   **James I**: b. 1394, son of Robert III. m. Joan (d. 1445),
             daughter of John Beaufort, earl of Somerset. Assassinated.

1437–60   **James II**: b. 1430, son of James I. m. Mary (d. 1463), daugh-
             ter of Arnold, duke of Gelders. Killed at the siege of
             Roxburgh.

1469–88   **James III**: b. 1452, son of James II. m. Margaret (d. 1486),
             daughter of Kristian I of Denmark. Assassinated.

1488–1513   **James IV**: b. 1473, son of James III. m. Margaret Tudor
             (1489–1541), daughter of Henry VII of England. Killed at
             the battle of Flodden.

1513–42   **James V**: b. 1512, son of James IV. m. Mary (1515–60),
             daughter of Claude, duke of Guise. Their daughter was
             Mary, Queen of Scots.

4.33   Sicily: kings

1377–   **Maria**: b. 1367, daughter of Federico III. m. Martí, heir to
1401   crown of Aragon.

1391–1409   **Martí I**: b. 1374, son of Martí I of Aragon; king of Sicily by
             virtue of his first marriage. m. (1) Maria, queen of Sicily,
             (2) Blanche, daughter of Charles III of Navarre.

1409–12   **Martí II**: d. 1412, son of Pedro IV of Aragon; father of
             Martí I. *Other title*: Martí I of Aragon. m. (1) Maria de Luna
             (d. 1407), (2) Margarita de Pardes (d. 1451).

Thereafter, as kings of Aragon.

4.34   Sweden: elected kings

1389–97   **Margrete** (Margaret): b. 1353, daughter of Valdemar
             Atterdag of Denmark, wife of Haakon VI of Norway; gener-
             ally accepted as queen of Sweden. d. 1412. Union of Kalmar
             (1397) formally united the crowns of Denmark, Norway
             and Sweden.

1397–1435   **Erik** of Pomerania: b. 1382, great-nephew of Margrete. *Other title*: king of Denmark and Norway (1412–39). m. Philippa (1394–*c.* 1430), daughter of Henry IV of England. Deposed in Sweden in a revolt led by Engelbrekt Engelbrektson (d. 1436), who was elected regent. d. 1459.

1438–40   Regent: Karl Knutsson Bonde: b. 1409, future King Karl VIII. d. 1470.

1441–48   **Kristoffer**: b. 1418, nephew of Erik of Pomerania. *Other titles*: duke of the Upper Palatinate, king of Denmark and Norway (1439–48).

1448–57   **Karl VIII**: First reign: details as above, Karl Knutsson Bonde.

1457–64   **Kristian I**: b. 1426. *Other titles*: count of Oldenburg, king of Denmark and Norway (1448–81). Deposed by insurgents. d. 1481.

1464–65   **Karl VIII**: Second reign: personal details as above.

1465–66   Regent: Jons Bengtsson Oxenstierna.

1466–67   Regent: Erik Axelsson Tott.

1467–70   **Karl VIII**: Third reign: personal details as above.

1470–97   Regent: Sten Sture the Elder.

1497–1501   **Hans II**: b. 1455, son of Kristian I. *Other titles*: king of Denmark and Norway (1481–1513). Deposed by insurgents. d. 1513.

1501–4   Regent: Sten Sture the Elder.

1504–12   Regent: Svante Nilsson Sture: cousin of Karl VIII.

1512–20   Regent: Sten Sture the Younger: Son of Svante Nilsson.

1520–21   **Kristian II**: b. 1481, son of Hans II. *Other titles*: king of Denmark and Norway (1513–23). Deposed in revolt led by Gustav Eriksson Vasa. d. 1559.

1521–23   Regent: Gustav Eriksson Vasa.

1523–60   **Gustavus I** (Gustav Eriksson Vasa): b. 1496. Previously regent; first king of the House of Vasa.

4.35   Urbino: counts, then (from 1474) dukes of the Houses of Montefeltro, Della Rovere and Medici

1377–1404   **Antonio da Montefeltro**: Son of Federico II.

1404–43   **Guidantonio da Montefeltro**: Son of Antonio. m. (1) Rengarda Malatesta of Rimini (d. 1423), (2) Caterina Colonna, niece of Pope Martin V.

1443–44   **Oddantonio da Montefeltro**: b. 1427, son of Guidantonio.

1444–82   **Federico II da Montefeltro**: b. 1422, illegitimate brother of Oddantonio. m. (1) Gentile (d. 1457), daughter of Bartolomeo Brancaleone, (2) Battista (1446–72), daughter

of Alessandro Sforza of Pesaro. Famous *condottiere*, friend of
humanists and patron of the visual arts.

1482–1508 **Guidobaldo I da Montefeltro**: b. 1472, son of Federico II.
m. Elisabetta (1471–1526), daughter of Federico Gonzaga
of Mantua. Duchy occupied by Cesare Borgia, June–
November 1502. Court in 1506 as setting for Castiglione's
Il libro del cortegiano (see 6.5.1).

1508–16 **Francesco Maria I della Rovere**: b. 1490, grandson of
Federico da Montefeltro, nephew of Guidobaldo I and of
Pope Julius II. First rule. m. Eleonora (d. 1543), daughter of
Francesco Gonzaga of Mantua and Isabella d'Este. d. 1538.

1516–19 **Lorenzo de' Medici**: b. 1492, son of Piero di Lorenzo *il
magnifico* and nephew of Leo X. m. Madeleine de la Tour
d'Auvergne (1501–19).

1519–20 Papal rule, in the name of Leo X.

1520–38 **Francesco Maria I della Rovere**: Seond rule: details as above.

5　Genealogical tables

5.1   The Sforza of Milan: at the crossroads of Renaissance Europe

Note: Except where indicated, the dates given are those of birth and death.

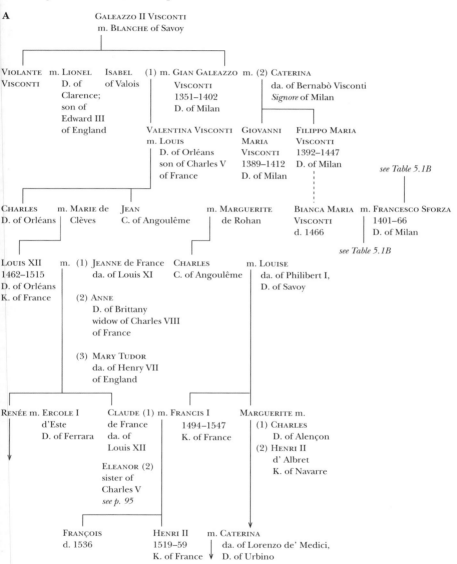

A

GALEAZZO II VISCONTI
m. BLANCHE of Savoy

VIOLANTE   m. LIONEL   ISABEL   (1) m. GIAN GALEAZZO   m. (2) CATERINA
VISCONTI   D. of   of Valois   VISCONTI   da. of Bernabò Visconti
              Clarence;   1351–1402   *Signore* of Milan
              son of   D. of Milan
              Edward III
              of England   VALENTINA VISCONTI   GIOVANNI   FILIPPO MARIA
                                     m. LOUIS   MARIA   VISCONTI
                                       D. of Orléans   VISCONTI   1392–1447
                                       son of Charles V 1389–1412   D. of Milan   *see Table 5.1B*
                                       of France   D. of Milan

CHARLES   m. MARIE de   JEAN   m. MARGUERITE   BIANCA MARIA   m. FRANCESCO SFORZA
D. of Orléans | Clèves   C. of Angoulême   de Rohan   VISCONTI   1401–66
                                                        d. 1466   D. of Milan

                                                              see Table 5.1B

LOUIS XII   m. (1) JEANNE de France   CHARLES   m. LOUISE
1462–1515   da. of Louis XI   C. of Angoulême   da. of Philibert I,
D. of Orléans   D. of Savoy
K. of France
               (2) ANNE
                   D. of Brittany
                   widow of Charles VIII
                   of France

               (3) MARY TUDOR
                   da. of Henry VII
                   of England

RENÉE m. ERCOLE I   CLAUDE (1) m. FRANCIS I   MARGUERITE m.
       d'Este   de France   1494–1547   (1) CHARLES
       D. of Ferrara   da. of   K. of France   D. of Alençon
                       Louis XII   (2) HENRI II
                                                        d' Albret
                       ELEANOR (2)   K. of Navarre
                       sister of
                       Charles V
                       see p. 95

       FRANÇOIS   HENRI II   m. CATERINA
       d. 1536   1519–59   da. of Lorenzo de' Medici,
                      K. of France   D. of Urbino

B

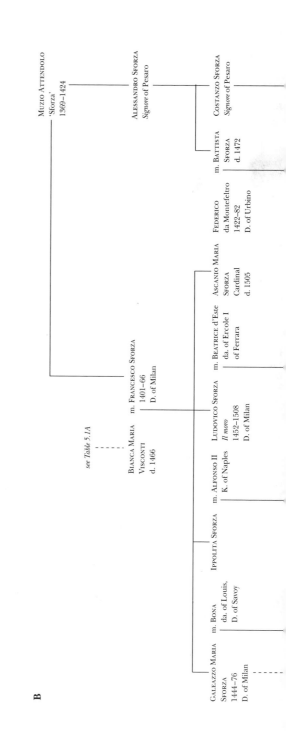

MUZIO ATTENDOLO
'SFORZA'
1369–1424

ALESSANDRO SFORZA
Signore of Pesaro

BIANCA MARIA   m. FRANCESCO SFORZA
VISCONTI   1401–66
d. 1466   D. of Milan

see Table 5.1A

COSTANZO SFORZA
Signore of Pesaro

m. BATTISTA
    SFORZA
    d. 1472

FEDERICO
da Montefeltro
1422–82
D. of Urbino

ASCANIO MARIA
SFORZA
Cardinal
d. 1505

m. BEATRICE d'ESTE
da. of Ercole I
of Ferrara

LUDOVICO SFORZA
Il moro
1452–1508
D. of Milan

m. ALFONSO II
    K. of Naples

IPPOLITA SFORZA

m. BONA
    da. of Louis,
    D. of Savoy

GALEAZZO MARIA
SFORZA
1444–76
D. of Milan

MASSIMILIANO SFORZA
1493–1530
D. of Milan

FRANCESCO II
MARIA SFORZA
1495–1535
D. of Milan

GUIDOBALDO da Montefeltro
D. of Urbino
m. ELISABETTA GONZAGA
da. of Federico,
M. of Mantua

GIOVANNI SFORZA
Signore of Pesaro
m. LUCREZIA BORGIA
1480–1519
da. of Pope
Alexander VI;
she also married
(2) Alfonso
D. of Bisceglie
illegitimate son
of Ferrante, K. of
Naples
(3) Alfonso I
d'Este
D. of Ferrara

ANNA SFORZA
m. Alfonso I d'Este
D. of Ferrara

BIANCA MARIA SFORZA
m. MAXIMILIAN I
Holy Roman Emperor
previously married to
Mary, D. of Burgundy

ERMES SFORZA

GIAN GALEAZZO II SFORZA
1469–94
D. of Milan
m. ISABELLA d' Aragona
da. of K. Alfonso II
of Naples

CATERINA SFORZA
c. 1462–1509

m. (1) GIROLAMO RIARIO
Signore of Imola and Forlì,
nephew of Pope Sixtus IV
d. 1488

(2) GIACOMO FEO

(3) GIOVANNI DE' MEDICI

GIOVANNI delle Bande Nere

m. MARIA SALVIATI
granddaughter of
Lorenzo de' Medici
(*il magnifico*)

COSIMO I
1519–74
D. of Florence
Grand Duke of Tuscany

5.2 Iberia, the Empire and the dynastic policy of Ferdinand of Aragon

Note: Except where indicated, the dates given are those of birth and death.

A HOUSE OF TRASTÁMARA

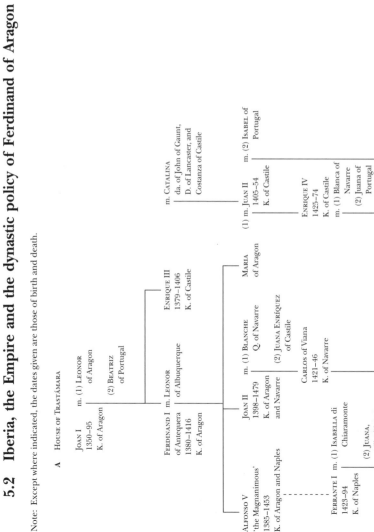

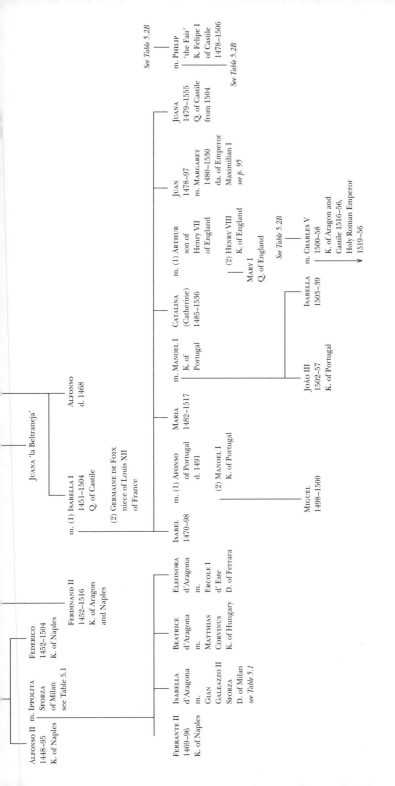

See Table 5.2B

ALFONSO II m. IPPOLITA
1448–95   SFORZA
K. of Naples   of Milan
           see Table 5.1

FEDERICO
1452–1504
K. of Naples

ALFONSO
d. 1468

JUANA 'la Beltraneja'

m. (1) ISABELLA I
1451–1504
Q. of Castile

(2) GERMAINE DE FOIX
niece of Louis XII
of France

FERDINAND II
1452–1516
K. of Aragon
and Naples

JUANA
1479–1555
Q. of Castile
from 1504

m. PHILIP
'the Fair'
K. Felipe I
of Castile
1478–1506

See Table 5.2B

JUAN
1478–97
m. MARGARET
1480–1530
da. of Emperor
Maximilian I
see p. 95

m. (1) ARTHUR
son of
Henry VII
of England

(2) HENRY VIII
K. of England

See Table 5.2B

MARY I
Q. of England

CATALINA
(Catherine)
1485–1536

m. MANOEL I
K. of
Portugal

ISABELLA
1503–39

m. CHARLES V
1500–58
K. of Aragon and
Castile 1516–56,
Holy Roman Emperor
1519–56

MARIA
1482–1517

JOÃO III
1502–57
K. of Portugal

ISABEL
1470–98

m. (1) AFONSO
of Portugal
d. 1491

(2) MANOEL I
K. of Portugal

MIGUEL
1498–1500

FERRANTE II
1469–96
K. of Naples

ISABELLA
d'Aragona
m.
GIAN
GALEAZZO II
SFORZA
D. of Milan
see Table 5.1

BEATRICE
d'Aragona
m.
MATTHIAS
CORVINUS
K. of Hungary

ELEONORA
d'Aragona
m.
ERCOLE I
d'Este
D. of Ferrara

B   HOUSE OF HABSBURG

FREDERICK III   m. LEONOR
1415–93   da. of Duarte I
Holy Roman Emperor   of Portugal

MAXIMILIAN I   m. (1) MARY of Burgundy
1459–1519   1458–82
Holy Roman Emperor   da. of Charles the Bold

                (2) BIANCA MARIA SFORZA
                   see Table 5.1

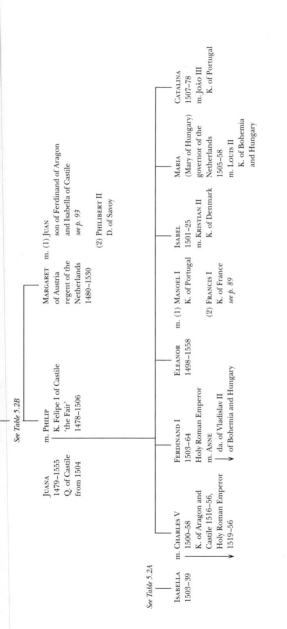

See Table 5.2B

JUANA
1479–1555
Q. of Castile
from 1504

m. PHILIP
K. Felipe I of Castile
'the Fair'
1478–1506

MARGARET
of Austria
regent of the
Netherlands
1480–1530

m. (1) JUAN
son of Ferdinand of Aragon
and Isabella of Castile
see p. 93

(2) PHILIBERT II
D. of Savoy

See Table 5.2A

m. CHARLES V
1500–58
K. of Aragon and
Castile 1516–56,
Holy Roman Emperor
1519–56

FERDINAND I
1503–64
Holy Roman Emperor
m. ANNE
da. of Vladislav II
of Bohemia and Hungary

ELEANOR
1498–1558

m. (1) MANOEL I
K. of Portugal

(2) FRANCIS I
K. of France
see p. 89

ISABEL
1501–25
m. KRISTIAN II
K. of Denmark

MARIA
(Mary of Hungary)
governor of the
Netherlands
1505–58
m. LOUIS II
K. of Bohemia
and Hungary

CATALINA
1507–78
m. JOÃO III
K. of Portugal

ISABELLA
1503–39

6   Courts and households

6.1   Introduction

The vast majority of people in western Christendom lived under the rule of princes. During this period the courts with which princes surrounded themselves tended to become larger, more elaborate and to be housed in ever more splendid palaces. Courts reflected the princes' magnificence and, together with the buildings in which they were housed, could be employed to impress foreign dignitaries and overawe potentially rebellious subjects. If the glory of a king was reflected by the presence of princes and dukes so, in their own domains, those princes and dukes in turn became the centres of smaller courtly cults. Courts also existed to meet the practical requirements of government, for councillors, secretaries and other officials also counted as courtiers, and might be of illustrious birth even without being ennobled by their grateful employers. While only the elite might be termed courtiers, people of all conditions belonged to households, noble and non-noble, settled or peripatetic. Hierarchy was important in courts and households of all sizes, reinforcing the importance of the great man or woman around whom they were centred.

6.2   French royal residences

In an age when the government of larger states depended less on bureaucracy and more on personal contact between the ruler and the ruled, monarchs and their courts were frequently on the move. Ferdinand of Aragon and Isabella of Castile provide the most notable examples of such a policy, but the peripatetic nature of French kingship in the Renaissance is reflected in the map opposite, which locates a number of royal residences in the northern half of the kingdom.

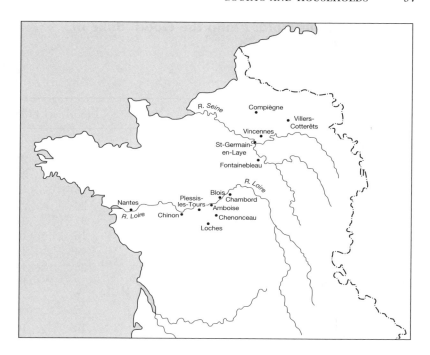

6.3   Royal household: kings of France, 1463–1516

	1463	1484	1498	1499	1505	1512	1516
Chamber/table	77	70	107	86	92	108	154
Chapel	—	7	15	15	13	10	30
Wardrobe	—	5	9	13	—	10	24
Medical service	3	6	18	15	13	11	16
Administration							
and guards	3	37	47	31	5	29	20
Kitchen	—	83	123	119	—	137	168
Others	—	8	10	8	—	9	10
Music	—	—	—	2	—	—	11

Source: D. Potter, *A History of France, 1460–1560*, pp. 66–69.
Note: These figures are distorted by the fact that some sub-categories of
personnel, listed under the general headings given above, are clearly
omitted in some years. Thus it should not be concluded that the king
was any less well guarded in 1463 and 1505 than in the other years.

6.4   Royal household: Philip the Good, duke of Burgundy, 1426–38

	1426	1433	1438
First chamberlain and knight-councillor-chamberlains	9	21	21
Other chamberlains	24	28	28
Stewards	5	5	5
Bread-pantry personnel	18	26	27
Cup-bearers and wine-pantry personnel	22	31	31
Trencher-squires	12	16	16
Kitchen staff	41	44	41
Equerries	39	c. 38	44
Mounted messengers	12	12	12
Quartermasters	5	7	8
Heralds and Kings-of-Arms	3	7	7
Trumpets and minstrels	9	10	10
Falconers and assistants	16	20	c. 13
Archers and bodyguard	12	24	50
Secretaries	7	7	9
Councillors	—	13	29
Total	234	309	351

Source: R. Vaughan, *Philip the Good: the Formation of the Burgundian State* (London, 1962), p. 140.

This table provides indications of the duke's governmental responsibilities, in the form of councillors and secretaries, of the hospitality expected of so great a lord, and of the pleasures of the courtly elite, attended as they were by minstrels and falconers. Like other rulers of the period, the Valois dukes of Burgundy headed a peripatetic court reflecting of their ever-increasing domains. Philip the Bold and John the Fearless resided in Paris a good deal, but Philip the Good preferred Brussels, Bruges, Lille, the castle of Hesdin in Artois and Dijon, capital of the duchy of Burgundy proper. This practice corresponded to the widening political breach between the kings of France and the dukes of Burgundy.

6.5   Noble court: the Montefeltro at Urbino

Federico da Montefeltro (1422–82) was lord of the papal vicariate of Urbino from 1444, before being created duke of the same in 1474 when his daughter married a nephew of Pope Sixtus IV. Federico embodied the Renaissance ideal of mastery of the arts of peace and those of war, being as notable for his patronage of the visual arts and genuine love of learning as for his prowess as one of the most successful *condottieri* of the fifteenth century. His humanist education had been acquired at Vittorino da Feltre's school at Mantua, a connection reinforced dynastically by the marriage of his son and heir Guidobaldo with Elisabetta Gonzaga. It was Federico's building projects at Urbino which went on to provide the setting for the best-known account of Renaissance court life.

6.5.1   Il libro del cortegiano *and the court at Urbino*

Thanks to *Il libro del cortegiano* (*The book of the courtier*) by Baldassare Castiglione (1478–1529), the court at Urbino is frequently thought of as a model of the civilised noble life. Castiglione came from a family of minor Lombard nobles which also produced a number of bishops, and was related to the Gonzaga of Mantua. He served the dukes of Milan and Mantua before taking holy orders and being appointed papal nuncio to the imperial court in Spain from 1525 until his death. Castiglione's 1506 visit to the Montefeltro court at Urbino provided the inspiration for *Il libro del cortegiano*, published in Venice in 1528, in which his characters discuss the attributes and accomplishments of ideal male and female courtiers, whose literary, artistic, sporting, musical and conversational skills should all be demonstrated with *sprezzatura*, unforced ease.

Castiglione's speakers include:

Pietro Bembo (1470–1547): Distinguished Venetian man of letters who championed both Ciceronian Latin and the vernacular of Petrarch and Boccaccio and became associated with a series of courts presided over by women – those of Caterina Cornaro at the Veneto hill-town of Asolo, celebrated by Bembo in *Gli Asolani* (written *c.* 1497, published 1505), Lucrezia Borgia, duchess of Ferrara, to whom he dedicated works on the nature of love, and Elisabetta Gonzaga at Urbino. Bembo's principal role in *Il libro del cortegiano* is to articulate the virtues of platonic love, as developed by fifteenth-century humanist philosophers such as Marsilio Ficino.

Bernardo Dovizi (1470–1520): Known as 'Il Bibbiena' from his Tuscan birthplace, this man of letters and Medici protégé followed his patrons into exile in 1494 and was rewarded by Leo X with important diplomatic missions and a cardinal's hat.

Ottaviano Fregoso (1470–1524): One of three siblings from this distinguished Genoese dynasty to feature in Castiglione's dialogue, he stayed in Urbino while in exile. Back in Genoa he was elected doge in 1513, but lost power in 1522 due to over-reliance on French protection.

Elisabetta Gonzaga (1471–1526): Daughter of Federico Gonzaga of Mantua. In the absence of her ailing husband, Guidobaldo da Montefeltro, the duchess of Urbino presides over the civilised debates which Castiglione sets in their palace.

Giuliano de' Medici (1479–1516): Youngest son of Lorenzo de' Medici (d. 1492) and brother of Leo X; duke of Nemours. His tomb and statue by Michelangelo are in the New Sacristy, S. Lorenzo, Florence.

Emilia Pia (d. 1526): From the Pio family, lords of Carpi, a dynasty otherwise noted for providing employment for the future printer Aldo Manuzio.

Francesco Maria della Rovere (1490–1538): The nephew of Guidobaldo da Montefeltro and of Julius II who was created duke of Urbino by the pope upon Guidobaldo's death in 1508. He was restored to that position in 1520 after Leo X had imposed his own nephew, Lorenzo de' Medici, on the duchy in 1516 (see 4.35).

6.6   Noble household: Elizabeth Berkeley, Countess of Warwick, 1420–21

Gentlewomen	6
Women of the chamber	3
Gentlemen	9
Yeomen (usher, cook, butler, 2 valets of the chamber)	5
Grooms (inc. servants of pantry, buttery, kitchen and head gardener)	26
Chaplain	1
Total	50

Source: J.C. Ward, *English Noblewomen in the Later Middle Ages* (London, 1992), Chapter 3.

Elizabeth Berkeley (d. 1422) was the first wife of Richard Beauchamp, earl of Warwick (d. 1439) and one of fifteenth-century England's most important heiresses. Her account book survives for the year 1420–21, illustrating the composition of her household, the hospitality she offered and the countess's travels between her various estates as both good lord and consumer of local produce. At that point Richard Beauchamp was engaged in Henry V's French war, leaving his wife responsible for the management of his estates and retainers as well as for her own. The fact that a number of her gentlewomen were the wives of her husband's retainers and that they, in turn, were members of the West Midlands gentry, suggests that the lord's household could be used as a means of establishing and maintaining control over a region.

6.7   Cardinal's household: Cardinal Giovanni Battista Zen, 1501

Prelates (including 1 archbishop and 2 bishops)	6
Nipoti ('nephews')	2
Chaplains	8 or 10
Chamberlains	2
Secretaries	2
Shield-bearers	2
Doctor	1
Others (including familiars of familiars)	*c.* 40
Total	*c.* 65

Source: Archivio di Stato di Venezia, Consiglio dei Dieci, Carte di Benedetto Soranzo, arcivescovo di Cipro, ser. V, busta VI. This source is seriously fragmented, many of the names have been lost. At the time of Cardinal Zen's death in 1501 he was based in Padua rather than Rome and most of his household originated in the Veneto region.

Like all households, those of Rome-based curial cardinals existed to serve the practical needs of the great man, through an inner circle of secretaries, treasurers and chaplains, and an outer one of servants. Princes of the Church, no less than secular lords, were also expected to offer hospitality on a level appropriate to their position. Cardinals' households did, however, demonstrate certain distinctive characteristics. They were in some respects miniature versions of the papal court and supplied personnel for papal service and were also the natural homes in Rome for men from the cardinals' native regions. In the sixteenth century cardinals' households lost the latter function and were reduced in size accordingly. Unlike other households, they were exclusively male in composition with many of their more senior members in holy orders, including at least one bishop. The term *familiaris continuus commensalis* was used to refer to permanent members of the household, those who habitually dined with the cardinal, as distinct from artists and other temporary members of the household.

Opinion varied on the size of household suitable for a cardinal. In 1493 Cardinal Ippolito d'Este of Ferrara planned to head a household of 136 servants and familiars. Between his promotion to the Sacred College in December 1471 and his death in January 1474, Sixtus IV's nephew Pietro Riario was said to have assembled a household of 500 persons in his palace at SS. Apostoli, but this figure was certainly exceptionally large.

6.8   Merchant's household: Andrea Barbarigo, 1442

Andrea Barbarigo (1399–1449) was a Venetian patrician merchant whose small household was fairly typical of the urban elite. In 1442 it consisted of Andrea himself, his wife, mother-in-law and two sons, whose needs were so amply met by a male slave, a female slave and a wet nurse for the younger son that a third slave was rented out to another household. This more or less conforms to the pattern of one free servant or unfree slave serving each adult member of a household.

Source: D. Romano, *Housecraft and Statecraft: Domestic Service in Renaissance Venice, 1400–1600* (Baltimore, MD, and London, 1996).

7 Republican government

7.1 Renaissance republicanism

In the Renaissance period republics existed only in Italy and had evolved
out of the communes which, in turn, had filled the power vacuum created by the breakdown of imperial government and administration south
of the Alps in the eleventh and twelfth centuries. Each commune was
initially composed of a political class of two or three hundred individuals who were often landowners or lawyers. By *c.* 1250 the addition
of merchants and guildsmen multiplied the number of men eligible
for political office which, in larger cities, could be as great as two, three or
four thousand. In Genoa and Venice, patrician merchants, generators
of the cities' wealth, had dominated government from at least the
beginning of the communal period and continued to do so, albeit with
dramatically different consequences. The evolution of communal constitutions coincided with the subjugation of the countryside (*contado*) which
surrounded and provisioned the cities. The few communes which did
not fall under the domination of party leaders, despots or *signori* such as
the Visconti of Milan or the Este of Ferrara, were governed by a combination of paid officers, generally a *podestà* and *capitano del popolo*, and a
series of committees on which citizens sat in rotation.

Self-conscious republicanism was apparent in Florence at the beginning of the fifteenth century and is associated with the writings of Coluccio
Salutati and Leonardo Bruni who, as students of antiquity, were aware of
the parallels between their city and ancient republican Rome. Republican
states were commonly depicted as new Romes, but the example of the
Greek *polis* may also be traced in Renaissance Italy. The fourteenth-
century Florentine chronicler Giovanni Villani described his city as 'the
daughter and creation of Rome' which rose to prominence as Rome
itself declined, but Villani's claim was merely a harbinger of panegyrics
to come. In addition to the established republican regimes of Florence,
Genoa, Lucca, Siena and Venice, republican enthusiasm was also mani-
fested in the short-lived Ambrosian Republic (1447–50) in Milan and
by thwarted Roman revolutionaries, most notably Stefano Porcari
(d. 1453).

7.2   Republican writers

Aurelio 'Lippo' Brandolini (*c.* 1440–97)
De comparatione reipublicae et regni (*A Comparison of Republics and Kingdoms, c.* 1490). Brandolini was a Florentine humanist who spent time in Naples, Rome (from 1480) and Hungary (1489). Returning to Italy, he taught at Florence and Pisa, but dedicated the last years of his life to missionary preaching.

Leonardo Bruni (*c.* 1374–1444)
Laudatio Florentinae urbis (*Panegyric on the City of Florence, c.* 1401). For a survey of the writings of this Florentine chancellor, see 15.4, p. 175.

Gasparo Contarini (1483–1542)
De magistratibus et republica Venetorum (*On the Commonwealth and Republic of Venice,* written 1523–24, published 1531): a significant plank in the construction of the Myth of Venice (see 7.7), presenting the Venetian constitution as an Aristotelian balance of monarchical, aristocratic and democratic elements. In this work, Contarini sought to remind his fellow patricians of the ideals from which he considered that they had fallen. For Contarini as a Christian writer, see 12.10.

Donato Giannotti (1492–1573)
Libro della repubblica de Viniziani (1520s) and *Della repubblica fiorentina* (pre-1527): accounts of the two leading republican regimes of the fifteenth century by a Florentine writer.

Bernardo Giustiniani (1408–89)
De origine urbis Venetiarum (*History of the Origin of Venice,* 1493). Giustiniani was a leading Venetian statesman and diplomat.

Paolo Morosini (*c.* 1406–*c.* 1482)
Defensio venetorum ad Europea principes contra obtrectatores and *De rebus ac forma reipublicae venetae*: a defence of Venice to counter its critics and a description of the same. Morosini held many Venetian governmental offices and, as Venetian ambassador to the Holy See, accepted the gift of Bessarion's library on behalf of the Republic.

7.3   Florence

In contrast to the republic of Venice, famed for the stability of its constitution, each of the three Tuscan republics experienced changes of government in the course of the fifteenth century. Most interpretations of Florentine government in this period emphasise the steady erosion of democratic elements by the ambitions of a faction-riven oligarchy. Only members of guilds were eligible for public office, nobles having been excluded by the 1293 anti-magnate Ordinances of Justice. The names of the politically eligible were placed in bags and then drawn when offices were to be filled, a process known as sortition. The apparent fairness of this system was countered by the problem of determining whose names should be placed in the bags in the first place, lists of those eligible being drawn up in scrutinies held every five years (until 1466, after which there were only two more scrutinies before the beginning of the principate). The officers responsible for supervising this crucial process were *accoppiatori*. As in the other republics, the ineligible included those individuals and families who had been sentenced to exile, a frequent practice in the faction-torn states of Italy. Among notable Florentine exiles were members of the Alberti (from 1395), Medici (1433–34, 1494–1512) and Strozzi (1434–66) families.

In spite of their inflated reputation, the fifteenth-century Medici were, strictly speaking, merely office-holding citizens of the republic. At the same time, through the judicious use of patronage, often based on neighbourhood ties, they built up a faction or group of supporters whose own chances of holding lucrative offices were thereby enhanced. This should not be thought exceptional, for interconnected patronage or client-age networks provided the lifeblood of fifteenth-century western European society. When assessing the position of the Medici in Florentine government these considerations should be balanced against the importance of their contacts with foreign princes, who preferred to deal with individuals rather than faceless republican committees.

Under Roman law, power was vested in the people, who could yield it to executive bodies. In Florence, the supreme executive magistracy was the Signoria, composed of eight Priori di Giustizia (Priors) and the Gonfaloniere di Giustizia (Standard-bearer of Justice). Together with the colleges of Buonuomini (Twelve Good Men) and Gonfalonieri (Sixteen Standard Bearers of the Companies), they made up the main executive committees. During their term of office the Signoria lived in the Palazzo della Signoria, now the Palazzo Vecchio. The Signoria initiated legislation which it then submitted to the Councils of the Commune and of the People. The subsidiary organs of government included the Dieci di Balìa (Ten of War) which had extraordinary military and diplomatic powers in time of war, the Otto di Guardia (Eight of Ward) which had extraordinary judicial power in time of peace, along with judicial officials, the Podestà and Capitano del Popolo (Captain of the People). A *balìa* was a temporary council with exceptional powers, often appointed in periods of crisis.

7.3.1   Selective chronology of Florentine constitutional change

1378   Revolt of the Ciompi cancelled out Guelf/Ghibelline factionalism, leaving the great *ottimati* families in control of government. Of these the Albizzi became the most dominant force in the regime.

1434   Return of the Medici from exile, their control of a faction following in the tradition established by Maso degli Albizzi. After 1434 the *accoppiatori* supervised a more controlled system of sortition, whereby the number of names in the electoral bags for specific offices was severely limited.

1458   Replacing the Councils of 200 and 131, which had been created in 1411, the Cento (Council of One Hundred) was created as a permanent legislative body with powers over taxation and the hiring of troops. The numerical reduction apparent here was part of the narrowing of the political elite. The Cento was one of a number of extraordinary councils instituted during the mid-century and given executive or legislative functions.

1471   The Cento was given executive authority in all important matters, including foreign affairs and taxation, but not over the *Monte*, the state-funded debt. The authority of the Signoria was thereby seriously threatened.

1480   In the wake of the Pazzi Conspiracy, the numbers involved in decision-making were further narrowed by the establishment of the Settanta (Council of Seventy) which effectively prevented the Signoria initiating legislation. It elected two committees, the Otto di Pratica and Dodici Procuratori, eight- and twelve-man magistracies given charge of foreign and domestic affairs respectively.

1494   When Piero de' Medici was outlawed for making an invalid treaty with the invading Charles VIII of France, the various magistracies created since 1434 were abolished and, inspired by a Savonarolan sermon, three draft constitutions all recommended that Florence follow some variation on the Venetian model of government. In December, the new 3,000-member Consiglio Maggiore (Great Council), the Ottanta (Council of Eighty) and a ten-man foreign affairs magistracy to replace the Otto di Pratica formed the broadest-based government in Florentine history.

1495   Scrutinies abandoned and elections introduced.

1498–1502   Period of near anarchy, including a governmental crisis in 1499 over taxation to meet the cost of the war to recover Pisa.

1502   Rejecting the broad-based Consiglio Maggiore as unwieldy, a compromise was achieved by the political elite with the election of Piero Soderini to the doge-like post of Gonfaloniere di Giustizia for life.

1512   Sack of Prato by Spanish troops allied with Julius II and the deposition of Piero Soderini, who fled to Dalmatia (see pp. 41–42). Within days the Medici were permitted to return and the constitution was reformed, with the Gonfaloniere di Giustizia appointed for one year, while a new Council of 120 had the power to elect to the Signoria, Otto di Guardia and Dieci di Balìa. *Accoppiatori* were appointed and a new scrutiny undertaken.

1513   Election of Giovanni de' Medici as Pope Leo X marked the beginning of a period in which the governance of Florence was determined by papal policy. Between 1513 and 1517 the organs of 'Medicean' government were reinvigorated or reintroduced, the Medici themselves returning with greater powers than they had enjoyed in the fifteenth century.

1523   Election of Giulio de' Medici as Clement VII. He had been the family's principal representative in Florence during Leo's pontificate and left in his stead the Medici bastards Ippolito and Alessandro, but they were too young to exercise power.

1527   Sack of Rome precipitated the restoration of popular government, with a constitution based on that of 1494, as amended in 1502 and 1512.

1530   End of the republic and creation of the first duke of Florence.

7.3.2   Sixty leading Florentine families

No attempt is made here to identify families who were pro- or anti-Medicean, nor does this list account for all those families who took part in government at its highest levels during the period 1390–1530. Whether as a result of noble status or of non-membership of a guild, a small minority of the families were ineligible for public office.

Acciauoli	Canigiani	Filicaia	Medici	Rondinelli
Alamanni	Capponi	Frescobaldi	Morelli	Rucellai
Alberti	Carnesecchi	Gianfiliazzi	Nardi	Salviati
Albizzi	Castellani	Ginori	Nerli	Soderini
Altoviti	Cavalcanti	Guaconi	Pandolfini	Spini
Antella	Cerretani	Guadagni	Pazzi	Strozzi
Antinori	Corbinelli	Guicciardini	Peruzzi	Tedaldi
Bardi	Corsini	Lanfredini	Pitti	Tornabuoni
Baroncelli	Davanzati	Machiavelli	Pucci	Valori
Benci	Della Stufa	Mancini	Ricasoli	Velluti
Biliotti	Dietisalvi	Mannelli	Ricci	Vespucci
Buondelmonti	Donati	Martelli	Ridolfi	Vettori

7.3.3   Chancellors of the Florentine republic

The First Chancellor was the principal officer of the administrative arm of government. Following the lead set by Coluccio Salutati, this office was held by a number of distinguished men of letters in the course of the fifteenth century.

1375–1406	Coluccio Salutati	1458–64	Benedetto Accolti
1406	Benedetto Fortini	1464/65–94 ⎫	
1406–10	Pietro di ser	1494–1497 ⎬	Bartolomeo Scala
	Mino Dettatore	1494–98?	Pietro Beccanugi
1410–11	Leonardo Bruni	1498–1521	Marcello Virgilio
1411–27	Paolo Fortini		Adriani
1427–44	Leonardo Bruni	1522–31	Alessio Lapaccini
1444–53	Carlo Marsuppini	1532	Francesco Campana
1453–58	Poggio Bracciolini		

In 1494 the Medicean Bartolomeo Scala fled from Florence, was rapidly replaced by Pietro Beccanugi, but no less rapidly restored to office, after which salaries were paid to both men.

7.4   Genoa

In the course of the fifteenth and early sixteenth centuries the republic of Genoa, which had been the dominant naval power in the Mediterranean before being eclipsed by Venice, was more often than not governed by foreign powers, generally due to the utter confusion of its domestic politics. As in Venice, the head of state was an elected doge. Between 1415 and 1528 all the doges came from the important Adorno and Fregoso (or Campofregoso) dynasties, but political instability meant that they each held office for only a few months at a time. The Casa di S. Giorgio was both the state treasury and a private bank.

Periods under foreign rule

1396–1409	France	1464–78	Milan
1409–13	Monferrato	1488–99	Milan
1431–35	Milan	1499–1512	France
1458–64	France	1515–22	France

7.5   Lucca

Between 1400 and 1430 Lucca was ruled by the despot Paolo Guinigi, after which it reverted to a republican constitution. The state's independence was maintained in spite of Florentine attempts to conquer it up to 1433. Senior government office-holders were drawn from the

Consiglio Generale and the executive committee was the College of nine Anziani, one of whom was the Gonfaloniere di Giustizia.

Some politically active Lucchese families

Balbani	Burlamacchi	Gentili	Guinigi	De' Nobili
Bernardi	Castracani	Da Ghivizzano	Malaspina	Di Poggio
Bernardini	Cenami	Gigli	Martini	Del Portico
Bertini	Franciotti	Guidiccioni	Neri	Rapondi
Buonvisi				

7.6   Siena

Like its painting and architecture, the republic of Siena flourished in the fourteenth century, prior to the territorial expansion of Florence on its northern border, which threatened to swallow up Siena itself. Executive authority in Siena was vested in the Signoria or Concistoro, nine Priors headed by the Capitano del Popolo. Membership of the Concistoro, as well as of other senior public offices, rotated on a regular basis and personnel were drawn from the Consiglio del Popolo. As in Florence and Lucca, names were drawn from bags to determine appointments, but other considerations made the Sienese system more complex. The city itself was divided geographically into three *terzi*: Città, S. Martino and Camollia, each of which had to be equally represented. Furthermore, the political class was divided into five parties, called *monti*: Dodici, Gentiluomini, Noveschi, Popolari, Riformatori. For much of the fifteenth century the Monte dei Dodici and Monte dei Gentiluomini were excluded from government, while a balance had to be struck between the other three in terms of office-holding. In 1487 this system of checks and balances was abandoned when Pandolfo Petrucci (d. 1512), of the Monte dei Nove (Noveschi), took power, he and his heirs ruling otherwise republican Siena until the 1520s.

Some politically active Sienese families

Bandini	Chigi	Martini	Salimbeni	Spannocchi
Bichi	Forteguerri	Petrucci	Saracini	Tegliacci
Buoninsegni	Gallerani	Piccolomini	Scotti	Tolomei
Buonsignori	Marsili			

7.7   Venice

As articulated by writers such as Gasparo Contarini (see 7.2), the stability of Venetian government, the balanced nature of the republic's constitution and the impartiality of its justice came to acquire legendary proportions. This is known for convenience as the Myth of Venice.

7.7.1 Doges

The doge was the head of state and elected to that post for life. With the exception of Francesco Foscari, all those listed below did indeed die in office. The only other doge to be deposed in the entire history of the Venetian republic was Marin Falier (1274–1355), decapitated because of his attempts to undermine the constitution.

1382–1400   **Antonio Venier**: Tomb in SS. Giovanni e Paolo.

1400–13   **Michele Steno**: Important *terraferma* expansion took place at this time. Tomb in SS. Giovanni e Paolo.

1414–23   **Tommaso Mocenigo**: Allegedly made a deathbed speech counselling against the election of Francesco Foscari as his successor, on the grounds that Foscari would dissipate Venetian wealth in war; Mocenigo favoured Venetian strength at sea rather than on land. Tomb in SS. Giovanni e Paolo.

1423–57   **Francesco Foscari**: Against the grain of well-known Venetian gerontocracy, Foscari was elected at the age of forty-nine. He presided over the acquisition of Brescia and Bergamo but involved Venice in protracted war with Milan. His princely self-aggrandisement, contrary to the Venetian ideal of selfless devotion to the state, included the building of a magnificent *palazzo* on the Grand Canal, and led to his deposition in 1457. Death followed so swiftly that he was buried with full ducal honours. Tomb in S. Maria Gloriosa dei Frari.

1457–62   **Pasquale Malipiero**: Tomb by Pietro Lombardo in SS. Giovanni e Paolo.

1462–71   **Cristoforo Moro**: An important cultural patron, during whose *dogado* many of the leading names associated with the Venetian Renaissance arrived in the city. Tomb in S. Giobbe.

1471–73   **Nicolò Tron**: Tomb by Antonio Rizzo in S. Maria Gloriosa dei Frari.

1473–74   **Nicolò Marcello**: Tomb by Pietro Lombardo in SS. Giovanni e Paolo.

1474–76   **Pietro Mocenigo**: Noted naval commander. Tomb by Pietro Lombardo in SS. Giovanni e Paolo.

1476–79   **Andrea Vendramin**: Another important cultural patron. Tomb by Tullio Lombardo in SS. Giovanni e Paolo.

1478–85   **Giovanni Mocenigo**: Brother of Pietro Mocenigo. Tomb by Tullio Lombardo in SS. Giovanni e Paolo.

1485–86   **Marco Barbarigo**: Distantly related to the merchant Andrea Barbarigo (see 6.8).

1486–1501   **Agostino Barbarigo**: Brother of Marco Barbarigo.

1501–21   **Leonardo Loredan**: Head of state during the difficult period of the War of the League of Cambrai, when almost

1521–23	all Venice's *terraferma* possessions were lost. Tomb in SS. Giovanni e Paolo.

1521–23 **Antonio Grimani**: At eighty-seven, the oldest doge ever elected. For his place in the Grimani dynasty, see 12.4.

1523–38 **Andrea Gritti**: A military and naval expert who, as doge, inspired important urban regeneration in Venice, including major building projects by Jacopo Sansovino around the Piazzetta de S. Marco. Tomb in S. Francesco della Vigna.

7.7.2   Venetian constitution

The structure of Venetian government is frequently presented in the shape of a pyramid, with the doge at the apex and Maggior Consiglio (Great Council) at the base. The doge, together with the six Ducal Councillors, one from each *sestiere* of the city (see 24.7), formed the Minor Consiglio. When the Minor Consiglio sat with the three Capi della Quarantia, heads of the Council of Forty, the appeals court of Venice, they became the Signoria, the executive body.

Below the Signoria came the Collegio (College) or Pien Collegio (Full College), the cabinet, comprising the Minor Consiglio and the three boards of *savi* (lit. 'wise ones'), the six *savi del consiglio* or *savi grandi*, the five *savi agli ordini*, originally responsible for maritime affairs, and the five *savi di terraferma*, responsible for the mainland interests acquired by Venice in the early fifteenth century. The Collegio prepared business for the Senate and was responsible for executing decisions taken by that larger body.

The Senate, properly the Consiglio dei Pregadi (lit. 'called ones'), was the principal assembly for debate and decision-making on both domestic and foreign affairs. By the fifteenth century it numbered over two hundred members, some elected and others, such as the forty members of the Quarantia, there by virtue of holding other offices. The Senate also included a sixty-man Zonta, a permanent version of the *ad hoc* committees which could be appointed to deal with specific tasks.

The Maggior Consiglio had originally been an elective sovereign assembly, but membership became hereditary after the 1297–98 Serrata ('closing'), which limited it to male patricians over the age of twenty-five whose family names were listed in the *Libro d'oro* (Golden book). Numbering up to two thousand men, it was too unwieldy to be more than a pool from which members were elected to sit on the various smaller committees and magistracies. It met on Sundays after Mass.

The pyramid model fails to account for the body responsible for state security and foreign policy in times of crisis, the Consiglio dei Dieci (Council of Ten). It consisted of ten elected members, the doge and Ducal Councillors, making a total of seventeen.

7.7.3   *Venetian patrician families*

Although the composition of the patriciate ought to be easy to establish with reference to the *Libro d'oro*, in practice it is difficult to be precise about which families were entitled to take part in the government of Venice. Politically active families are listed below, twenty-four being identified as *case vecchie* (V) and others as *case nuove* (N), 'old' and 'new', terms which were of more consequence in earlier centuries, but which certainly indicated venerability by the Renaissance period.

Aurelio	De Lege	Michiel (V)
Badoer (V)	Del Mezzo	Minio
Balbi	Diedo	Mocenigo (N)
Barbarigo (N)	Dolfin (V)	Molin
Barbaro	Donà/Donato (N)	Moro (N)
Barbo	Duodo	Morosini (V)
Barozzi (V)	Emo	Pesaro
Baseggio (V)	Erizzo	Pisani
Bembo (V)	Falier (V)	Polani (V)
Bernardo	Foscari (N)	Priuli (N)
Boldù	Foscarini	Querini (V)
Bollani	Gabriel	Salamon (V)
Bondimero	Giustiniani (V)	Sanuto (V)
Bragadin (V)	Gradenigo (V)	Soranzo (V)
Capello	Grimani (N)	Steno
Civran	Gritti (N)	Tiepolo (V)
Cocco	Lando (N)	Trevisan (G)
Condulmer	Leone	Tron (N)
Contarini (V)	Lippomano	Vendramin (N)
Cornaro/Corner (V)	Loredan (N)	Venier (N)
Correr	Malipiero (N)	Vitturi
Da Canal	Marcello (N)	Zane (V)
Da Mosto	Memmo (V)	Zen (V)
Dandolo (V)	Miani	Zorzi (V)

8   Urban life

8.1   Corporate life: guilds and confraternities

The purpose of trade guilds was to set and maintain standards of work and the prices charged for the same. Guilds also held monopolies in their particular fields of competence. Although the guild system operated throughout western Europe, it was particularly strong in Florence, where membership of one of the seven greater or fourteen lesser guilds was an essential prerequisite for participation in government, and guilds acted as major cultural patrons (see 22.2 for their commissioning of statues at Orsanmichele).

Corporate patronage was also undertaken by confraternities, brotherhoods which partly developed out of the flagellant movement of the thirteenth century and which undertook a range of pious activities, including the provision of dowries for poor girls and ensuring that deceased *confrères* had honourable funerals. In Venice, confraternities were known as *scuole*, of which there were many *scuole piccoli* but only five of the more prestigious *scuole grandi* (sing. *scuola grande*), until a sixth was founded in 1552. The charitable activities of the *scuole grandi* took the place of welfare provision by the state, while the building and decoration of their meeting-houses were among the most important artistic commissions in Renaissance Venice.

8.1.1   Florentine guilds

Seven greater guilds

Arte del Cambio	bankers and money changers
Arte della Calimala	importers and finishers of cloth
Arte della Lana	cloth manufacturers
Giudici e Notai	judges and notaries
Medici e Speziali	physicians and spice/drug dealers
Arte della Seta	leading manufacturers and retailers of silk
Vaiai e Pelliciai	furriers and skinners

The fourteen lesser guilds were those of the linen-makers and mercers, shoemakers, smiths, salters, butchers and slaughterers, wine dealers, innkeepers, harness-makers, leather-dressers, armourers, ironmongers, masons, carpenters, and bakers.

8.1.2   Venetian scuole grandi with dates of foundation and numbers of brethren

S. Giovanni Evangelista	1261	550 brethren
S. Marco	1261	600 brethren
S. Maria della Carità	1261	550 brethren
S. Maria della Misericordia	1308	550 brethren
S. Rocco	1478	550 brethren
S. Teodoro	1552	550 brethren

S. Rocco was recognised as a *scuola grande* in 1489.

The business of each *scuola* was organised by the *banca*, a committee consisting of the *guardian grande* (leader), *vicario* (his deputy), *scrivano* (record keeper) and twelve *degani* (deacons, two from each of the city's six *sestieri*: see 24.7). The book of statutes which determined the organisation of the *scuola* was called the *Mariegola*.

8.2   Hospitals and almshouses

The close association between sickness and poverty makes it appropriate to group together hospitals and almshouses, which were founded with pious intentions throughout this period. The Hôtel-Dieu, Paris (seventh century), St Thomas's and St Bartholomew's, London (founded 1106 and 1123, respectively), were among those hospitals founded prior to the fifteenth century but which remained important features of urban life. Notable foundations for the relief of sickness and poverty were:

1419	Ospedale degli Innocenti, Florence: the first foundling hospital
1436	God's House, Ewelme, Oxfordshire: almshouses founded by Alice Chaucer, wife of William de la Pole, duke of Suffolk
1427	St Nikolausspital, Kues (Germany)
1440	Second Hospital of the Knights of St John, Rhodes
1440	St Cross, Winchester: almshouses founded by Cardinal Henry Beaufort
1443	Hôtel-Dieu, Beaune: founded by Nicolas Rolin, Chancellor of Burgundy
1456	Ospedale Maggiore, Milan: Filarete's design created the first cruciform hospital, with four wards meeting at a central altar
1474	S. Spirito in Sassia, Rome: re-founded by Sixtus IV
1479	Ospedale di S. Maria Nuova, Florence
1499	Hospital Real, Santiago de Compostela
c. 1500	Hospital de Santa Cruz, Toledo
1509	Savoy Hospital, London: founded by Henry VII

8.3   Public brothels

Prostitution was a ubiquitous feature of urban life. The founding of public brothels by the secular authorities, sometimes with the approval of the Church, was a response to the problems caused by men remaining single until they were sufficiently wealthy to marry. The widespread practice of sodomy among youths and young adults in fifteenth-century Florence was the sort of consequence which civic authorities wished to avoid. Some cities where public brothels were opened:

1360	Venice	1421	Siena
1385	'Great House' of Dijon	1433	Munich
1396	Frankfurt	1454	Memmingen
1400	Nuremberg	1469	Strasbourg
1403	Florence		

8.4   Selective glossary of terms relating to urban life

campanilismo   It. term deriving from *campanile* (bell tower) and referring to extreme devotion to one's home city/town.

clientage   Social relationship between a superior and an inferior characterised by mutual back-scratching in terms of acquiring and retaining political office, arranging marriages, loans and so forth.

corregidores   Spanish officials appointed by the Crown who, after 1480, brought the municipalities under royal control after the near anarchy of previous decades.

hermandades   Sp. 'brotherhoods', municipal institutions combining the functions of police force and judicial tribunal, coordinated by Ferdinand and Isabella under the Santa Hermandad from 1476.

menu peuple   Fr. term for labourers, servants and other low-ranking urban dwellers.

patriciate   Urban elite, deriving from the ancient Roman division between patricians and plebeians; of particular significance in republican cities such as Florence and Venice where they were the natural governors. In a Florentine context the terms *ottimati* and *grandi* can be used to refer to this elite.

popolani   It. 'commoners'.

popolo grasso   Upper middling sort, especially in Florence; *haute bourgeoisie*.

popolo minuto   Lower middling sort, especially in Florence.

9 Population

9.1 Introduction

The difficulty of establishing population figures for either states or cities in the late medieval and early modern periods is reflected in the differing estimates to be found in the secondary literature. Thus, for example, France in 1500 has been variously estimated to have had a population of between sixteen and nineteen million, while the city of Genoa, also in 1500, has been given a population of either *c.* 60,000 or *c.* 85,000 souls. These problems derive from the limitations of the primary sources. If households or hearths were counted by contemporaries, which multiplier should be used to estimate the total population? Do the records tell us only of the Christian population? If so, how many Jews were there? Do they tell us only of the free population? If so, how many slaves?

The Black Death (1348–50) and subsequent outbreaks of plague resulted in the loss of up to a third or a half of the population in certain areas, with only a few isolated pockets being spared altogether. Those losses were not made up in the Renaissance period: some land inside medieval city walls remained uninhabited for centuries.

Throughout the late medieval period the most densely populated regions of Europe were the Low Countries and northern Italy, both major centres of manufacturing and consumption. By contrast, France had a predominantly rural population, with only six to twelve per cent of the total living in urban centres.

9.2 European population by region: estimates for 1450 and 1500

c. 1450	millions	*c.* 1500	millions
Greece and Balkans	4.5	Balkans	7
Italy	7.5	Italy	11
Iberia	7	Iberia	9
France and Low Countries	12	France	16
		Low Countries	2
British Isles	3	British Isles	5
Germany and Scandinavia	7.5	Germany	13
		Switzerland	0.8
		Scandinavia	—
Russia	6	Russia	10
Poland–Lithuania	2	Poland	4
Hungary	1.5	Danubian region	6
European total	50	European total	73.8

Sources: J.C. Russell, 'Population in Europe 500–1500', in C.M. Cipolla, ed., *Fontana Economic History of Europe*, vol. I: *the Middle Ages* (London, 1972), p. 36; C.M. Cipolla, *Before the Industrial Revolution: European Society and Economy, 1000–1700* (London, 1976), p. 4.

9.3 Urban population

Estimated population in 1500	Cities
150–200,000	Constantinople, Naples, Paris
100–150,000	Milan, Venice
60–100,000	Cordoba, Florence, Genoa, Granada, Seville
40–60,000	Antwerp, Augsburg, Barcelona, Bologna, Brescia, Cologne, Cremona, Ghent, Lisbon, London, Lyon, Palermo, Rome, Rouen, Toulouse, Valencia

Source: R. Mols, 'Population in Europe, 1500–1700', in C.M. Cipolla, ed., *Fontana Economic History of Europe*, vol. II: *the Sixteenth and Seventeenth Centuries* (London, 1974), pp. 412–13.

10 Money and commerce

10.1 Systems of reckoning

With certain regional variations, the system of pounds, shilling and pence (£.s.d.) operated widely.

British Isles	£.s.d. and marks: 12d. = 1s., 20s. = 1li.; 13s. 4d. = 1m.
Portugal	£.s.d.
Castile	maravedis and dineros: 10d = 1m.
Granada	besants (dinars) and millarenses (dirhams): 10m. = 1b.
France Low Countries Aragon Navarre N. Italy Swiss Confederation SW. Germany	£.s.d.: 12d. = 1s.; 20s. = 1li.
S. Italy	uncie, tari and grani: 20g. = 1t.; 30t. = 1u.
Greece	hyperpyra and carats: 24c. = 1h.
E. Europe	sommi and aspers: the number of aspers to a sommo varied from place to place
Bavaria Austria	£.s.d. but: 30d. = 1s.; 8s. = 1li.
Bohemia	schocks, groschen and pfennigs: 12d. = 1gr.; 60gr. = 1sch.
Poland	grzywnas (marks) and groszy: 48g. = 1grz.
Prussia	marks, sköter and pfennigs: 30d. = 1s.; 24s. = 1m.
Denmark, N. Germany	marks, schillings and pfennigs: the number of schillings to a mark varied from place to place

Based on: P. Spufford, *Handbook of Medieval Exchange* (London, 1986), p. xxii.

10.2 Currencies

British Isles	Scottish Sterling; English Sterling
Iberia	Reis of Portugal; Doblas of Granada; Reales of Majorca; Alfoninos of Sardinia; Reales of Valencia; Maravedís, Reales and Doblas of Castile; Iaccenses of Aragon; Florins of Aragon; Ternales of Barcelona; Tolza (Pyrenees), Melgorian (Pyrenees), Carlines and Sanchetes of Navarre
France	Bordelais; Poitevins; Angevins; Bretons; Mansois; Royal Tournois; Ecus and Francs (central region); Viennois; Paparini Cameral Florins of Avignon; Mixed Money of Marseille, Royal Parisis of Normandy; Provinois of Champagne; Digenais; Estevenantes; Florins of Dauphiné; Raymondins; Royaux Coronats of Provence; Nicienses. French currency also included: Agnel/Mouton, Salut, Écu, Teston, Denier, Liard, Maille, and Marc
Low Countries	Flemish Parisis and Groten; Payement and Gros of Brabant; Tournois of Hainault; Witten of Utrecht
Swiss Confederation	Geneva, Lausannois and Konstanzer Pfennig; Züricher Pfennig
Baltic region	Marks of Denmark; Marks of Lübeck; Sundisch Marks; Sköter of Prussia; Marks of Riga
E. Central Europe	Grosz of Cracow; Ducats of Hungary; Prague Groschen
German-speaking lands	Weiner Pfennig; Regensburger Pfennig; Augsburger Pfennig; Heller; Strassburger Pfennig; Rheinguilden and Weisspfennig; Pagament of Aachen; Marks and Pagament of Cologne; Pagyment of Westphalia
Italy	£.s.d. imperiale of Bergamo; £.s.d. imperiale of Milan; £.s.d. papiensis (Pavia); £.s.d. astenses (Asti); Florins of Savona; Genovini; £.s.d. Genovese; £.s.d. of Lucca; £.s.d. Pisani; Aquilini (Pisa); £.s.d. of Volterra; £.s.d. of Siena; £.s.d. of Perugia; £.s.d. of Cortona; Florins, £.s.d. piccoli, £.s.d. affiorino (Florence); Bolognini, £.s.d. of Bologna; £.s.d. Ravennantes; £.s.d. of Ferrara; £.s.d. of Mantua; £.s.d. Veronenses; £.s.d. of Cremona; £.s.d. imperiale of Brescia; Kreutzer (Trent, Alto Adige); £.s.d. of Aquileia; Ducats, £.s.d. di piccoli, di grossi,

a grossi (Venice); Anconitani; Provisini of Rome; Uncie, carlini and d. of Naples; Uncie, tari and grani of Sicily. Fifteenth-century popes struck coins like those of Bologna.

Based on information in: P. Spufford, *Handbook of Medieval Exchange* (London, 1986), p. xxv.

10.3   Bills of exchange

Bills or letters of exchange facilitated long-distance trade between cities where banks operated. Practice varied in detail, but bills of exchange were due for payment within a given number of days, depending on the distance between the two cities concerned; that period was termed 'usance'. The standard procedure is illustrated here with reference to an importer in Florence paying his correspondent in Bruges:

1. Payee (e.g. importer's correspondent or agent) in Bruges enters in his books debit for goods to creditor.
    Goods from payee to deliverer (e.g. an importer, who delivers money for exchange and names the recipient).
    Deliverer in Florence enters in his books credit for goods to payee.
2. Deliverer in Florence enters in his books debit for money paid for bill of exchange.
    Payment in florins from deliverer to drawer (e.g. a 'banker' who draws bill and names payer), both in Florence.
3. Drawer in Florence enters in his books credit to payer for bill.
    Drawer in Florence notifies drawee/payer (e.g. banker's correspondent or agent who pays bill) in Bruges that bill has been drawn.
    Drawer sends three copies of bill to deliverer, both in Florence.
4. Bill pays for goods – sent by deliverer in Florence to payee in Bruges, in triplicate by three successive couriers.
5. Presentation of first copy of bill to arrive from payee to drawee/payer, both in Bruges.
6. Acceptance of bill from drawee/payer to payee.
7. Payee in Bruges enters in his books credit for money received from bill of exchange.
    Payee in Bruges enters in his books debit for bill to drawer.
    Payment in money groot from drawee/payer to payee, both in Bruges.

Adapted from: P. Spufford, *Handbook of Medieval Exchange* (London, 1986), p. xxxii.

10.4   Communications

Couriers provided a quick but expensive means of communicating between cities, and were employed by governments and wealthier merchants. Courier times from the 1442 notebook of Giovanni da Uzzano are tabulated below. Some of the times are mutually inconsistent.

Journey	Time, in days	Journey	Time, in days
Genoa – Avignon	7–8	Florence – London	25–30
Genoa – Montpellier	9–11	Florence – Bruges	20–25
Genoa – Barcelona	18–21	Florence – Milan	10–12
Genoa – Bruges	22–25	Florence – Rome	5–6
Genoa – Paris	18–22	Florence – Brescia	10–11
		Florence – Naples	11–12
Avignon – Barcelona	7–9	Florence – Seville	29–32
Avignon – Montpellier	2–3	Florence – Paris	20–22
Avignon – Paris	15–16	Florence – Barcelona	20–22
Avignon – Florence	12–14	Florence – Montpellier	15–16
		Florence – Avignon	12–14
Barcelona – Bruges	19–20	Florence – Genoa	5–6
Barcelona – Paris	22–24	Florence – Fabriano	6–7
Barcelona – Montpellier	8–9	Florence – Aquileia	5–6
Barcelona – London	16–18	Florence – Cremona	5–6

Source: P. Spufford, *Handbook of Medieval Exchange* (London, 1986), pp. 320–1.

10.5   Double-entry book-keeping

Double-entry book-keeping was common practice among businessmen prior to Luca Pacioli's account of it in his *Summa de arithmetica* (Venice, 1494), but it has become popularly associated with that publication. Pacioli describes the procedure thus:

> There are two unique expressions used in the journal: one is called Per (Debit) and the other A (Credit). . . . An ordinary item is never entered in the journal (which will later be posted to the ledger) unless it contains the two expressions. . . . Each of the entries made in the journal must be posted twice in the ledger, one to the debit and the other to the credit. In the journal the debit is indicated by Per and the Credit by A. You must have an entry for each of them

in the ledger, the debit entry on the left hand side and the credit on the right. . . . All the items in the ledger are cross-referenced and you must never post a transaction to the debit without posting the related credit, nor must you make a credit entry without its respective amount being ready to be entered as a debit. The balancing of the ledger depends on this. The books cannot be closed unless the debits equal the credits.

For further information see L. Pacioli, *Summa di arithmetica*, with introduction by B. Yamey (Venice, *c.* 1994).

10.6   Banks, bankers and entrepreneurs

Banking facilities existed to meet a range of needs, from those of rich merchants to poorer families saving for their daughters' dowries. Bankers employed skilful ruses to avoid charges of usury, the practice of charging interest on the repayment of loans. This was condemned by the Church, particularly by Observant Franciscan preachers, though Jews were exempted from this ban by the Fourth Lateran Council (1215) and were frequently to be found as money-lenders. In Italy the pious response to this problem was the creation of public pawn shops, *Monti di pietà*, such as that founded in Florence (1495) at the height of Savonarola's influence, which enabled wealthier citizens to assist their poorer neighbours. *Monti delle doti*, on the other hand, were funds operated in Italian cities in which parents deposited money which matured to form their daughters' dowries. That in Florence was established in 1425.

10.6.1   Medici Bank

In 1397 Giovanni di Bicci de' Medici (d. 1429) transferred the main branch of his bank from Rome to Florence. Giovanni's fortune was inherited by his son Cosimo, an astute businessman, who widened the geographical interests of the bank, employed the profits in business enterprises such as silk manufacturing and effectively bought support among the Florentine political class as well as financing Francesco Sforza's 1450 coup in Milan. Following the death of Piero di Cosimo de' Medici (1469), General Manager Francesco Sassetti assumed effective control of the bank instead of Piero's inexperienced sons Lorenzo and Giuliano. A sequence of problems beset the bank before its final collapse when the Medici fled from Florence in 1494: the loss of papal business, liquidation of the Bruges and Milanese branches in the wake of the 1478 Pazzi Conspiracy and difficulties at the Lyon branch.

Branches of the Medici Bank

Rome	1400–94	Bruges	1439–80
Tavola in Florence	1406–94	Pisa	1442–89
Naples	1400–94	Avignon	1446–79?
Venice	1402–81	London	1446–80
Geneva-Lyon	1426–94	Milan	1452–78
Basel	1438–43		

General Managers of Medici Bank

1402–20	Benedetto de' Bardi
1420–33	Ilarione de' Bardi
1433–35	Lippaccio de' Bardi
1435–43	Antonio Salutati and Giovanni Benci
1443–55	Giovanni Benci alone
1455–63	Giovanni di Cosimo de' Medici
1459–63	Francesco Sassetti, assistant to Giovanni di Cosimo de' Medici
1463–90	Francesco Sassetti alone
1490–94	Giovambattista Bracci with the assistance of Filippo da Gagliano

10.6.2   Fugger Bank

From humble origins as peasant weavers, the Fugger of Augsburg grew increasingly wealthy in the fifteenth century on a variety of commercial fronts, including silver, copper and mercury mining, as well as the cinnabar and gold trades. They enjoyed monopoly rights over both their mining interests and revenue collection activities. As bankers to Charles V they helped to secure his imperial election in 1519. Jakob Fugger (d. 1525) amassed a particularly enormous fortune and is consequently known as 'the Rich'. Like the Medici, the Fugger employed some of their wealth in cultural patronage and the embellishment of their native city.

Agencies of the Fugger Bank

Antwerp	Danzig	Leipzig	Mogilen	Seville
Breslau	Frankfurt	Lisbon	Nuremberg	Venice
Buda	Gastein	Madrid	Rome	Vienna
Cologne	Halle	Milan	Salzburg	Villach
Cracow	Innsbruck			

10.6.3   Agostino Chigi

The immensely wealthy papal banker Agostino Chigi (1465–1520) of Siena was one of Renaissance Rome's most munificent cultural patrons, particularly at his villa, now the Farnesina. The artists patronised by Chigi included Peruzzi, Raphael, Sebastiano del Piombo, Sodoma and Ugo da Carpi (see 20.1, p. 221 and 20.4, p. 238).

10.6.4   Jacques Coeur

Born into a wealthy Bourges family Coeur (c. 1395–1456) became the richest man in Europe through mastery of France's Levantine trade and the favour of Charles VII. He financed the French reconquest of Normandy and Gascony from the English and reorganised the French coinage, but opposition to his success was appeased when Charles ruined and imprisoned him. Undaunted, Coeur escaped to Rome, was appointed commander of the papal fleet and died on Chios while on campaign, leaving his extravagantly Gothic house in Bourges as a monument to his wealth (see 20.4, p. 234).

10.7   Hanseatic League

Cities which coordinated their trade in the Baltic region and dealt with western Europe mostly through Bruges and London:

Bergen	Cologne	Hamburg	Reval	Stendal
Bremen	Danzig	Lübeck	Riga	Stralsund
Brunswick	Dortmund	Lüneburg	Soest	Wisby

10.8   Secular taxes

Aides   Indirect taxes in France.

Alcabala   Castilian sales tax from which the monarchs gained a substantial amount of their income

Catasto   Florentine means test for tax purposes established by a law of 22 May 1427. The catasto provided a thorough survey of the wealth of fifteenth-century Florentine families. Returns were intended to be made every three years, but this evidently proved unmanageable.

1st catasto	1427		6th catasto	1451
2nd catasto	1430		7th catasto	1457
3rd catasto	1433		8th catasto	1469–70
4th catasto	1442		9th catasto	1480–81
5th catasto	1446			

In 1427 the wealthiest men in Florence, those with net capital of over 30,000 florins, were as follows:

101,422 fl.	Palla di Nofri Strozzi
79,472 fl.	Giovanni di Bicci de' Medici
78,166 fl.	Gabbriello di Messer Bartolommeo Panciatichi
55,815 fl.	Alessandro di Ser Filippo Borromei (and sons)
48,820 fl.	Giovanni di Messer Bartolommeo Panciatichi
46,402 fl.	Niccolò di Giovanni da Uzzano
46,320 fl.	Francesco and Niccolò di Simone Tornabuoni (and nephews)
41,727 fl.	Bernardo di Lamberto Lamberteschi
34,987 fl.	Francesco di Francesco di Pierozzo della Luna
31,480 fl.	Bernardo di Giannozzo Manetti
31,245 fl.	Giovanni di Nofri Bischeri
31,000 fl.	Andrea di Guglielmo de' Pazzi

Decima Venetian property tax, assessed at 10 per cent of annual income.

Gabelle (Fr.) **gabella** (It.) Commodity tax, most commonly levied on salt (France), but also on wheat, livestock and the retail sale of wine.

Taille Most significant direct tax levied in France.

11 Warfare

11.1 Introduction

The fifteenth and early sixteenth centuries witnessed not only a constant succession of full-scale wars and internal rebellions, each notable for sieges and pitched battles, but also dramatic developments in the practice of warfare. Gunpowder, a Chinese invention, was known in Europe from the thirteenth century, and employed first in large siege artillery and then in hand-held firearms in the fourteenth and fifteenth centuries. While bows remained more accurate and had a greater range – in the case of the English longbow up to 200 metres – ever-increasing firepower came to be of particular significance in siege warfare, and greater accuracy was possible when metal replaced stone shot. In their final defeat of the kingdom of Granada in 1492 Ferdinand of Aragon and Isabella of Castile had a siege-train of c. 180 guns, while Machiavelli and Guicciardini considered French firearms, though not as numerous as in the Iberian example, the crucial advantage enjoyed by Charles VIII over the Italian cities in 1494. In response to the challenge posed by siege artillery, new styles of fortification, based around the angled bastion, were developed. Artillery also determined the creation of better plate armour to protect individual soldiers. The most highly prized armour was made in Milan.

At the same time infantry tactics were transformed by the highly disciplined squares of Swiss pikemen, whose 'victims' included Charles the Bold, duke of Burgundy. Just as both cavalry and the chivalric ethos were defeated by English longbows at Agincourt (1415), so they were dealt another blow by the impregnable pike squares. At the same time the degree of discipline demonstrated by the Swiss could only be countered by a more professional approach to warfare, something which was possible for the larger powers but not for the smaller states of Italy.

Many leading architects undertook military engineering projects. Fra Giocondo (Giovanni da Verona, 1433–1515) was a hydraulic specialist and architect to the Venetian Council of Ten in 1506, working mainly on *terraferma* fortifications. Michele Sanmicheli (c. 1487–1559) worked on fortifications at Parma, Piacenza and Legnano, but is best known for his work at Verona and elsewhere in the Veneto, which formed an essential part of Venetian *terraferma* strategy after the republic's humiliation in the War of the League of Cambrai. His contemporary, Michelangelo, was employed on Florentine fortifications in 1528–29. Francesco di Giorgio Martini also made significant contributions to both the theory and practice of military engineering.

Naval warfare in northern Europe relied on the requisitioning of merchantmen; vessels were not specially built for military purposes. In the Mediterranean, by contrast, there was not only increasing specialisation in ship design, for mercantile and military uses, but also the emergence of permanent navies in Aragon and the major Italian states. The most important type of vessel used in naval warfare was the galley, a highly manoeuvrable oared ship which could carry up to 400 men and which was armed with guns raised on castles fore and aft.

11.2   Glossary of terms relating to warfare

arquebus   Highly effective hand-gun developed in the 1420s and 1430s.

bastion   Or *trace italienne*: a low-walled, earth-packed fortification, devised to counter the ease with which artillery could destroy the traditionally high walls of cities and fortresses (illustrated, 11.3). Infantry on the attacking side found it difficult to negotiate the crossfire from guns covering the various angles, so that the only way to take a fortified town was by siege, which was expensive in manpower. The bastion was developed in northern and central Italy in the second half of the fifteenth century, after which its popularity spread widely throughout Europe.

bombard   Large breechloading piece of siege artillery, a famous surviving example of which is the 8.5 ton 'Mons Meg', cast for Philip the Good of Burgundy in 1449, which threw stone shot 500mm in diameter.

compagnies d'ordonnance   Companies of heavy cavalry created in France from 1439 as part of Charles VII's imposition of royal authority in the wake of civil turmoil and the English invasion. With captains appointed by the crown and troops paid by the government, rather than by their commanders, the core of a standing army was thereby created.

condotta   Term used in Italy for an agreement between a mercenary leader – hence *condottiere* – and his employer, specifying the numbers of men to be recruited, the duration of the agreement, rates of pay in times of peace and war and other pertinent matters.

condottieri   It.: mercenaries, whether employed for land or naval warfare. The hiring of mercenaries was common practice in the Renaissance period. Mercenary companies fought in the Anglo-French Hundred Years War, some of them subsequently seeking employment in Italy. Among them was the Englishman Sir John Hawkwood (*c.* 1320–94).

Known in Italy as 'Giovanni Acuto', he commanded the White Company and was employed by a number of Italian states before forming an unusually long-lasting relationship with Florence, where he was celebrated by a fresco in the Duomo (see 20.1, p. 210). In the absence of standing armies, mercenary warfare became the norm in fifteenth-century Italy, as states entered into contracts with mercenary captains who, in turn, recruited men-at-arms. By the mid-fifteenth century some longer-term contracts provided the potential bases of permanent armies, but there was still a considerable amount of fluidity in employment patterns. While some *condottieri* acquired lands and fortunes in the course of their careers, others were already of landed or even noble status. Federico da Montefeltro is the classic example here. By the end of the century, Swiss infantry had gained a reputation for effectiveness as mercenaries. By advocating the superiority of citizen militias over unreliable mercenaries, who allegedly owed no real loyalty to their employers and were not prepared to take risks, Machiavelli has coloured posterity's view of Renaissance mercenaries. Militias, on the other hand, could not be as highly trained as were professional mercenaries. See 11.4 for details of some of the most distinguished *condottieri*.

culverin   A long, muzzle-loading gun cast in bronze or iron which threw a ball of *c.* 18lb. Demi-culverins threw shot of half the weight.

franc-archers   Partly trained infantry militia introduced in France in 1448 as part of Charles VII's military reforms. Recruited in specific towns or localities, the groups consisted of archers, crossbowmen, pikemen and, in due course, handgunners, but their effectiveness was short lived.

janissaries   Ottoman crack troops, recruited from among the Christian population of their Balkan acquisitions.

jinetes   Spanish light horse used to great effect in the final stages of the reconquest of Granada.

lance   Standard military unit of which armies were composed, though the size and composition of lances varied geographically and over time. Essentially, it consisted of a man-at-arms and his attendants and horses, the man-at-arms being recruited by a mercenary or other captain and in turn undertaking to provide the whole lance.

Landsknechte   Lit. 'companions of the country': independent bands of mercenaries in Upper Germany which were organised into a significant fighting force in the later fifteenth century. They fought with pikes and halberds in imitation of their Swiss neighbours. Georg von Frundsberg (1473–1528), a soldier of the Swabian League who fought at the battle of Pavia (1525), was known as the 'father of the German Landsknechts'.

lanze spezzate   Lit. 'broken lances', these were men-at-arms, with their attendants and horses, employed directly by Venice and other states in the fifteenth century rather than by mercenary captains. They tended to be veterans recruited in an attempt to create a standing army without recourse to mercenary companies. The term refers to their broken contracts with the *condottiere* captains.

provveditori   Members of the Venetian government who acted as links in the field between the state and mercenary captains, with responsibility for the provisioning and payment of troops.

Stradiots   Light cavalrymen recruited by Venice in Dalmatia, Albania and Greece, who were employed to great effect against the Turks in the 1470s.

trace italienne   See *bastion*.

11.3   Angled bastion

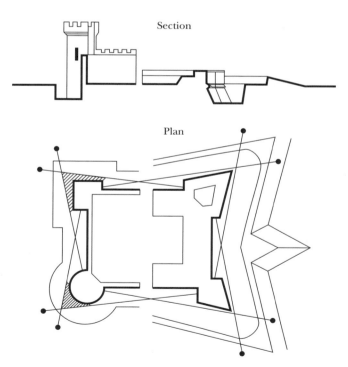

Adapted from: S. Pepper and N. Adams, *Firearms and Fortifications: Military Architecture and Siege Warfare in Sixteenth-century Siena* (Chicago and London), p. 4.

Traditional medieval defences, consisting of a combination of tall curtain walls and corner towers, are contrasted overleaf with low angled bastions, such as were developed during the Renaissance period. Most obviously the bastion eliminates blind spots, the hatched areas on the left hand side.

11.4   *Condottieri*

For the circumstances in which these military captains fought, see Chronology of Public Events.

Carmagnola Francesco Bussone, count of Carmagnola (*c.* 1385–1432): While employed by Filippo Maria Visconti of Milan, Carmagnola defeated the Swiss at Arbedo (1422), but his ambition caused him to break with Milan and seek employment with Venice (from 1425), for whom, with Niccolò da Tolentino (*c.* 1350–1435), he was victorious over his former employers at Maclodio (1427). Divided loyalty between Venice and Milan led to his trial in Venice for treason and execution between the columns of the Piazzetta di S. Marco.

Bartolomeo Colleoni (1400–76): Originating near Bergamo, Colleoni served under Braccio da Montone and Muzio Attendolo Sforza early in his career before serving Venice under the command of Gattamelata and Francesco Sforza during the wars with Milan. He rose to become Venetian captain-general and the most highly esteemed commander of his day, an esteem reflected in Verrocchio's bronze equestrian statue of him in Venice (see 20.3, p. 230). In later life Colleoni also became renowned as a cultural patron, surrounded by the trappings of courtly life.

Federico da Montefeltro, *Signore* and (from 1474) duke of Urbino (1422–82): In his military capacity, the humanist-educated bibliophile and leading cultural patron made a point of being employed by his fellow princes instead of entering into full-scale alliances with them. These flexible terms allowed him to serve successively Venice, the papacy, Naples and Florence, acquiring experience of fighting with or against all the leading commanders of his day and an illustrious reputation in the process. For his cultural patronage, see 20.1, p. 214 and 20.4, p. 235.

Braccio da Montone Fortebraccio (1368–1424): Perugian Captain-General of the Church (from 1414), who used papal forces to secure personal control over his native city. Among the commanders of his day Francesco Sforza was his greatest rival. His much-feared followers were known as *Bracceschi*.

Gattamelata Erasmo da Narni (1370–1443): Celebrated in his native Padua by Donatello's equestrian statue, Gattamelata, as Erasmoda Narni was known, had trained in arms with Braccio da Montone and Piccinino. After serving Florence and the papacy, he rose to become Venetian captain-general in the republic's wars with Milan.

Niccolò Piccinino (1386–1444): Of lowly Umbrian origins, he succeeded his master Fortebraccio as leader of the *Bracceschi* and went on to serve first Florence and then Filippo Maria Visconti of Milan, in which capacity his great rival was Francesco Sforza, future duke of Milan; he was then employed by Venice. Piccinino's defeat at S. Romano (14.32) was depicted by Paolo Uccello.

Francesco Sforza, duke of Milan (1401–66): Son of the *condottiere* Muzio Attendolo, known as 'Sforza', to the command of whose company he succeeded. Though the family had been based in the Marche region, Francesco Sforza's contracts with Filippo Maria Visconti of Milan and his marriage with the duke's illegitimate daughter Bianca Maria resulted in the Sforza becoming a Lombard dynasty. Between 1447 and 1450 he fought for Venice against the Ambrosian Republic.

11.5   Combatants in the Italian Wars

Numbers engaged in the battles in the Italian Wars. Figures in parentheses indicate the ratio of cavalry to infantry. For information about the contexts in which these battles were fought, see Chronology of Public Events.

Date	Battle	Composition of armies	
1494	French army invading Italy	31,000 (2:1)	
1495	Fornovo	French 9,000 (2:1)	Italians 22,000 (1:1)
1503	Cerignola	French 12,000 (2:1)	Spanish 11,500 (1:2)
1503	Garigliano	French 35,000 (1:1)	Spanish 22,000 (4:7)
1509	Agnadello	French 40,000 (3:5)	Venetians 36,000 (2:5)
1512	Ravenna	French 33,000 (2:3)	Spanish 20,000 (1:2)
1515	Marignano	French 48,000 (5:11)	Swiss 22,000 (0:1)
1525	Pavia	French 31,000 (1:3)	Spanish 25,000 (1:4)

Source: M.E. Mallett, 'The Art of War', in T.A. Brady, H.A. Oberman and J.D. Tracy, *Handbook of European History 1400–1600*, vol. I: *Late Middle Ages, Renaissance and Reformation* (Leiden, 1994), p. 550, Table 1.

11.6   Holy warfare

The Christian reconquest, *reconquista*, of Iberia from Moorish rule was an ongoing process pursued with varying degrees of intensity throughout the high and later Middle Ages. Independent military captains were given leave by the Christian monarchs to recruit soldiers for this pious enterprise, and given permission to hold whatever land they occupied in the king's name. These 'capitulations' provided the model for agreements between the Spanish monarchs and conquistadors in the New World. A prominent part in this holy war was also played by the military-religious orders of Alcántara, Calatrava and Santiago. The *reconquista* was resumed by Ferdinand of Aragon and Isabella of Castile, culminating in the fall of Granada on 2 January 1492.

Another relic of the crusading past was found at the opposite end of Christendom, where the Teutonic Knights were engaged in Christian warfare against the pagan peoples to the east. From 1309 they were based at Marienburg, south-east of Danzig. War with Poland in the mid-fifteenth century resulted in territorial losses for the order, whose knights steadily retreated into Germany.

11.7   Chivalric Orders

The foundation (1348) of the Order of the Garter by Edward III of England with a membership of just twenty-five knights, heralded a revival in the fortunes of chivalric orders throughout western and central Europe. With few serious crusading opportunities remaining in the fifteenth century, the orders acquired a more overtly political character. Thus, in the later fifteenth century, hostility between the king of France and the duke of Burgundy was manifest in the fact that it was not possible to be a member of both the French Order of St Michael and the Burgundian Order of the Golden Fleece. Membership of the latter was limited to thirty knights and, at various times, members included Alfonso the Magnanimous of Naples, Joan II of Aragon, Edward IV of England and Ferdinand II of Aragon. Lesser orders included those of the Ear of Corn and Ermine of Brittany, the Elephant of Denmark, the Lily of Aragon, St Maurice of Savoy and the Tower and Sword of Portugal.

Date of foundation	Order	Founder
1351	Star	Jean II, king of France
1381	Ship	Charles III of Durazzo, king of Naples
c. 1413	Dragon	Emperor Sigismund
1430	Golden Fleece/ *Toison d'Or*	Philip the Good, duke of Burgundy
1444	Swan	Albrecht III Achilles, duke of Brandenburg
1448	Crescent/ *Croissant*	René, duke of Anjou
1465	Ermine	Ferrante, king of Naples
1469	St Michael/Saint-Michel	Louis XI, king of France

11.8   Wars of words

The most prized classical works on the art of war were Frontinus, *Stratagemata* and Vegetius, *De re militari*. Contemporary works on the subject included: Honoré Bonet, *L'arbre des batailles*; Christine de Pisan, *Le livre des fais d'armes et de chevalerie* (for her other works see 15.3); Conrad Kyeser, *Bellifortis*; Niccolò Machiavelli, *Arte della guerra* (*Art of War*); Bérault Stuart (d. 1508), *Traité sur l'art de la guerre*; and Roberto Valturio (1405–75), *De re militari libri XII*.

12 Church and churchmen

12.1 Roman Curia

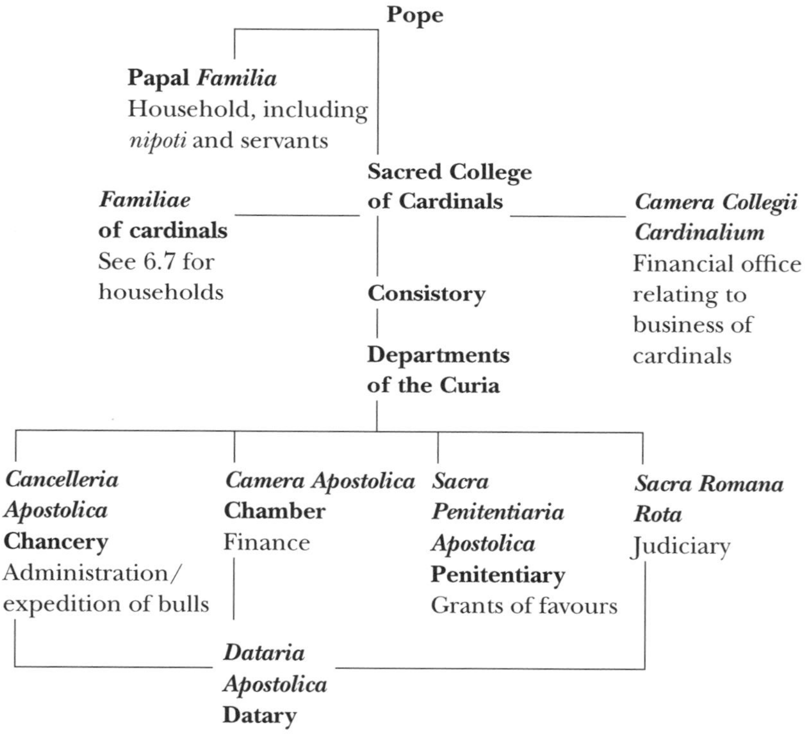
Pope
Papal *Familia*
Household, including *nipoti* and servants
Sacred College of Cardinals
Familiae of cardinals
See 6.7 for households
Camera Collegii Cardinalium
Financial office relating to business of cardinals
Consistory
Departments of the Curia
Cancelleria Apostolica
Chancery
Administration/ expedition of bulls
Camera Apostolica
Chamber
Finance
Sacra Penitentiaria Apostolica
Penitentiary
Grants of favours
Sacra Romana Rota
Judiciary
Dataria Apostolica
Datary

Based on: John F. D'Amico, *Renaissance Humanism in Papal Rome: Humanists and Churchmen on the Eve of the Reformation* (Baltimore, MD, and London, 1988), p. 22.

Papal Familia As the chart indicates, a distinction was made between the papal household, consisting of the pope's relatives and personal servants, and the papal court or *curia*, composed of the various administrative departments responsible for the organisation of the Church throughout western Christendom. While the papal household was based at the Vatican, the curia was divided between offices there and elsewhere in Rome. For the careers of individual popes, see 2.2.

Sacred College of Cardinals   The Third Lateran Council (1179) recognised cardinals as being alone responsible for the election of popes, which they did when meeting in conclave. In addition to the six cardinal bishops of dioceses in the vicinity of Rome (Albano, Ostia and Velletri, Porto, Palestrina, Sabina, Tusculum), there were cardinal priests and cardinal deacons, originally clergy in the city of Rome who served their bishop, the pope. Numbers fell as low as eighteen in 1374 after many had been killed by plague, and rose as high as thirty-six in 1478. There was an attempt at the Council of Constance to abolish the Sacred College completely, but the anti-conciliar Eugenius IV issued the Bull *Non mediocri* in 1439, giving cardinals precedence over archbishops and bishops. Cardinals based in Rome acted as protectors of the interests of nations, cities or religious orders, gaining income in the process, as they also did from the division of their half of the common and minute service taxes exacted from new appointments to bishoprics and important abbeys. Existing cardinals frequently objected to an increase in their numbers for it meant that income from such sources had to be divided among more people. This income was not available to non-curial cardinals, some of whom acted as legates, the pope's powerful representatives in certain states or regions.

Consistory   Between conclaves, cardinals acted collectively as the pope's innermost council of advisers, meeting with him in public and secret consistories. Ambassadors from foreign powers were among those who could attend and address public consistories.

Chancery   As in other states, the secretarial department was nominally headed by the powerful vice-chancellor, a post generally held by a cardinal and enjoyed by Rodrigo Borgia (the future Alexander VI) between 1457 and 1492. The Chancery was based in the Palazzo Sforza-Cesarini from the mid-fifteenth century until 1521, when it was housed in the building still known as the Palazzo della Cancelleria. It was responsible for the production of bulls (*bulla* = seal), briefs and other documents, and worked closely with the Datary, which dated the finished products. Taxes were charged for writing, sealing and other production processes, putting judicial and other appeals to Rome beyond the means of the poor.

Camera Apostolica   The financial department, headed by the Camerarius or Camerlengo, which post was held by a cardinal from the fifteenth century, and staffed by Chamber clerks, but had strong associations with the pope's secular bankers, whose facilities transferred money over long distances. Its records of income and expenditure covered a wide range of business, including the collection of ecclesiastical taxes such as crusading tithes, annates and Peter's Pence from agents (papal collectors) throughout western Christendom. In its judicial capacity it was responsible for judging financial suits.

Datary An office created during the fifteenth century to prepare and date papal grants of favour, particularly certain dispensations, reflecting the distinction between the signing and dating of papal letters.

Penitentiary Headed by the Cardinal Penitentiary and staffed mostly by clerics who often had other curial posts, this office dealt with dispensations and matters of conscience.

Rota Its name deriving form the circular table at which its judges (Auditors) had sat at Avignon, the *Rota* was the curia's judicial department and dealt with disputes over benefices as well as cases concerning legitimation, religious profession, betrothal, and the nullification of marriage. As an extension of the Chancery, the vice-chancellor also headed this department.

12.2   Cardinals: promotions and places of origins

The table opposite is derived from details of promotions to the cardinalate given by C. Eubel, *Hierarchia catholica medii aevi*, vols I–III (Münster, 1901–13), although other published lists of cardinals differ, reflecting discrepancies in the original sources. Wherever possible geographical origin has been interpreted as the cardinal's place of birth; where this is unclear appointments to benefices have been used as a guide.

	Gregory XI	Urban VI	Boniface IX	Innocent VII	Clement VII	Benedict XIII	Gregory XII	Alexander V	John XXIII	Martin V	Eugenius IV	Felix V	Nicholas V	Calixtus III	Pius II	Paul II	Sixtus IV	Innocent VIII	Alexander VI	Pius III	Julius II	Leo X	Adrian VI	Clement VII
Rome/Papal States	1	9	3	7	1	1	0	0	2	4	2	1	1	3	3	1	8	0	3	0	3	11	0	0
Tuscany	0	3	0	0	1	1	3	0	0	1	1	0	0	3	3	1	8	1	1	0	4	12	0	4
Liguria	0	3	0	0	0	0	0	0	0	0	2	0	0	0	0	0	8	1	1	0	8	2	0	3
Milan/Lombardy	1	0	0	0	1	0	0	0	1	1	2	0	1	0	0	0	3	3	3	0	0	2	0	0
Savoy/Monferrato	0	0	0	1	0	0	0	0	0	0	0	1	1	0	0	0	0	0	0	0	0	1	0	3
Mantua	0	0	0	0	0	0	0	0	0	0	0	0	0	0	1	0	0	0	2	0	1	0	0	2
Ferrara/Modena	0	1	0	0	0	0	0	0	0	0	0	0	0	0	1	1	0	0	1	0	1	1	0	0
Venice & its empire	0	3	2	0	0	0	0	0	3	0	3	1	0	0	0	3	0	2	3	0	1	2	0	2
Naples/Sicily	0	17	1	0	0	0	0	0	2	0	3	1	0	0	0	1	2	1	1	0	1	1	0	4
Russia/Byzantium	0	0	0	0	0	0	0	0	0	0	2	1	0	0	0	1	1	0	1	0	1	1	0	0
Poland	0	0	0	0	0	0	0	0	0	0	1	0	0	0	1	0	0	0	0	0	0	0	0	0
Hungary	0	2	0	0	0	0	0	0	0	0	1	2	0	0	0	0	0	0	1	0	1	0	0	0
Bohemia	0	1	0	0	0	0	0	0	0	0	0	0	0	0	0	0	0	0	0	0	0	0	0	0
Germany/Austria	0	0	0	0	0	0	0	0	0	1	0	2	1	0	1	1	0	0	1	0	1	3	1	1
Swiss Confederation	0	0	0	0	0	0	0	0	0	0	0	1	1	0	0	0	0	0	0	0	0	0	0	0
Low Countries	0	0	0	0	0	0	0	0	0	0	0	0	0	0	0	0	0	0	0	0	0	0	0	0
France	17	2	1	1	23	3	0	0	6	5	4	10	5	2	2	1	6	2	0	0	5	2	0	7
Spanish kingdoms	2	0	0	0	4	8	1	0	0	3	3	4	1	3	1	0	4	6	18	0	2	3	0	7
Portugal	0	0	0	0	1	1	0	0	1	0	1	0	0	0	1	0	1	0	0	0	0	1	0	0
England/Scotland	0	2	0	0	1	0	1	0	2	1	0	0	0	0	0	1	0	0	1	0	1	0	0	0
Total	21	43	6	11	34	15	13	0	18	16	27	25	11	9	12	10	34	8	43	0	27	43	1	33

12.3 Western Christendom's wealthiest archbishoprics and bishoprics

In 1418 there were 717 sees (bishoprics and archbishoprics) in western Christendom. For the purposes of this exercise, wealth has been measured in terms of the common service taxes (*servitiae*) which were assessed at one-third of the estimated income of the bishopric. Of the fifty-seven sees listed below, only two (Aquileia and Ravenna) are in Italy, reflecting the fact that Italian bishoprics were generally smaller and poorer than their counterparts beyond the Alps. The figures are taken from C. Eubel, *Hierarchia catholica medii aevi*, vol. II (Münster, 1901); they relate to the period 1431–1503 and are given in cameral gold florins.

12,000fl.	Rouen, Winchester
10,000fl.	Aquileia, Auch, Canterbury, Cologne, Mainz, Salzburg, Trier, York
9,000fl.	Durham, Langres, Narbonne
8,000fl.	Toledo
7,500fl	Ely
7,200fl.	Liège
6,000fl.	Braga, Carcassonne, Exeter, Metz, Sens
5,000fl.	Gniezno, Nicosia, Norwich, Passau, Seville, Thérouanne, Toulouse, Tournai, Valencia, Zaragoza
4,600fl.	Beauvais, Utrecht
4,500fl.	Salisbury
4,400fl.	Bayeux, Verdun, Viviers
4,300fl.	Bath & Wells
4,200fl.	Amiens
4,000fl.	Autun, Arras, Bordeaux, Bourges, Bratislava, Cashel, Châlons-sur-Marne, Chartres, Cominges, Dol (Brittany), Esztergom, Freising, Laon, Lisieux, Maguelone, Ravenna, Rheims, Santiago de Compostela

12.4   Clerical nepotism: the Grimani of Venice

The best-known examples of clerical nepotism in this period are those of papal families such as the Della Rovere and the Borgia (see 2.2 for details). The history of the Grimani family of Venice, however, may be used to illustrate the way in which senior benefices effectively became the fiefdoms of particular clerical dynasties, often resigned by one relative in favour of another instead of being retained until death, when an entirely new appointment would have been made.

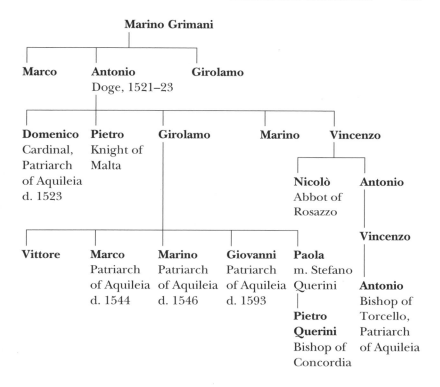

The Grimani held the patriarchate of Aquileia between 1498 and 1550, and again from 1585 to 1593. Their possession of the bishopric of Ceneda provides a parallel case.

Aquileia		Ceneda	
1498–1517	Domenico (resigned)	1508–17	Marino (resigned)
1517–29	Marino (resigned)	1517–31	Domenico (resigned)
1529–33	Marco (resigned)	1520–31	Giovanni (resigned)
1533–45	Marino (resigned)	1532–40	Marino (resigned)
1545–50	Giovanni (resigned)	1540–45	Giovanni (resigned)
1585–93	Giovanni	1545–46	Marino (resigned)

12.5   Popes and prelates: General Councils

The French pope Clement V (1305–16) officially transferred the papacy from Rome to Avignon. Six pontificates later, Gregory XI tried to reverse that process but died before it could be brought to effect. From 1378 western Christendom was split between two obediences, those of

Urban VI based at Rome and of antipope Clement VII at Avignon (see 2.1 for details of popes). The allegiances of the secular powers were determined by political considerations. If the kingdom of France was officially Clementine, then the enemies of France were Urbanist. Secular support for the Avignon obedience came from Aragon, Castile, France, Naples, Navarre and Scotland, while the Urbanist popes received more moral than practical support from England, many of the German and Italian states and Portugal.

Members of the University of Paris were at the forefront of calls for a General Council of the Church to break the deadlock caused by the papal contenders refusing to give way to each other. Conciliar thought, based on the experience of the early Church, maintained that the decisions of a General Council, bringing together representatives from throughout western Christendom and not favouring one region over another, could initiate binding decisions in matters of faith and ecclesiastical discipline, providing they were ratified by the pope.

Pisa (1409–10): Twenty-four cardinals from the Roman and Avignonese obediences met as equals and elected first Alexander V and then John XXIII as unsuccessful solutions to the papal schism.

Constance (1414–18): Called by John XXIII on the initiative of Emperor Sigismund with the result that John fled and was arrested (1415), Gregory XII resigned (1415) and antipope Benedict XIII was deposed (1417). The decree *Sacrosancta* (6 April 1415) proclaimed: 'The ecumenical Council assembled at Constance represents the whole Church. It derives its authority from Christ. Everyone, even the Pope, owes obedience to it in all that concerns the faith, the unity of the Church and the reform of both head and members.' Voting was by 'nation' (e.g. Italy, France, Germany), with Henry V's dynamic foreign policy gaining the English 'national' independence from Germany. An electoral college of cardinals and six deputies from each nation elected Oddone Colonna as Martin V (11 November 1417). The burning of Jan Hus for heresy was one of a number of anti-Hussite measures taken by the Council. Reinforcing the importance of councils, the decree *Frequens* (9 October 1417) called for frequent councils, the next to meet five years after Constance ended.

Pavia–Siena (1423–24): Called by Martin V in compliance with *Frequens*, but poorly attended and lacking the secular support which had made Constance successful.

Basel (1431–37, but continued without papal sanction until 1449): The clearest example of tension between Conciliarism and papal supremacy, the Council being dissolved in 1431 by Eugenius IV who declared all councils heretical in 1433 but was swiftly forced to reverse his decision. Between 1433 and 1435 payments to the Roman Camera were transferred to Basel, depriving Eugenius of his usual sources of revenue. In 1437 Eugenius ordered the Council to move to Ferrara but few obeyed, the assembly largely broke up, but the remaining rump 'deposed' Eugenius and elected Amadeus of Savoy as antipope Felix V (June and November 1439 respectively). Finally petered out at Lausanne.

Ferrara–Florence (1438–39, but met in Rome until 1442/43): Called by Eugenius IV with a view to reunifying the Latin and Orthodox churches to meet the threat posed by the advancing Ottoman Turks. The Greek party, led by the Byzantine emperor and the patriarch of Constantinople arrived in Ferrara in March 1438, but the council transferred to Florence (January 1439) where the fugitive Eugenius was based and the meeting was largely financed by the Medici Bank as papal bankers. After debate on matters such as the procession of Holy Ghost (the *filioque* – 'and the Son' – clause in the Nicene Creed), the decree of union was signed by both sides (July 1439) but later rejected by the Orthodox hierarchy in Constantinople. When the Council transferred to Rome acts of union were signed with representatives of the Mesopotanian, Chaldean and Maronite churches.

Pius II's 1460 Bull *Execrabilis* declared it anathema to undermine papal authority by appealing to a council, though such threats, mostly from secular powers, did not cease.

Fifth Lateran (1512–17): Called by Julius II in response to the anti-papal council which met at Pisa (1511) and was supported by France. This hostility prompted the Council to declare the Pragmatic Sanction of Bourges null and void. Backed by Emperor Maximilian, Ferdinand of Aragon and Henry VIII of England as enemies of France, it was never-theless almost entirely Italian in composition. After the death of Julius (20 February 1513), Louis XII ceased to oppose the Council, paving the way for the Concordat of Bologna (1516).

12.6   Popes and princes: concordats

Treaties between popes and secular powers are called concordats. The circumstances in which the more important concordats were concluded, as well as some of their terms, are given in the Chronology of Public Events. The powers involved were as follows:

1418	France; German princes; Spanish kings; England	1448	Holy Roman Emperor
1426	France (Concordat of Gennazzano)	1472	France
1441	Brittany (Concordat of Redon)	1516	France (Concordat of Bologna); Portugal
1447	German princes	1519	Poland

12.7   Popes and pilgrims: Holy Years

The granting of special indulgences which promised a reduction of time in Purgatory, encouraged pilgrims to visit the great basilicas of Rome during Holy Years or Jubilees. The celebration of Jubilees paralleled the fortunes of the papacy during this period. Other indulgences were suspended in Jubilee years to encourage pilgrims to go to Rome.

1300   Jubilee certainly celebrated.

1350   Jubilee certainly celebrated.
Urban VI (d. 1389) decided that Jubilees should be celebrated not every fifty years, but every thirty-three, corresponding to the span of Christ's life.

1390   Clement VII at Avignon denounced Jubilee celebrations held in Rome which attracted many pilgrims to Rome from Germany, Hungary, Poland, Bohemia, England and other places of the Roman obedience. Apart from that denunciation nothing more is known of the event.

1400   Uncertain whether a Jubilee was celebrated.

1423   If there was a Jubilee in 1390 and they were held every thirty-three years, then this ought to have been the next such year.

1450   So many pilgrims flocked to Rome that many were killed by an outbreak of plague and others died when the Ponte Sant'Angelo collapsed due to the weight of numbers on it.

1475   Following Paul II's decree that Jubilees should be held every twenty-five years, Sixtus IV duly presided over that of 1475, marking it with a programme of urban improvements, which included building the Ponte Sisto over the Tiber.

1500   Muted celebrations during the pontificate of Alexander VI.

12.8   Saints and *beati*

About forty men and women whose adult lives fell between 1390 and 1530 have been canonised by the Catholic Church. They include martyrs, preachers of crusades against the enemies of Christendom, founders and members of religious orders, lay people of exceptional piety, and children allegedly murdered by Jews. Among their contemporaries who have been beatified and accorded the title of 'Blessed' are the painter Fra Angelico (*c.* 1395/1400–55), Bernardino da Feltre (*c.* 1439–94), who encouraged the foundation of public pawn shops, *monti di pietà*, in Italy, the mystic Julian of Norwich (d. *c.* 1423) and the Camaldolese scholar Ambrogio Traversari (*c.* 1386–1439). Some of the more prominent saints of the period are listed below in alphabetical order of Christian name. Names have been anglicised to match their published lives.

Antoninus or Antonino; Antonio Pierozzi (1389–1459)   Florentine Observant Dominican based successively at Fiesole, Rome (S. Maria Sopra Minerva) and Florence, where he founded the convent of S. Marco (1436) and was prior of same (1439–44); archbishop of Florence (1446). He led the reform of the Dominican Order and wrote an influential manual for confessors and preachers, *Summa theologia moralis*.

Bernardino of Siena Bernadino da Siena; Bernardino degli Albizzeschi (1380–1444)   Known as the Apostle of the Holy Name from his promotion of the IHS monogram for the name of Jesus. Elected vicar-general of the Italian Observant Franciscans (1438), he undertook reforms of his order and played a prominent part in the Council of Florence (1439). The most notable preacher of his generation, in whose message there was a strong anti-Jewish theme.

Cajetan Gaetano da Thiene (1480–1547)   Priest from Vicenza who, with Pietro Carafa (later Pope Paul IV), founded the Theatine Order (1524) in Rome.

Casimir of Poland (1458–84)   The ascetic third child of Kazimierz IV of Poland and Elizabeth, daughter of Emperor Albert II. He was sent as a military commander against Matthias Corvinus of Hungary in 1471, but turned back and devoted the remainder of his short life to prayer and study.

Catherine of Bologna (d. 1463)   Visionary Poor Clare originally from Ferrara.

Catherine of Genoa (1447–1510)   Noble widow notable for her works of piety.

Colette (1381–1447)   Visionary from Corbie who revised the rule of the Poor Clares (female Franciscan order) and founded seventeen new convents.

Frances of Rome Francesca Romana (1384–1440)   Married laywoman who devoted her life to caring for the poor of her native city and founded a society of laywomen dedicated to works of charity.

Francis of Paola Francesco da Paola (1416–1507)   Calabrian hermit and founder of the Minim Friars, summoned to France in 1481 by the dying Louis XI.

Ignatius of Loyola Íñigo López de Recalde (1491–1556)   Spaniard of noble birth who had a powerful conversion experience while recuperating after being injured in the defence of Pamplona against the French (1521). He wrote *Ejercicios espirituales* (*Spiritual exercises*) at Manresa in 1522. While studying at Salamanca (1527), the Inquisition suspected him of being an *alumbrado* ('enlightened one'), a mystic of doubtful orthodoxy but of a type then fashionable in Spain. In 1534 he and six close associates founded the Society of Jesus (Jesuits), the most notable of the new orders of the Counter Reformation.

Jadwiga or Hedwig (1374–99)   Queen of Poland: see 4.28. Canonised in 1997.

James of the Marches Giacomo della Marca (1394–1476)   Observant Franciscan and close associate of Giovanni da Capistrano. He undertook preaching missions in central and eastern Europe and his message contained a strong anti-Jewish element.

Jeanne de France (1464–1505)   Daughter of Louis XI and Charlotte of Savoy who married Louis, duke of Orléans (1476), but the marriage was nullified upon his inheritance of the French throne (1498), after which she founded the contemplative order known as the Annonciades of Bourges.

Joan of Arc Jeanne d'Arc (d. 1431)   Peasant girl from Domrémy in Champagne who claimed to hear the voices of Saints Michael, Margaret of Antioch and Catherine of Alexandria, urging her to save the kingdom of France from the invading English and from civil conflict. For her political role, see Chronology of Public Events (pp. 11–12). Canonised 1920; France's second patron saint. She is venerated as a virgin rather than as a martyr.

John Fisher (1469–1535)   Bishop of Rochester and chancellor of the University of Cambridge (for which see 14.4), but whose opposition to Henry VIII's ecclesiastical policy resulted in his martyrdom. Days before his execution, Clement VII made him a cardinal. Together with Thomas, More, canonised in 1934.

John of Capistran Giovanni da Capistrano (1386–1456)   Franciscan from the Abruzzi who studied under S. Bernardino da Siena, becoming a popular preacher involved in the reform of his order. As inquisitor-general in Austria (1451) he was zealous in preaching against the Bohemian Hussites. The fall of Constantinople (1453) prompted similar fervour in the crusading cause. He died after the successful Christian defence of Belgrade (see p. 21).

John of Kanti (1390–1473)   Professor of theology at the University of Cracow.

John of Sahagun (1419–79)   Spanish Augustinian friar.

Lorenzo Giustiniani (1381–1455)   First patriarch of Venice after the suppression of the neighbouring patriarchate of Grado.

Nicholas von Flüe (1417–87)   Swiss layman who adopted the eremitical life in 1467.

Peter Arbues (d. 1485)   Martyred Aragonese Inquisitor.

Peter Regalatus (d. 1456)   Austere Spanish Franciscan.

Simon of Trent (d. 1475)   Two-year-old boy supposedly killed by Jews at Trento in northern Italy, around whom a miracle cult developed. Known as the 'Child Simon' (see 12.11, p. 148).

Thomas More (1479–1535)   For the career of this distinguished public figure and man of letters, see 15.5, p. 183. Like John Fisher, he was martyred for refusing to accept the diminution of papal power implied in Henry VIII's ecclesiastical policy.

Vincent (or Vicent) **Ferrer** (c. 1350–1419)   Widely travelled, Valencian-born preacher of English or Scottish extraction, whose priorities included converting Jews and healing the papal schism. For his contribution to the persecution of the Jews, see 12.11, p. 147.

12.9 Religious orders

Criticism of the religious orders by writers such as Erasmus, himself an Augustinian canon, and the rejection of monasticism by the former Augustinian Martin Luther has tended to obscure the achievements of monks and friars during the century prior to the Reformation. Strict allegiance to the Rules of their orders distinguished the Observant Franciscans and Dominicans in reaction to the perceived shortcomings of their Conventual brethren. Sixtus IV (d. 1484) who, as Francesco della Rovere, was General of the Franciscan Order, was the only mendicant pope in this period and increased privileges for the various mendicant orders during his pontificate.

Distinguished monks and friars arranged by order include:

Benedictine
Ludovico Barbo (c. 1381–1443)   Abbot of S. Giustina at Padua, from where he provided the initiative for an important tradition of ecclesiastical reform and spiritual renewal in Venice and the Veneto. S. Giustina became the mother house of a Congregation within the Benedictine Order.

Observant Dominicans Order of Preachers
Fra Angelico (see 20.1, p. 211).
S. Antonino/Antonius (see 12.8).
Fra Bartolommeo (see 20.1, p. 219).
Girolamo Savonarola (1452–98)   Preacher and theologian from Ferrara who became prior of the Medici-supported convent of S. Marco in 1491.

After the fall of the Medici (1494), Savonarola's preaching inspired a moral crusade in Florence characterised by bonfires of 'vanities', but the enthusiasm of all but the most committed *piagnoni* ('snivellers') soon waned. See Chronology of Public Events (pp. 34–36) for his dramatic rise and fall.

Juan de Torquemada (1388–1468)   Spanish theologian.

Tomás de Torquemada (1420–98)   Nephew of Juan; first Inquisitor-General of the independent Spanish Inquisition (1483).

Observant Franciscans Friars Minor
S. Bernardino da Siena (see 12.8).
S. Giovanni da Capistrano (see 12.8).
S. Giacomo della Marca (see 12.8).
Cardinal Francisco Jiménez de Cisneros (1436–1517)   Franciscan Provincial in Castile (1494); for his political and cultural impact, see 4.9, 14.2, 15.2, 17.2.

Minim Frairs Franciscan
S. Francesco da Paola (see 12.8).

12.10   Selected Christian writers

The four authors included here have been selected to illustrate certain traditions or schools of thought within fifteenth- and early sixteenth-century Christianity, namely reform of the Church and interior spirituality. They should not be regarded in isolation from Christian scholars such as Erasmus, who are featured elsewhere.

Gasparo Contarini (1483–1542)   *De officio viri boni ac probi episcopi* (*c.* 1516): treatise on the office of a bishop. At that stage Contarini was still a layman. A Venetian patrician, Contarini studied Latin with Marcantonio Sabellico (*c.* 1436–1506) and Giorgio Valla (*c.* 1447–1500), Greek with Marcus Musurus (*c.* 1470–1517), and philosophy and theology at Padua. Among Contarini's Paduan friends were fellow patricians Vincenzo Querini (1479–1514) and Tommaso Giustiniani (1476–1528) who both joined the Order of Camaldoli and whose *Libellus ad Leonem X* (1513) was presented at the Fifth Lateran Council and became a model for subsequent ecclesiastical reform programmes. Contarini's spiritual crisis (1511) defined his faith, as expressed in a treatise defending the immortality of the soul, but also led him to pursue an evangelical mission in the world, his secular appointments including that of Venetian ambassador to Charles V (1521–25). Along with the aristocratic poet Vittoria Colonna (1490–1547), the part-royal Cardinal Reginald Pole (1500–58) and others, Contarini became identified as a figurehead of evangelism in Italy, which attempted to combine emphasis on personal faith in a manner akin to Lutheranism with loyalty to the Church, and offered the potential to heal the schism between Catholics and Protestants. Though still a layman, Contarini was made a cardinal in 1535. For his political writing, see 7.2.

Marguerite of Angoulême Queen of Navarre (1492–1549)   *Miroir de l'âme pécheresse* (*Mirror of the sinful soul*, printed 1531): an expression of her identification with Évangélisme, the scripturally inspired French reform movement led by humanist Jacques Lefèvre d'Étaples and Guillaume II Briçonnet (1472–1534), bishop of Meaux, but opposed by Noël Béda of the University of Paris. Évangélisme was a reform movement within the Church, but many of its adherents, most significantly Jean Calvin, became convinced Protestants. Marguerite, like her mother Louise of Savoy, protected reformers such as Louis de Berquin (d. 1529) and Guillaume Farel (1489–1565), leading to Francis I taking an interest in his sister's clients and their cause in the 1520s. The poet Clément Marot (1496–1544), who also had Protestant sympathies, acted as her secretary. After the Affaire des Placades (1534), the reformers were dispersed and Marguerite retired to her court at Nérac where she wrote the *Héptameron*, stories printed in 1559.

Nicholas Krebs Nicholas of Cusa (1401–64)   *De docta ignorantia* (*On learned ignorance*, 1440): on the relativity of human knowledge. In addition to rediscovering a substantial number of classical texts (see 15.1, pp. 163, 165), Nicholas of Cusa, an active churchman as well as a scholar, was one of the most erudite men of his time. He was educated by the Brethren of the Common Life at Deventer and at the universities of Heidelberg and Padua.

Thomas à Kempis Thomas Hemerken (*c.* 1380–1471)   *De imitatione Christi* (*The imitation of Christ*, pre-1418): the author of this masterpiece of interior Christianity was educated at Deventer by the Brethren of the Common Life and spent his entire adult life in the monastery at St Agrientenberg near Zwolle. The text was popular in both northern and southern Europe.

12.11   Jews and Moors: a chronology of persecution

1412–15   Preaching by the Valencian Dominican Vicent Ferrer resulted in the passing of anti-Jewish laws in Aragon. This campaign built on the 'Holy War' (1391) of Archdeacon Ferrán Martínez against the Jews of Seville, which spread to many parts of Castile and Aragon, as a result of which Jews were massacred. Spain had an exceptionally large Jewish population, as well as many *conversos*, Jews who claimed to have converted to Christianity but whose sincerity was frequently doubted. This accounts for the Christian obsession with *limpieza de sangre*

	(purity of blood). By this date Jews had already been expelled from France, England, Ireland and parts of Germany.
1421	Jews expelled from Austria headed eastwards.
1445	Expulsion of Jews from Lithuania. Further expulsions followed in 1495, the majority of the victims heading southwards.
1449	Rebellion by Jews in Toledo, as a result of which *conversos* were, for the first time, specifically excluded from public offices, both ecclesiastical and secular, in Castile.
1475	Jews suspected of the ritual murder of the 'Child Simon' at Trento, northern Italy, leading to a serious anti-Jewish backlash.
1480	First Castilian inquisitors appointed: tribunals of the Inquisition established at Cordoba in 1482, Jaén and Ciudad Real in 1483. The Spanish Inquisition was independent of that in Rome and dealt initially with *conversos* rather than practising Jews. As in Rome, inquisitors were members of the Dominican Order. In 1483 Jews were expelled from the diocese of Seville and the city of Cadiz.
1484	Spanish Inquistion extended to the kingdom of Aragon, more as a means to unify the kingdoms than to deal with a genuine problem.
1492	Spanish edict offering Jews the choice of conversion to Christianity or exile, on the grounds that professing Jews were leading *conversos* astray; *c.* 15,000 Jews converted, while an estimated 100,000 fled to Portugal, Italy, Germany, the Balkans, North Africa and the Near East.
1494	Savonarola-inspired anti-Jewish legislation in Florence, where Jews had been tolerated since the return of Cosimo de' Medici in 1434. Jews expelled from Cracow in Poland.
1496	Edict for the expulsion of Jews from Portugal, a condition of the marriage between King Manoel of Portugal and Isabel, daughter of Ferdinand of Aragon and Isabella of Castile: they fled to North Africa and Portuguese-held Brazil.
1502	Enforced baptism of Castilian Muslims after the First Revolt of the Alpujarras (1498) in the mountains around Granada.
1510	Many Jews ordered to leave the Spanish-held kingdom of Naples, but total expulsion did not take place until the mid-sixteenth century.
1516	All Venetian Jews ordered to live in a strictly segregated area, the original *ghetto*, thereby providing a model adopted by many other cities.
1526	Spanish Inquisition extended to the former kingdom of Granada.
1527	Expulsion of Jews from republican Florence, where they had again been tolerated by the Medici after 1512.

13 Glossary of terms relating to literary culture

Academies The scholarly counterpart of confraternities, in which the learned met to discuss literary matters in an informal atmosphere, academies were inspired by the example of Plato's school at Athens. Most obviously Platonic in all respects was the circle associated with Marsilio Ficino (1433–99) at Cosimo de' Medici's suburban villa at Careggi, near Florence, though it would be misleading to think of it as a scholarly community leading an idyllic life, for it may be that comments by Ficino have been exaggerated to create such an impression. A similar 'academic' environment was to be found in the meetings of Florentine intellectuals in the Orti Oricellari (Rucellai Gardens) in the early sixteenth century. Machiavelli found congenial company there, the dialogues in his *Arte della guerra* (*Art of War*) being set in the gardens. The leading figure of the fifteenth-century Roman Academy was Pomponio Leto (1428–98), who encouraged in his associates so thorough a devotion to all aspects of classical civilisation that many of its members were arrested (1468) by Pope Paul II on charges of conspiracy against his person, imprisoned and tortured to extract confessions. The pope certainly suspected them of neo-paganism, republicanism and sexual immorality. In addition to himself, Platina (see 15.4) listed the academicians as Leto, Callimachus, Demetrius, Campanus, Mursus, Augustinus, Lucidius, Glaucus, Lucilius and Petreius. Callimachus – Filippo Buonaccorsi – sought sanctuary in Poland where, with Conrad Celtis, he founded the Sodalitas Vistulana at Cracow, another variation on the academic theme (see 15.1, p. 168). The Neapolitan Academy enjoyed the patronage of King Alfonso I and was the focus of cultural life in the city. It was led by Antonio Beccadelli (called 'il Panormita' from his birthplace of Palermo, 1394–1471) and Giovanni/ Gioviano Pontano (1426–1503), the most important humanist in fifteenth-century Naples. Other members included Giannozzo Manetti, Bartolomeo Fazio, Lorenzo Valla and Theodore Gaza. The scholars attracted to the Venetian printshop of Aldus Manutius formed an academy which vowed to speak only Greek at its meetings. The term 'academy' has also been applied to the groups of scholars who gathered around humanist-minded ecclesiastics such as Cardinal Bessarion in Rome and Archbishop János Vitéz in Hungary.

Aristotelianism In spite of the criticisms levelled by humanists against Aristotelian-based scholasticism, the works of Aristotle himself, with their emphasis on logic and empirical investigation, found many translators and commentators, including Ermolao Barbaro (d. 1493), in the Renaissance period, and were still more widely read than those of any other classical writer. The University of Padua was an important centre of Aristotelian philosophy while the leading name in Italian Aristotelianism was that of Pietro Pomponazzi (1462–1525), who taught at the universities of Padua and Bologna, and whose *De immortalitate animae* (1516), was exceptionally controversial, since it stated that there was no rational proof for the immortality of the soul.

Cabbalism From the Hebrew *Kabbalah*: Jewish mystical writings which were believed by Renaissance scholars to have been written in the age of the patriarchs and were thus reliable, if highly cryptic, interpretations of the Old Testament. Christian humanists and philosophers of the fifteenth and sixteenth centuries endeavoured to use this theosophy to understand the relationship between Judaism and Christianity. Johannes Reuchlin was the most committed of these enthusiasts, as articulated in his *De verbo mirifico* (*The Wondrous Word*, 1494) and *De arte cabbalistica* (1517) (see 15.5, p. 184). In Italy Marsilio Ficino and Giovanni Pico della Mirandola both sensed the potential of cabbalistic texts and among the younger scholars influenced by them in this respect was Henricus Cornelius Agrippa of Nettesheim (1486–1535). Many of the texts by which these humanists set so much store actually dated from the thirteenth century.

Christian humanism This was the most conspicuous variation on the humanistic theme, being the application of humanist textual criticism to Christian texts. The deeply entrenched nature of Christian scholasticism in the universities of northern Europe, together with the greater availability of Christian rather than pagan classical texts in that region has resulted in Christian humanism being generally associated with north European scholars such as Erasmus and Colet, but this is deceptive and one should not think in terms of a Christian north and a pagan south. The reality was by no means so clear-cut.

Ciceronianism While all variations on the humanistic theme were inspired by the history and texts of the ancient Greek and Roman worlds, not all humanists concurred on the degree to which fidelity to the ancients should be taken. Poggio Bracciolini and Pietro Bembo were among those who sought to cultivate the purest Latin prose, after the manner of Cicero. In his *Ciceronianus* (1528) Erasmus was heavily critical of such slavish devotion and advocated the creative use of Latin as a supposedly living language.

Civic humanism   A concept associated with the work of Hans Baron (d. 1988), who studied the impact in early fifteenth-century Florence of Cicero and other classical authors writing on the importance of the individual participating in public life and the manner in which this should be done. The message was best suited to a republican environment in which many men held public office and, according to Baron, struck a particular chord in the Florence of Coluccio Salutati and Leonardo Bruni, threatened as it was in *c.* 1402 by the forces of the 'tyrant' Gian Galeazzo Visconti.

Dignity of man   A concept most commonly associated with Giovanni Pico della Mirandola's *Oratio de dignitate hominis* (*Oration on the Dignity of Man*, 1496), but also familiar from the philosophical work of Marsilio Ficino. Deriving from Greek thought, man is presented as occupying a uniquely privileged place between the physical world and that of the intellect or spirit. Just as the Greeks had no concept of original sin but regarded a human being as a *tabula rasa* on which could be imprinted good or bad influences, so 'dignified' man was capable of making a free choice about whether to be more earthly or more spiritual. This bore a close resemblance to Pelagianism, the Christian heresy which asserts that man can contribute towards his own salvation instead of relying entirely on God's grace, and was thus a contentious subject.

Hermeticism   As with Cabbalistic texts, so the supposed writings of an ancient Egyptian magus Hermes Trismegistus ('thrice great'), also identified as the god Thoth, were believed by Renaissance philosophers to be of great antiquity and to contain mysteries which would be of help in interpreting the truth of Christianity. The manuscripts in question (the *Corpus hermeticum*) were taken from Greece to Italy in 1460 at the behest of Cosimo de' Medici, who was already intrigued by Platonic texts. Hermes was thought to have had access to wisdom that pre-dated Plato and Moses, and which they both might have discovered in Egypt. The texts in question were subsequently found to have been produced in the second and third centuries of the Christian era.

Humanism   A nineteenth-century term derived from the Italian *umanista*, teacher of the *studia humanitatis*, the arts syllabus in schools and universities, which was 'human' in the sense of being distinct from the study of divinity. Humanists devoted themselves to the study of, first, Latin and, later, Greek literature, grammar and rhetoric, together with other aspects of the ancient world, including its history, jurisprudence, philosophy, poetics and political theory. Beginning with Petrarch's analysis of classical texts, humanism's Latin phase lasted essentially from *c.* 1330 to 1420, while the Greek phase followed between *c.* 1400 and *c.* 1490, by which time a humanistic appreciation of such texts had become commonplace, in spite of the academic conflict which continued to rage in Germany, France and other regions of Europe between those who accepted this New Learning and their 'scholastic' critics. In a narrow interpretation of the term, humanists collected manuscripts of the works of Cicero, Livy, Quintilian, Vitruvius and a host of other classical authorities, subjecting the texts to philological criticism, attempting to identify the originals from copies, and disseminating their discoveries, first in manuscript and later in print. From this developed a more general appreciation of all aspects of classical civilisation. It is not surprising that the attractions of antiquity were felt most profoundly in Italy, divided as it was into city-states which resembled in size and constitution those of the ancient world, but also because the ruins of classical Rome were at hand. Thus ancient Greece and Rome came to provide models for statecraft, the waging of war, the public role of the individual, and works of art and architecture. 'Humanism' should not be used as an all-encompassing term to refer to Renaissance philosophy, however tempting it may be to present it as a convenient contrast to Scholasticism; their interrelation-ship was considerably more complex.

Platonism and Neoplatonism   In a Renaissance context this is more likely to refer to the study of Neoplatonists of the Christian era, prin-cipally Plotinus (204–70), rather than to the dialogues of Plato himself, in which is conveyed the great wisdom of his master, Socrates. In contrast to the logical and empirical philosophy of Plato's own pupil, Aristotle, the Platonic tradition evolved a distinctly spiritual interpretation of the universe and of the relationship between macrocosm and microcosm, the universe and the human soul. Interpreted Platonically, art and architecture, literature and music should emulate the essential harmony of the universe, everything on earth being but an imperfect copy of its heavenly exemplar or reality. Thus the Renaissance Neoplatonists, ex-emplified by Marsilio Ficino and Giovanni Pico, had little difficulty in presenting Plato as perfectly compatible with Christianity. The migration of Greek scholars to Italy in the fifteenth century introduced western philosophers to much of the Platonic corpus for the first time.

Scolasticism   A blanket term used to refer to the method of education in medieval schools and universities based on the formalised question-ing of texts, and application of logic to the same, in order to reveal the truths they contain. The texts in question could be biblical, patristic or from the more recent Christian past, but there was also a strong depend-ence on the works of Aristotle; the great Schoolmen, such as the Do-minicans St Thomas Aquinas and St Albertus Magnus, sought to prove that these sacred and secular traditions were not incompatible. This basic objective was no less a feature of Renaissance philosophy but, from Petrarch in the fourteenth century through to Lorenzo Valla in the fifteenth and Erasmus in the sixteenth, humanist scholars soundly rejected scholastic methods as both too arid and too subtle to be of genuine help to Christians in their spiritual lives.

virtù Particularly associated with the writings of Machiavelli, this term derives from the Latin *vir*, 'man' and refers to the human capacity for prowess and creativity; it should not be confused with notions of moral virtue, Christian or otherwise.

14 Education

14.1 Schools

Although practice varied to some degree throughout Europe, schooling in Renaissance Italy consisted of a three-stage process:

1. Elementary education, consisting essentially of reading and writing, for pupils of the age of four and above. Children destined for employment requiring a limited range of skills did not need to continue beyond this stage.
2. *Abbaco*, mathematical education, available at *abbaco* schools, for pupils aged between roughly ten and fifteen. This was particularly appropriate for boys destined for a mercantile career, who had no need of study beyond this level.
3. Grammar, essentially Latin but with some Greek, as a prelude to university studies and the higher professions. Latin grammar was frequently taught from the *Donatus* or *Ars minor*, attributed to the fourth-century grammarian Aelius Donatus, and the *Doctinale* (*c.* 1199) of Alexander of Villedieu. Emphasis was also placed on the epistolary art or *Ars dictaminis*. Humanist educators, most notably Guarino da Verona and Vittorino da Feltre (see 14.4), sought to rejuvenate these tired teaching practices. Humanist educational theories were characterised by a combination of intellectual instruction, spiritual edification and physical training, so that the individual student might realise his (or even her) potential in all spheres. Christian and pagan classical studies were regarded as complementary rather than in conflict with each other.

14.2 Universities with their dates of foundation

An alphabetical list of European universities functioning during the period 1390–1531, with dates of foundation, adapted from H. de Ridder-Symoens, ed., *A History of the University in Europe*, vol. II (Cambridge, 1996). It must be remembered that some universities ceased to operate during this period and that some universities had already disappeared before 1390.

Aberdeen (Old)	1495
Aix-en-Provence	1409
Alcalá de Henares	1499 (Founded by Cardinal Francisco Jiménez de Cisneros, but not inaugurated until 1508)
Angers	c. 1250
Avignon	1303
Barcelona	1450
Basel/Basle	1459
Bologna	Late twelfth century (Included a college for Spaniards. Important centre of medical studies. In contrast to Paris, the model of a student-led university)
Bordeaux	1441
Bourges	1464 (Important centre of legal studies)
Bratislava/ Pressburg/ Pozsony	1465 (Probably ceased to exist after 1492)
Buda	1389 (Suppressed 1400; re-established 1410– c. 1460; then disappeared)
Caen	1432
Cahors	1332
Cambridge	1209–25
Catania	1444
Cologne	1388
Copenhagen	1475
Cracow	1364
Dôle	1422
Erfurt	1379
Ferrara	1391 (Ceased to exist 1394, but was re-established 1430; important centre of medical studies)
Florence	1349 (Reorganised 1472, when all but *studia humanitatis* moved to Pisa)
Frankfurt-an-der-Oder	1498 (Opened in 1506)
Freiburg im Breisgau	1457
Genoa	1471 (Opened in 1513)
Glasgow	1451
Granada	1531
Greifswald	1456 (Closed 1527–39)
Grenoble	1339
Heidelberg	1385
Huesca	1354
Ingolstadt	1459
Leipzig	1409
Lérida	1300

Lisbon	1290 (Transferred to Coimbra 1308–38, 1354–77 and from 1537)
Louvain	1425
Lucca	1369
Mainz	1476
Marburg	1527
Montpellier	Early thirteenth century (Important centre of medical studies)
Nantes	1460
Naples	1224 (Suppressed 1458, but re-established 1465)
Orange	1365
Orléans	c. 1235 (Important centre of legal studies)
Oxford	Early thirteenth century
Padua	1222 (Effectively the University of Venice, where Venetian patricians received their higher education; important centre of medical studies and stronghold of Aristotelianism)
Palma, Majorca	1483
Paris	Early thirteenth century (Important centre of theological studies; in contrast to Bologna, the model of a master-led university)
Parma	1412 (Disappeared before 1500, but restored 1512)
Pavia	1361 (Effectively the University of Milan; transferred to Piacenza, 1489–1502)
Perpignan	1350
Perugia	1308
Pisa	1343 (Also see Florence)
Poitiers	1431
Prague	1347
Rome, Sapienza/ Studium Urbis/	1303
Rostock	1419
Salamanca	pre-1218/19 (Spain's premier university)
Salerno	1231 (Status as a university in doubt)
Seville, Santa María de Jesús	1505
Seville, Santo Tomás (Dominican)	1516
Siena	1246
Sigüenza	1489
St Andrews	1411
Toledo	1521

Toulouse	1229
Trier	1454
Tübingen	1476
Turin	1404
Uppsala	1477 (Suppressed 1515)
Valence	1452
Valladolid	Late thirteenth century
Venice	1470 (Medical faculty only, but with university status)
Vienna	1365
Wittenberg	1502 (Lutheran from as early as 1517, but other universities followed this lead as the Reformation gathered pace)
Würzburg	1402 (No sign that it existed after 1413)
Zaragozo/Saragossa	1474

14.3   Glossary of terms relating to universities

Colleges of doctors   In contrast to 'master-led' universities of the Paris or Oxford type, teachers in so-called 'student-led' universities such as Bologna were hired by the university or the communal government. Nevertheless, they formed themselves into colleges of doctors, who examined candidates and awarded degrees: the examining board and the teaching faculty were not always the same body of men. Colleges of doctors are not to be confused with University colleges (see below).

Faculties   The most inferior faculty was that of Arts, which taught the traditional *trivium* (grammar, rhetoric, dialectic) and *quadrivium* (the four sciences – music, arithmetic, geometry, astronomy) as a first degree programme. From Arts, students could move on to more advanced studies in one of three other faculties – Medicine, Law and Theology. The most important medical faculties were at Bologna, Montpellier, Paris and Padua. Medical students studied the works of Galen and Hippocrates from the Hellenistic world, together with those of Avicenna and other Islamic authorities, much of whose knowledge ultimately derived from those same Greek sources. Civil law and canon (ecclesiastical) law were both taught in most faculties of law, the former on the basis of the sixth-century *Code* and *Digest* of Roman Law, the latter from the twelfth-century *Decretum* of Gratian and thirteenth-century *Decretals* of Pope Gregory IX. Graduates of both civil and canon law (*in utriusque juribus*) went on to occupy senior positions in church and state. Theology was the most prestigious field of study and Paris the pre-eminent centre for theological studies, which were taught on the basis of the Bible and the twelfth-century *Sentences* of Peter Lombard, a theological textbook. The university authorities were wary of teaching theology and civil law in close proximity, which helps to account for the reputation of Italian universities for legal studies, while civil law was not taught at Paris.

Nations   Students were frequently divided into groups according to their geographical origins. The 'nations' of which a particular university was composed depended on its catchment area. Thus the University of Paris had four nations – France, Picardy, Normandy and England – the last including students from central and northern Europe, while Prague's four nations were for Czechs, Poles, Bavarians and Saxons. Students at Bologna were divided into about twenty nations and those at Orléans into ten, though Vienna, Leipzig, Louvain and Salamanca each had four.

Rectors   These were the elected heads of universities, elected by the students in Bologna-type universities and by the masters in the Paris type. The Rector was required to be a graduate, a cleric and of sufficient wealth and social standing to carry weight within and beyond the university.

University colleges   These evolved out of the tradition of each religious order having its own hostel or hospice in a university city. Pious endowments led to the creation of such hostels for students whose poverty was not the result of a monastic vow, though university tuition fees were introduced in the fifteenth century. The collegiate structure was stronger in some universities than in others, with Paris and the English universities among the best examples. Parisian colleges included the Sorbonne (graduates only), Collège de Boncourt, Collège de Coqueret, Collège de Montaigu and Collège de Navarre. Oxford colleges founded during this period included All Souls College, founded by Henry VI and Archbishop Chichele of Canterbury in 1437, and Cardinal College (now Christ Church), founded by Cardinal Wolsey in 1525. Cambridge foundations of the period which enjoyed royal patronage were King's College (Henry VI, 1441), Queens' College (Margaret of Anjou and Elizabeth Woodville, 1448), Christ's College and St John's College (Lady Margaret Beaufort, 1505 and 1511 respectively).

14.4   Notable educators

Inevitably this is a very small selection of the potential whole, since the majority of humanist and other literary figures held teaching posts, whether at university or pre-university level. The emphasis here is on teachers of theology and of Greek and Latin grammar; there is no attempt to account for the careers of eminent teachers of law or medicine, though examples of the latter may be found in 18.2.

Gasparino Barzizza (c. 1360–1431)   Humanist professor of grammar, rhetoric and moral philosophy from Bergamo, whose educational ideas influenced both Guarino da Verona and Vittorino da Feltre. Taught at Pavia (1403–7) and Padua (1407–21), where his students included Francesco Filelfo and Francesco Barbaro, thereafter moving to Milan (1421–28), before returning to Pavia.

Noël Béda (*c.* 1470–1537)   Educated at the Collège de Montaigu, of which he was principal from 1504. Dominated the Paris theology faculty in the 1520s. Staunch critic of Erasmus, Lefèvre and the Meaux circle, whom he accused of promoting Lutheranism in France. Royal protection of the reformers resulted in Béda's loss of public posts and exile from Paris in 1533 and 1535.

John Colet (1467–1519)   Educated at Oxford and in Italy, where he discovered Ficinian Neoplatonism. From 1496 he lectured at Oxford on the New Testament, taking a humanistic approach in reaction to traditional word-by-word teaching methods. Dean of St Paul's, London, from 1505, in which capacity he founded St Paul's School (1509). Colet was a friend of More and the other English humanists, as well as of Erasmus, who valued him as a model Christian humanist.

Francesco Filelfo (1398–1481)   Humanist from Tolentino in the Italian Marches who was educated with Barzizza at Padua and acquired knowledge of Greek while secretary to the Venetian ambassador at Constantinople (1421–27). This short-tempered, wandering scholar taught at Bologna (1428), at the Florentine Studium until banished from Florence in 1434, at Siena until 1438, Bologna and then Pavia for over three decades. Visconti and Sforza patronage made him the highest-paid professor of his day, but in 1474 he accepted a post at the Roman Studium for 600 florins, though disputes about remuneration led to his departure from Rome and, after further travels, he accepted a chair in Greek at Florence (1481). At various times he also taught in Ancona, Bergamo, Marseille, Naples and Turin.

John Fisher (1469–1535)   The martyred bishop of Rochester who, with Thomas More, refused to take the Oath of Allegiance, but is otherwise remembered as confessor to Lady Margaret Beaufort and for guiding her benefactions to the University of Cambridge, of which he was chancellor.

Jean Gerson (1363/4–1429)   Chancellor of the University of Paris from 1395/96 who represented the University at the Council of Constance and also supported Christine de Pisan's defence of women.

Guarino da Verona (Guarino de' Guarini) (1374/75–1460)   Taught grammar in private schools in Venice, Verona and Bologna and Greek at the Florentine Studium (from 1408), where he held Chrysoloras's former post. Taught in Venice (1414–19) where his students included the patricians Bernardo Giustiniani (1408–89) and Francesco Barbaro, the latter being one of the first Venetians to study Greek. Thanks to Este patronage, Guarino moved to Ferrara in 1429 and taught there until his death. He divided the curriculum into three parts – elementary, grammatical and rhetorical – a pattern derived from Quintilian, and placed emphasis on the cultivation of both mind and body. This regime attracted students from throughout Europe, including the Englishmen William Grey (d. 1478), future bishop of Ely, John Free (*c.* 1430–65), who became bishop of Bath and Wells, and Robert Flemmyng (d. 1483), bibliophile, poet and king's proctor in Rome. Guarino also taught the humanist George of Trebizond and fellow educator Vittorino da Feltre.

William Lily (*c.* 1468–1522)   First high master of Colet's St Paul's School, London, who was himself educated at Oxford. He heard Leto lecture in Rome and wrote Latin epigrams with Thomas More.

Thomas Linacre (*c.* 1460–1524)   A man of two interconnected capacities: Paduan-educated physician who numbered Erasmus, More and Cardinal Wolsey among his patients, and classical scholar of great renown who was tutor to Arthur, prince of Wales, and the Mary Tudors who went on to be queens of France and England respectively. Linacre himself studied with Poliziano and Chalcondyles, assisted the printer Aldus Manutius in Venice, taught Greek to More, translated Galen from Greek to Latin and founded medical lectureships at Oxford and Cambridge, as well as the (Royal) College of Physicians (1518).

Vittorino da Feltre (Vittorino de' Rambaldini) (*c.* 1378–1446)   Began teaching in Padua in 1396, moved to Venice in 1415 and succeeded Barzizza as professor of Latin at Padua in 1422. The following year he moved to Mantua under the patronage of the Gonzaga, where his pupils included Lorenzo Valla and Federico da Montefeltro, the future duke of Urbino.

Juan Luis Vives (1492–1540)   Born in Valencia of *converso* parents and educated at the Collège de Montaigu, Paris, from 1509, Vives reacted against the Parisian educational establishment in the same way as Erasmus. Moving to Bruges, he became tutor to Guillaume de Croy (1500–21), who was briefly archbishop of Toledo, taught at Louvain and moved to England in 1523. An associate of More, Fisher and Linacre, he was tutor to Henry VIII's daughter Mary and supported her mother, Catherine of Aragon, throughout the divorce controversy. Vives wrote on pedagogy, Latin grammar, philosophy and political thought.

15   Letters and lives

15.1   Chronology of the Latin and Greek revivals

The origins of the Latin revival are commonly associated with the career of Petrarch (Francesco Petrarca, 1304–74), although interest in Latin letters can be traced throughout the medieval period, including a outburst of enthusiasm in early fourteenth-century Padua. By the end of the fifteenth century, it was common for Italian humanists to have mastered Greek as well as Latin, while a number of north Europeans were also being initiated into the mysteries of the more venerable classical tongue. This chronology focuses on the most notable achievements of the classical revival and the most illustrious names, but it also gives an impression of the itinerant careers of Renaissance scholars.

1394	Greek scholar **Manuel Chrysoloras** (1350–1415) travelled to Italy to seek support for beleaguered Byzantine Empire.
1397–1400	Thanks to the humanist interests of Florentine chancellor **Coluccio Salutati** (1331–1406), Chrysoloras was appointed professor of Greek in Florence, where his pupils included future historian of Florence Leonardo Bruni (c. 1374–1444), Niccolò Niccoli (1365–1437), Roberto de' Rossi (c. 1355–1417), Palla Strozzi (d. 1462), and Pier Paolo Vergerio (1370–1444). Chrysoloras's enthusiasm for Greek language, literature, thought and art was infectious, with this group of acolytes forming the core of the early fifteenth-century classical revival in Florence.
1400–3	Chrysoloras travelled to Pavia, before returning to Constantinople. He was joined by **Giacomo Angeli de Scarperia** (c. 1360–1411), who sent back to Italy manuscripts of the complete works of Plato and Plutarch, Greek historians, Homer and other poets, together with manuals of mythology, grammars and vocabularies.
1403–8	**Guarino (de' Guarini) da Verona** (1374/75–1460) travelled to Constantinople, returning to Italy with numerous manuscripts. Among authors not represented in Angeli's finds but collected by Guarino were Xenophon, Aristophanes, Aristotle and Hesiod.

1405–13   **Giovanni Aurispa** (1369–1459) followed in the footsteps of Angeli and Guarino: his manuscript finds included works of Euripides, Sophocles and Thucydides.

1407   Apostolic Scriptor **Poggio Bracciolini** (1380–1459) and Leonardo Bruni visited the monastery of Montecassino (kingdom of Naples), which housed the largest library in medieval Europe and from which they 'rescued' a number of classical texts.

1408   **Chrysoloras** visited France before moving on to England (1409), Spain and Bologna (1410), Rome (1411), Florence again (1413), and attending the ecumenical Council at Constance, where he died, 15 September 1415.

1414–18   General Council of the Church at Constance provided opportunities for scholarly exchanges and searches for manuscripts, since many humanists were employed as secretaries to senior churchmen and other delegates. Barzizza, Poggio and Vergerio were there in papal service, while Bruni was also present. Poggio's first expedition from Constance was to the monastic libraries at Cluny and Langres, where he discovered manuscripts of Ciceronian orations.

1416   June–July: with Cencio de' Rustici and Bartolomeo Aragazzi of Montepulciano, **Poggio** made his first expedition from Constance to the monastery of St Gall, where his important manuscript finds included Quintilian, *Institutiones oratoriae* (*On the instruction of an orator*), together with further Ciceronian orations, works by Valerius Flaccus, Lactantius and the *De architectura* of Vitruvius. Petrarch's 1333 discovery at Liège of Cicero's *Pro Archia* oration had marked the revival of classical rhetoric.

1417   **Lorenzo Valla** taught Greek in Florence.

1417   January: **Poggio** returned to St Gall, making manuscript discoveries there and at neighbouring monasteries, including Vegetius, *Epitoma rei militaris* (Epitome of military science). Spring: Poggio's expedition to the monastery at Fulda yielded works by Tertullian and other classical authors. Summer: Poggio's fourth journey from Constance took him to a number of French and German libraries, including Langres (Cicero's *Pro Caecina* speech) and Cologne (seven more Ciceronian orations). Poggio was in regular contact with book collectors in Italy, particularly Niccolò Niccoli, but also with Leonardo Bruni, Ambrogio Traversari, Guarino da Verona and the Venetian Francesco Barbaro (d. 1482), so his discoveries were soon shared with fellow enthusiasts.

1418–22	**Poggio** in England under the patronage of Cardinal Henry Beaufort, but the limitations of English libraries confined him to patristic studies.
1418	**Ciriaco d'Ancona** (Ciriaco Pizzicolli, *c.* 1390–1455) to Constantinople for mercantile purposes, but also collected Greek manuscripts, gems and other antiquities. Other expeditions followed.
1419	**Guarino da Verona** discovered letters of the Younger Pliny in Venice.
1420	Death of **Laurant de Premierfait**, whose translations from Latin and Italian into French included works by Cicero and Boccaccio.
1420–27	**Francesco Filelfo** in Constantinople. Authors who did not feature in Aurispa's list but who were collected by Filelfo included Homer, Hesiod, Herodotus, Theocritus, Aeschines, Lysias, Polybius, Aristides, Hermogenes, Philo, St John Chrysostom, Apollonius of Perga, Filostratus, Libanius, Suidas and Nonnus.
1421–23	**Aurispa**'s second Byzantine expedition, undertaken for Gian Francesco Gonzaga of Mantua. Among his finds were texts by Sophocles, Aeschylus and Apollonius Rhodius, Homeric hymns, Pindar, Aristophanes, Aristotle, Xenophon, Demosthenes, Apollonius Dyscolus, Callimachus, Oppiano, Hephaestion, Strabo, Plutarch, Diodorus Siculus, Orpheus and Procopius.
1422	Discovery at Lodi, near Milan, probably by **Gerardo Landiano**, bishop of Lodi, of the complete text of Cicero, *De oratore*, and of his *Brutus*. Vittorino da Feltre succeeded Barzizza as professor of Latin at Padua.
1423	**Vittorino da Feltre** moved to Mantua, where his pupils included Lorenzo Valla and Federico da Montefeltro, future duke of Urbino.
c. 1425	Poggio's first contact with **Heinrich von Grebenstein**, the 'monk of Hersfeld', who supplied him with more manuscripts.
1426	Paduan-educated **Nicholas Krebs** of Kues (Nicholas of Cusa, 1401–64), in the service of Cardinal Giordano Orsini, found *c.* 800 manuscripts at Cologne cathedral, including Cicero, *De re publica*. He later made his name as a distinguished theologian, cardinal and papal legate to Germany and the Low Countries (see 12.10).
1427	Monk of Hersfeld returned to Poggio at Rome with a list of 'new' manuscripts, including Ammiano Marcellino, the *First Decade* of Livy and further Ciceronian orations, though many of these were already known to bibliophiles.

1429	**Guarino da Verona** moved to Ferrara, where he taught until his death in 1460. Poggio returned to Montecassino, where his discoveries included Frontinus on aquaducts.
1431	As legate to Bohemia, Moravia, Germany, Hungary and Poland, Cardinal **Giuliano Cesarini** used the opportunity to search for more manuscripts. He was also in contact with Niccoli's circle in Florence.
1431	**Carlo Marsuppini** (1398–1453) of Arezzo appointed to the Florentine chair of Greek after the departure of Filelfo; he went on to become chancellor of Florence.
1432–34	**Ambrogio Traversari**, biblical and patristic scholar as well as General of the Camaldolese Order, undertook a visitation of its houses, taking this opportunity to search out manuscripts in Bologna, Mantua, Verona, Venice, Treviso, Vicenza, Faenza, Ravenna.
1432–40	More discoveries made during the Council of Basel, as there had been at Constance; these were mainly by **Tommaso Parentucelli** (future Nicholas V), Aurispa and Bartolomeo Capra, archbishop of Milan. In 1433 Aurispa visited Mainz, Cologne and Strasbourg. Pietro Donato, bishop of Padua, made important discoveries at Speyer in 1436.
1434	**Palla Strozzi**, collector of manuscripts and sometime pupil of Chrysoloras, exiled from Florence following the return of Cosimo de' Medici. He was based in Padua thereafter, where his library, hospitality to scholars and patronage of promising university students, made him a 'foundation stone' of the Renaissance in the Veneto.
1435–38	Tuscan **Giovanni Tortelli** (*c.* 1400–66) went to Constantinople to study Greek. He returned to Italy with manuscripts of Hermes Trismegistus, Dioscorides and Thucydides.
1435–40	**Pietro del Monte**, papal collector in England, inspired Humphrey, duke of Gloucester, to employ humanists, including Tito Livio Frulovisi, whose *Vita Henrici Quinti* marked the arrival of humanist history writing in England.
1437	**Nicholas of Cusa** sent to Constantinople by Eugenius IV and the Council of Basel. He used this opportunity to acquire a considerable number of manuscripts.
1438	Francesco Filelfo visited Milan. Bruni's translation of Aristotle's *Politics* reached Humphrey of Gloucester. Death of **Niccolò Niccoli**, who wrote nothing but was a speaker in Bruni's dialogues, expressed enthusiasm for all facets of the classical past and collected an important library which he left to Traversari's Camaldolese monastery in Florence but

which soon passed to Cosimo de' Medici and then to the Dominican house of S. Marco.

1438–39   Council of Ferrara–Florence, at which the Byzantine contingent included the great Platonic scholar **Gemistos Plethon** (*c.* 1355/60–1452), Isidore of Kiev, Bessarion of Trebizond and possibly Theodore Gaza (1400–75/77). Plethon, the arch-Platonist who taught Bessarion, possibly motivated Cosimo de' Medici's interest in Platonic writings. Other Greek humanists who first went to Italy for the Council, whose academic careers prospered there and who were associates of Bessarion included: Calixtus Andronicus (d. *c.* 1487), Janus Argyropulos (1415–87) and Demetrius Chalcondyles (1423–1511). On the Latin side, Ambrogio Traversari was among those who helped to write the deed of Union.

1440   **Lorenzo Valla**'s *Elegantiarum linguae latinae* (*On the elegancies of the Latin tongue*) completed: it began to circulate in 1444.

1443   Humphrey of Gloucester received **Pier Candido Decembrio**'s translation of Plato's *Republic*. Decembrio (1392–1477), a Milanese humanist, had been a pupil of Chrysoloras.

1445   Theodore Gaza's Greek grammar circulated.

1445   **William Grey** arrived at Ferrara to study with Guarino, patronised the promising young humanist Niccolò Perotti (1429–80) and, in 1446, became the king of England's proctor in Rome. Grey's library, assembled in Italy, contained many treatises on grammar and rhetoric and was bequeathed to Balliol College, Oxford. Grey was on good terms with Poggio and Bessarion.

1447   Election of the humanist **Tommaso Parentucelli** as Pope Nicholas V. His pontificate witnessed the gathering in Rome of a number of humanists including Giannozzo Manetti, Lorenzo Valla, Francesco Filelfo, Bessarion and Theodore Gaza.

1447–58   Visit to Italy of Hungarian poet known as **Janus Pannonius** (1434–72), during which he attended Guarino's school at Ferrara and the University of Padua. A book collector and humanist, he was nephew of János Vitéz (*c.* 1408–72), himself mentor to Matthias Corvinus, archbishop of Esztergom and primate of Hungary (from 1465). Vitéz was in contact with numerous Italian humanists and was a patron of the short-lived Hungarian Renaissance.

1451–54   Cardinal **Nicholas of Cusa**'s legation to Germany, Bohemia, Prussia, England and the Low Countries provided excellent opportunities for manuscript-hunting.

1451	**Enoch d'Ascoli** returned from a manuscript-hunting mission to the Near East, where he had been sent by Nicholas V, and was dispatched on a similar tour of northern Europe, during which he discovered Tacitus's *Germania* at the abbey of Hersfeld.
1452	**Niccolò Perotti** visited Trebizond, from where he sent manuscripts to Nicholas V.
1453	Fall of Constantinople to the Turks made western European scholars more dependent on émigré Greeks for knowledge of the language and literature.
1455	Gutenberg Bible printed: the development of printing with moveable type exercised an even greater influence on classical scholarship than did the fall of Constantinople.
1457	Death of arch-classicist **Lorenzo Valla** (see 15.5, p. 185), whose expertise was in Latin, but not Greek.
1458	Death of **Íñigo López de Mendoza**, marquis of Santillana (b. 1398), who read neither Latin nor Greek, but commissioned so many Spanish translations of classical texts that he may be regarded as the father of the classical revival in Spain. He was also a notable poet, the first to write Petrarchan sonnets in Castilian. His sons, including Cardinal Pedro Mendoza (d. 1495), not only proved significant supporters of Isabella of Castile, but were also among the leading cultural patrons of later fifteenth-century Spain.
1465	First printing press in Italy founded at Subiaco by **Konrad Sweynheim** and **Arnold Pannartz**, both from Mainz.
1467	**Sweynheim** and **Pannartz** transferred their press to Rome, where their first publication was Cicero, *Epistolae ad familiares.*
1468	**Bessarion**'s donation of his library to the Republic of Venice, though he retained use of it during his lifetime.
1468	Members of Roman Academy arrested by Paul II, who feared that they were plotting to kill him and certainly disapproved of their devotion to pagan culture. This Academy was founded by **Pomponio Leto** (1428–98), humanist and long-serving teacher at the Roman Studium, whose students included Jacopo Sannazaro (1457/58–1530), Pontano, Platina, Marcantonio Sabellico, Alessandro Farnese (the future Paul III), Reuchlin, the future imperial councillor Konrad Peutinger and 'Publio' Fausto Andrelini (*c.* 1462–1518). Leto was in Venice when the arrests took place, but was sent back to Rome and imprisoned in Castel Sant'Angelo.
1469	**Johann of Speyer** founded the first Venetian printing press, its first publication also being Cicero, *Epistolae ad familiares.*

1476	**Calixtus Andronicus** sold six cases of manuscripts in Milan, where a Greek printing press was also established that year.
After 1479	German humanist **Rodolphus Agricola** Senior (1444–85) wrote *De inventione dialectica* on logic and rhetoric, in addition to making translations from Greek to Latin, and was duly praised by Erasmus for bringing true learning out of Italy.
1480	**Angelo Poliziano** (Angelo Ambrogini, 1454–94) was appointed to the chair of Greek and Latin eloquence at the Florentine Studium, where he had also studied. A native of Montepulciano, from which his literary name derived, he had been tutor to Lorenzo de' Medici's children in the 1470s and celebrated Lorenzo's brother Giuliano in the vernacular *Stanze per la giostra di Giuliano de' Medici* (*Verses for the joust of Giuliano de' Medici*) (1475–78). His textual scholarship was most clearly expressed in his influential *Miscellanea* (1489).
1481	Publication of the Latin grammar *Introductiones latinae* by **Elio Antonio de Nebrija** (or Lebrija, 1441/44–1527), professor of grammar and rhetoric at Salamanca. The work was initially intended for use at Salamanca, but created a sensation throughout literate Europe. This self-proclaimed 'vanquisher of barbarism' had been educated at the Spanish college of the University of Bologna, added the classicising 'Elio' to his name, won the approval of Isabella of Castile and worked on the Complutensian Polyglot Bible from 1513.
1482	**Johannes Reuchlin** (1454/55–1522) in Rome, reflecting the common practice of German humanists heading south early in their careers.
1485	**Thomas Linacre** went to Italy (see 14.4).
1486	**Giovanni Pico della Mirandola** offered to debate his 900 *Conclusiones*, which relied heavily on Jewish and Arabic sources, thereby sparking ecclesiastical censure (see 15.5).
1487	First Latin–French dictionary printed at Geneva.
1487	Venetian **Cassandra Fedele** (*c.* 1465–1558), a classical scholar whose correspondents included Poliziano, began teaching informally at Padua.
1488	First printed edition of Homer printed in Florence.
1489	**Aurelio 'Lippo' Brandolini** (d. 1497), who wrote on rhetoric and philosophy, as well as Latin verse, left Rome for Hungary and the patronage of Matthias Corvinus, but returned after the king's death and became an Augustinian friar.

1491	After studying with Poliziano and Chalcondyles in Florence and Aldus in Venice, **William Grocyn** (*c.* 1446–1519) became the first Englishman to teach Greek in his native country. His friends included Erasmus, Linacre and Latimer, and his pupils included Thomas More.
1493	**Giorgio Merula** (1430/31–94), former pupil of Francesco Filelfo, made major literary finds at Bobbio, between Piacenza and Genoa, marking the end of the heroic age of manuscript discoveries.
1493	Death of the great Venetian humanist **Ermolao Barbaro** (the younger, b. 1453/54), grandson of Francesco Barbaro, whose short but distinguished career combined embassies on behalf of the Venetian Signoria with important textual work, particularly on Aristotle, a reflection of his Paduan education. Erasmus travelled to Italy 'to hear Barbaro'.
1494	Greek humanist **Janus Lascaris** (*c.* 1445–1535), transferred his allegiance from Florence to the invading French, going on to work with Guillaume Budé (see 15.5, p. 179) in the royal library at Fontainebleau and to serve as French ambassador to Venice (1504–9), where he enjoyed close contacts with the circle of Aldus Manutius.
1495	**Aldus Manutius** began printing in Venice.
1499	**Erasmus**'s first visit to England.
1500	Publication in Paris of **Erasmus**'s *Adagiorum collectanea* (*Adages*), a collection of sayings with explanations, designed as teaching aids. The expanded version was printed by Aldus in Venice in 1508.
1501	Death of the Byzantine scholar **Constantine Lascaris** (b. 1434), who bequeathed seventy-six manuscripts to the city of Messina, Sicily, where his appointment as professor at the Gymnasium was due to Bessarion's support.
1508	Death of Latin poet laureate, playwright and editor of Seneca, **Conrad Celtis**, (Konrad Bickel or Pickel, b. 1459), who visited Italy and promoted humanism in Hungary, Germany and Poland, founding sodalities (academies) in Buda, Heidelberg and Cracow, the last of which was known as the Sodalitas Vistulana, and was co-founded with Filippo Buonaccorsi (1437–96), the poet known as Callimachus, who fled from Rome when the Academicians were arrested in 1468.
1517	Corpus Christi College, Oxford, founded by **Richard Fox** (*c.* 1448–1528), bishop of Winchester, as the first 'trilingual' college in England, for the teaching of Latin, Greek and Hebrew, though the last was taught as part of Divinity.

Fox had inherited the library of John Shirwood (d. 1494), whom he succeeded as bishop of Durham and who was himself the most committed collector of humanist manuscripts in later fifteenth-century England (this collection remains at Corpus Christi). Shirwood's impressive collection of manuscripts and printed books, including editions by Sweynheim and Pannartz, was assembled while he served as king's proctor at Rome.

1518   **Philipp Melanchthon** (lit. 'black earth', 1497–1560), nephew of Reuchlin, appointed professor of Greek at the University of Wittenberg. He became a leading Protestant reformer, retaining a particular interest in educational matters.

1527   Debate at Valladolid between Spanish Erasmians and Dominican theologians resulted in victory for the Erasmians. With links perceived between humanists and Lutherans, Erasmians in Spain and elsewhere found themsleves persecuted, parallelling the fall of **Erasmus** as Europe's intellectual darling.

1528   In the *Ciceronianus,* **Erasmus** criticised those scholars who advocated slavish devotion to Ciceronian Latin, instead of employing the language creatively.

1529–34 French legal humanist **Lazaire de Baïf** (d. 1547), whose writings on that subject were regarded as second only to those of Budé, served as French ambassador to Venice, where he enjoyed contacts with many humanists, having already studied with Janus Lascaris and Marcus Musurus.

1530   Inspired by **Guillaume Budé**, Francis I sponsored the *Lecteurs royaux* in Hebrew, Greek, Latin and mathematics, forming the nucleus of the future Collège de France.

1531   Publication of the *Emblemata* of **Andrea Alciati** (1492–1550), a collection of 104 mottoes representing virtues and vices, and illustrated by woodcuts and poems. Alciati thereby created the distinctive Renaissance genre of the emblem book (It. *impresa* = emblem).

15.2   Christian humanism: a chronology of biblical scholarship

c. 1382   'Wycliffe's' English translation of the Bible, with heavy input by his Lollard followers. Another such was made *c.* 1388.

1444   **Lorenzo Valla,** *Adnotationes* on the standard Latin Vulgate text of St Jerome. By studying Greek manuscripts, Valla 'revolutionised' biblical scholarship.

1466   *Biblia Germanica* printed at Strasbourg, the first vernacular printing of the Bible in any language. Between 1461 and 1520, however, there were eighteen German translations, fourteen in High German, and four in Low German, all based on a fourteenth-century translation of the Vulgate.

1471   First translation of the Old and New Testaments into Italian.

1477   First Dutch translation of the Old and New Testaments printed at Delft.

1478   First Catalan translation of the Old and New Testaments.

1487   First French translation of the Old and New Testaments, made by royal confessor **Jean de Rély**.

1488   First Czech translation of the Old and New Testaments printed at Prague.

1489   **Giovanni Pico**, *Heptaplus*: allegorical version of the Creation.

1502   Work on the six-volume Complutensian Polyglot Bible begun under the patronage of Cardinal Cisneros. Led by **Diego López de Zúñiga**, the team of translators included Antonio de Nebrija, the Cretan Demetrios Doukas, Hernan Núñez, Alfonso de Zamora, Alfonso de Alcalá and Pablo Coronel. The Bible was printed 1514–17, but not published until 1522. Texts in Hebrew, Chaldean and Greek appear alongside the Vulgate Latin in parallel columns. 'Complutensian' refers to the Latin for Alcalá de Henares, where the project was undertaken.

1506   **Johannes Reuchlin**, *De rudimentis hebraicis* printed at Pforzheim. This opened up Hebrew studies to northern scholars.

1509   **Jacques Lefèvre d'Étaples** (1450–1537), *Quincuplex Psalterium*: parallel texts of Old Latin, Gallican, Roman and Hebrew Psalters, with commentary.

1512   **Lefèvre**'s Latin translation of, and commentary on, the Pauline Epistles.

1516   **Erasmus**'s Latin translation of the New Testament, which he entitled *Novum Instrumentum*, printed by Froben at Basel. This provided the basis for Luther's German translation.

1518   **Lefèvre**, *De Maria Magdalena*: debate on the various Marys in the New Testament.

1519   **Erasmus**, *Novum Testamentum*, second edition of his 1516 translation, for which the title was changed, together with his *Annotationes* on the same.

1519   Parts of the New Testament translated into Russian.

1522   **Luther**'s High German *Das Newe Testament deutsch* published at Wittenberg with woodcut illustrations by Cranach.
         Lefèvre, *Commentarii initiatori in quatuor Evangelica*.

1523   **Lefèvre**'s French translation of the New Testament published.

1523-24 **Luther,** *Das Alte Testament deutsch* published at Wittenberg: drew on the scholarship of Melanchthon, Reuchlin and others.

1524 First translation of the New Testament into Danish.

1525 English Bible of **William Tyndale** (*c.* 1494–1536), based on Erasmus's Greek and Latin editions, began to appear in parts the year after he fled persecution in England for his Protestant beliefs.

1526 First translation of the New Testament into Swedish.

1527 German translation to rival Luther's. Translator **Hieronymus Emser** (1477/78–1527) was a student of Reuchlin.
Lefèvre, *Commentarii in Epistolas catholicas.*

1528 **Lefèvre**'s French translation of the Old Testament published.

1530 **Lefèvre**'s French translation of the Old and New Testaments printed at Antwerp (known as the Antwerp Bible): based very firmly on the Vulgate, in contrast to the freer translations of many of his contemporaries, but with reference to Jean de Rély.

1530 **Tyndale**'s English translation of the Pentateuch printed at Marburg: based on Hebrew originals with reference to the Vulgate, Erasmus and Luther.

1531 **Tyndale**'s English translation of Jonah.

1534 **Luther**'s *Deutsche Bibel,* German Old and New Testaments, printed at Wittenberg: based on sources in original languages.

1535 **Pierre Robert Olivetan** (*c.* 1506–38) completed the first French Protestant translation of the Bible, printed at Neuchâtel: based on Lefèvre's scholarship.

1535 English translation of complete Bible by **Miles Coverdale** (1488–1569) printed: not based on original languages.

15.3 Chronology of vernacular literature

c. **1390** **John Gower** (*c.* 1330–1408), *Confessio amantis:* most important English work by a poet who also wrote in French and Latin. A younger generation of Englishmen writing in the vernacular included Thomas Hoccleve (*c.* 1370–1430) and John Lydgate (*c.* 1370–1449), a client of Humphrey of Gloucester.

1404/5 **Christine de Pisan** (b. 1364), *Le livre de la cité des dames:* derived from Boccaccio's *De claris mulieribus* (*Of famous women*) and followed by *Le livre des trois vertus/ Trésor des dames* (*Treasure of the city of ladies,* 1405). Christine was born in Venice but moved to France when her father became physician to Charles V. Widowed in 1390, she turned to writing for royal patrons to support her family, thereby gaining the reputation of being the first professional female writer. Other works included: *Livre des faicts et bonnes moeurs du roi Charles* [V] (a biography of the late king), *Ditié en l'honneur de Jeanne d'Arc* (in praise of her contemporary) and *Le livre des fais d'armes et de chevalerie* (on chivalry) (1410).

1415–40 Confinement in England of **Charles d'Orléans**, prince and poet, whose *Livre de la prison* reveals him as the last of the courtly poets.

1424 **Alain Chartier**, *La belle dame sans merci*: by a poet whose work reflects both humanist influence and post-Agincourt gloom in France. Chartier undertook diplomatic missions to Germany, Venice and Scotland.

c. 1433–34 **Leon Battista Alberti** (1404–72), *Della familia* (*On the family*): in addition to his theoretical works on the visual arts, Alberti also wrote vernacular treatises such as this, and others on moral philosophy, horses, the ruins of Rome, secret codes and mathematics, and a grammar to demonstrate the nobility of the Tuscan language.

1450–52 **Jacques Milet** (*c.* 1428–66), *Istoire de la destruction de Troye la grant*: a play for performance over four days.

1452 Poet **François Villon** (*c.* 1431–after 1463), author of *Le Lais* (*Petit Testament*) and *Le Testament* (*Grand Testament*) received his MA at Paris. He disappeared in the 1450s after committing crimes in Paris but returned to both the city and a life of crime in 1462.

c. 1460 **Joanot Martorell** (d. 1470), *Tirant lo blanch*: an important work of chivalric literature, written in Catalan and completed by Martí Joan de Galba, but not printed until 1490.

c. 1460 Anon., possibly **Antoine de la Salle**, *Cent nouvelles nouvelles*: stories modelled on Boccaccio's *Decameron* and presented to Philip the Good of Burgundy.

1470 **Sir Thomas Malory** (*c.* 1434–71), *Le morte d'Arthur*: based on French sources and printed by Caxton in 1485, days before Arthurian enthusiast Henry Tudor assumed the English crown.

1483 **Matteo Maria Boiardo** (1441–94), *Orlando innamorato* (*Roland in love*), books I and II; complete text published 1495: this chivalric romance by a Ferrarese poet includes Arthurian and Carolingian elements. A Tuscan Italian version by Francesco Berni (*c.* 1497–1535) was more influential than the original.

c. 1487 **Girolamo Benivieni** (1453–1542), *De lo amore celeste*: influential poem inspired by Ficinian Neoplatonism, which this Florentine author later repudiated.

1492	**Antonio de Nebrija**, *Gramática sobre la lengua castellana*: the first Castilian grammar, published at Salamanca.
1494	**Sebastian Brant** (1457/58–1521), *Das Narrenschiff* (*The ship of fools*), printed at Nuremberg. Brant was an academic lawyer and edited humanist texts for Froben and other printers. His text highlighted human folly and exhorted Emperor Maximilian to champion the reform of clerical abuses.
1495	**Juan del Encina** (1468–*c.* 1530), *Cancionero de palacio*: anthology of Spanish plays and poems to which this composer, poet and playwright was principal contributor. Encina, a priest, was popular in Spanish court circles and enjoyed the patronage of the Catalan pope Alexander VI, dividing his time between Spain and Rome.
1499	**Fernando de Rojas** (*c.* 1465–1541), *La tragicomedia de Calisto y Melibea*, better known as *La Celestina*, published in Burgos: the most popular fictional work of the day in Spain.
1502	**William Dunbar** (*c.* 1456–*c.* 1513), *The thistle and the rose*: poem by this Scottish 'Chaucerian' to celebrate the marriage of James IV of Scotland with Margaret Tudor of England. Dunbar was possibly killed at the battle of Flodden. Another poet of the same school was Robert Henryson (d. 1506).
1503	**Symphorien Champier** (*c.* 1474–1539), *La Nef des Dames vertueuses*. Champier was a poet of the Lyon School.
1505	**Pietro Bembo** (1470–1547), *Gli Asolani*: dialogues probably written between 1497 and 1502, inspired by Caterina Cornaro's court at Asolo, dedicated to Lucrezia Borgia, duchess of Ferrara, and notable for its account of platonic love, firmly in the Ficinian tradition. Son of Venetian diplomat Bernardo Bembo (1433–1519), Pietro wrote in both Latin and Italian, was an editor of the Aldine press, was appointed Venetian state librarian and historiographer (1530) and made a cardinal (1538). See also 6.5.1.
1508	**Garci Rodríguez de Montalvo** and others, *Amadís de Gaula* (*Amadis of Gaul*): chivalric novel published at Zaragoza, which became an international bestseller. It was written *c.* 1492.
1511	Various, *Cancionero general de Hernando del Castillo*: 1,033 poems by various authors, edited by **Hernando del Castillo** and published at Valencia.
c. 1513	**Niccolò Machiavelli** (1469–1527), *Il principe* (*The prince*): the epoch-making study of classical and modern statesmanship.
1516	**Ludovico Ariosto** (1474–1533), *Orlando furioso* (first edition, the second and third following in 1521 and 1532 respectively): a continuation of Boiardo's themes but with evidence

of additional classical inspiration. Begun in 1503, it partly celebrates the founding of the Este dynasty, by whom Ariosto was employed. A great sensation, it was soon translated into French, Spanish and English.

c. 1518 **Niccolò Machiavelli**, *La mandragola* (*The mandrake root*): stage comedy for which its author was best known in his lifetime.

1524 **Pietro Aretino** (1492–1556) was forced to flee from Rome after publishing sixteen obscene sonnets to match Giulio Romano's erotic engravings, *I modi* (see 20.2). Aretino, whose name derived from his birthplace, Arezzo, was a master of vernacular verse and prose who moved to Rome under the patronage of Sienese banker Agostino Chigi, was part of the city's vibrant cultural life but rejected Christianity and lived in Venice from 1527.

1528 **Baldassare Castiglione** (1478–1529), *Il libro del cortegiano* (*The book of the courtier*): the tip of the 'advice literature' iceberg. See also 6.5.1.

1531 **Sir Thomas Elyot** (c. 1490–1546), *The boke named the governour*: one of many spin-offs from Castiglione's work.

1532 **François Rabelais** (1494–c. 1553), *Pantagruel*: comic novel about a giant, the first of a series of works by this failed monk which had a tremendous impact on French language and literature. Rabelais was influenced by the unorthodox Florentine poet Luigi Pulci (1432–84), who also fell foul of the ecclesiastical authorities.

1534 **Rabelais**, *Gargantua*: sequel to *Pantagruel*, Gargantua being the father of Pantagruel; notable for its satire on humanist education.

1536 Death in battle of **Garcilaso de la Vega**, Spanish courtier poet who, with Juan Boscán de Almogaver (c. 1490–1542), cultivated Italian poetic forms in Spain, most notably the Petrarchan sonnet.

15.4   Historians of their own times

This period witnessed significant evolution in the writing of history. While the chronicle tradition remained vibrant, it was challenged by humanistically trained writers who sought to emulate ancient historians such as the Greek Polybius and the Romans Livy, Sallust and Julius Caesar, in both choice of subject matter and execution.

Flavio Biondo (1392–1463)
Historiam ab inclinatione Romani imperii decades: European history from AD410 to 1441; written from the mid-1430s; printed at Venice in 1483.

Biondo, from Forlì, contributed to the classical revival through archaeo-logical studies published as *Roma instaurata*: written 1444–46; printed at Rome in 1471. His other works included: *De verbis Romanae locutionis* (*Concerning the words of Roman speech*, 1435); *Italia illustrata*, completed 1453, printed at Rome in 1474; *Roma triumphans* (printed at Brescia, 1473–75). Biondo's plans to become Venetian state historiographer were thwarted in 1462.

Poggio Bracciolini (1380–1459)
Historiae Florentini populi (*History of the Florentine people*): covers the period 1350–1455 and, not surprisingly, given the author's humanist creden-tials, is modelled on Sallust (see also 15.5, pp. 178–9).

Leonardo Bruni (*c.* 1374–1444)
Historiae Florentini populi (*History of the Florentine people*), books I–VI written 1415–29, books IX–XII written 1437/38–44, covering the period up to 1404: humanist history inspired principally by Polybius and trans-lated into Italian by Donato Acciauoli (1429–78), grandson of Palla Strozzi. Other works include: *Commentarium rerum gestarum commentarius* (*Commentary on the history of his own times*), 1440–41, and *Laudatio Florentinae urbis* (*Panegyric of the city of Florence*), *c.* 1401.

John Capgrave (1394–1464)
Nova legenda Angliae: chronicle of English history in the vernacular, cover-ing the period to 1417. He also wrote a life of Humphrey, duke of Gloucester, whose client he was.

Georges Chastellain (*c.* 1404/5–1475)
Chronique de choses de ce temps. This Flemish historian of Valois Burgundy wrote in the mould of Froissart.

Philippe de Commynes (Commines) (*c.* 1447–1511)
Mémoires, written 1489–98. Commynes was a Flemish noble who served Charles the Bold until defecting to Louis XI in 1472. Driven from court after Louis' death, he was imprisoned (1487–89), but rehabilitated and accompanied Charles VIII to Italy (1494–95). Commynes is a valuable source because of his experience of high office.

Sigismondo de' Conti (1432–1512)
Historia sui temporis (*History of his own time*) in seventeen books, written 1475–1510. Conti studied with a number of leading humanists and was papal secretary to Sixtus IV, Innocent VIII, Alexander VI and Julius II.

Bernal Diaz del Castillo (1492–*c.* 1576)
Historia verdadera de la conquista de Nueva España (*True history of the con-quest of New Spain*): first-hand account by a man who accompanied Cortes.

Jean Froissart (d. *c.* 1410)
Written between *c.* 1360 and *c.* 1400, Froissart's *Chroniques* provide the classic source for the Anglo-French Hundred Years War. He was a widely travelled cleric who also wrote poetry and romance.

Tito Livio Frulovisi (*c.* 1400–*c.* 1464)
Vita Henrici Quinti, written for Humphrey of Gloucester after 1437, was the first biography of an English subject to be given humanist treatment. Frulovisi was born at Ferrara, educated in Venice with Guarino and in contact with many leading humanists.

Robert Gaguin (*c.* 1423–1501)
Compendium supra Francorum gestis (1497) covers French history from Pharamond to 1491. Gaguin was dean of the faculty of canon law at the University of Paris, General of the Trinitarian Order from 1473, a noted writer of French verse, and translator of Latin works, who also helped Fichet to establish the first Parisian press. He undertook diplomatic missions to Germany, Italy and England for the French crown.

Paolo Giovio (1483–1552)
Historia sui temporis (History of his own time), 1550–52: covers the period 1494–1547, unreliably.

Francesco Guicciardini (*c.* 1483–1540)
Florentine patrician contemporary of Machiavelli, with whose historical work his are frequently compared. *Storie fiorentine* covers the period from 1378 and was written in 1508–9; *Storia d'Italia* evolved from his memoirs, written after 1537, and deals with the period 1494–1532. Although not as devoted to ancient subject matter as Machiavelli, Guicciardini wrote humanist history in the style of Livy. It is in his work, in particular, that one senses the significance of the death of Lorenzo de' Medici (1492), the end of the perceived Italian 'balance of power' and the French invasion of 1494.

Jean Juvenal des Ursins (1388–1472)
Continuator of *Grandes Chroniques de France* to cover the reign of Charles VI.

Niccolò Machiavelli (1469–1527)
Istorie fiorentine (History of Florence), 1520–25: commissioned by Leo X and presented to Clement VII, the Medici popes. As a convinced Florentine republican writing for the Medici, Machiavelli set himself the difficult task of writing a Florentine history which avoids mentioning that family, subverters of republican liberties, as much as possible. Influenced by Livy. For his other works see 15.5, pp. 182–3.

Olivier de la Marche (*c.* 1425–1502)
Mémoires: covers Burgundian history in the period 1435–67.

Andrea Navagero (1483–1527)
Navagero was appointed Venetian state historiographer and librarian (1516), but his history of Venice did not proceed beyond draft; he also held ambassadorial posts.

Il Platina (Bartolomeo Sacchi) (1421–81)
Liber de vita Christi ac omnium pontificum (*Lives of Christ and all the popes*, completed 1474). His birthplace of Piadena, near Mantua, provided this humanist with his literary name. Gonzaga patronage in Mantua preceded his move to Rome in 1462, where he was employed in the College of Abbreviators until Paul II reduced their numbers in 1464. There followed two periods of imprisonment in Castel Sant'Angelo, the second after he was arrested as one of Leto's Academicians (1468). Rehabilitation was confirmed by his appointment as papal librarian (1475–81).

Marcantonio Sabellico (*c.* 1436–1506)
Sabellico wrote the first thirty-two books of a history of Venice (Venice, 1487), and a universal history *Enneades sive rhapsodia historiarum* (Venice, 1498). He taught at the S. Marco School, Venice, and was custodian of what became the Biblioteca Marciana.

Marin Sanudo (1466–1536)
His *Diarii* cover the period 1496 to 1533. This most famous of Venetian diarists also wrote *Le vite dei dogi* (*Lives of the doges*) in the chronicle tradition.

Bartolomeo Scala (1430–97)
Historia Florentinorum (*History of the Florentine people*), *c.* 1480–97. Scala was Florentine chancellor from 1465 (see 7.3.3).

Hartmann Schedel (1440–1558)
Weltchronik (Nuremberg Chronicle, 1493): notable for its woodcut illustrations (see 20.2). Schedel was a Paduan-educated Nuremberg physician and bibliophile.

Polidore Vergil (Polidoro Vergilio) (*c.* 1470–1555)
Anglica Historia: covers the period up to death of Henry VII (1509); written 1512–13, published at Basel in 1534. Vergil was an Urbino-born cleric who travelled to England in 1502 as assistant to the papal collector Adriano Castellesi (*c.* 1461–*c.* 1521). He wrote an *Adagia* (1498) similar to that of Erasmus.

Vespasiano da Bisticci (1421–98)
Le vite d'uomini illustri del secolo XV (*Lives of illustrious men of the fifteenth century*), published in 1839: by a Florence-based bookseller whose customers included Cosimo de' Medici, Federico da Montefeltro, Nicholas V, the Este of Ferrara, Neapolitan royals and the king of Hungary, and whose

biographical subjects were frequently determined by his personal connections with the same.

Jacob Wimpfeling (1450–1528)
Epithoma rerum Germanicarum usque ad nostra tempora (*Epitome of German affairs*, 1505): a patriotic history of Germany to counter Italian taunts about German barbarism. Wimpfeling claimed to be opposed to humanism but was not unaffected by the anticlericalism with which it was associated.

15.5   Profiles of major literary figures

Bessarion (*c.* 1403–72)
Education: With Gemistos Plethon, 1431–36.
Offices: Orthodox delegate to the Council of Ferrara–Florence (1438–39); cardinal of the Roman Church (1439); papal legate to Bologna, the Romagna and the March of Ancona (1450), Germany (1460) and Venice (1462); protector of monastic orders. In papal conclaves he was repeatedly considered *papabile*, likely to be elected, but was passed over as a convert whose loyalty to Rome was doubted.
Works: *In calumniatorem Platonis libri IV* (printed Rome, 1469, but written a decade earlier). A defence of Plato which was part of an ongoing debate about the relative strengths of Plato and Aristotle. Bessarion was accused of incoherence and of making errors of interpretation, though most of the Greek humanists in Italy sided with him.
Other scholarly significance: The cardinal's clients among Greek scholars in Italy included George of Trebizond, Theodore Gaza, Demetrius Chalcondyles and Constantine Lascaris, to whom were added the Italians Pomponio Leto, Flavio Biondo, Platina, Domizio Caldarini and Niccolò Perotti. Bessarion's Roman palace at SS. Apostoli was an important humanist centre in the 1460s. In 1468 he donated his library to the Republic of Venice, but retained the use of it while he lived.

Poggio Bracciolini (1380–1459)
Education: In Arezzo and Florence; Latin skills acquired in Salutati's circle.
Offices: Papal scriptor (1403–17), in which capacity he attended the Council of Constance; returned to papal employment in 1423 after a period in England under the patronage of Cardinal Henry Beaufort.
Works: Dialogues *De avaritia* (*On avarice*, 1428), *De nobilitate* (*On nobility*, 1440), *De infelicitate principum* (*On the unhappiness of princes*, 1440), *De miseria humanae conditionis* (*On the misery of human condition*, 1445), *De varietate fortunae* (*On the vicissitudes of fortune, c.* 1448), *Contra hypocritas* (*Against hypocrites*, 1449), *Historiae Florentini populi* (*History of the Florentine people*, see 15.4).

Other scholarly significance: Scoured Europe's monastic libraries for hitherto lost or better texts of classical authors. In a famous letter he describes his heroic rescue of Quintilian's *De institutione oratia* (*On the education of an orator*) from 'imprisonment' in the monastic library of St Gall. Arranging for the texts to be copied and sold through Florentine book dealers, he ensured that his friends, including Leonardo Bruni and Niccolò Niccoli, were able to fill their private libraries with fine copies of ancient writings. In England (1418–22) under the patronage of Cardinal Beaufort, Poggio was academically frustrated but inspired a number of English scholars with enthusiasm for humanistic studies.

Guillaume Budé (*c.* 1467–1540)
Education: Universities of Paris and Orléans; Greek with Janus Lascaris.
Offices: Secretary to Charles VIII of France; Louis XII's ambassador to Rome (1501, 1505); secretary to Francis I and (first) royal librarian.
Works: Translation of Plutarch from Greek to Latin. *Annotations on the Pandects* (1508) was his passport to humanist renown, in which he attacked medieval commentators and urged readers to study Roman law directly, championing the necessity of philology to do so. Shots were also aimed at the Parlement of Paris and its judges, under-age bishops and worldly clerics. This work gave birth to the French 'legal Renaissance', most famously expressed by Jean Bodin (1530–96) in *The six books of the commonwealth* (1576). Budé's treatise *De asse et partibus ejus* (1514) dealt with ancient coins and demonstrated a profound knowledge of the differences between Greek and Roman civilisation and an analysis of the basic rules of economic life. Also wrote *Commentarii linguae graecae* (1529).
Other scholarly significance: Met Thomas More at the Field of the Cloth of Gold (1520). Thanks to Budé, Francis I established the *lecteurs royaux* in Hebrew, Greek, Latin and mathematics (1530).

Erasmus (Desiderius Erasmus, Erasmus of Rotterdam) (*c.* 1469–1536)
Education: Schools at Gouda, Deventer (Brethren of the Common Life) and Utrecht; theology at Collège de Montaigu, University of Paris, from 1495; doctorate in theology, Turin (1506).
Offices: Ordained priest (1492) after making his profession as an Augustinian Canon at Steyn (*c.* 1488), but was partially dispensed from his vows (1506); imperial councillor (1515).
Works (with dates of publication): *Adagiorum collectanea* (*Adages*, 1500) a collection of proverbs and maxims which Erasmus extracted from classical authors; the 1500 edition contained 838 of them, mainly from Latin sources, though the expanded Aldine edition of 1508 contained 3,260 – to Erasmus they distilled the wisdom of the ancients. Edition of Cicero, *De officiis* (1501); *Enchiridion militis christiani* (*Manual of a Christian knight*, 1503), a devotional manual on how to live the Christian life; edition of

Valla's *Adnotationes Novum Testamentum* (1503); *Epigrammata* (1506), a translation of Lucian undertaken with Thomas More; *Adagiorum Chiliades* (1508); *Moriae Encomium* (*Praise of Folly*, 1511): written for More, it went through thirty-seven Latin editions before 1536; *De ratione studii* (1511); *De copia* (1511); *Julius exclusus* (*c.* 1513), portraying Julius II's frustrated attempt to enter Heaven (during his visit to central Italy Erasmus had become familiar with the activities of this warlike pontiff); *Cato* (1513); *Parabolae* (1513); *De constructione orationis* (1514); *Epistolae* (1515); *Institutio principis christiani* (1515), for the instruction of the future Charles V; commentaries on the Psalms (1515), *Paraclesis* (1516); *Querela pacis* (1516). Edition of the New Testament, *Novum Instrumentum*, with commentary (1516): a Greek text was used to produce this new Latin version, which in turn provided the basis for vernacular translations in French, English, German and other languages. Edition of St Jerome (1516). *Colloquia* (*Colloquies*, 1518): these started out as dialogues in elementary Latin for children, though they contained satire and topical allusions which caught the imagination of adults. *Antibarbari* (1518, but written early in his career): conveys the classic humanist concept of true learning vanquishing barbarian ignorance. *Declamationes* (*Encomium matrimonii* and *Encomium medicinae*, 1518); *Ratio verae theologiae* (1519); *Progymnasmata* (1519); *De conscribendis epistolae* (1520); *De contemptu mundi* (1521); *De immensa Dei misericordia* (1523); *De libero arbitrio* (1524), part of the controversy with Luther over free will; *Exomologesis* (1524); *Lingua* (1525); *De civilitate* (1526); *Institutio Christiani matrimonis* (1526); commentary on Origen (1527); *Ciceronianus* (1528), in which Erasmus is critical of slavish devotion to Ciceronian Latin; *Dialogus de recta Latini Graecique serminis pronuntiatione* (1528); *Paraphrasis in Elegantias L. Vallae* (1529); *De pueris statim ac liberaliter instuendis* (1529); *Vidua christiana* (1529); *Consultatio de bello Turcio* (1530); *Apophthegmata* (1531); *Explanatio symboli apostolorum* (1532); *Liber de Sarcienda Ecclesiae concordia* (1533); *Praeparatione ad mortem* (1534); *Ecclesiastes* (1535); *Precationes* (1535); edition of the works of Origen (1536); *De puritate ecclesiae* (1536). This list does not include the majority of Erasmus's work on the Bible and Fathers of the Church, all of which he edited. His complete works were printed at Basel in 1540.

Other scholarly significance: As tutor to William Blount, Lord Mountjoy, himself the future tutor of Henry VIII, Erasmus's English contacts were established. During visits to England (1499, 1505–6, 1509–14) he met Colet, More and the other humanists of their circle, was introduced to Florentine Neoplatonic thought and lectured at Cambridge (1511–14). Colet persuaded him to turn from classical to theological studies. His Italian travels (1506–9) included a nine-month stay with Aldus Manutius in Venice. The later career of this most distinguished of humanists highlighted the difficulties experienced by his contemporaries in distinguishing between calls for internal reform of the Church, as advocated by the Dutchman, and outright Lutheran rejection of the hierarchy.

Marsilio Ficino (1433–99)

Education: Florentine Studium.

Offices: In holy orders from 1473.

Works: For Cosimo de' Medici, Ficino translated (1463–69) all the dialogues then attributed to Plato, of which only four out of ten were genuine; there followed commentaries on Plato and Plotinus (from 1469); *Theologia Platonica de immortalitate animae* (*Platonic theology concerning the immortality of the soul,* 1469–74); *Pimander* (a Hermetic text, 1471); *De christiana religione* (*Concerning the Christian religion,* c. 1475); *Liber de vita* (*Book of life,* 1489), a work on astrology and white magic which was condemned by the Church. Ficino was also a prolific letter-writer.

Other scholarly significance: Medici patronage continued after the death of Cosimo (1464), though doubt has been cast on the existence of a formal Platonic academy, centred on Ficino, at the Medici villa at Careggi, near Florence. Lefèvre and Colet were among the non-Italians influenced by Ficino's Platonic philosophy. Together with Leon Battista Alberti and Lorenzo de' Medici, he was one of the speakers in the *Disputationes Camaldulenses* of Cristoforo Landino (1424–98), discussing the relative merits of the active and contemplative life.

George of Trebizond (Georgius Trapezuntius) (1395–1472/73)

Education: In his native Crete.

Offices: Taught Greek in Vicenza, Venice and Mantua; in papal service from at least 1444, or even from the time of the Council of Florence (1439); went to Venice in 1458.

Works: *Comparatio philosophorum Aristotelis et Platonis* (1458): this made him the 'calumniator' to whom Bessarion responded with *In calumniatorem Platonis* (1459). Made translations of many Greek authors, Christian and non-Christian, into Latin, some at the invitation of Nicholas V.

Other scholarly significance: Notable for various disputes with fellow scholars, George was so irascible that Nicholas V exiled him and Paul II imprisoned him in Castel Sant'Angelo.

Ulrich von Hutten (1488–1523)

Education: Universities of Cologne, Erfurt, Frankfurt, Leipzig, Greifswald and Bologna (law, 1512); learned Greek.

Works: Composed poetry of sufficient distinction to win praise from Erasmus and the title of poet laureate from Emperor Maximilian (1517). In 1515 he contributed to the pro-Reuchlin volume of *Letters of obscure men,* a devastating satire aimed at the 'obscurantist' theologians of Cologne, who allegedly sought to obstruct the path of humanistic learning. A second volume was more political in nature and critical of the Church, the life of monks and the trade in relics and indulgences. He edited Lorenzo Valla's *On the Donation of Constantine* (1518) and wrote dialogues in which he blamed the Roman Church for destroying German 'virtue' and impeding the progress of learning.

Other scholarly significance: An early supporter of Luther.

Jacques Lefèvre d'Étaples (1450–1537)

Education: University of Paris; studied in Florence with Ficino, in Rome with Ermolao Barbaro and visited Aldus Manutius in Venice; knew Greek.

Offices: Taught at the University of Paris.

Works: From 1490 Lefèvre singlehandedly produced the first thorough humanist edition of the bulk of Aristotle's works, including the *Metaphysics* (printed in 1515), *Nichomachean ethics, Politics, Logic* and *Organon*. In 1509 he turned to Christian texts, publishing the *Quincuplex Psalterium* (*Fivefold Psalter*), a milestone in biblical studies, followed by the translation of and commentary on the Pauline Epistles (1512) and *De Maria Magdalena* (1518). His French translations of the New and Old Testaments were published in 1523 and 1528 respectively (see 15.2). He also edited the Fathers of the Church, Flemish mystics and the principal medieval Christian texts. Many of his works were printed by Henri Estienne.

Other scholarly significance: Lefèvre's interest in Dionysius, the Pseudo-Areopagite (an author then assumed to have been St Paul's first Athenian convert, but actually sixth-century), and in Hermetic writings is explained by the influence of Pico. His biblical and patristic work, highlighting issues such as justification by faith, made Lefèvre an inspiration to the younger ecclesiastical reformers associated with Guillaume II Briçonnet, bishop of Meaux, whose tutor, Josse Clichtove (d. 1543), was a pupil of Lefèvre. Though initially championed by the crown, Lefèvre became the target of persecution by conservatives in the Church, and accordingly moved first to Strasbourg (1525) and then to the court of Marguerite of Navarre at Nérac (1530) (see 12.10).

Niccolò Machiavelli (1469–1527)

Education: School in Florence.

Offices: Florentine civil servant, secretary to the Dieci di Balìa, in which capacity he was responsible for the organisation of the Florentine militia (1506–12), which was created on his initiative, and took part in a number of diplomatic missions to the leading political players of the day. A close associate of Piero Soderini, he was dismissed from office when the Medici returned to Florence in 1512.

Works: *Il principe* (*The Prince*, 1513): portraying statesmen as they are and not as they might be, this is the best-known work of Renaissance political theory and gained its author a posthumous Europe-wide but unjustified reputation as the personification of evil. *Discorsi sopra la prima deca di Tito*

Livio (*Discourses on the First Decade of Livy, c.* 1515–17); *Belfagor* (short story, *c.* 1515–20); stage comedies *Mandragola* (1518) and *Clizia* (*c.* 1524–25); *Arte della Guerra* (*Art of War*, 1519–20); *La Vita di Castruccio Castracani da Lucca* (life of the fourteenth-century Lucchese despot, 1520); *Discorse delle cose fiorentine dopo la morte di Lorenzo* (on recent Florentine history, 1519–20); *Istorie fiorentine* (*History of Florence*: see 15.4); minor works including poetry and government reports.

Other scholarly significance: The return of the Medici to Florence in 1512 and Machiavelli's implication in an anti-Medicean plot led to his enforced retirement at S. Andrea in Percussina, south of Florence, where he had leisure to compose the works on which his reputation is based. A staunch republican, he was also inspired by ancient history without being a humanist in the strictest philological sense. Between 1515 and 1519 he was associated with a group of Florentine intellectuals who met in the Orti Oricellari, gardens belonging to Cosimo Rucellai.

Thomas More (1479–1535, canonised 1934)
Education: University of Oxford (*c.* 1492) where he came under the influence of the New Learning; legal studies in London from 1494; learned Greek in London with Grocyn and Linacre (*c.* 1500–4).
Offices: Elected to Parliament (1504); Under-Sheriff of London (1510); royal councillor (1517); Speaker of the House of Commons (1523); Chancellor of the Duchy of Lancaster (1525); Lord Chancellor after the fall of Wolsey (1529), which post More resigned (1532) in protest against Henry VIII's self-appointed headship of the Church in England. With John Fisher, bishop of Rochester, More refused to take the Oath of Succession, on the grounds that it implied a diminution of papal authority. They were both executed under the 1535 Treason Act, Fisher on 22 June that year, More on 6 July.
Works: *The history of King Richard III*, now accepted as a parody of humanist historiography rather than as the accurate account it was once believed to be; *Lyfe of Johan Picus erle of Mirandula* (*c.* 1510), a translation of Gianfrancesco Pico's biography of his uncle; with Erasmus, translations of Lucian of Samosata from Greek; *Utopia* (1516 in Latin, 1551 in English) (see 23.2, p. 268); devotional works, including *Dialogue of comfort*.
Other scholarly significance: Friendship with Erasmus began in 1499. In 1521 Henry VIII called on him to help with an anti-Lutheran work in defence of the seven sacraments.

Giovanni Pico della Mirandola (1464–94) From the ruling family of the small Lombard territory of Mirandola.
Education: Universities of Ferrara (1479), Padua (1480–82), Florence (1484) and Paris (1485); not actually a pupil of Ficino but generally regarded as close to him in thought.

Works: Publication in Rome of 900 *Conclusiones* (*Theses*), the preface of which is known as *Oratio de dignitate hominis* (*Oration on the dignity of Man*, 1486), in which Pico privileges Christianity but aims to synthesise all known religious belief in the quest for ultimate truth. Papal examination of the *Conclusiones* in 1487 resulted in the condemnation of seven of them as heretical, with another six being declared of doubtful orthodoxy. Pico presented his self-defence in the *Apologia* (1487), but was arrested and briefly imprisoned on Innocent VIII's order (1488), after which he lived in Florence. Other works include *Heptaplus* (1488) which interprets Christian doctrine in the light of the Jewish Cabbala; *De ente et uno* (*On being and the One*, 1492); *Disputationes adversus astrologiam* (*Disputations against astrology*, c. 1493/4).

Other scholarly significance: Thought of as a member of Lorenzo de' Medici's circle in Florence and close associate of the Neoplatonist Ficino, but was also a friend of the Paduan Aristotelian Ermolao Barbaro. He was instrumental in Savonarola being invited to Florence and his work became an important influence on Erasmus and More.

Johannes Reuchlin (1454/55–1522)

Education: Universities of Freiburg im Breisgau, Paris, Basel, Orléans and Tübingen; Greek and Hebrew studies in Germany.

Offices: Lawyer to the duke of Württemberg; judge of the Swabian League (1502–13); taught at the Universities of Ingolstadt (1519) and Tübingen (1521).

Works: Latin comedies, editions of Demosthenes, Hippocrates and Homer, but his chief contribution was as a Hebraicist, particularly with *De rudimentis hebraicis* (1506), a Hebrew grammar, and *De arte cabbalistica* (1517).

Other scholarly significance: He made three trips to Italy as a young man, coming into contact with Pico and Ficino and being greatly impressed by Pico's theses on cabbalistic knowledge and stress on Hebrew studies. He corresponded with Erasmus and entered into a literary feud with Johannes Pfefferkorn (c. 1469–c. 1522), a former Jew who became fervently anti-Jewish: Reuchlin considered it unnecessary to destroy Hebrew works in which Christianity is not slandered and which could be useful for scholarly purposes, but Pfefferkorn's *Der Handspiegel* (1511) attacked him and led to Reuchlin's supporters compiling *Epistolae obscurum vivorum* (*Letters of obscure men*, 1515–17), of which Johannes Crotus Rhubianus and Ulrich von Hutten were the main authors, directing their ire against the Dominican theologians of the University of Cologne. Reuchlin was summoned to appear before the Inquisition and the tract he wrote in his own defence was denounced as heretical by Leo X. Although not a supporter of the Reformation, he had some sympathy with Luther's protest.

Alfonso de Valdés (*c.* 1490–1532)

Education: Possibly with Pietro Martire d'Anghiera.

Offices: Secretary to the imperial Chancellor Gattinara and to Charles V; mediator at the Diet of Augsburg (1530).

Works: *Diálogo de las cosas ocurridas en Roma* (*Dialogue on the things occurring at Rome*, 1530), an anonymously published defence of the 1527 Sack of Rome by the armies of Charles V, presenting it as God's judgement on the papacy and on all churchmen for their belligerency and corruption, and for ignoring warnings of men like Erasmus; *Diálogo de Murcurio y Carón* (1528).

Other scholarly significance: Valdés was of *converso* origin. He took part in the 1527 Valladolid debate between Erasmians and their Dominican adversaries. His brother Juan de Valdés (*c.* 1491–1541), author of *Diálogo de doctrina cristiana* (*Dialogue on Christian doctrine*), was one of Spain's leading Erasmians, but accepted Lutheran teachings, principally justification by faith, and was also in contact with mystical *alumbrados*. Fleeing from a heresy trial, Juan went into religious exile in Italy in 1531.

Lorenzo Valla (1407–57)

Education: In his native Rome; self-taught knowledge of Latin.

Offices: Taught at Padua (1431–33), then privately in Milan; to Genoa (1434–35); in the service of Alfonso of Naples (from 1435); to Rome 1448; apostolic secretary (from 1455).

Works: *De voluptate* (*On pleasure*, 1431), later known as *De vero falsoque bono* (*On the true and the false good*); *De falso credita et ementita Constantini donatione* (*On the donation of Constantine*, 1440), revealing his discovery that the document which supposedly gave the pope extensive dominion in western Christendom was an eighth-century forgery; *De libero arbitrio* (*On free will*, *c.* 1440); *Dialecticae disputationes*; the extremely influential *Elegantiarum linguae latinae* (*On the elegancies of the Latin tongue*, completed in 1440, printed in Rome, 1471); *Adnotationes in Novum Testamentum* (or *Collatio Novi Testamenti*, 1443/44), the 1505 printing of which was made at the instigation of Erasmus and which applied the new philology to the Vulgate, foreshadowing Erasmus's own achievements.

Other scholarly significance: Invited to work in Rome by the humanist pope Nicholas V.

16 Libraries

This list is not intended to represent the largest libraries of the time, but rather interesting cases of public, semi-public and private collections, which in turn enable patterns of scholarship and patronage to be traced. Private collections dominate the list, since the initiative in book collecting came from individuals rather than institutions, with many university libraries augmented by the bequest of private libraries.

Date	Collector	Location	Number of volumes/ manuscripts, some estimated, others based on detailed catalogues
1406	Coluccio Salutati	Florence	*c.* 800: a reflection of Salutati's place in the Florentine classical revival
1407	Gonzaga family	Mantua	*c.* 300, Latin
1411	French royal library	Paris	941, based on the collection of the bibliophile king Charles V (d. 1380)
1416	Jean, duke of Berry	Paris	297, including the books of hours for which this connoisseur is best known. The collection also reflects Berry's genuine interest in classical scholarship
1418	Cosimo de' Medici	Florence	*c.* 65, mostly Latin, some vernacular
1420	Philip the Good, duke of Burgundy	Brussels	*c.* 250, a figure quadrupled by the duke's death in 1467
1424	French royal library	Paris	843, a reduced figure reflecting the adverse fortunes of war, including the sale of some of Charles V's collection to John, duke of Bedford

Date	Collector	Location	Number of volumes/ manuscripts, some estimated, others based on detailed catalogues
c. 1425	Antonio Corbinelli	Florence	173 Latin, 64 Greek: Corbinelli was one of the bibliophiles in the circle of Poggio Bracciolini and Niccolò Niccoli
1426	Visconti family of Milan	Pavia	998, including 4 Greek manuscripts
1433	Amplonius Ratingk	Erfurt	637, bequeathed to the college founded by this former rector of the university
1436	Niccolò Niccoli	Florence	Over 800, which were bequeathed to the Dominican convent of S. Marco, Florence, but held by Cosimo de' Medici until Michelozzo's library at S. Marco was ready to receive them in 1444
1436	Niccolò III d'Este	Ferrara	279, including 1 Greek manuscript
1439	Cardinal Giordano Orsini	Rome	254: Orsini was a contact of Poggio Bracciolini and other bibliophiles
1439	Humphrey, duke of Gloucester	Oxford	129, donated to the University of Oxford; followed by a further 16 in 1441 and 134 in 1444; the building designed to house them was not completed until 1488
c. 1440	Emperor Frederick III	Vienna	Foundation of the Imperial Library
1443	Eugenius IV	Rome	338, Latin
1455	Nicholas V	Rome	807 Latin and c. 414 Greek: a reflection of this pope's genuine humanist interests
1456	Cosimo de' Medici	Florence	158

Date	Collector	Location	Number of volumes/ manuscripts, some estimated, others based on detailed catalogues
1468	Cardinal Bessarion	Rome	482 Greek, 264 Latin, at the time of the donation of his library to the Republic of Venice
1472	Cardinal Bessarion	Rome	c. 1,000, at the time of his death. The books arrived in Venice at various dates between 1469 and 1474 but may not have been housed in Jacopo Sansovino's purpose-built Biblioteca Marciana until 1565
c. 1482	Federico da Montefeltro, duke of Urbino	Urbino	772, including 93 Greek, though higher total estimates have been made. The date of Federico's death is given here. Purchases from the Florentine bookseller Vespasiano da Bisticci formed a substantial proportion of this collection
c. 1490	Matthias Corvinus, king of Hungary	Buda	Estimates vary, with c. 2,500 at the higher end of the range
1494	Medici family	Florence	A minimum of 971, of which approximately half were Greek
1495	Ercole I d'Este, duke of Ferrara	Ferrara	512, including 2 Greek
1518	Francis I, king of France	Blois	1,626, including 41 Greek, 2 Hebrew and 2 Arabic. The king's library was moved from Blois to Fontainebleau in 1544, at which time the Blois collection contained 1,894 volumes, including 109 printed books

Date	Collector	Location	Number of volumes/ manuscripts, some estimated, others based on detailed catalogues
1523	Cardinal Domenico Grimani	Venice	*c.* 15,000, including the library of Giovanni Pico, bought by Cardinal Grimani in 1498, which consisted of 1,190 items, including many works of Hebrew scholarship
1524	Niccolò Leoniceno	Ferrara	*c.* 117 Greek volumes, with emphasis on scientific and medical works: probably the largest such collection of the day

17 Printing

17.1 Dates of foundation of printing presses in fifteenth-century Europe

Bohemia and Moravia

1470s Pilsen
1480s Bratislava (Pressburg/Pozsony), Brno, Kuttenberg, Prague, Vimperk (Winterberg)
1490s Olomouc (Olmütz)

England

1470s Oxford, Westminster
1480s London, St Albans

French-speaking regions (excluding Swiss Cantons)

1470s Albi, Angers, Chablis, Lyon, Paris, Poitiers, Toulouse, Vienne
1480s Abbeville, Besançon, Bréhan-Loudéac, Caen, Chambéry, Chartres, Embrun, Lantenac, Moûtiers en Tarantaise, Rennes, Rouen, Salins-les-Bains, Tréguier, Troyes
1490s Angoulême, Avignon, Cluny, Dijon, Dôle, Grenoble, Groupillières, Limoges, Mâcon, Nantes, Narbonne, Orléans, Périgueux, Provins, Tours, Uzès, Valence

German-speaking regions (excluding Swiss Cantons)

1450s Mainz, Strassburg (Strasbourg)
1460s Augsburg, Bamberg, Cologne, Eltville
1470s Blaubeuren, Breslau, Erfurt, Esslingen, Lauingen, Lübeck, Magdeburg, Marienthal im Rheingau, Merseburg, Nuremberg, Reutlingen, Rostock, Schussenried, Speyer, Ulm, Urach, Würzburg
1480s Dillingen, Eichstätt, Freising, Hagenau, Heidelberg, Ingolstadt, Kirchheim, Leipzig, Meissen, Memmingen, Metz, Munich, Münster, Passau, Regensburg (Ratisbon), Schleswig, Stendal, Stuttgart, Trier, Vienna, Zweibrücken

1490s   Danzig, Freiberg in Sachsen, Freiburg im Breisgau, Hamburg,
        Lüneburg, Marienburg, Offenburg, Pforzheim, Tübingen, Zinna

Hungary

1473   Buda

Italy

1460s   Rome, Subiaco, Venice
1470s   Ascoli Piceno, Bologna, Brescia, Cagli, Caselle, Colle di Val d'Elsa,
        Como, Cosenza, Cremona, Faenza, Ferrara, Fivizzano, Florence,
        Foligno, Genoa, Jesi, Lucca, Mantua, Matelica, Messaga, Messina,
        Milan, Modena, Mondovì, Naples, Padua, Palermo, Parma, Pavia,
        Perugia, Piacenza, Pieve di Sacco, Pinarolo, Pogliano, Reggio
        Calabria, Sant'Orso, Savigliano, Savona, Torre Belvicino, Tos-
        colano, Trento, Trevi, Treviso, Turin, Verona, Vicenza, Viterbo
1480s   Aquila, Capua, Casale, Casalmaggiore, Chivasso, Cividale del
        Friuli, Gaeta, Nonantola, Novi Ligure, Pescia, Pisa, Portese, Reggio
        Emilia, Saluzzo, San Germano, Siena, Soncino, Udine, Vercelli,
        Voghera
1490s   Barco, Cagliari, Cesena, Forlì, Nozzano, San Cesario, Scandiano,
        Urbino

Low Countries

1460s   Utrecht
1470s   Alost, Bruges, Brussels, Delft, Deventer, Gouda, Louvain,
        Nijmegen, Sint Maartensdijk, Zwolle
1480s   Antwerp, Ghent, Haarlem, Hasselt, 's Hertogenbosch, Kulienburg,
        Leiden, Oudenaarde
1490s   Schiedam, Schoonhaven

Montenegro

1490s   Cetinje

Poland

1474   Cracow

Portugal

1480s   Faro, Lisbon
1490s   Braga, Leiria, Oporto

Scandinavia

1480s   Odense, Stockholm
1490s   Copenhagen, Gripsholm (Mariefred monastery), Vadstena

Spain

1470s   Barcelona, Lérida, Segovia, Seville, Tortosa, Valencia, Zaragoza
         (Saragossa)
1480s   Burgos, Coria, Gerona, Guadalajara, Híjar, Huete, Mallorca,
         Murcia, Pamplona, Salamanca, San Cucufate (San Cugat), San-
         tiago de Compostela, Tarragona, Toledo, Valladolid, Zamora
1490s   Granada, Monterrey, Montserrat

Swiss Cantons

1470s   Basel, Beromünster, Burgdorf, Constance, Geneva, Zürich
1480s   Promenthoux, Rougemont
1490s   Lausanne

Adapted from C. Clair, *A History of European Printing* (London, 1976),
pp. 431–6. In cases of doubt, the earlier date is given.

17.2   Chronology of early printing

1430s–1440s   Printing with moveable type developed by Mainz goldsmith **Johann Gutenberg** (*c.* 1399–1468). A simple screw
press was adapted from those used for pressing cheese or
grapes. Type metal was made from an amalgam of lead,
tin and antimony. The printing of single-sheet indulgences
often preceded larger works in the output of the early
presses. Mainz was the first centre of this new industry.

c. 1448–55   Gutenberg's 42-line Bible or Mazarin Bible, printed in
two volumes, with a total of 643 two-column folios. Of
thirty-five copies printed on vellum and 165 on paper,
only forty-eight are now known. Gutenberg's press was
established with the aid of a loan from Johann Fust.
Inability to repay resulted in Gutenberg's bankruptcy in
1458 and to his firm being taken over by Fust and the
latter's son-in-law Peter Schöffer, Gutenberg's foreman.

1457   Mainz Psalter printed by Fust and Schöffer.

c. 1459   Anonymously printed 36-line Bible of 884 two-column
folios.

1462	Schöffer's 48-line Bible printed at Mainz, in the same year as a rebellion by the burghers of Mainz against their archbishop, Adolph von Nassau, resulted in the city's sack by the archbishop's troops. An important consequence was that printers took their skills elsewhere.
1465	Germans **Konrad Sweynheim** and **Arnold Pannartz** began printing at Subiaco, east of Rome, their first publication being Cicero, *De oratore*. In 1467 their press was transferred to Rome, where the humanist bishop and papal librarian Giovanni Andrea Bussi (1417–75) was closely involved with their work. Giovanni Antonio Campano (1429–77), another bishop, edited texts for the printers Ulrich Hahn and Giovanni Filippo Lignamine during the early years of Roman printing.
1469	Printing began in Venice, which rapidly became the print capital of Europe. The first generation of Venetian printers included the Germans Johann and Windelin of Speyer, and the Frenchman Nicolas Jenson.
1470	**Johan Heynlin** began printing in Paris with the collaboration of the humanist rector of the university, Guillaume Fichet, their first publication being Gasparino Barzizza, *Epistolarum libri*. Another early publication was Lorenzo Valla's *De elegantiarum linguae latinae* (1471). In 1472 Fichet gave up both his academic career and printing to devote himself to the crusading cause.
1471–72	First major printed book with woodcut illustrations, *Legenda aurea* (*Golden legend*: saints' lives) of Jacobus de Voragine, printed by Günther Zainer in Augsburg.
1472	Johann Neumeister of Mainz printed the first edition of Dante, *La divina commedia*, at Foligno.
c. **1475**	First Hebrew works published.
1476	**William Caxton** (*c.* 1420/24–*c.* 1491) established the first English press, in the precincts of Westminster Abbey. He had previously been head of the English merchant community in Bruges, where he enjoyed the patronage of Margaret of York, duchess of Burgundy, and learned printing in Cologne. His English patrons included Edward IV's brother-in-law, Anthony Woodville, and Henry VII's mother, Lady Margaret Beaufort (1443–1509), otherwise distinguished as an educational benefactor. Among Caxton's most notable publications were Chaucer's *Canterbury Tales* (1478) and Sir Thomas Malory's *Morte d'Arthur* (issued as *King Arthur*, 1485).

1491   **Johann Froben** (c.1460–1527) began printing in Basel the
year after he moved there from Nuremberg, and went on
to achieve renown as a close associate of Erasmus and
printer of his works. His firm remained in business until
1603.

c. **1491**   Fleming **Wynkyn de Worde** (d. 1535) took over Caxton's
press at Westminster.

1493   Copiously illustrated Nuremberg Chronicle (*Weltchronik*),
a particularly impressive history of the world, written by
Hartmann Schedel with woodcuts by Michael Wolgemut
and Wilhelm Pleydenwurff (son of Hans; see p. 225),
printed by Anton Koberger (1440–1513) (see also 20.2
and 15.4).

1495   **Aldo Manuzio** (*c.* 1452–1515; Latinised as Aldus Manutius),
who had previously acted as tutor to members of the Pio
family at Carpi, together with his future father-in-law
Andrea Torresani, began printing in Venice, establishing
a reputation for producing Latin and Greek classical texts
to a high standard of scholarship and production. Between
1495 and 1515 the Aldine press, at the sign of the
dolphin and anchor, produced 126 editions, including ninety-four first editions of classical or post-classical
Greek authors, together with many Latin works and a
small number in Italian. Erasmus was the most eminent
of the humanist scholars associated with the Aldine press
in authorial or editorial capacities, others including
Girolamo Aleandro (1480–1542), better known for his
1520 mission to Germany to enforce the anti-Lutheran
Bull *Exsurge Domine*, together with the Greeks Janus
Lascaris and Marcus Musurus, and the Venetian Andrea
Navagero.

1499   *Hypnerotomachia Polifili* (*The erotic dream of Polyphilus*) by
Francesco Colonna (*c.* 1433–1527) printed at Venice by
the Aldine press with *c.* 168 striking woodcut illustrations
by an anonymous artist.

1501   Francesco Griffo's cursive (italic) type first used by the
Aldine press.

1501   **Ottaviano Petrucci** (1466–1539) revolutionised music
publishing with *Harmonice musices Odhecaton A*, a collection
of polyphonic music containing seventy-five French songs,
five Italian and thirteen others, printed in Venice in a
three-stage process, printing first staves, then notes and
finally text. This was followed by *Canti B* and *Canti C*
(Venice, 1502–3).

1502	Henri Estienne (1460–1520) began printing in Paris. His son Robert (1503–59) went on to become printer to Francis I, but went into exile for his Protestant allegiance and continued printing at Geneva.
1514–17	Complutensian Polyglot Bible printed at Alcalá under the aegis of Cardinal Cisneros, but not published until 1520.
1515	Death of Aldus Manutius, whose business was continued by members of his family.
1521	**Johann Siberch** of Cologne became the first printer to Cambridge University.
1530	**Geofroy Tory** (c. 1480–1533), grammarian and printer, appointed *Imprimeur du roi* to Francis I.

17.3   Selected glossary of terms relating to early printing

fount/font   A complete cut set of upper and lower case letters, accented letters, ligatures, numbers, symbols and punctuation.

incunable/incunabulum (pl. incunabula)   From Latin *cunae* = 'cradle', so refers to printed books in their infancy, that is before 1500.

typeface   The design of all early typefaces was based on handwriting, so that printed books could resemble manuscripts. Since printing originated in Germany, the earliest typefaces were based on German hands, known as Gothic, black letter or textura. Germans Konrad Sweynheim and Arnold Pannartz, working in Italy, cut the first roman type, based on ninth-century Carolingian script. Nicolas Jenson's roman type of 1470 has been particularly influential. The first cursive or italic type was designed by Francesco Griffo for the Aldine press in Venice in 1501.

17.4   Censorship of printed books: a chronology

1479	Sixtus IV commissioned the University of Cologne to impose ecclesiastical penalties upon anyone printing, selling or reading heretical texts.
1480	Specific publications approved by the Church in Venice.
1486	Archbishop of Mainz prohibited the printing in his diocese of any works not authorised by the University of Erfurt.
1487	Bull of Innocent VIII to the University of Cologne is considered to be the first general instruction on printing issued by the papacy.
1491	*Constitution* of Niccolò Franco, papal legate to Venice, was the first printed ecclesiastical statute concerning censorship and the earliest proscription of printed books.

1501   Bull *Inter multiplices* issued by Alexander VI to the archbishop of Magdeburg, outlining both the positive and the harmful implications of printing.

1512   A heretic and his books burned by the Inquisition in The Hague.

1513   *Constitution* of Leo X, warning against the misuse of classical studies, had implications for printed works. Reuchlin's *Der Augenspiegel* (1511) condemned as heretical by the universities of Louvain, Cologne, Mainz and Erfurt; his works ultimately appeared in an Index of prohibited books.

1515   Archbishop of Mainz appointed a 'commissary' to examine and censor books proposed for printing privileges. Bull *Inter solicitudines*, according to which no works could be printed without permission from the papal Vicar or Master of the Sacred Palace in Rome or from bishops or Inquisitors-General elsewhere. This created the model for future press regulation.

1517   Leo X condemned *Letters of obscure men*, written in defence of Reuchlin (see 15.5).

1518   Some works of Erasmus had been placed on the Index by this date, and his *Colloquia* was condemned by the Sorbonne.

1519   University of Louvain issued an edict condemning all Luther's works.

1520   A tribunal of cardinals confirmed the condemnation of Reuchlin's works of Hebrew scholarship. Luther's works condemned by the University of Cologne; his excommunication in the same year included a condemnation by the papacy of all his works.

c. **1520**   *Directorium inquisitorium*, a list of heretical works, published in Venice.

1521   Francis I decreed that all books printed in France had to have prior licence from the University of Paris. The Edict of Worms marked a new unity of purpose between the ecclesiastical and secular authorities in their condemnation of heretical works. First prohibition of Lutheran works in England. Brief from Leo X to the Spanish government ordering measures to be taken against the importation of Lutheran literature. Luther's works condemned by the Sorbonne.

1522   Charles V appointed an Inquisitor in the Low Countries. Adrian of Utrecht, shortly before his election to the papacy, called for the destruction of all heretical works in Spain.

1523   Diet of Nuremberg confirmed the Edict of Worms, including measures on the censorship of printing.

1524   In the Low Countries the confiscation of goods and corporal punishment was decreed for association with heretical books.

1525   Condemnation by the Sorbonne of works by Erasmus.

1526   Henry VIII's 'Index', condemning the works of Luther, Zwingli and Brenz.

1528   Provincial Council of the Church, held at Sens, issued a decree forbidding the possession of Lutheran works in France; similar decreed at Bourges.

1529   In England, Henry VIII's second catalogue of prohibited works listed eighty-five titles, including works by Luther, Wycliffe and Zwingli. In the Low Countries, the death penalty was instituted for association with heretical books.

1530   In England, the reading of Scripture in the vernacular was forbidden, together with the importation, sale or possession of any books containing heretical doctrines or threats to the rule of the king and of law. In France, inquisitors of literature were appointed. The 1521 regulations in Spain were confirmed and tightened by the Inquisitor-General. Further censorship of the press was announced by the Diet of Augsburg.

17.5   Typefaces

Samples taken from incunables:

Gutenberg, 42-line Bible (Luke 1: 28–38)
Source: V. Scholderer, *Johann Gutenberg: the Inventor of Printing*, (London, 1970), plate V.

multa fagaciores acutioresq; fint: Nam de Aegyptiis quidé nefcio qd
dicere oporteat: bæluas enim & ferpétes & uiuos & mortuos uenerant.
Hæc igitur ifpiciés diuinus ille uir mœnibus ferreis & iuiolabili uallo
a cæteris gétibus fepare nos uoluit: quo pacto facilius corpore atq; aio
imaculatos lōgeq; ab huiufcemodi falfis opinioíbus remotos fore uide-
bat: ut folū uerū deum præter cæteras gentes adorantes illi folūmodo
inhæreamus. Vnde factūm eft ut a nōnullis ægyptiorum facerdotibus
qui difciplinam noftram altius cōfiderarunt dei homines gens noftra
fit appellata: quod nemini nifi deū uerū colat accidere poteft. Nec id
iniuria: reliquis enim cibo potui ueftituiq; inhiantibus noftri omibus
iftis contemptis per totam uitam de omnipotétia dei cogitant. Ne igit
conuerfatione atq; confuetudine aliorum corrupti ad ipietaté eorum
deferamur: cibi & potus tactus & auditus atque uifionis purificatione
legali nos a cæteris feparauit. Cuncta enim ab una potentia oipotentis

Jenson, roman type
Source: M. Lowry, *The World of Aldus Manutius*, (Oxford, 1979), p. 39.

yn eupæncæs Wryton in olæ englyffhe foz to reduce it in to
our englyffhe noW Bfid/ And certaynly it Was Wreton in
fuche Wyfe that it Was more lyke to dutche than englyffhe
J coux not reduce ne Brynge it to be Bnærftonæn/ And certaynly our langage noW Bfed Baryeth ferre from that. Whi
che Was Bfed and fpoken Whan J Was borne/ For We englyffhe men/ ben borne Bnær the compnacyon of the mone.
Whiche is neuer fteðfafte/ But euer Waueryngæ/Weyyngæ o-
ne feafon/ and Waneth & opfcreafeth another feafon/ And
that compn englyffhe that is fpoken in one fhyre Baryeth
from a nother. Jn fo moche that in my dayes happened that

Caxton, type 6
Source: Caxton's own prologue to *Eneydos* (1490)

T elephus?aut summi plena iam margine libri
S criptus, et in tergo nec dum finitus, Orestes?
N ota magis nulli domus est sua, quam mihi lucus
M artis, et æoliis uicinum rupibus antrum
V ulcani · Quid agant uenti, quas torqueat umbras
A eacus, unde alius furtiuæ deuehat aurum
P elliculæ, quantas iaculetur Monychus ornos,
F rontonis platani, conuulsáq; marmora clamant
S emper, et assiduo ruptæ lectore columnæ ·
E xpectes eadem a summo, minimóq; poeta ·

Aldine italic, cut by Francesco Griffo (1501)
Source: M. Lowry, *The World of Aldus Manutius* (Oxford, 1979), p. 139.

18 Science

18.1 The essence of Renaissance science distilled

As in the medieval period, western Christendom's scientific appreciation of Nature and its laws still derived in many respects from works written in the Roman, Greek and Hellenistic worlds, the last often mediated by Islamic scholars. Aristotle's scientific thought was widely known thanks to his centrality in university syllabuses. Appreciation of geometry and optics derived from Euclid (fl. *c.* 300BC), Archimedes (*c.* 287–212BC) provided the foundations for the study of physics, while Pythagoras (fl. *c.* 530BC) meshed the study of mathematics with mysticism, and was, in consequence, a particularly significant source of inspiration throughout the Renaissance period. Hippocrates (*c.* 460–*c.* 377BC) and Galen (*c.* AD130–*c.* 200) were the great medical authorities. The second-century astronomer Claudius Ptolemy of Alexandria was among those who provided scientists and explorers with an appreciation of the globe, the inhabitants of which were accounted for by the Elder Pliny (AD23–70) in his immensely influential *Historia naturalis* (see 23.2).

During the fifteenth and early sixteenth centuries significant developments were made in many branches of scientific study, but number symbolism still featured prominently in mathematical thought, astronomy was not yet divorced from astrology, nor modern chemistry from alchemy. Above all, the arts and science syllabuses had yet to be divided, so that overlaps may be found in areas such as the study of optics and linear perspective, for the application of which in the visual arts see 20.1, 20.4 and 21, p. 244.

18.1.1 Magic squares

At a simple level the mystical aspects of Renaissance mathematics can be demonstrated by magic squares, in which numbers in lines, columns and the longest diagonals add up to the same total. This one appears in Dürer's engraving *Melancholia I* (1514):

16	3	2	13
5	10	11	8
9	6	7	12
4	15	14	1

18.1.2 Golden Section

Harmony between the arts and sciences, a product of the university curriculum, also reflected Neoplatonic emphasis on the harmony of the heavenly spheres. Harmonious proportion, one of the most characteristic features of Renaissance mathematics, was the subject of Fra Luca Pacioli's *De divina proportione* (Venice, 1509). According to Pacioli, the most perfect proportion, as useful for artists as for type designers, is that in which the ratio of the smaller part (A–B) to the larger part (B–C) is the same as the ratio between the larger (B–C) and the whole (A–C):

A   B   C

This is known as the Golden Section, Golden Mean or Golden Ratio. The ratio in question is irrational but roughly 8:13. Pacioli emphasised its spiritual significance as a reflection of the Holy Trinity, Three-in-One.

18.2 Scientific chronology

Pre-1439   Distinguished physician **Ugo Benzi** (or Benci, 1376–1439) wrote commentaries on Avicenna, Galen and Hippocrates, as well as treatises on practical medicine.

1475   **Regiomontanus** (originally Johann Müller, 1436–76) published *Tabulae directionum* (*Table of directions*) on trigonometry: this mathematician and astronomer, educated at Leipzig and Vienna, was involved in the proposed reform of the calendar.

1489   **Marsilio Ficino** (1433–99) published *Liber di vita* (*Book of life*), of which the third, *De vita coelitus comparanda* (*On the life to be obtained from the heavens*), deals with connections between astrology and medicine, and attracted much notoriety. Ficino was both a priest and a physician.

1492   **Niccolò Leoniceno** (1428–1524) published *De Plinii et aliorum erroribus in medicina* (*On the errors of Pliny and other doctors in medicine*) at Ferrara, where he taught at the university and collected an extensive medical library.

1493   **Giovanni Pico della Mirandola** (1463–93), *Disputationes adversus astrologiam divinatricem* (*Disputations against astrology*) compiled at the end of his life, but published in 1496.

1494   **Luca Pacioli** (*c.* 1445–1517), *Summa de arithmetica, geometrica, proportioni et proportionalita*, which includes the best-known account of double-entry book-keeping, was published in Venice (see 10.5). The author was a wandering Franciscan scholar from Sansepolcro who, at various times, taught mathematics at Perugia, Naples, Rome, Florence and Bologna.

1509   **Luca Pacioli**, *De divina proportione*, illustrated by Leonardo da Vinci and published in Venice. Covering mathematical and artistic proportion, it is clearly based on the then unpublished theoretical works of Piero della Francesca (1410–92), *De prospettiva pingendi* (*On linear perspective in painting*) and *De quinque corporibus regularibus* (*On the five regular bodies*) (see 20.5). Piero also wrote *De abaco*, a treatise on mathematics. By this date, Leonardo (1452–1519) had devoted decades to various forms of scientific study, particularly anatomy, but also technology, mechanics, mathematics and geology, though his work long remained unpublished.

1513   **Eucharius Rösslin** (d. 1536), *Rosengarten* (*A garden of roses for pregnant women and midwives*): mostly derived from ancient and medieval authorities.

1518   **Thomas Linacre** (*c.* 1460–1524) founded the College of Physicians in London. This became the Royal College of Physicians. For further biographical information, see 14.4.

1521   **Francesco Maurolico** (1494–1575), *Photismi de lumine et umbra* (published in 1611): a study of various phenomena including rainbows, vision, lenses and photometry, by a multi-talented Sicilian.

1521   From this year the Ferrarese **Giovanni Manardo** (1462–1535) published his *Epistolae medicinales*. Manardo's distinctive contribution to medical study was to separate medicine from astrology while recognising astronomy as an entirely distinct branch of research. In the course of his career he helped to edit the works of Giovanni Pico della Mirandola, served as royal physician in Hungary, travelled in Austria and Poland, and succeeded his master Leoniceno as professor of medicine at Padua in 1524. From Leoniceno he inherited the Galenic tradition, but combined this with alternative approaches.

1522   **Giacomo Berengario da Carpi** (*c.* 1460–*c.* 1530), *Isagogue breves* . . . : an anatomical work published in Bologna where its author practised and lectured in surgery.

1530   **Girolamo Fracastoro** (*c.* 1478–1553), poem *Syphilis sive morbus gallicus* (*Syphilis, or the French pox*): Veronese physician writing on the disease that first appeared in Italy in 1495 and may have arrived in Europe from the New World, in exchange for the various Old World diseases to which the Amerindians had no immunity. Fracastoro later published important research on the spread of disease, *De contagione et contagionis morbis* (*On contagion and contagious diseases*, 1546).

1530   **Theophrastus Paracelsus** (originally von Hohenheim, 1493–1541) completed his *Volumen paramirum* on the cause and nature of disease. This Ferrarese-educated professor of medicine at Basel rejected many features of traditional medicine and used chemically prepared drugs rather than herbal remedies.

1543   **Nicolaus Copernicus** (1473–1543), *De revolutionibus orbium coelestium* (*Concerning the revolutions of the heavenly spheres*): the controversial work in which this Polish scholar expressed his rejection of the Ptolemaic system in favour of a sun-centred universe.

1543   **Andreas Vesalius** (1514–64), *De humani corporis fabrica* (*On the fabric of the human body*): an extremely influential and strikingly illustrated anatomical text by the most notable medical authority of the day, whose teaching at Padua emphasised hands-on experience.

1543   First edition of Euclid's *Elements* printed at Venice in the translation of **Niccolò Tartaglia** (1499/1500–57), a mathematician who also made an important contribution to the study of ballistics.

1545   Tartaglia's rival **Girolamo Cardano** (1501–76) published his greatest mathematical work, *Artis magnae sive de regulis algebraicis liber unus.* Cardano was also a medical practitioner.

19 Music and musicians

19.1 Music

Mass settings, motets and other pieces of liturgical music form the majority of works surviving from the fifteenth and early sixteenth centuries. This reflects the fact that musicians were more likely to find employment with the Church than elsewhere. One interesting feature to trace in the Mass settings of this period is the use of the French folk-song *L'homme armé* ('The armed man') as the melody in what are polyphonic compositions.

There is also ample evidence of secular music-making in both courtly and urban environments. Dance and vocal music formed a central part of multi-media court entertainments. Many secular vocal compositions of the period are known as *chansons* or *frottole* (sing. *frottola*), both of which were essentially simpler versions of the technically complex madrigals so characteristic of the sixteenth century.

Two of the most notable features of musical life in this period were the excellence of Franco-Flemish composers, many of whom found work in Italy, and the influence of particular patrons, such as the Este dukes of Ferrara. Both points are illustrated in the biographical profiles below.

19.2 Musicians

Alexander Agricola (*c.* 1446–1506): Flemish composer active in France, Milan, Florence, Naples and Spain. Died in Spain shortly after travelling there with Philip the Fair and Juana of Castile.

Gilles Binchois (*c.* 1400–60): Renowned Franco-Flemish organist and composer of sacred and secular works. Client of Philip the Good in the 1420s.

Antoine Brumel (*c.* 1460–*c.* 1520): Franco-Flemish composer mainly of sacred music, based at Geneva (1486–92), Chartres (1493–96), Laon (1497), Paris (1498–1500), the Savoyard capital Chambéry (1501–2) and at the Ferrarese court (1506–9). Esteemed as second only to Josquin Després in his day.

Antoine Busnois (*c.* 1430–92): Franco-Flemish composer, possibly a pupil of Ockeghem and certainly in the service of Charles the Bold and his daughter Mary of Burgundy, after whose death (1482) he was based in Bruges.

Loyset Compère (*c.* 1445–1518): Franco-Flemish composer, possibly a pupil of Ockeghem, active at the Sforza court in Milan (1474–76), but who received French nationality (1494) and attended Charles VIII in Italy (1494–95). A prolific composer, though few of his works survive.

William Cornysh (Cornish) (*c.* 1460–1523): English composer whose work for the royal court included supervising music at the Field of the Cloth of Gold (1520). A member of the Chapel Royal from 1496 and Master of Children of the Chapel Royal (1509–23).

Guillaume Dufay (Du Fay) (1397–1474): Acclaimed Franco-Flemish composer who found fame in Italy. In Rome by 1428, where he sang in the papal choir and remained until Eugenius IV transferred his court to Florence. Allegedly, he wrote a motet for the dedication of Brunelleschi's dome (1436), but this has been disputed. Returned to his home town of Cambrai by 1439, thereafter dividing his time between the Low Countries and Savoy. Wrote the earliest known Requiem Mass setting.

John Dunstaple (Dunstable) (*c.* 1390–1453): English composer influenced by Dufay and Binchois. Enjoyed both a European reputation and the patronage of Henry V's brothers John, duke of Bedford, and Humphrey, duke of Gloucester.

Juan del Encina (1468–*c.* 1530): Spanish composer, poet and playwright who, as a result of the patronage of Alexander VI, divided his time between Spain and Rome (see also 15.3, p. 173).

Robert Fayrfax (1464–1521): English composer and organist who sang in the Chapel Royal from 1496 and received the first doctorate in music awarded by the University of Oxford (1511).

Costanzo Festa (*c.* 1490–1545): Piedmontese composer who achieved musical eminence in Italy at a time when the leading practitioners there were north Europeans. He sang in the papal choir for twenty-eight years and his setting of the *Te Deum* is still sung at papal elections.

Francesco Gaffuri (Gaffurio) (1451–1522): Lombard musical theorist best known for his *Practica musicae* (Milan, 1496).

Nicolas Gombert (*c.* 1500–*c.* 1560): Prolific Flemish composer of both sacred and secular works. In the service of Charles V from 1526 to 1540.

Paul Hofhaimer (1459–1537): Austrian composer and organist active in Innsbruck and Salzburg. In the service of Emperor Maximilian from 1489 to 1519.

Heinrich Isaac (*c.* 1450–1517): Prolific Flemish composer who beat the well-trodden path from the Low Countries to Italy, albeit via Innsbruck (1484). In Florence (1485–93) he taught the children of Lorenzo de' Medici, thereafter finding employment with the Este of Ferrara and Emperor Maximilian.

Josquin Desprès (des Pres) (*c.* 1440–1521): Franco-Flemish composer, possibly a pupil of Ockeghem, reputed to have been both the leading composer of his day and a temperamental genius. He was active in Milan from 1459 before entering the service of Cardinal Ascanio Maria Sforza, with whom he travelled to Rome (1484), where he belonged to the papal choir (1486–99). After serving as *maestro di capella* to Ercole d'Este at Ferrara (1503–4), he returned to the Low Countries. He wrote over seventy secular works, nearly 100 motets and eighteen Masses. His fame was established by the publication of his works by Ottaviano Petrucci (see 17.2).

Cristóbal de Morales (1500–53): Spanish composer, principally of sacred works, active at Ávila (1526–28), Plasencia (1528–31) and Rome (1535–45). His last years were spent in Spain.

Jean Mouton (*c.* 1459–1522): Franco-Flemish composer active at the courts of Louis XII and Francis I of France. A pupil of Josquin Desprès and master of Willaert.

Jacob Obrecht (*c.* 1450/1–1505): Composer of Dutch origin active throughout the Low Countries as well as in Ferrara (1487–88), where he died. Cabbalistic influences and number mysticism have been traced in his work.

Johannes Ockeghem (*c.* 1420–97): Franco-Flemish composer traceable in Antwerp (1443), Moulins, at the French royal court (from *c.* 1452/53), in Italy and Spain (1470). Though few of his works remain, contemporaries regarded him as a leading composer of his generation.

Pierre de la Rue (*c.* 1460–1518): Franco-Flemish composer active in Italy (early 1480s) and at the Burgundian court (1492–1516). His two journeys to Spain can be attributed to royal patronage and the dynastic connections between Iberia and the Low Countries.

John Taverner (*c.* 1490–1545): English composer noted for writing polyphonic settings and as the organist and choir master of Wolsey's Cardinal College (now Christ Church), Oxford (1526–30).

Johannes de Tinctoris (*c.* 1436–*c.* 1511): Franco-Flemish composer active in the Low Countries and Italy, whose importance lies in his theoretical publications, including *Terminorum musicae diffinitorium* (Treviso, 1495), which provides 299 definitions of musical terms then in use.

Bartolomeo Tromboncino (*c.* 1470–after 1535): Prolific Veronese composer based in Florence (1489–94), but who thereafter lived in Mantua until 1513. In 1499 he murdered his wife and her lover, was pardoned, but fled to Ferrara and the temporary patronage of Lucrezia Borgia. Lived in Venice from 1521.

Sebastian Virdung (b. *c.* 1465): German musician and author of the earliest-known book on musical instruments, *Musica gututscht und ausgezogen* (Basel, 1511).

Adriaan Willeart (*c.* 1490–1562): Franco-Flemish composer who was active in Rome (1515), Hungary (1517–19), Ferrara and Venice, where he was *maestro di capella* at S. Marco from 1527 and remained for the rest of his life. His work included early examples of the madrigal form.

20 Chronologies of the visual arts

20.1 Painting, including manuscript illumination

The majority of the works listed below are panel paintings, with frescoes specifically identified as such. Media are distinguished in a few particularly significant cases, though as a general rule egg tempera tended to predominate for panel paintings earlier in the period, with the use of oil paint spreading from the Low Countries in the early fifteenth century to become the principal medium by the end of the period.

The current locations of portable works appear in parenthesis; if no gallery is mentioned, then the work is still in the location for which it was created.

1396	Death of **Agnolo Gaddi**, son of painter Taddeo Gaddi, who in turn was trained by Giotto.
c. 1400	Anon., poss. French: *Wilton Diptych* (London, National Gallery, hereafter NG) for Richard II of England: best-known English example of the International Gothic style.
c. 1405–8	**Pol, Jean** and **Herman Limbourg** (all d. 1416): *Belles Heures* (New York, Metropolitan Museum of Art) for Jean, duke of Berry, brother of Charles V of France. The Limbourg brothers were all painters and illuminators whose careers took them from Nijmegen to Paris and who all died in 1416, probably of plague. Pol and Jean also worked for Philip the Bold, duke of Burgundy and brother of Jean de Berry. The Limbourgs' uncle Jean Malouel (d. 1415) also served as court painter to successive dukes of Burgundy.
1408	**Gentile da Fabriano** (c. 1385–1427): Frescoes, Sala del Maggior Consiglio, Palazzo Ducale, Venice (destroyed 1557): executed during a five-year visit to the city.
Up to 1409	Poss. **Jacquemart de Hesdin**: *Grandes Heures* (Paris, Bibliothèque Nationale) for Jean, duke of Berry.
c. 1413–16	**Pol, Jean** and **Herman Limbourg**: *Très Riches Heures* (Chantilly, Musée Condé) for Jean, duke of Berry.
1423	**Gentile da Fabriano**: *Adoration of the Magi* (*Strozzi Altarpiece*; Florence, Galleria degli Uffizi, hereafter Uffizi)

for the Florentine patrician Palla Strozzi: the master-piece of an artist whose work marked the height of International Gothic in Italy and who influenced Jacopo Bellini, Pisanello, Fra Angelico and Domenico Veneziano. Strozzi was also a patron of Sienese painter and illuminator Lorenzo Monaco (Piero di Giovanni, *c.* 1370/5–*c.* 1425/30), a Camaldolese monk in Florence.

c. 1423   Anon. Parisian: *Bedford Hours* (London, British Library) for John, duke of Bedford, then English Regent in France.

c. 1423–32   **Hubert** and **Jan van Eyck** (*c.* 1395–1441 and *c.* 1385/90–1426 respectively): *Adoration of the Lamb* (Ghent Altarpiece), St Bavo, Ghent, for Jodocus Vijd and his wife Elisabeth Burlunt: Hubert's only known work. Jan van Eyck is acknowledged as the founder of the Early Netherlandish School of painters and 'inventor' of oil painting (see p. 243). He served John of Bavaria, count of Holland, after whose death (1425) he entered the service of Philip the Good, duke of Burgundy, by whom he was employed as both painter and emissary, under-taking a diplomatic mission to Portugal and Spain. His influence was particularly marked among Spanish and Italian painters, including Lluís Dalmau (fl. 1428–61) and Antonello da Messina.

c. 1424–27   **Masolino** (Maso di Cristoforo Fini, Il Masolino da Panicale) (*c.* 1383–1447) and **Masaccio** (Tommaso di Ser Giovanni di Mone Cassai) (1401–28): Petrine fresco cycle, Brancacci Chapel, S. Maria del Carmine, Florence, for Felice Brancacci. Masolino, a Florentine influenced by Ghiberti and Gentile da Fabriano, is thought to have contributed *St Peter preaching* and *St Peter curing a cripple and the raising of Tabitha* (*c.* 1424–25). Among Masaccio's contributions are *The tribute money* and *St Peter healing with his shadow*. The precise chronolgy of the chapel's decoration is difficult to reconstruct. The project was eventually completed by Filippino Lippi, *c.* 1485–87.

c. 1425   **Masolino** and **Masaccio**: *Madonna and Child with St Anne* (Florence, Uffizi). In 1425 Masolino moved to Hungary to work for the *condottiere* Filippo Scolari (Pippo Spano), but by *c.* 1428 he was in Rome, after which he worked in Umbria and Lombardy.

c. 1425–27   **Masaccio**: *Trinity* fresco, S. Maria Novella, Florence, for Domenico Lenzi: notable features include the illusion-istic barrel vault.

1426	**Masaccio**: *Pisa Altarpiece* (London, NG, Berlin Gemäldegalerie, and Naples, Museo di Capodimonte) for S. Maria del Carmine, Pisa. He died suddenly in Rome, 1428.
1430	Death of **Andrei Rublev**, most celebrated of Russian icon painters, whose *Old Testament Trinity* (Abraham's three angels; Moscow, Tret'yakov Gallery) is dated *c*. 1411 or 1425–27.
c. 1431	**Jan van Eyck**: *Madonna of Chancellor Rolin* (Paris, Musée du Louvre, hereafter Louvre) for Nicolas Rolin, chancellor of Philip the Good, duke of Burgundy.
1434	**Jan van Eyck**: *Arnolfini Marriage* (London, NG), for Giovanni Arnolfini, a Lucchese banker in Bruges, marking his marriage to Giovanna Cenami.
1436	**Jan van Eyck**: *Madonna with Canon van der Paele* (Bruges, Groeningemuseum).
1436	**Paolo Uccello** (Paolo di Dono) (*c*. 1397–1475): Fresco of the *condottiere* Sir John Hawkwood (d. 1394), Duomo, Florence. Uccello had been apprenticed as a painter in Ghiberti's workshop.
c. 1437–39	**Fra Filippo Lippi** (Filippo di Tommaso) (*c*. 1406–69): *Barbadori Altarpiece* (Paris, Louvre) for Gherardo Barbadori. The Florentine Lippi was influenced by Masaccio, Rogier van der Weyden, Jan van Eyck and Fra Angelico, being in turn master of Botticelli. He took monastic vows at S. Maria del Carimine, Florence (1421) but was released from them after he abducted a nun, by whom he had two children, including painter Filippino Lippi.
c. 1438–45	**Fra Angelico** (Fra Giovanni da Fiesole or Guido di Pietro da Mugello) (*c*. 1395/1400–1455): Frescoes, including those in the friars' cells, S. Marco, Florence. This painter and Dominican friar was based at S. Domenico, Fiesole, from *c*. 1417, before moving to the Medici-financed convent of S. Marco, Florence. His Florentine followers included Benozzo Gozzoli and Fra Bartolommeo. After attracting the attention of Eugenius IV, he worked in Orvieto, Perugia and Rome.
c. 1440–45	**Stefan Lochner**: *Adoration of the Magi*, known as the 'Dombild' (Cologne Cathedral) for Cologne town hall: Lochner's career is difficult to reconstruct from documentary sources.
1442	**Rogier van der Weyden** (*c*. 1399/1400–1464): *Descent from the Cross* altarpiece (Madrid, Museo del Prado,

hereafter Prado). Pupil of Robert Campin (d. 1444) who in turn is now identified as the Master of Flémalle (fl. *c.* 1420–*c.* 1440). Van der Weyden, from Tournai, was made official city painter of Brussels in 1436.

c. 1445   **Domenico Veneziano** (d. 1461): *St Lucy Altarpiece* (central panel, Florence, Uffizi; predella panels, Cambridge, Washington and Berlin). A painter of Venetian origin active in Florence, in whose art no Venetian influences have been discerned. Is thought to have been Piero della Francesca's master.

c. 1445   **Piero della Francesca** (Piero de' Franceschi) (*c.* 1415–92): *Madonna della Misericordia* (Sansepolcro, Pinacoteca): an example of this important Umbrian painter's early work which remains in his home town (then known as Borgo S. Sepolcro). Although strongly associated with his native region, Piero did work in Ferrara, Rimini, Rome and Florence at various times.

1447–48   **Pisanello** (Antonio Pisano) (*c.* 1390–1455): Fresco fragments of chivalric subjects, Palazzo Ducale, Mantua, for Ludovico III Gonzaga. Pisanello, a painter and medallist, presumably from Pisa, was based in Verona, but worked in Mantua, Ferrara, Pavia, Milan, Naples and Rome, and is credited with inventing the commemorative medal, producing portrait medals of, among others, Emperor John VIII Palaeologus and Francesco Sforza. In painting he is associated with the International Gothic style.

1447–50   **Fra Angelico**: Frescoed *Scenes from the lives of Saints Stephen and Lawrence* for Nicholas V's private chapel in the Vatican. Fra Angelico was beatified in 1984, but the formula 'beato Angelico' was in popular use long before that.

From 1448   **Andrea Mantegna** (1430/31–1506): Frescoes, funerary chapel of Antonio Ovetari, church of the Eremitani, Padua (bombed 1944). Mantegna was born near Padua and had been adopted by his master Francesco Squarcione (*c.* 1397–*c.* 1468) by 1442. His work is distinguished by a passion for the ancient world. He married Nicolosa, daughter of Jacopo Bellini, in 1452/53.

Late 1440s   **Piero della Francesca**: *Baptism of Christ* (London, NG) for Sansepolcro cathedral: particularly instructive for Piero's interest in perspective.

c. 1452–*c.* 1465   **Piero della Francesca**: *Legend of the True Cross* fresco cycle, S. Francesco, Arezzo.

From 1453	**Andrea del Castagno** (Andrea di Bartolo di Bargiella) (pre-1419–57): Frescoes of *Last Supper* and *Passion*, SS. Annunziata, Florence: these are considered his masterpieces, while his other fresco work is found, *inter alia*, in the chapel of S. Tarasio, S. Zaccaria, Venice (1442) and the Florentine convent of S. Apollonia (1447–48).
Mid-1450s	**Uccello**: *Battle* (or *Rout*) *of S. Romano*, three panels for Cosimo de' Medici (Florence, Uffizi, London, NG, and Paris, Louvre): Florentine victory over Sienese troops, 1 June 1432 (see p. 12), depicted through striking use of linear perspective. Uccello's later works include *St George and the dragon* (London, NG).
Mid-1450s(?)	**Piero della Francesca**: *Flagellation of Christ* (Urbino, Galleria Nazionale delle Marche) has generated considerable comment both for its distinctive treatment of the subject and for its attention to rules of perspective.
c. 1455	**Mantegna**: *Agony in the Garden* (London, NG); *Presentation in the Temple* (Berlin, Gemäldegalerie).
1455–56	**Andrea del Castagno**: Frescoed equestrian portrait of *condottiere* Niccolò da Tolentino, in Florentine employ 1427–34, commissioned to match Uccello's of Hawkwood (1436) on north nave wall of Duomo, Florence.
c. 1455/56	**Rogier van der Weyden**: *Crucifixion* (Madrid, Escorial): among the few authenticated works of this influential master.
1456–59	**Mantegna**: *S. Zeno Altarpiece*, S. Zeno, Verona.
Post-1458	**Piero della Francesca**: *Resurrection* fresco (Sansepolcro, Museo Civico).
1459–61	**Benozzo Gozzoli** (Benozzo di Lese) (*c.* 1420/22–97): Fresco cycle *Journey of the Magi*, Palazzo Medici, Florence, for Piero de' Medici, executed after training as a goldsmith. He worked with Ghiberti on the Florentine Baptistery doors, breaking his Baptistery contract to assist Fra Angelico in Rome and Orvieto.
1460	**Mantegna** took up post of court painter to Ludovico Gonzaga and remained in Mantua for the rest of his life, with the exception of a period in Rome (1488–90) to paint Innocent VIII's chapel in the Vatican Belvedere (work destoyed 1780). Towards the end of his career he contributed two paintings to the *studiolo* of Isabella d'Este.
1460–62	**Alesso Baldovinetti** (*c.* 1425–99): *Nativity* fresco, atrium, SS. Annunziata, Florence. This Florentine painter,

mosaicist and stained glass artist was inspired by Andrea del Castagno.

early 1460s **Giovanni Bellini** (*c.* 1431/36–1516): *Agony in the Garden* (London, NG). Son and pupil of Jacopo Bellini, brother of Gentile and brother-in-law of Mantegna, who also influenced him. The leading Venetian painter of his generation, highly praised by contemporaries including Dürer, and particularly noted for his altarpieces and abandonment of egg tempera for oils, which had already revolutionised Netherlandish painting.

c. 1460–65 **Antonello da Messina** (*c.* 1430–79): *St Jerome in his study* (London, NG): once thought to have been by a Netherlandish master, since this Sicilian painter is generally held to be the first Italian to be influenced by van Eyck's development of oil painting, knowledge he probably acquired in Naples, where Netherlandish art was then in vogue.

c. 1461 **Mantegna**: *Death of the Virgin* (Madrid, Prado) contains a view of Mantua in background.

1464–68 **Dirk/Dieric Bouts** (*c.* 1415–75): *Holy Sacrament* altarpiece, St Peter's, Louvain. Haarlem-born painter linked to the shadowy figure of Albert van Ouwater (fl. *c.* 1440–65) and Geertgen tot Sint Jans.

c. 1465–70 **Martin Schongauer** (*c.* 1435/50–91): *Orlier Altarpiece* (Colmar, Musée d'Unterlinden). This painter and engraver from Colmar was greatly esteemed by his contemporaries.

1465–74 **Mantegna**: Frescoes, Camera degli Sposi or Camera Picta, Palazzo Ducale, Mantua, for Ludovico Gonzaga: Mantegna's most notable Mantuan creation features the Court Scene (*c.* 1470), including portraits of Ludovico, his wife Barbara of Brandenburg, their children, courtiers and servants, the Meeting Scene (1474) between Ludovico and his son Cardinal Francesco Gonzaga, and the oculus.

c. 1467/68 **Vincenzo Foppa** (*c.* 1427/30–1515/16): Fresco cycle, Portinari Chapel, S. Eustorgio, Milan.

1467–*c.* 1484 **Benozzo Gozzoli**: Old Testament fresco cycle, Campo Santo, Pisa; seriously damaged in 1944.

Late 1460s/ early 1470s **Francesco del Cossa** (*c.* 1435–76/77): Frescoes, Salone dei mesi (Room of the months), Palazzo Schifanoia, Ferrara, for Borso d'Este: disputed payment for this project resulted in Cossa leaving Ferrara for Bologna.

1470/71 Death of **Jacopo Bellini** (b. *c.* 1400), father of Gentile and Giovanni Bellini and father-in-law of Mantegna.

Although a small number of paintings are attributed to him, including frescoes in Padua and Verona, he is best known for *c.* 300 highly finished drawings, now in two books (Paris, Louvre and London, British Museum).

Post-1472   **Piero della Francesca**: Matching portraits of Federico da Montefeltro of Urbino and his wife Battista Sforza (Florence, Uffizi) probably painted after her death.

1473   **Schongauer**: *Madonna of the Rose Garden*, St Martin's, Colmar.

1473–74   **Joos van Wassenhove** (fl. *c.* 1460–80): *Institution of the Eucharist* (Urbino, Galleria Nazionale delle Marche), the only work linked to this Netherlandish painter by documentary evidence. 'Justus of Ghent' was based at Urbino by 1472, questions of attribution arising due to the presence of the Flemish-influenced Spanish painter Pedro Berruguete (*c.* 1450–pre-1500) there in the same decade. Portraits of famous men in Federico da Montefeltro's *studiolo* are attributed to Joos Justus, together with a portrait of Federico with his son Guidobaldo (Urbino, Galleria Nazionale delle Marche).

1473–78   **Hugo van der Goes** (*c.* 1440–82): *Portinari Altarpiece* (Florence, Uffizi) commissioned for Hospital of S. Maria Nuova, Florence, by Tommaso Portinari, agent of Medici Bank in Bruges and patron of Memling.

c. 1474–77   **Francesco Botticini** (1446–97): *Assumption of the Virgin* (London, NG) for the painter's fellow Florentine, Matteo Palmieri.

c. 1475   **Piero della Francesca**: *Madonna and Child with Federico da Montefeltro* (Milan, Brera).

1475–85   **Andrea del Verrocchio** (Andrea di Cione) (1435–88) assisted by **Leonardo da Vinci** (1452–1519): *Baptism of Christ* (Florence, Uffizi): the versatile painter, draughtsman and musician born at Anchiano, near Vinci in Tuscany, was apprenticed to Verrocchio and is said to have contributed an angel to this painting, which was for S. Salvi, Florence.

1476/77   Death of Bruges-based painter **Petrus Christus** (b. *c.* 1450), of whose life little is known.

1475–76   **Antonello da Messina**: *S. Cassiano alterpiece* (fragments, Vienna, Kunsthistorisches Museum hereafter Kunst. Mus.) for Pietro Bon: Antonello used his stay in Venice to disseminate appreciation of Netherlandish techniques among Venetian painters, including Giovanni Bellini and Alvise Vivarini.

c. 1476–77 **Melozzo da Forlì** (Melozzo degli Ambrogi) (1438–94): Fresco (now on canvas; Vatican, Pinacoteca) depicting Sixtus IV's appointment of Platina as papal librarian. This Romagnole painter was influenced by Piero della Francesca and worked in Urbino from *c.* 1465 before moving to Rome (1475–81). His frescoes in SS. Apostoli, Rome, for Giuliano della Rovere exist only as fragments. Later work was undertaken at Loreto and Forlì.

c. 1477 **Master of Mary of Burgundy**: *Hours of Mary of Burgundy* (Vienna, Östrreichisches Nationalbibliothek) for the eponymous duchess, daughter of Charles the Bold, for whom this Ghent-based illuminator also worked.

c. 1477–78 **Domenico Ghirlandaio** (1448/49–94): Frescoes, chapel of S. Fina, Collegiata Pieve, S. Gimignano, which was built by the Florentine architect Giuliano da Maiano (1432–90). Ghirlandaio's workshop included his brother Davide (1452–1525), while Giuliano da Maiano's brother Benedetto da Maiano (1442–97) was a leading Florentine architect and sculptor.

c. 1478 **Sandro Botticelli** (Alessandro di Moriano Filipepi) (1444/45–1510): *Primavera* (Florence, Uffizi) for Lorenzo di Pierfrancesco de' Medici. A Florentine, Botticelli trained with Fra Filippo Lippi and had documented connections with Lorenzo de' Medici and his circle.

1479–80 **Hans Memling** (Memlinc) (*c.* 1430/40–94): Triptych (London, NG) for Sir John Donne. Of German origin, Memling was active in Bruges, where he introduced the style of his probable master, Rogier van der Weyden. His patrons included Angelo Tani and Tommaso Portinari of the Medici Bank in Bruges and his surviving works include *c.* 20 altarpieces and over thirty portraits.

1480 Death of **Jean Fouquet** (b. *c.* 1415/20), whose reputation as France's greatest fifteenth-century painter rests on portraits, including that of Charles VII (Paris, Louvre).

1480 **Gentile Bellini** (*c.* 1429–1507): Portrait of Sultan Mehmet II (London, NG): painted during Bellini's mission to Constantinople (1479–81). Venetian painter named after Gentile da Fabriano, his father Jacopo's master. One of the official painters to the Republic, his smaller works also include portraits of successive doges and of Venice's first patriarch, S. Lorenzo Giustiniani (Venice, Accademia delle Belle Arti, hereafter Accad.).

c. 1480 **Giovanni Bellini**: *S. Giobbe Altarpiece*, for S. Giobbe, Venice (Venice, Accad.).

c. 1480	**Hieronymus Bosch** (Jeroen van Aken, in Spain 'El Bosco') (*c.* 1450–1516): *The Seven Deadly Sins* (Madrid, Prado): a circular table top. Painter from 's Hertogenbosch, Brabant, where he lived throughout his life. A lucrative marriage enabled him to follow his artistic instincts rather than the dictates of the art market, with highly remarkable results.
c. 1480–95	**Mantegna**: *Triumph of Caesar* (London, Hampton Court Palace): nine-part picture based on ancient sources and later acquired by Charles I of England.
1480s	**Leonardo da Vinci**: *Virgin of the Rocks* (Paris, Louvre); cf. London version, mid-1490s (see p. 218).
c. 1481	**Leonardo da Vinci**: *Adoration of the Magi* (Florence, Uffizi) belongs to Leonardo's first Florentine period (1472–*c.* 1482), after which he was based in Milan until 1499 under Sforza patronage.
1481–82/83	**Botticelli, Domenico Ghirlandaio, Pietro Perugino** (Pietro Vannucci) (*c.* 1450–1523), **Pinturicchio** (Bernardino di Betto) (*c.* 1452–1513), **Cosimo Rosselli** (1439–1507) and **Luca Signorelli** (*c.* 1450–1523): Frescoes, Sistine Chapel, Vatican, for Sixtus IV: see 22.3 for distribution of work. Perugino's nickname derived from his native Perugia, where he was mainly active. According to Vasari he was a pupil of Verrocchio and Piero della Francesca. Though his fortunes waned later, Raphael trained in his studio. He was possibly assisted in the Sistine Chapel by Pinturicchio. Signorelli, from Cortona, worked extensively in Tuscany and Umbria, and was possibly a pupil of Piero della Francesca.
1482–1515	**Giovanni Bellini**: Contributions to history cycles, Palazzo Ducale, Venice; assisted by Alvise Vivarini (1442/53–1503/5), a member of a Venetian family of painters who worked especially in Venice and Padua.
c. 1484	**Botticelli**: *Birth of Venus* (Florence, Uffizi) probably for a Medici patron.
c. 1484–94	**Geerten tot Sint Jans** ('Little Gerard of the Brethren of St John') (*c.* 1460–*c.* 1495): Altarpiece (partially destroyed, remainder in Vienna, Kunst. Mus.) for the Commandery of the Knights of St John, Haarlem by this Leiden-born painter identified from his relationship with this order.
c. 1485	**Botticelli**: *Mars and Venus* (London, NG) possibly for members of the Florentine Vespucci family.

c. 1485	**Botticelli:** *Pallas and the Centaur* (Florence, Uffizi) for Lorenzo di Pierfrancesco de' Medici.
c. 1485	**Ghirlandaio:** Fresco cycle, Sassetti Chapel, S. Trinità, Florence, for Francesco Sassetti, General Manager of the Medici Bank (see 10.6.1, p. 123).
c. 1485–87	**Filippino Lippi** (*c.* 1457–1504) *Vision of St Bernard* (Florence, Badia). In addition to this altarpiece, the son of Filippo Lippi is known for his fresco cycles in Florence and Rome.
1485–90	**Ghirlandaio:** Fresco cycle, *Scenes from the lives of the Virgin and St John the Baptist*, Cappella Maggiore, S. Maria Novella, Florence, for Giovanni Tornabuoni, brother-in-law of Piero de' Medici. It provides a useful record of later fifteenth-century Florentine interiors and social life in general.
1486	**Ercole de' Roberti** (*c.* 1455–96) succeeded Cosimo Tura (*c.* 1430–95) as Este court painter at Ferrara; died in poverty.
1486	**Carlo Crivelli** (*c.* 1430/35–94): *Annunciation* (London, NG): a well-known example of the work of this Venetian-born painter whose working life was spent in Zara in Dalmatia and Fermo and Ascoli Piceno in the Italian Marches. The influence of Mantegna has been detected in his highly dramatic works.
1487	**Leonardo da Vinci:** Unexecuted model for the crossing of Milan Cathedral. Another of his unrealised Milanese projects was a giant equestrian monument to Francesco Sforza.
1488	**Giovanni Bellini:** *Frari Altarpiece*, S. Maria Gloriosa dei Frari, Venice.
c. 1490–91	**Leonardo da Vinci:** *Lady with an ermine* (Cracow, Czatoryski Collection): portrait of Ludovico Sforza's mistress, Cecilia Gallerani.
1490–95	**Vittore Carpaccio** (Vittore Scarpazza) (*c.* 1460/66–1525/26): *Life of St Ursula* narrative cycle, for Scuola di S. Orsola, Venice (Venice, Accad.). Although Carpaccio is best known for his narrative paintings, he also produced altarpieces and portraits.
1490s	**Botticelli:** *Calumny of Apelles* (Florence, Uffizi): based on Lucian's essay on Slander.
1492–94/5	**Pinturicchio:** Frescoes, Borgia Apartments, Vatican, for Alexander VI. For Della Rovere patrons he decorated four chaples in S. Maria del Popolo, Rome.

1492–1504	**Michael Sittow** (*c.* 1468–1525/26) worked in Spain for Isabella of Castile before returning to his native Estonia. He painted in the tradition of Memling and made his name in Bruges.
c. 1494–1505/10	**Lazzaro Bastiani** (d. 1512), **Gentile Bellini**, **Carpaccio**, **Benedetto Diana** (*c.* 1460–1525), **Giovanni Mansueti** (fl. 1485–1526/27) and **Perugino**: *Miracles of the True Cross* panels, for Scuola Grande di S. Giovanni Evangelista, Venice (Venice, Accad.): together with other narrative paintings by Carpaccio, these detailed studies greatly enhance our knowledge of Venice and Venetian life in this period.
1494	The death of Memling left **Gerard David** (*c.* 1460–1523) as the leading painter in Bruges, though none of his works are signed.
Mid-1490s	**Leonardo da Vinci**: *Virgin of the Rocks* (London, NG); cf. Paris version, 1480s (see p. 216).
Begun 1495	**Leonardo da Vinci**: Fresco, *Last Supper*, S. Maria delle Grazie, Milan: has deteriorated dramatically due to the employment of unconventional techniques.
c. 1495–1500	**Bosch**: *Haywain* (Madrid, Prado).
1496–1504	**Juan de Flandres** (*c.* 1465–1519) travelled from his native Flanders to serve as court painter to Isabella of Castile until her death.
1498	**Albrecht Dürer** (1471–1528): Self-portrait (Madrid, Prado). Painter, printmaker and draughtsman, Dürer is held to be Germany's greatest artist. Apprenticed in his native Nuremberg to painter Michael Wolgemut. Worked on book illustrations in Basel (*c.* 1492) and Strasbourg (1494) on his way to Venice (1494–95), which he revisited 1505–7, determined to challenge Venetian artists in the realm of colour.
c. 1498–1500	**Giorgione** (Giorgio da Castelfranco) (1476/78–1510): *Virgin enthroned with Saints George and Francis* (Castelfranco Altarpiece), S. Liberale, Castelfranco Veneto, Giorgione's home town. Academic studies of Giorgione, who moved to Venice, centre on problems of chronology and attribution since none of his works are signed and Titian's early work is difficult to differentiate from that of Giorgione, whose name is mainly associated with smaller compositions often of mythical and even confusing subjects: *The Tempest* (Venice, Accad.), *The Three Philosophers* (Vienna, Kunst. Mus.), *Sleeping Venus* (Dresden, Gemäldegalerie).

From 1499	**Leonardo da Vinci** spent periods in Mantua under the patronage of Isabella d'Este, of whom he made a drawing (Paris, Louvre), and in Florence (1500–6), after the fall of Ludovico Sforza of Milan.
1499	**Fra Bartolommeo** (Baccio della Porta) (1472–1517): *Last Judgement* (Florence, Museo di S. Marco) exhibits a mystical element which may be attributable to Savonarolan influences. After training with Cosimo Rosselli, he became a Dominican in 1500 and was based at S. Marco, Florence, though he travelled elsewhere.
c. 1499–1515	**Leonardo da Vinci**: Cartoon, *Virgin, Child and St Anne* (London, NG); cf. Paris version, c. 1515 (see p. 222).
1500	**Dürer**: Self-portrait (Munich, Alte Pinakothek).
1500	**Botticelli**: *Mystic Nativity* (London, NG): example of Botticelli's later, Savonarola-inspired work.
c. 1500	**Mantegna**: *Dead Christ* (Milan, Brera): even this is distinctly classical in treatment.
c. 1500–5	**Piero di Cosimo** (1461/62–c. 1521): *Death of Procris* (London, NG). Mythological subjects formed Piero's most distinctive subject matter, though this Florentine pupil of Cosimo Rosselli, from whom his name derived and whom he assisted on the Sistine chapel frescoes, also painted a good range of portraits and sacred subjects.
c. 1500–6	**Leonardo da Vinci**: *Mona* [Madonna] *Lisa* or *La Gioconda*, portrait of Lisa Gherardini, wife of Francesco del Giocondo (Paris, Louvre).
c. 1501	**Giovanni Bellini**: Portrait of Doge Leonardo Loredan (London, NG).
1502–3	**Leonardo da Vinci** employed by Cesare Borgia as a military engineer.
1502–7	**Carpaccio**: Narrative cycle, *Scenes from the lives of St George and St Jerome*, Scuola di S. Giorgio degli Schiavoni, Venice.
1502–7/8	**Pinturicchio**: Frescoes, *Scenes from the life of Aeneas Sylvius Piccolomini* (Pius II), Piccolomini Library, Siena Cathedral, for Cardinal Francesco Todeschini-Piccolomini, later Pius III.
1503	**Dürer**: Watercolour, *Large piece of turf* (Vienna, Graphische Sammlung Albertina) exhibits attention to detail also apparent in his woodcuts, etchings and engravings.
1503–6	**Leonardo da Vinci**: Fresco, *Battle of Anghiari*, Salone dei Cinquecento, Palazzo della Signoria, Florence (destroyed): depiction of Florence's 1440 victory over Milan. Michelangelo's matching *Battle of Cascina* was not executed.

1504	**Raphael** (Raffaello Santi) (1483–1520): *Betrothal of the Virgin* (Milan, Brera): early work by this High Renaissance master, whose father Giovanni Santi (*c.* 1435/40–94) was a painter at the Montefeltro court in Urbino; Raphael was at least influenced by Perugino, if not his pupil. Based in Florence 1504–8.
c. 1504	**Bosch**: *Garden of earthly delights* (Madrid, Prado): like his other works, this deals with human sinfulness and folly and exhibits a strong eschatological emphasis. In Bosch's lifetime his work attracted the interest of Isabella of Castile, Philip the Fair and Margaret of Austria, but was later systematically collected by Philip II of Spain.
1505	**Giovanni Bellini**: *S. Zaccaria Altarpiece*, S. Zaccaria, Venice.
1505	**Raphael**: *Madonna of the Meadow* (Vienna, Kunst. Mus.).
1505	After making his name in Vienna as an etcher, **Lucas Cranach** the Elder (1472–1553) was summoned to Wittenburg by Frederick the Wise, Elector of Saxony, to succeed Jacopo de' Barbari as court artist. Cranach produced many paintings of both Christian and classical subjects as well as portraits of his patrons and of Martin Luther.
1506	**Lorenzo Costa** (*c.* 1460–1535) succeeded Mantegna as Gonzaga court painter at Mantua.
1506	**Giorgione**: *Laura* (Vienna, Kunst. Mus.).
1506	**Dürer**: *Virgin of the Rosegarlands* for the Scuola dei Tedeschi, S. Bartolomeo di Rialto, Venice (Prague, National Gallery).
c. 1506–8/pre-1511	**Giorgione** and **Titian** (Tiziano Vercellio) (*c.* 1488/90–1576): Frescoes (Venice, Accad., fragments only), exterior of Fondaco dei Tedeschi, headquarters of the German merchant community in Venice. Titian, from Cadore, trained with Giovanni Bellini.
1506/8–13	**Leonardo da Vinci** based in French-occupied Milan and briefly in Rome (1513).
1507	**Dürer**: *Adam and Eve* (Madrid, Prado).
1507–8	**Giorgione**: Frescoes, Palazzo Ducale, Venice (destroyed).
To 1508	**Jean Bourdichon** (1457–1521): *Hours of Anne of Brittany* (Paris, Bibliothèque Nationale) for Louis XII's consort by this court painter to Louis XI, Charles VIII, Louis XII and Francis I.
1508–9	**Jan Gossaert** (Jan Mabuse) (*c.* 1478–1532): A diplomatic embassy from Margaret of Austria, regent of the

	Netherlands, to Julius II duly resulted in the incorporation of classical architecture into the work of this Netherlandish painter and printmaker.
1508–12	**Raphael**: Frescoes, Stanza della Segnatura, Vatican, for Julius II; including *Disputa* of Church Fathers over the Sacrament, *Parnassus*, abode of Apollo and the Muses, and *School of Athens*, which depicts Leonardo da Vinci as Plato, Michelangelo as Aristotle and Bramante as Euclid.
1508–12	**Michelangelo Buonarroti** (1475–1564): Frescoes, Sistine Chapel ceiling, Vatican, for Julius II, nephew of Sixtus IV, founder of chapel (see 22.3).
1510	**Botticelli** died in obscurity, his style outdated by High Renaissance masters.
c. 1510	Attrib. **Giorgione**: *Concert Champêtre* (Paris, Louvre).
c. 1510	**Sebastiano del Piombo** (Sebastiano Luciani) (*c.* 1485–1547): *Salome* (London, NG): an example of work from Sebastiano's Venetian period, when he was influenced by Giovanni Bellini and Giorgione, whose *Three Philosophers* (Vienna, Kunst. Mus.) he possibly completed. In 1511 wealthy Sienese banker Agostino Chigi visited Venice and took Sebastiano with him to Rome, where the latter remained, except for brief periods, for rest of his life. For Chigi, he contributed to the decoration of Villa Farnesina. His position as keeper of the papal seals (from 1531) accounts for nickname 'del Piombo'.
1511	**Titian**: Frescoes, Scuola di S. Antonio, Padua.
c. 1512	**Raphael**: Fresco, *Galatea*, Villa Farnesina, Rome, for Agostino Chigi; Raphael's portrait of Julius II (London, NG) is also dated *c.* 1512.
1512–14	**Raphael**: Frescoes, Stanza d'Eliodoro, Vatican, for Julius II, including *Expulsion of Heliodorus from the Temple*, *Miracle of the Mass at Bolsena*, *Repulse of Attila by Leo I* and *Deliverance of St Peter from Prison*. Giulio Romano assisted with the decoration of the Stanze.
1512/13–15	**Mathias Grünewald** (1475/80–1528): *Isenheim Altarpiece* for Isenheim Abbey, Alsace (Colmar, Musée d'Unterlinden): masterpiece of the greatest German painter of his day, who was also an architect and hydraulic engineer. His career is rather shadowy, but it is known that he met Dürer at Charles V's coronation at Aachen (see p. 45) and was court painter to the archbishops of Mainz until this became incompatible with his Protestant sympathies.

c. 1512–15	**Raphael**: *Sistine Madonna* (Dresden, Gemäldegalerie Alte Meister).
1513	**Giovanni Bellini**: Altarpiece, S. Giovanni Crisostomo, Venice.
1513	**Quentin Metsys** (Massys) (c. 1466–1530): *Money-changer and his wife* (Paris, Louvre), a van Eyckian piece set in the 1440s. Based in Antwerp, Metsys worked in the tradition of Rogier van der Weyden, but with Italian influences.
1514	**Giovanni Bellini**: *Feast of the gods* (Washington, National Gallery).
c. 1514	**Titian**: *Sacred and Profane Love* (Rome, Galleria Borghese) possibly to celebrate a marriage.
1514–17	**Raphael**: Frescoes, Stanza dell'Incendio, Vatican, for Julius II: subject matter inspired by the rebuilding of St Peter's basilica, of which Raphael, along with Fra Giocondo and Antonio da Sangallo, was architect following Bramante's death in 1514 (see 20.4, p. 238).
1515	**Giovanni Bellini**: *Woman at her toilet* (Vienna, Kunst. Mus.).
c. 1515	**Leonardo da Vinci**: *St John the Baptist* (Paris, Louvre); *Virgin and Child with St Anne* (Paris, Louvre), the cartoon of which is in London, NG.
c. 1515	**Raphael**: Portrait of Baldassare Castiglione (Paris, Louvre).
From c. 1515	**Raphael**: Vatican Logge frescoes; Raphael's cartoons (London, Victoria and Albert Museum) for the decoration of the Sistine Chapel date from 1515–16.
c. 1515–18	**Titian**: *Assumption of the Virgin*, S. Maria Gloriosa dei Frari, Venice: monumental altarpiece.
1516	A painter of Netherlandish origin, **Jean Clouet** (c. 1485–1540/41) began to receive a French royal pension. His son François (c. 1516–72) succeeded him as court painter.
1516	**Titian** appointed official painter to the Venetian Repub-, lic, in which capacity he worked in the Palazzo Ducale.
1516/17	**Leonardo da Vinci** Travelled to France under the patronage of Francis I, who provided him with a home at Cloux, near Amboise, where Leonardo died in 1519. Leonardo's designs for a city and royal castle at Romorantin were not executed. His anatomical drawings and optical studies are contained in notebooks at Windsor Castle.
1517	**Andrea del Sarto** (Andrea d'Agnolo) (1486–1530): Altarpiece *Madonna of the Harpies* (Florence, Uffizi).

This Florentine painter, whose nickname derives from his father being a tailor, was apprenticed under Piero di Cosimo and, apart from a period as Francis I's court painter (1418–19), spent his career in Florence, where he created frescoes at SS. Annunziata and for the Compagnia dello Scalzo.

1517/18   Death of **Giovanni Battista Cima da Conegliano** (b. *c.* 1459), the leading painter in Venice between Giovanni Bellini and Giorgione. Most of his surviving works are altarpieces.

1518   **Alonso Berruguete** (*c.* 1488–1561) appointed court painter to Charles V. Probably trained by his father Pedro, Alonso worked in Italy and Spain.

1518   **Bernard van Orlay** (*c.* 1488–1541) appointed court painter to Margaret of Austria, regent of the Netherlands; served her successor Mary of Hungary, in the same capacity. Jan Mostaert (*c.* 1475–1555/56) was another of Margaret's Netherlandish painters.

1519–36   **Titian:** *Madonna di Ca' Pesaro,* S. Maria Gloriosa dei Frari, Venice, for the Pesaro family of Venice.

1520   **Vincenzo Catena** (*c.* 1470–1531): *Christ saving St Christina from drowning,* S. Maria Mater Domini, Venice: Catena continued the style of Giovanni Bellini and was a friend of Giorgione.

c. 1520–22   Netherlandish painter **Jan van Scorel** (1495–1562) made a pilgrimage to Holy Land and worked for fellow Dutchman Adrian VI in Rome.

1521/22   **Hans Holbein** (the Younger) (1497/98–1543): *Dead Christ* (Basel, Kunst. Mus.). Holbein moved from his native Augsburg to Basel in 1515, resulting in portraits of Erasmus, who had moved there in 1514, but travelled in Italy (1516–17) and was based in Lucerne (1517–19).

1522–23   **Titian:** *Bacchus and Ariadne* (London, NG) for Alfonso d'Este, duke of Ferrara.

1525–31   **Giulio Romano** (Giulio Pippi) (1492/99–1546): Frescoes, including those in the Sala dei Giganti (Room of the Giants), Palazzo Te, Mantua, for Federico II Gonzaga, a building which Giulio also designed (see 20.4, p. 239). His craft as both painter and architect had been learned from Raphael, whom he assisted in the Stanza dell'Incendio.

1525–32   **Lorenzo Lotto** (*c.* 1480–1556) worked in his native Venice after periods in Rome (1508–12) and Bergamo (1513–25).

Up to 1526	**Dürer**: *Four Apostles* (Munich, Alte Pinakothek): presented by the artist to the town of Nuremberg in 1526.
1526	**Jerg Ratgeb** (b. *c.* 1480), a painter, executed for his part in the German Peasants' War.
1526–27	**Holbein**: *Sir Thomas More and his family* (destroyed 1752), a group portrait set in their Chelsea home. Patronage in Basel had dried up due to the Reformation, so Holbein tried his luck in England (1526–28) and was introduced to More's circle by Erasmus.
1528	Death of **Palma il Vecchio** (Jacopo Negreti, b. *c.* 1480), painter of undated altarpieces and portraits in Venice. Palma il Giovane (1544–1628) was his great-nephew.
1529	**Albrecht Altdorfer** (*c.* 1480–1538): *Battle of Alexander at Issos* for Wilhelm IV, duke of Bavaria (Munich, Alte Pinakothek). Altdorfer, a painter and engraver of Regensburg, also worked for Emperor Maximilian.
c. 1530	**Correggio** (Antonio Allegri) (*c.* 1489–1534): Fresco, *Assumption of the Virgin*, dome, Parma cathedral. Inspired by Andrea Mantegna and influenced by Leonardo da Vinci, Correggio was known by the name of city where he was born and died.
c. 1530	**Lucas Cranach** (1472–1553): *Golden Age* (Munich, Alte Pinakothek).
1532	**Francesco Primaticcio** (1504/5–70) travelled to France, where he decorated Francis I's chateau at Fontainbleau with elaborate combinations of fresco and stucco. He was a native of Bologna and had assisted Giulio Romano on decoration of Palazzo Te at Mantua.
1533	**Holbein**: *The Ambassadors* (London, NG), portraits of Jean de Dinteville and Bishop Georges de Selve. Holbein's second period in England began in 1532; he was appointed King's Painter in 1536.
c. 1534–40	**Il Parmigianino** (Girolamo Francesco Mazzola) (1503–40): *Madonna of the long neck* (Florence, Uffizi): best-known work of this Mannerist painter and printmaker from Parma (hence his nickname), who worked briefly in Rome before the Sack of 1527.
1534–41	**Michelangelo**: *Last Judgement* fresco, Sistine Chapel, Vatican, for Paul III (see 22.3).
1536–39	**Rosso Fiorentino** (Giovanni Battista di Jacopo Rosso) (1494–1540): Galerie François I, Chateau de Fontainebleau, for Francis I: Mannerist style of this Florentine painter put to flamboyant use.

20.2 Engravings

1493   **Michael Wolgemut** (1434–1519): Illustrations for Hartmann
             Schedel's *Weltchronik* (Nuremburg Chronicle, see 15.4,
             p. 177). In 1472 Wolgemut had married the widow of painter
             and stained glass designer Hans Pleydenwurff (*c.* 1425–72)
             and took over the latter's prosperous workshop. As a de-
             signer of woodcuts, he was Dürer's master.

1497–1500   **Jacopo de' Barbari** (d. *c.* 1516): Large woodcut bird's-eye
             view of Venice (dated 1500), both the earliest and the best-
             known work of this Venetian painter and engraver. It exists
             in twelve copies, blocks of which are in the Museo Correr,
             Venice. He travelled in Germany, becoming court artist to
             Emperor Maximilian in 1500, and later enjoyed the patron-
             age of Margaret of Austria, regent of the Netherlands.

1498   **Albrecht Dürer** (1471–1528): Fifteen woodcuts illustrating
             the *Apocalypse*.

1503   Death of **Israhel van Meckenem** the Younger (b. *c.* 1440/
             45), the most prolific fifteenth-century German wood en-
             graver, to whom *c.* 600 pieces have been attributed.

1513   **Dürer**: Engraving *Knight, death and the Devil.*

1514   **Dürer**: Engravings *St Jerome in his study* and *Melancholia I*
             (see 18.1.1). Swabian painter and engraver Hans Baldung
             'Grien' (1484/85–1545); notable for his depictions of
             witches and witchcraft, was among those trained in Dürer's
             Nuremberg workshop.

1515   Swiss engraver, goldsmith, painter and mercenary **Urs Graf**
             (*c.* 1485–1527/29) fought at battle of Merignano.

1522–34   **Lucas Cranach** (the Elder) (1472–1553): Dürer-inspired
             woodcuts for his friend Luther's German translation of the
             New Testament. Friendship with Luther did not prevent
             Cranach working for Catholic patrons.

c. 1524   **Marcantonio Raimondi** (*c.* 1470/82–1534): *I modi*, a set of
             sixteen engravings of erotic subjects based on paintings
             by Giulio Romano (see also 15.3, p. 174). On the respect-
             able level, this prolific engraver from near Bologna, who
             trained with Francesco Francia, pioneered the use of prints
             to reproduce the paintings of Raphael and others, which
             thereby gained great popularity. His career never recov-
             ered after the Sack of Rome in 1527.

1525   **Hans Sebald Beham** (1500–50) and **Bartel Beham** (1502–
             40) expelled from Nuremberg for extreme Protestant views.
             Their engravings were influenced by Dürer.

| 1531 | Death of **Hans Burgkmair** the Elder (b. 1473) of Augsburg, among whose *c.* 800 extant woodcuts are those for Emperor Maximilian's own publications. |
| 1533 | Death of **Jacob Cornelisz van Oostanen** (b. *c.* 1472/77), engraver of over 200 woodcuts. Death of **Lucas van Leyden** (b. *c.* 1494), Dürer-influenced Netherlandish painter and engraver who produced at least 168 engravings. |

20.3 Sculpture

Apart from in exceptional cases media are not identified. The current locations of portable works appear in parenthesis. If no gallery is mentioned, then the work is still in the location for which it was created.

c. 1396–1403	**Claus Sluter** (*c.* 1360–1405/6): *Moses Fountain* (partly destroyed), Chartreuse de Champmol, Dijon, for Philip the Bold, duke of Burgundy, whose service this important Netherlandish sculptor entered in 1385 and whose tomb he began in 1404.
1401	**Lorenzo Ghiberti** (1378–1455) won competition for the Florentine Baptistery doors, other competitors including his fellow Florentine Filippo Brunelleschi and the Sienese Jacopo della Quercia. Ghiberti's successful gilded bronze low relief, *Sacrifice of Isaac* (Florence, Museo Nazionale Bargello, hereafter Bargello), provided a model for the twenty-eight panels of which the North doors are composed, though their subjects are New Testament scenes. Brunelleschi thereafter devoted himself to architecture.
1403–24	**Ghiberti**: North doors, Baptistery, Florence: originally placed on the East side, opposite the entrance to the Duomo, but were replaced by Ghiberti's 'Gates of Paradise'; earlier doors (*c.* 1336) by Andrea Pisano were moved and are now on the South side.
1405–7/8	**Jacopo della Quercia** (Jacopo della Fonte) (*c.* 1374–1438): Tomb of Ilaria del Carretto, wife of the Lucchese despot Paolo Guinigi, Lucca cathedral. This serene figure established Jacopo's reputation.
1408–19	**Jacopo della Quercia**: *Fonte gaia/Fountain of joy* (Siena, Palazzo Pubblico) for Piazza del Campo, Siena.
1411–13	**Donatello** (Donato di Niccolò di Betto Bardi) (1386/87–1466): *St Mark*, Orsanmichele, Florence, for the Linaiuoli (see 22.2). The leading sculptor of his day, Donatello served his apprenticeship with Ghiberti, 1404–7.

c. 1411–13   **Nanni di Banco** (*c.* 1384–1421): *Quattro Santi Coronati* (Four Crowned Saints), Orsanmichele, Florence, for the Maestri di Pietra e Legname: masterpiece of this Florentine sculptor (see 22.2).

1414   **Ghiberti**: *St John the Baptist,* Orsanmichele, Florence, for the Calimala (see 22.2).

c. 1415–17   **Donatello**: *St George,* Orsanmichele, Florence, for the Corazzai (Florence, Bargello) (see 22.2).

1417   **Donatello**: Relief, *St George and the Dragon,* Orsanmichele, Florence (Florence, Bargello).

c. 1418–22   **Donatello**: *St Louis of Toulouse,* Orsanmichele, Florence, for the Parte Guelfa (Florence, Museo dell'Opera di S. Croce) (see 22.2).

1419–21   **Ghiberti**: *St Matthew,* Orsanmichele, Florence, for the Cambio (see 22.2).

After 1419   **Donatello** and **Michelozzo di Bartolomeo** (1396–1472): Tomb of Baldassare Cossa, antipope John XXIII, Baptistery, Florence, for Cosimo de' Medici. Like Donatello, Michelozzo, a Florentine sculptor and architect, was a pupil of Ghiberti and assisted on the Florentine Baptistery doors until *c.* 1420.

1423   **Giovanni di Martino da Fiesole**: Tomb of Doge Tommaso Mocenigo, SS. Giovanni e Paolo, Venice.

c. 1426–52   **Ghiberti**: East doors of Florentine Baptistery, known as 'Gates of Paradise', were also commissioned by the Arte di Calimala and depict Old Testament subjects in ten square panels, which occupied almost the remainder of Ghiberti's career, though other works were undertaken simultaneously.

1427–34   **Giovanni** and **Bartolomeo Bon** or **Buon** the elder (*c.* 1360–1442 and *c.* 1400/10–*c.* 1464/67 respectively): Sculptural decoration, Ca' d'Oro, Venice, for Marino Contarini: Venetian Gothic *tour de force.* This father-and-son team had worked at Madonna dell'Orto, Venice (1392). Bartolomeo was the most important sculptor in Venice before Antonio Rizzo.

1428   **Ghiberti**: *St Stephen,* Orsanmichele, Florence, for Arte della Lana (see 22.2).

1431–38   **Luca della Robbia** (1399/1400–82): *Cantoria* (singing gallery), Duomo, Florence (Florence, Museo dell'Opera del Duomo).

1433–39   **Donatello**: *Cantoria* (singing gallery), Duomo, Florence (Florence, Museo dell'Opera del Duomo), to match that of Luca della Robbia.

1438–42	**Giovanni** and **Bartolomeo Bon**: Porta della Carta, Palazzo Ducale, Venice, incorporating the figure of Doge Francesco Foscari.
c. 1443–45	**Filarete** (Antonio Averlino) (*c.* 1400–69): Bronze doors, old St Peter's, Rome: later transferred to the new basilica. This work is possibly an indication of his training with Ghiberti. 'Filarete' means 'lover of virtue'.
c. 1446–48	**Bernardo Rossellino** (*c.* 1409–64): Tomb of Leonardo Bruni, S. Croce, Florence: a suitably classical design for Florence's humanist chancellor.
1447–53	**Donatello**: Equestrian monument to the *condottiere* Gattamelata, Piazza del Santo, Padua: inspired by the Capitoline statue of Marcus Aurelius in Rome and, in turn, the inspiration for Verrocchio's Venetian monument to Bartolomeo Colleoni. Donatello was based in Padua in the period 1443–57.
1449–56	**Agostino di Antonio di Duccio** (1418–*c.* 1481): Work on Alberti's Tempio Malatestiano, Rimini (see 20.4, p. 234), by a Florentine sculptor whose career took him to Modena, Venice, Cesena, Forlì, Bologna and Perugia.
1440s/1450s	**Donatello**: Bronze *David* (Florence, Bargello) for Cosimo de' Medici: this piece originally stood in the *cortile* of the Palazzo Medici, Florence.
1453–60	**Desiderio da Settignano** (1429/32–64): Tomb of humanist chancellor Carlo Marsuppini, S. Croce, Florence: stands opposite Bernardo Rossellino's tomb for Marsuppini's predecessor, Leonardo Bruni. Desiderio, a Florentine sculptor inspired by Donatello, is otherwise notable for creating marble low reliefs.
c. 1456–60	**Donatello**: *St Mary Magdalene* (Florence, Museo dell'Opera del Duomo) in polychrome and gilt wood.
1455–58	**Francesco Laurana** (*c.* 1430–1502), **Pietro da Milano** and others: Decoration of triumphal arch, Castel Nuovo, Naples, for King Alfonso I. Laurana, from Dalmatia, also spent periods at the Provençal court of René of Anjou. A series of female portrait busts in Naples has been attributed to him.
Later 1450s	**Donatello**: *Judith slaying Holofernes* (Florence, Palazzo Vecchio; copy, Florence, Loggia dei Lanzi) for Cosimo de' Medici.
1461–66	**Antonio Rossellino** (1427/28–79): Tomb of Cardinal-Prince of Portugal, S. Miniato al Monte, Florence: the cardinal died in Florence in 1459 and requested burial

there. Antonio was a leading figure in his brother Bernardo's Florentine workshop.

1466　　At his death Donatello left two unfinished pulpits for the Medici church of S. Lorenzo, Florence.

c. 1466–83　　**Andrea del Verrocchio** (Andrea di Cione) (1435–88): *Christ and St Thomas*, Orsanmichele, Florence, for the Tribunale della Mercanzia (see 22.2).

1467　　Death of Moravian sculptor **Hans Multscher** (b. c. 1400), whose innovative work is found extensively in Germany.

1467–70　　**Pietro Lombardo** (c. 1435–1515): Tomb of Doge Pasquale Malipiero, SS. Giovanni e Paolo, Venice. Together with other Lombard artists, Lombardo was intrumental in introducing the classical revival to Venice.

c. 1470–75　　**Giovanni Antonio Amadeo** (c. 1447–1522): Funerary chapel for the *condottiere* Bartolomeo Colleoni, S. Maria Maggiore, Bergamo. Amadeo, apprenticed at the Certosa in his native Pavia, supervised various building projects in Milan and elsewhere in Lombardy, being chief architect of Milan cathedral, 1480s to c. 1512.

1471–81　　**Michael Pacher** (d. 1498): St Wolfgang Altarpiece, St Wolfgang im Salzkammergut: important example of the work of this painter and sculptor who worked in the Austrian Tyrol.

c. 1473　　Death of Netherlandish sculptor **Nicolaus Gerhaert** whose career was short but influential due to his mobility; among other places, he worked in Trier and Strasbourg, and was invited to Vienna by Frederick III.

c. 1473　　Attrib. **Antonio Rizzo** (pre-1440–c. 1499): Tomb of Doge Nicolò Tron, S. Maria Gloriosa dei Frari, Venice. Rizzo originated in Verona and was master of works at the Palazzo Ducale, Venice.

1474–80　　**Mino da Fiesole** (1429–84): This Florentine sculptor undertook many works in Rome, where he collaborated with Andrea Bregno (1418–1503) and the Croatian Giovanni Dalmata (c. 1440–after 1509) and created a number of tombs, including that of Paul II (reconstructed in the Vatican Grotte). Dalmata worked in Hungary between 1481 and the death of his patron Matthias Corvinus in 1490.

1475　　**Verrocchio**: Bronze *David* (Florence, Bargello).

1476–81　　**Pietro Lombardo**: Tomb of Doge Pietro Mocenigo, SS. Giovanni e Paolo, Venice.

1477–89　　**Veit Stoss** (c. 1450–1533): Altarpiece, St Mary's, Cracow: largest work of this Nuremberg craftsman, whose other significant work in Cracow was the tomb of King Kazimierz IV (1492). Together with Tilman Riemenschneider (*c.* 1460–1531), Stoss was regarded as the leading master of the time.

1478   **Bertoldo di Giovanni** (*c.* 1430/40–91): Medal cast to commemorate the defeat of the Pazzi conspirators in Florence. This Florentine sculptor was noted for his statuettes and reliefs. He completed the pulpits of his supposed master, Donatello, in S. Lorenzo, Florence, and worked for Lorenzo de' Medici at the Palazzo Medici and Poggio a Caiano. He is often referred to as the head of the informal sculpture academy which met in the Medici garden at S. Marco, Florence, and included the youthful Michelangelo.

c. 1479–92   **Verrocchio**: Equestrian monument to *condottiere* Bartolomeo Colleoni, Campo SS. Giovanni e Paolo, Venice.

1489–93   **Gil de Siloé** (d. *c.* 1501): Tombs of Juan II of Castile, his consort Isabel of Portugal and son Alfonso, Charterhouse of Miraflores, near Burgos, for Isabella of Castile. Siloé was possibly from Antwerp. His son Diego (*c.* 1490–1563) was also a sculptor and architect, in whose work at various Spanish cathedrals Italianate influences can be found.

Up to 1493   **Antonio** and **Paolo Pollaiuolo** (Antonio and Paolo di Jacopo Benci) (*c.* 1432–98 and *c.* 1441–*c.* 1496 respectively): Bronze tomb of Sixtus IV, St Peter's, Rome (Vatican, Museum of St Peter's). Antonio's workshop in Florence was second only to that of Verrocchio in the 1460s and 1470s. He was a painter, sculptor and goldsmith, his brother Paolo specialising in painting. Their nickname derives from their father's work as a poulterer.

Early 1490s **Tullio Lombardo** (*c.* 1455–1532): Tomb of Doge Andrea Vendramin, SS. Giovanni e Paolo, Venice. Tullio and his brother Antonio (*c.* 1458–*c.* 1516), another sculptor, were sons of the architect and sculptor Pietro Lombardo, but their style was more overtly classical.

c. 1492   **Michelangelo Buonarroti** (1475–1564): *Battle of Lapiths and Centaurs* (Florence, Casa Buonarroti). Apprenticed to the painter Domenico Ghirlandaio in 1488 and traditionally associated with the Medici sculpture 'academy' at S. Marco, Florence, early influences on Michelangelo also included the preaching of Savonarola. With Leonardo da Vinci and Raphael, he is regarded as one of the High

Renaissance greats, being all the more notable for his exceptionally long career and for his reputation, created by a combination of extensive output and eulogistic biographies by Ascanio Condivi and Giorgio Vasari.

1497–1500 **Michelangelo**: *Pietà* for Cardinal Jean Villiers de la Grolais (Rome, St Peter's): the fall of the Medici in 1494 had prompted moves to Venice and Bologna before Michelangelo was called to Rome (*c.* 1496) by Cardinal Raffaele Riario.

1499–1507 **Michel Colombe** (*c.* 1430–*c.* 1514) with **Jean Perréal** (Jean de Paris) (*c.* 1455–1530) and **Girolamo da Fiesole**: Tomb of François II of Brittany and Marguerite de Foix, Nantes cathedral, for their daughter Anne of Brittany, queen of France. Little of the Breton Colombe's work remains. The French invasions allowed Perréal to visit Italy three or four times.

Early 1500s **Tullio Lombardo**: Tomb of Doge Giovanni Mocenigo, SS. Giovanni e Paolo, Venice.

1501–4 **Michelangelo**: *David*, Piazza della Signoria, Florence (Florence, Accademia; copy Florence, Piazza della Signoria): an expression of Michelangelo's republican sympathies during the 1501–5 visit to his native city.

1505 Death of South German mason **Matthaus Böblingen** who worked with his father Hans (d. 1482) at Esslingen before becoming master mason at Ulm Minster in 1480.

c. 1505–10 **Andrea Riccio** (Andrea Brioso) (*c.* 1470–1532): Bronze statuette, *Shouting horseman* (London, Victoria and Albert Museum): a typical example of this Paduan-based sculptor's work.

From 1505 **Michelangelo**: Tomb of Julius II, designed for St Peter's, Rome (Rome, S. Pietro in Vincoli; figures also in Florence, Accademia, and Paris, Louvre): intended to be exceptionally imposing, the project was scaled down after Julius's death (1514) and was eventually but a fraction of the proposed whole. Figures of captives slaves for the tomb are now divided between the Louvre and the Florentine Accademia.

1506 Classical group, *Laocoön* and his sons attacked by sea monsters, discovered at Rome.

From 1507 **Colombe, Perréal, Conrat Meit** (*c.* 1475–1550/51), **Jan van Roome** and others: Tombs of Margaret of Austria, regent of the Netherlands (d. 1530), her second husband Philibert of Savoy (d. 1504) and Philibert's mother, Marie of Bourbon, mausoleum at Brou, Bourg-en-Bresse, near Lyon, for Margaret of Austria: precise division of labour remains subject to conjecture. Meit was from Worms.

1509–13   **Sebastian Loscher, Hans Daucher** and others: Sculptural decoration, Fugger Chapel (bombed 1944), St Anna, Augsburg for Jakob Fugger II: first important Renaissance-style funerary chapel in Germany.

1511   Julius II purchased the classical figure of *Apollo Belvedere*, which had recently been discovered at Porto d'Anzio.

1511   **Pietro Torregiano** (1472–1528): Tomb of Lady Margaret Beaufort, mother of Henry VII of England, Westminster Abbey, London. Florentine sculptor who trained with Benedetto and Giuliano da Maiano.

1512–13   **Domenico Fancelli** (1469–1519): Tomb of Infante Juan, only son of Ferdinand of Aragon and Isabella of Castile, Santo Tomás, Ávila. Trained in the circle of Bernardo Rossellino and Mino da Fiesole, Fancelli introduced Renaissance sculptural styles to Spain.

1512   **Andrea Sansovino** (*c.* 1467–1529): *Virgin and Child with St Anne*, S. Agostino, Rome: technically ambitious group by a Tuscan sculptor with Medicean connections who also created the tombs of Cardinals Ascanio Maria Sforza and Girolamo Basso della Rovere in S. Maria del Popolo.

1512–18   **Torregiano**: Tomb of Henry VII of England and Elizabeth of York, Westminster Abbey, London. Torregiano arrived in Spain by 1522, was arrested by the Inquisition and died in prison (1528).

1514–17   **Fancelli**: Monument to Ferdinand of Aragon and Isabella of Castile, Capilla Real, Granada.

1515   Death of Moravian mason and sculptor **Anton Pilgrim** (b. *c.* 1450) whose work is found most notably at Brno and Heilbronn.

1515–42   **Roulland Le Roux** (d. *c.* 1527): Tombs of Cardinals Georges I and Georges II d'Amboise (1460–1510 and 1488–1550 respectively), archbishops of Rouen, Rouen Cathedral.

1516–31   **Guido Mazzoni** or **Jean Perréal**: Tomb of Louis XII of France and Anne of Brittany, Abbey of Saint-Denis, north-east of Paris.

c. 1519   **Bartolomé Ordóñez** (*c.* 1485–1520): Tomb of Cardinal Cisneros at Alcalá de Henares. Ordóñez died at Carrara while obtaining marble for the tomb of Philip the Fair and Juana of Castile, Capilla Real, Granada, a task he had

	inherited from Fancelli. He had previously worked with Diego de Siloé in Naples and at Barcelona cathedral.
1519–34	**Michelangelo**: Tombs of Lorenzo de Medici, duke of Urbino (d. 1519), and Giuliano de' Medici, duke of Nemours (d. 1516), which feature figures representing *Day, Night, Dawn* and *Dusk*, New Sacristy, S. Lorenzo, Florence (see 20.4, pp. 238–9).
1527	According to his autobiographical account, Florentine goldsmith, sculptor and Medicean **Benvenuto Cellini** (1500–71) was among the defenders of Castel Sant'Angelo during the imperialists' Sack of Rome, after which he retreated to Mantua and worked in France (1540–45) for Francis I.
1527–34	**Baccio Bandinelli** (1488–1560): *Hercules and Cacus*, Piazza della Signoria, Florence. This Florentine sculptor, painter, draughtsman and staunch Medicean enjoyed the patronage of Leo X and Clement VII in Florence and Rome, but excited the enmity of the republican Michelangelo and the animosity of his rival Cellini.

20.4 Architecture

c. 1394	**Henry Yevele** (d. 1400): Westminster Hall, London, with its dramatic hammerbeam roof.
1418–36	**Filippo Brunelleschi** (1377–1446): Although involved with the construction of the Duomo in Florence from 1404, his design for a dome to span the huge octagonal drum was not adopted until 1418, construction starting in 1420. In spite of the claim that it was inspired by Roman examplars, nothing like it actually existed in Rome. Here and elsewhere, Brunelleschi's distinctive style meshed classical vocabulary with traditional Florentine elements. The first phase of the classical revival in architecture is most closely associated with his name.
1419–24	**Brunelleschi**: Ospedale degli Innocenti/Foundling Hospital, Florence: notable for its elegant portico. The famous blue and white roundels of babies on the façade were probably created by Andrea della Robbia (1435–1525), whose family produced this distinctive glazed terracotta work over a number of generations.
1420s	**Michelozzo di Bartolomeo** (1396–1472): Villa, Cafaggiolo, near Florence, for Averardo de' Medici, cousin of Cosimo.

1421–28	**Brunelleschi:** Old Sacristy, S. Lorenzo, Florence, for Giovanni di Bicci de' Medici and his neighbours; the body of the church was then reconstructed with the financial support of Cosimo de Medici; the Old Sacristy was later matched by Michelangelo's New Sacristy.
From 1429	**Brunelleschi:** Pazzi Chapel, S. Croce, Florence, commissioned by Andrea de' Pazzi 1429–30 and constructed 1442–*c.* 1465. Luca della Robbia provided roundels of Apostles (*c.* 1450–60) for the spandrels.
c. 1433	**Michelozzo di Bartolomeo:** Additions to villa, Careggi, near Florence, for Cosimo de' Medici.
1434	**Brunelleschi:** Scolari Oratory, S. Maria degli Angeli, Florence: first centralised Renaissance building.
1436	**Brunelleschi:** Won competition for lantern of Florentine Duomo, which was completed by Bernardo Rossellino.
From 1436	**Brunelleschi:** S. Spirito, Florence: traditional Latin cross design.
From 1436	**Michelozzo di Bartolomeo:** Cloisters, sacristy and library, S. Marco, Florence, which enjoyed the patronage of Cosimo de' Medici, who had his own cell there.
1443–53	House of Jacques Coeur, Bourges: lavishly decorated monument to the wealth of Charles VII's finance minister.
1444	**Michelozzo di Bartolomeo:** Palazzo Medici (now Medici-Riccardi), Florence, for Cosimo de' Medici: influential in the history of Florentine palace architecture: (see 22.1.1). From 1441 Michelozzo also supervised the building of Brunelleschi's S. Lorenzo, again for Cosimo de' Medici, and was appointed Master of the Florentine Cathedral Works after Brunelleschi's death in 1446.
1448	**Leon Battista Alberti** (1404–72): Made survey of St Peter's basilica, Rome, which was found to have slipped two metres on the south side. Alberti, Genoese-born illegitimate member of an exiled Florentine family, had already commenced his theoretical writings on the visual arts (see 20.5) before making his name as a practising architect.
From *c.* 1450	Ca' Foscari, Venice, built for Doge Francesco Foscari: a large Venetian Gothic *palazzo.*
From *c.* 1450	**Alberti:** S. Francesco (known as the Tempio Malatestiano), Rimini, for Sigismondo Pandolfo Malatesta, *signore* of Rimini: this thoroughly classical building, with triumphal arch façade, was left incomplete at Malatesta's death in 1461.

1453	**Bernardo Rossellino** (*c.* 1409–64): Began demolition of St Peter's basilica, Rome, in his capacity as architect (*ingegnere del palazzo*) to Nicholas V.
From *c.* 1453	**Alberti**: Palazzo Rucellai, Florence, for Giovanni Rucellai; completed 1460 by Bernardo Rossellino.
1456–65	**Filarete** (Antonio Averlino) (*c.* 1400–69): Ospedale Maggiore, Milan, for Francesco Sforza: partially executed.
c. 1458	**Alberti**: Façade, S. Maria Novella, Florence, for Giovanni Rucellai.
1459–64	**Bernardo Rossellino**: Cathedral, bishop's palace and town hall around the central piazza, Pienza, near Siena, for Pius II, whose humble birthplace, previously called Corsignano, was thereby transformed into a papal residence.
1460	Attrib. **Antonio Gambello** (d. 1481): Porta dell'Arsenale, Venice: triumphal arch design marked the arrival of classicising architecture in Venice.
From 1460	**Alberti**: S. Sebastiano, Mantua, for Ludovico Gonzaga: the first of two Gonzaga commissions resulting from Alberti's presence at Pius II's Congress of Mantua (1459–60). S. Sebastiano was the first Renaissance church built on a Greek cross plan.
1468–72	**Luciano Laurana** (*c.* 1420/25–79): Ducal Palace, Urbino, including *cortile*, for Federico da Montefeltro. Dalmatian-born Laurana, architect and military engineer, also worked at Fano (1464), Pesaro, Mantua and Naples (1472–74). Possibly related to Francesco Laurana. The Palazzo Ducale was completed by versatile Sienese painter, sculptor, architect, art theorist, medallist, military engineer and diplomat Francesco di Giorgio Martini (1439–1501) who may also have designed the intarsia work in Federico's *studiolo*.
1469–77	**Mauro Codussi** (Coducci) (*c.* 1440–1504): Camaldoese church of S. Michele in Isola, Venice. Born at Lenna, near Bergamo, but based in Venice by 1469, Codussi was one of those Lombards who introduced classical styles there. He clearly emerges as an architect in the modern sense rather than merely chief craftsman.
1471–85	**Pietro Lombardo** (*c.* 1435–1515): Chancel, S. Giobbe, Venice: first Renaissance interior in Venice.
From 1472	**Alberti**: S. Andrea, Mantua, for Ludovico Gonzaga. In contrast to Alberti's design for S. Sebastiano, Mantua, this is a Latin cross but has a triumphal arch façade.

From 1476   **Juan Guas** (*c.* 1430–96): Monastery of San Juan de los Reyes, Toledo, to commemorate Ferdinand and Isabella's victory over the Portuguese at the battle of Toro.

1479   Consecration of the Sistine Chapel, the shell of which was constructed by **Giovanni de' Dolci** for Sixtus IV.

1480–83   **Guas**: Palacio del Infantado, Guadalajara, Castile, for Íñigo Lopez de Mendoza, duke of Infantado: first large noble town house in Spain on the Italian model.

Began *c.* 1485   **Giuliano da Sangallo** (Giuliano Giamberti) (*c.* 1443/45–1516): Villa Medici, Poggio a Caiano, near Florence, for Lorenzo de' Medici. Giuliano was the principal figure in a family of architects, their collective soubriquet 'Sangallo' deriving from the location of their workshop at Florence's Porta San Gallo.

1480–1500   **Codussi**: Completion of S. Zaccaria, Venice.

1481–89   **Pietro Lombardo**: S. Maria dei Miracoli, Venice: marble-coated church.

1482–90   **Codussi**: Campanile, S. Pietro in Castello, Venice.

From 1484   Attrib. **Antonio Rizzo** (pre-1440–*c.* 1499): Scala dei Giganti, Palazzo Ducale, Venice.

1485–92   **Giuliano da Sangallo**: S. Maria delle Carceri, Prato: built on Greek cross plan.

c. 1485–*c.* 1511   **Baccio Pontelli** (1450–92/94): Palazzo della Cancelleria, Rome, for Cardinal Raffaele Riario: one of many Roman buildings of the 1480s conveniently attributed to this Florentine architect and military engineer, who certainly designed fortifications in the Papal States.

1486   **John Wastell** (d. *c.* 1515): Appointed master mason at King's College, Cambridge. In his time there the distinctive fan vault was constructed, perhaps to the design of **Reginald of Ely** (d. 1471).

c. 1486   Death of the Bolognese architect **Aristotele Fieravanti** (b. *c.* 1415) who worked in Milan and Hungary but whose most notable work was in Moscow, including two cathedrals in the Kremlin, part of Ivan III's ambitious urban planning.

1489–90   **Giuliano da Sangallo**: Model for Palazzo Strozzi, Florence, for Filippo Strozzi and family, later used by Benedetto da Maiano and Il Cronaca. Sangallo left Florence after the death of Lorenzo de' Medici (1492), finding a new patron in Cardinal Giuliano della Rovere, the future Julius II.

1490s   **Donato Bramante** (Donato di Pasuccio d'Antonio) (*c.* 1444–1514): Urban planning at Vigevano, south-west of Milan for Ludovico Sforza. Prior to the French invasion of 1499, the Umbrian Bramante also designed a number of Milanese churches and contributed to Pavia cathedral from 1488.

From 1490   **Codussi**: Palazzo Corner-Spinelli (formerly Lando), Venice.

c. 1490–1504   **Il Cronaca** (Simone del Pollaiuolo) (1457–1508): S. Salvatore al Monte, Florence: the masterpiece of an architect whose nickname derived from his study of antiquity.

1490–95   **Codussi**: Upper portion of façade and ceremonial staircase, Scuola Grande di S. Marco, Venice. The Scuola Grande di S. Giovanni Evangelista commissioned a similar staircase from Codussi in 1495.

1492–95   **Lorenzo Vasquez** (fl. 1490–1509): Medinaceli palace, Cogolludo, province of Guadalajara, Castile, for the duke of Medinaceli.

1492–1504   **Codussi**: Rebuilding of S. Maria Formosa, Venice.

From 1492   **Biagio Rossetti** (c. 1447–1516) and others: Addizione Erculea, Ferrara, one of the most important pieces of town planning in Renaissance Italy, for Ercole d'Este, duke of Ferrara: the design of at least four churches and eight palaces within the Addizione has traditionally been attributed to Rossetti, though his role has recently been reinterpreted as that of a practical engineer rather than a creative artist.

1495–96   **Il Cronaca** and others: Salone dei Cinquecento (Hall of the Great Council), Palazzo della Signoria, Florence: Savonarolan architect chosen for this Savonarolan project.

1496–1500   Attrib. **Codussi**: Procuratorie Vecchie (government buildings) and Torre dell'Orologio (clock tower), Piazza di S. Marco, Venice. Government building in Venice was supervised at that time by a father and son of Lombard origin, Bartolomeo (c. 1450–c. 1509) and Pietro (d. 1529) Bon or Buon.

1497–1504   **Codussi**: S. Giovanni Crisostomo, Venice, the city's first centrally planned church.

1502   **Bramante**: Tempietto, S. Pietro in Montorio, Rome, for Ferdinand of Aragon and Isabella of Castile.

From c. 1502   **Codussi**: Palazzo Vendramin-Calergi (formerly Loredan), Venice, for Andrea Loredan.

1503–9   Poss. **Robert Vertue** or **Robert Janyns** (both d. 1506): Henry VII's Chapel, Westminster Abbey, London, to

	house the tomb of Henry and his wife Elizabeth of York.
1505	**Giorgio Spavento** (d. 1506): Fondaco dei Tedeschi, Venice, for the use of the German merchant community.
1505	**Bramante**: Wholesale destruction of Constantinian basilica of St Peter's, Rome, by 'the master of the ruins'.
From 1505	**Bramante**: Cortile del Belvedere, Vatican, for Julius II: linked the Vatican palace with Nicholas V's Belvedere.
1506	18 Apr: foundation stone of the new St Peter's laid, following Bramante's design (see 22.1.2).
c. 1506–11	**Baldassare Peruzzi** (1481–1536): Villa (now Villa Farnesina), Rome, for Agostino Chigi: decorated by Peruzzi, who had moved from Siena to assist Raphael in the Vatican Stanze, Giulio Romano, Sodoma (Giovanni Antonio Bazzi, 1477–1549) and Ugo da Carpi (d. 1532).
From 1509	**Bramante**: Santa Casa (Holy House), Loreto, believed to have been mysteriously translated from Nazareth: Andrea Sansovino contributed to the decoration.
c. 1511	Death of the Spanish master mason **Simón de Colonia**. His son Francisco de Colonia (d. 1542) worked in both Gothic and classical styles.
c. 1511–12	**Raphael** (Raffaello Santi) (1483–1520): Design for S. Eligio degli Orefici, Rome, on which building began 1514 and was completed by Peruzzi.
1513	Work on St Peter's Basilica suspended at the death of Julius II, but **Bramante**'s Greek cross with Pantheon-inspired dome provided the basic scheme and dimensions for his successors.
1514	Death of **Bramante** led to **Raphael**'s appointment as architect of St Peter's basilica, in addition to which he became Superintendent of Roman Antiquities in 1515.
1515–24	attrib. **Domenico da Cortona** (c. 1470–c. 1549): Northwest wing, Château de Blois, for Francis I, where Louis XII had also built a wing.
From 1517–18	**Raphael**: Villa (now Villa Madama), Rome, for Cardinal Giulio de' Medici, the future Clement VII.
c. 1519	**Jacopo Sansovino** (Jacopo Tatti) (1486–1570): S. Giovanni dei Fiorentini, Rome. This Florentine architect and sculptor trained under Andrea Sansovino, whose name he adopted, worked in Rome from 1505, Florence (c. 1510–15) and again in Rome from 1518 until the Sack of 1527.
1519–34	**Michelangelo Buonarroti** (1475–1564): New Sacristy, S. Lorenzo, Florence, deigned to match Brunelleschi's

Old Sacristy and to house the tombs of the Medici *Magnifici* Lorenzo (d. 1492) and Giuliano (d. 1478) and *Principi* Lorenzo, duke of Urbino (d. 1519) and Giuliano, duke of Nemours (d. 1516), but only the last two tombs were executed by Michelangelo (see 20.3, p. 233).

From 1519   Attrib. **Domenico da Cortona**: Château de Chambord, near Blois, for Francis I.

1524–33   **Michelangelo**: Biblioteca Laurenziana (Laurentian Library), S. Lorenzo, Florence, to house the library of Lorenzo de' Medici (d. 1492); staircase in Vestibule completed in 1559.

1526   Death of the Spanish architect **Juan Gil de Hontañón** (b. *c.* 1480), a late exponent of the Gothic style. His legitimate son Juan worked in the Plateresque style and his illegitimate son Rodrigo (1500–77) designed the façade of the University of Alcalá de Henares (1549).

1527   **Peruzzi**: Returned to Siena following the Sack of Rome.

1527–34   **Giulio Romano** (Giulio Pippi) (1492/99–1546): Palazzo Te, Mantua, for Federico II Gonzaga (see 20.1, p. 223). After designing a number of buildings in Rome, Giulio was based in Mantua between 1524 and 1540.

1527–68   **Pedro Machuca** (*c.* 1490–1550): Palace adjacent to the Alhambra, Granada, for Charles V: includes a circular courtyard based on Hadrian's villa at Tivoli (see 22.1.3). Machuca was also a painter.

1528   Death of **Henry Redman**, who may have designed Hampton Court Palace for Cardinal Wolsey.

c. 1527–40   **Gilles Le Breton** (*c.* 1500–*c.* 1552): Master mason; Château de Fontainebleau, for Francis I, after work on Château de Chambord.

From 1528   **Girolamo della Robbia** (1488–1566) and others: Château de Madrid, Bois de Boulogne, Paris, for Francis I: Italianate in design but does not survive.

1529   **Jacopo Sansovino**: Appointed chief architect to the Procurators of S. Marco, Venice, in which capacity he designed the Zecca (Mint, *c.* 1535), Biblioteca Marciana (from 1537) and Loggietta at the foot of the Campanile (*c.* 1537–42). He also designed a number of Venetian churches: S. Francesco della Vigna, S. Spirito, S. Giuliano, S. Martino and S. Geminiano.

c. 1530   **Michele Sanmicheli** (*c.* 1487–1559): Palazzo Canossa, Verona, for Ludovico Canossa: an example of this Lombard architect's work in Verona, 1526/7–35, which also included the Porta Nuova. Sanmicheli's military

	engineering formed an essential part of Venetian *terraferma* strategy after the disastrous War of the League of Cambrai.
1532–36	**Peruzzi**: Palazzo Massimo delle Colonne, Rome, for Pietro Massimo: negotiates an awkward city-centre site with an ingenious curved façade.
c. 1534	Death of Spanish master mason **Enrique Egas** (b. 1494).
From 1534	**Michelangelo**: Redesign of Rome's ancient Capitol, an important piece of urban planning.
From 1534	**Antonio da Sangallo** (Antonio Giamberti) (1484–1546): Palazzo Farnese, Rome, for Cardinal Alessandro Farnese, later Pope Paul III, completed after 1546 by Michelangelo. Antonio was a nephew of Giuliano da Sangallo.

20.5   Art theory

c. 1390	**Cennino d'Andrea Cennini** (*c.* 1370–*c.* 1440): *Il libro dell'arte* (*The craftsman's handbook*): first treatise of its kind and one which enjoyed considerable popularity among artists.
1435	**Leon Battista Alberti** (1404–72): *De pictura*: first of Alberti's great treatises on the visual arts, devoted to painting; Italian translation, *Della pittura*, 1436. Alberti entered papal employment in 1432, so was based in Florence in 1434–43 as part of Eugenius IV's entourage. There he discovered the achievements of Brunelleschi, Masaccio and others, chanelling this enthusiasm into his theoretical works.
1452	**Alberti**: *De re aedificatoria*: on architecture; printed 1485.
1460s	**Alberti**: *De statua*: on sculpture.
1461–64	**Filarete** (Antonio Averlino) (*c.* 1400–69): *Trattato d'architettura*, printed in the nineteenth century: contains a design for the ideal city 'Sforzinda', named after Filarete's Milanese patron, Francesco Sforza.
c. 1482	**Francesco di Giorgio Martini** (1439–1501): *Trattato d'architettura civile e militare*: derived from Vitruvius and Alberti.
1492	**Piero della Francesca** (1410–92): At his death, his theoretical works remained unpublished: *De prospettiva pingendi* (*On linear perspective in painting*) and *De quinque corporibus regularibus* (*On the five regular bodies*).
1511	**Vitruvius** (*fl. c.* 40BC) First printed edition of *De architectura*, including 136 woodcut illustrations by Fra Giocondo (Giovanni da Verona, 1433–1515).
1525	**Albrecht Dürer** (1471–1528): *Underweyssung der Messung* (*Treatise on measuring*).

1528   **Dürer:** *Vier Bücher von menschlicher Proportion* (*Four books on human proportion*).

1537–51   **Sebastiano Serlio** (1475–*c.* 1554): *Tutte l'opere d'architettura et prospetiva*, published in six parts and later collectively (Venice, 1619): an immensely influential study, essentially an updated version of Vitruvius. Serlio was a Bolognese architect active in Rome from *c.* 1514, a pupil of Peruzzi and influenced by Bramante; he also worked in Venice and France.

21 Glossary of terms relating to the visual arts

altarpiece Painting or sculpted scene depicting a sacred subject, placed on or behind an altar.

book of hours Aid to devotion popular with the laity in the late medieval period, comprising prayers for the various canonical hours.

bottega It. 'shop', 'workshop'; can also refer collectively to a master and his apprentices.

cassone Italian marriage chest, often elaborately decorated with contemporary scenes which are useful sources for social history.

chiaroscuro It. 'light-dark'; use of contrasted light and shade to convey in pigment the appearance of a solid form, a technique originally associated with the innovative work of Leonardo da Vinci.

cortile It. 'courtyard', often surrounded by *logge*, arcades, on one or more storeys.

Dance of Death *Danse macabre*: *memento mori* depicting skeletons, popular with early print makers.

diptych Hinged, two-panel painting, generally an altarpiece such as the Wilton Diptych. A triptych is the tripartite version.

Flamboyant Late French Gothic architectural style, in use from *c.* 1460.

Fontainebleau School French artistic style, *c.* 1530–*c.* 1560, inspired by the ornate, Mannerist work of Primaticcio, Rosso Fiorentino and others for Francis I at Fontainebleau.

fresco It. 'fresh'; in this method of wall painting, a small area is covered with a layer of wet plaster or lime, on which the design is drawn in charcoal. The paint which is then applied comprises powdered mineral or earth pigment suspended in water. Rather than resting on the wall surface, the pigment becomes integrated with the plaster and thus with the wall. This represents a day's work. *Fresco* is not suited to damp conditions, rendering such experiments unsuccessful in Venice.

Greek cross One with four arms of equal length; used as the ground plan of many centralised churches.

High Renaissance Generally used with reference to the period *c.* 1495–1520 and the work of Leonardo, Michelangelo, Raphael and their contemporaries, particularly in Rome.

ignudo It. 'nude'; nude male figure, such as those which appear on Michelangelo's Sistine Chapel ceiling.

intarsia Intricate marquetry in Italy.

International Gothic Although Italians were frequently as dismissive of the 'gothic' art of northern Europe as of the literary culture north of the Alps, the International Gothic style which flourished between *c.* 1375 and *c.* 1425 was as apparent in the painting and sculpture of Italy as it was in France and elsewhere. Characterised by 'aristocratic elegance and delicate naturalistic detail', the leading practitioners included Gentile da Fabriano, Pisanello and the Limbourg brothers.

Latin cross One with three short arms and one long; used as the standard ground plan for churches, the long arm being the nave, the short ones the chancel/choir and north and south transepts.

Mannerism Twentieth-century term derived from It. *maniera*, 'style', to summarise the distortions from the classical norms of architecture which emerged *c.* 1515–*c.* 1610 and the parallel phenomena in painting and sculpture of the same period. Thus, while many Renaissance architects knew their Vitruvius backwards, Michelangelo actually applied the elements of classical architecture backwards. The elongated figures of Parmigianino are often regarded as the epitome of Mannerism in painting.

mudéjar As *mudéjares* were Muslims who remained in Christian Spain, so *mudéjar* art was either the work of Moors or in imitation of Moorish non-figurative design.

oculus Eye-like window or other opening, such as in the ceiling of Mantegna's Camera degli Sposi, Mantua.

oil paint The combination of pigment with certain vegetable oils, particularly linseed, poppy and walnut, which 'harden on exposure to air'. Although the first use of this technique is commonly attributed to Jan van Eyck, the first principal practitioner, its origins actually predate him. The use of oil paint spread from the Low Countries to Spain, Italy and elsewhere.

orders Divisions of classical architecture, whether in the ancient world or any other period, most obviously identified by their capitals: Tuscan, Doric, Ionic, Corinthian and Composite. The principal features of any order are to be found in columns (or pilasters) and the entablatures which surmount them:

Entablature { Cornice / Frieze / Architrave

Column { Capital / Shaft / Base

perspective   Means by which space or three-dimensional objects may be conveyed on a flat (painting, engraving) or nearly flat (low relief) surface. First appreciated by the architect Brunelleschi, it was employed to striking effect by Masaccio, Uccello and other *quattrocento* (fifteenth-century) painters, who revelled in its possibilities. Alberti publicised these achievements in his treatise *De pictura*. Linear perspective is based on the notion of a vanishing point on which a series of lines converge.

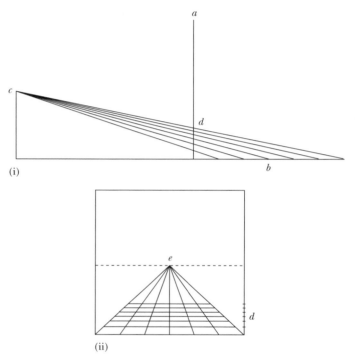

Alberti's 'visual pyramid': (i) side elevation: (a) picture plane;
(b) equal divisions behind the picture plane joined to the viewer's eye;
(c) viewer's eye; (d) points at which these lines cross the picture plane, which provide the horizontal divisions for (ii), a grid in perspective in which (e) is the 'centric' or 'vanishing' point.
Source: J. Turner, ed., *The Dictionary of Art*, vol. 24 London, 1996, p. 487.

Pietà   It. 'pity'; depiction of the Virgin Mary holding the dead Christ in her lap. The best-known example of this is Michelangelo's sculpture (1497–1500) in St Peter's basilica, Rome.

Plateresque   That ornately decorated, peculiarly Spanish combination of Gothic and classical styles of architecture which flourished in the early sixteenth century under the direction of masters such as Diego de

Siloé and Alonso de Covarrubias (1488–1570). The term derives from the intricate work of silversmiths. The equivalent Portuguese style is Manueline, dating from the reign of Manoel I (1495–1521).

predella   Smaller panel(s) placed at the foot of a painting, especially an altarpiece, the subject matter perhaps echoing that of the main picture.

'Primitives'   Nineteenth-century term for true pre-Raphaelite painting in an age when High Renaissance artists were popularly appreciated almost to the exclusion of their predecessors.

proportion   For the importance of balance and harmony in Renaissance art and architecture, see 18.1.2.

proto   Given the difficulty of distinguishing architects from master craftsmen in the fifteenth century, this term provides a useful combination of the two in an Italian context.

rustication   Large-cut masonry with deep joints, notable examples being the ground floor of Michelozzi's Palazzo Medici, Florence, and the diamond-like facing which gives the Palazzo dei Diamanti, Ferrara, its name.

sacra conversazione   'Holy conversation'; depiction of the Virgin and Child with saints apparently in dialogue.

Serliana   Tripartite window design in which two flat-topped sections flank an arched one, as first illustrated in Sebastiano Serlio's *Architettura* (1537). Also known as a Venetian window.

sfumato   It. 'smoky'; describes the immensely subtle fusion of different hues of which Leonardo was the supreme exponent.

studiolo   It. 'small study'; often used with reference to Federico da Montefeltro's intarsia-lined room in Urbino or that in Mantua in which Isabella d'Este collected works of art by the masters of her day.

tempietto   Small round temple-like building inspired by Bramante's original at S. Pietro in Montorio, Rome.

tempera   Egg-based medium generally used in painting prior to the development of oil paint in the fifteenth century.

terracotta   It. 'baked earth', burnt clay.

Venetian Gothic   Architectural style characterised by ogee arches and quatrefoil tracery which reached its most fully developed form in the fifteenth century and was lauded by Ruskin in *The Stones of Venice*.

villa   Inspired by literary accounts of villas and villa life in the ancient world, rich landowners developed medieval castles or farm buildings into rural outposts of urban civilisation and sophistication. The various Medici villas in the vicinity of Florence or, later, those of Palladio in the Veneto are well-known examples.

22 Plans and designs

22.1 Plans of Renaissance buildings

22.1.1 Micholozzo di Bartolomeo: elevation and ground floor plan, Palazzo Medici (now Medici-Riccardi), Florence, begun 1444

Cosimo de' Medici's imposing urban residence excited first resentment from his fellow citizens and then emulation, as Luca Pitti, Filippo Strozzi and others also chose the heavily rusticated look for their Florentine *palazzi*. The illustration above shows the main Via Larga (now Via Cavour) elevation of the Palazzo Medici. Opposite is the ground floor plan. The *cortile* once housed Donatello's bronze *David* (now Florence, Bargello).

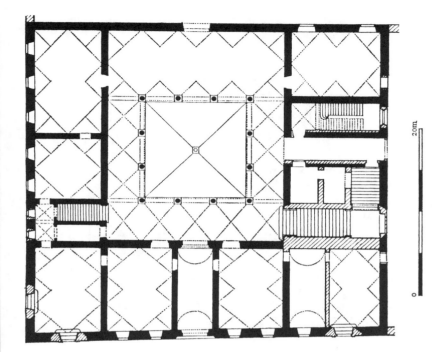

22.1.2 Donato Bramante: design for St Peter's basilica, Rome, c. 1506.

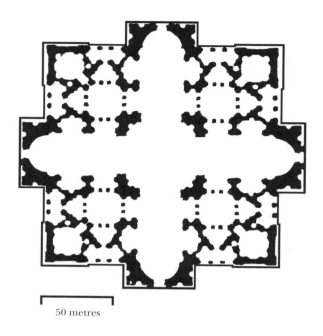

50 metres

Bramante, a keen student of classical architecture, chose a centralised, Greek cross plan for the rebuilding of the most important church in western Christendom. The four piers of the crossing were duly built to Bramante's design and thereafter determined the dimensions of the basilica for later architects, including Michelangelo, who designed the dome, and Carlo Maderno (1556–1629), who extended one of the arms to create a nave and thereby form a Latin cross.

22.1.3   Pedro Machuca: palace of Charles V, Granada, 1527–68

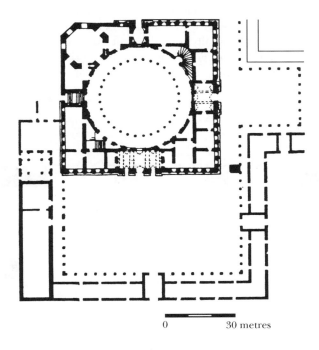

0   30 metres

This building, on which construction began in 1533, adjoins the Moorish palace of the Alhambra. The most prominent feature of this ground floor plan is the circular courtyard, inspired by Hadrian's villa at Tivoli, east of Rome, and a striking example of Renaissance preoccupation with harmony. It therefore reflects Charles V's imperial status as a new Caesar and forms a notably restrained and dignified contrast to traditionally ornate Spanish architectural design.

22.2   Orsanmichele, Florence, and its statues

Orsanmichele, now a church but formerly a grain market, occupies an important place in the history of Renaissance sculpture. The Florentine guilds were given responsibility for filling the fourteen niches around the exterior of the building. They commissioned work from the leading sculptors of the day, thereby creating a unique concentration of early Renaissance masterpieces. Unless otherwise stated, the statues remain *in situ.*

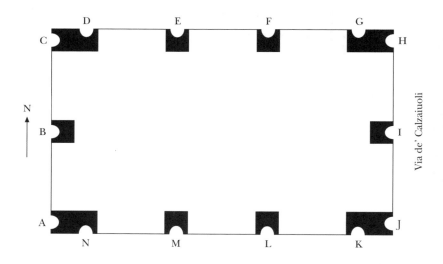

Notes to Plan 22.2

West Front

A   Nanni di Banco, *St Eligius, c.* 1411–14, for the Maniscalchi (farriers' guild)

B   Lorenzo Ghiberti, *St Stephen,* 1425–29, for the Arte della Lana (wool manufacturers' guild)

C   Lorenzo Ghiberti, *St Matthew,* 1419, for the Cambio (bankers' guild)

North Front

D   Donatello, *St George,* begun *c.* 1414/15 (now Florence, Bargello), for the Corazzai (armourers' guild)

E   Nanni di Banco, *Quattro santi coronati (Four crowned saints), c.* 1411–13, for the Maestri di Pietra e Legname (wood and stone workers' guild)

F   Nanni di Banco, *St Philip*, c. 1412–14, for the Calzaiuoli (shoemakers' guild)
G   Attrib. Bernardo Ciuffagni, *St Peter*, c. 1415, for the Beccai (butchers' guild)

East Front
H   Niccolò Lamberti, *St Luke*, c. 1405–10 (now Florence, Bargello), for the Giudici e Notai (magistrates' guild)
I   Donatello, *St Louis of Toulouse*, c. 1418–22 (now Florence, Museo dell'Opera di S. Croce); later replaced by Andrea del Verrocchio, *Christ and St Thomas*, c. 1463–80; both for the Tribunale della Mercanzia (merchants' court)
J   Lorenzo Ghiberti, *St John the Baptist*, 1414, for the Calimala (wool merchants' guild)

South Front
K   Attrib. Jacopo di Piero Guidi, *St John the Evangelist* (now Florence, Ospedale degli Innocenti), for the Arte della Seta (silk manufacturers' guild)
L   Simone Ferruci, *Virgin and Child*, 1399, for the Medici e Speciali (doctors' and pharmacists' guild)
M   Attrib. Piero di Niccolò Lamberti, *St James*, c. 1415, for the Vaiai e Pelliciai (furriers' guild)
N   Donatello, *St Mark*, 1411–13, for the Linaiuoli (linen weavers'/drapers' guild)

22.3   Sistine Chapel frescoes

Wall frescoes by Perugino, Botticelli and others 1481–83. Ceiling frescoes by Michelangelo 1508–12. See overleaf for plan. As in St Peter's basilica, liturgical East is actually at the western end of the building. The moses and Christ cycles are on the South and North walls respectively.

Perugino & Pinturicchio: Circumcision of Moses's son	Botticelli: Moses in Egypt and Midian	Rosselli: Crossing of the Red Sea

	Death of Haman		Salmon		Rehoboam	
		Jeremiah		Persian Sybil		Ezeki
Michelangelo: Last Judgement 1535–41 previously Perugino: Nativity of Christ, Finding of Moses and an altarpiece of the Assumption	Jonah	Separation of light from darkness	Creation of stars and planets	Separation of water from land	Creation of Adam	Creatie of Eve
	The Brazen Serpent	Libyan Sybil		Daniel		Cumae Sybil
			Jesse		Asa	

Perugino & Pinturicchio: Baptism of Christ; Christ preaching	Botticelli: Temptation of Christ	Ghirlandaio: Calling of the first apostles

selli: ses on Mount ai; Adoration of Golden Calf	Botticelli: Punishment of Korah and the sons of Aaron; Stoning of Moses	Signorelli: Last testament and death of Moses

Azariah		Zerubbabel		David and Goliath	
	Erythraean Sybil		Joel		
Fall of man and expulsion from Paradise	Sacrifice of Noah	The Flood	Drunkenness of Noah	Zechariah	
	Isaiah		Delphian Sybil		
Hezekiah		Josiah		Judith and Holofernes	

Ghirlandaio: Resurrection and Ascension of Christ Overpainted by Hendrik van den Broeck, 16C.

Signorelli: Fight for the body of Moses Overpainted by Matteo da Lecce, 16C.

sselli: mon on the unt; Healing the leper	Perugino: Christ giving the keys to St. Peter; Tribute money; Stoning of Christ	Rosselli: Last Supper; Agony in the garden; Betrayal; Crucifixion

23 Discovery and the world beyond Europe

23.1 Chronology of exploration

1390s   According to family papers, Venetians Antonio and Nicolò Zen (d. 1400), brothers of naval hero Carlo Zen, undertook explorations in the North Atlantic, possibly to Greenland and North America, though the fanciful nature of the narrative has caused doubt to be cast on its veracity.

1400   By this date the seafaring peoples of Genoa, Castile and Majorca had visited the Canary Islands and knew the coast of Africa as far south as Rio del Oro.

1402–5   Adventurers Jean de Béthancourt and Gadifer de la Salle undertook expeditions to the Canaries on behalf of the Crown of Castile.

1403–6   An embassy to the Mongol Timur (Tamerlane) at Samarkand by Ruy Gonzalez de Clavijo (d. 1412) resulted in the first account of oriental travel by a Spaniard.

1407   Italian Pietro Rombulo resident in Ethiopia until 1444.

1408   Documentary evidence tells of a wedding in Greenland, after which there were no known contacts between Europe and Greenland until at least the 1470s.

1415   Portuguese conquest of the Moroccan port of Ceuta, strategically placed opposite Gibraltar and at the end of caravan routes, was a prelude to sustained Portuguese interest in African commercial opportunities.

1419   Nicolò de' Conti (c. 1395–1469) of Venice left his home city on a twenty-five-year round trip which took him to Syria, India, Ceylon, Sumatra, Java, Burma, Malaya and the Holy Land. Infante Henrique of Portugal, Prince Henry 'the Navigator' (1394–1460), made governor of Algarve by his father João I, from where he sponsored voyages of exploration. The prince's interest lay in a combination of combating Islam, conquering the Holy Land (in alliance with the legendary Christian priest-king Prester John, supposedly a descendant of the Magi and variously located in Asia and Africa) and trading in African gold and slaves, though his role in Portuguese geographical discoveries has often been exaggerated.

c. 1419   Portuguese colonisation of Porto Santo and Madeira, where lucrative sugar plantations were established.

1427   Azores discovered by Diogo de Silves and colonised by Portuguese from 1439; cereals grown there.

1434   Portuguese Gil Enneas sailed beyond Cape Bojador, the limit of previous African exploration due to the shallowness of coastal waters and the notion that beyond it lay the 'torrid zone', a region too hot for human habitation.

1437   Abortive Portuguese attack on Tangier.

1441   Ethiopian and Coptic delegates excited great interest at the ecumenical Council of Florence. First black slaves taken from West Africa to Europe. Portuguese Nuno Tristão sighted Cape Branco (in modern Mauritania).

1444   Expeditions by Nuno Tristão and his fellow-countryman Dinis Dias venturing to the Senegal River and Cape Verde respectively. Nicolò de' Conti's return to Venice (see 1419, above).

1448   Foundation of a fort at Arguin, south of Cape Branco, the first of the factories which formed the basis of the Portuguese seaborne empire.

1454   Venetian patrician merchant Alvise Ca' da Mosto (Cadamosto, *c.* 1426–83) deserted the Flanders galleys to seek commercial ventures with Portuguese adventurers along the African coast, returning from his first Senegal expedition the following year.

1455   By means of the Bull *Romanus pontifex* Nicholas V confirmed the Portuguese in possession of all their African discoveries.

1456   Travelling with Antoniotto Usodimare, a Genoese mariner encountered during his first African venture, Ca' da Mosto undertook his second African exploration. His written account of these travels is notable not only for the sympathetic light in which he described the people of the region, but also for his claim to have discovered the Cape Verde Islands when blown off course *en route* for Senegal. This assertion has been contested.

1461–62   Diogo Afonso discovered the Cape Verde Islands.

1462   After discovering Sierra Leone *c.* 1460, Pedro da Sintra rounded Cape Mensurado (in modern Liberia) and entered the Gulf of Guinea.

1469   Fernão Gomes took up the baton of Portuguese African coastal trade and exploration until 1474.

1470s   Possible renewal of contacts between Denmark and Greenland.

1471   João de Santarém and Pero Escobar reinforced the Portuguese presence in the Gulf of Guinea. Venetian Caterino Zen sent as ambassador to the Persian court of Uzun Hasan, the republic's anti-Ottoman ally. Tangier taken by Portugal.

1474   Lopo Gonsalves reached Cape St Catherine (in modern Gabon). Florentine geographer and astronomer Paolo del Pozzo Toscanelli (1397–1482) conveyed to Afonso V of Portugal, in a letter which duly inspired Christopher Columbus (It. Cristoforo Colombo, Sp. Cristobal Colón, *c.* 1451–1506), his notion about the circumference of the globe and the possibility of sailing westwards from Europe in order to reach Cathay/China.

1474–78   Venetian patrician Giosafat Barbaro (1413–94) in Persia as the republic's ambassador to Uzun Hasan: this followed in the wake of his 1436–51 journey through Russia and the Black Sea region. He wrote accounts of both expeditions, as did his fellow-countryman Ambrogio Contarini (1429–at least 1496), whose career followed a similar pattern.

1475   Outbreak of the Castilian War of Succession, in which the Portuguese invaded Castile and the Castilians realised the potential of developing a naval dimension to meet the challenge set by their maritime neighbour.

c. **1476**   Columbus moved from Genoa to Lisbon, from where he voyaged to Iceland, Madeira and probably Elmina (see 1481 below).

1479   **4 Sept.**: Treaty of Alcaçovas acknowledged Portugal's monopoly over the Guinea trade and confirmed Portuguese possession of the Cape Verde Islands, Madeira and the Azores, leaving the Canaries as the only Atlantic island group in Castilian hands. This proved to be crucial for Columbus's plans for sailing west to Asia, since he set a course due west from the Canaries in 1492.

c. **1480**   English voyages in search of 'Brasill', one of a number of fabled Atlantic islands, probably began at this time.

1481   Foundation of the Portuguese fort at Elmina (São Jorge da Mina) on the Guinea coast.

1482–84   Voyage of the Portuguese Diogo Cão along the coasts of modern Gabon, Congo and Angola.

c. **1484**   Columbus sought Portuguese royal patronage for his westward voyage to Cathay, a journey to be broken at the allegedly pearl and gold-rich island of Cipangu (Japan), of which he read in Marco Polo's *Divisament du monde.*

c. **1485**   Columbus in Castile, continuing his quest for patronage for the proposed oceanic expedition.

1485–86   Diogo Cão's second voyage took him to Cape Cross (in modern Namibia).

1486–87   Columbus's claims were rejected by an investigating panel in Castile, prompting him to return briefly to Portugal and contributing to that sense of isolation and victimisation which increased throughout his subsequent career.

1487 Portuguese envoys Pero da Covilhã (d. 1526) and Afonso de Paiva sent to India and Ethiopia via Egypt, on a mission to contact Prester John. The former returned to Portugal in 1525 after many adventures, but the latter died in Ethiopia. Fleming Ferdinand van Olmen gained permission from the Portuguese King to look for the fabled Atlantic island of Antilia, but the consequences of this are not known. Bartolomeu Dias (*c.* 1450–1500) departed from his native Portugal on one of the most significant voyages undertaken during this period.

1488 Dias rounded the Cape of Good Hope, venturing as far as the Great Fish River, thereby opening up an alternative, Turk-free route to Asia and proving that the Indian Ocean was not an enclosed sea. He returned to Lisbon in December.

1489 Bartolomé Colón (d. 1514/15), brother of Christopher Columbus, travelled to England and France in search of patronage for his brother's westward voyage to the Indies.

1492 **17 Apr.**: Columbus finally received a contract – to find 'islands and mainland in the Ocean Sea' – from Isabella of Castile and Ferdinand of Aragon, heralding the first of his transatlantic voyages. Developing the tradition of the Spanish *reconquista*, Columbus was appointed hereditary admiral, viceroy and governor-general of any non-Christian territories discovered. Meanwhile, his self-appointed role became that of *Christo ferens*, bearer of Christ to the inhabitants of the Indies. **3 Aug.**: Columbus departed from the Andalusian port of Palos with a fleet of three ships, the *Santa Maria*, *Niña* and *Pinta*, the last of which probably took its name from Martín Alonso Pinzón (d. 1493) of Palos, Columbus's fellow commander on this expedition. **12 Oct.**: Columbus's ships landed in the Bahamas at an island which he called San Salvador (Watling Island), known to its inhabitants as Guanahani. The party discovered Cuba in October and Hispaniola in December. All of these discoveries Columbus thought of as outlying parts of Asia and also claimed them for the Crown of Castile. In the course of the expedition Columbus enslaved Arawaks from the larger Caribbean islands, whom he was subsequently ordered to release. According to natural law it would have been permissible to enslave man-eating Caribs of the Lesser Antilles. **25 Dec.**: Loss of flagship *Santa Maria* and foundation of a fort at Navidad on Hispaniola.

1493   **16 Jan.**: Departure of Columbus from Hispaniola.

3/4 May: Alexander VI's Bull of donation and demarcation, *Inter caetera*, which gave the Crown of Castile 'all islands and mainlands, discovered or yet to be discovered, sighted or not yet sighted, to the west and south of a line set and drawn from the Arctic or North Pole to the Antarctic or South Pole, the line to stand a hundred leagues to the west and south of the so-called Azores and Cape Verde Islands . . . if they are not actually possessed by another Christian prince . . .'

25 Sept.: Columbus departed from Spain on his second transatlantic voyage.

18 Nov.: He discovered Puerto Rico.

28 Nov.: Garrison of the fort at Navidad was found to have been massacred.

1494   **7 June**: Treaty of Tordesillas moved the line of demarcation 270 leagues further west, a development which inadvertently put Brazil in the Portuguese hemisphere.

24 Apr.–29 Sept.: Columbus explored Cuba and Jamaica, naming the islands Juana and Santiago respectively.

1495   **Mar.**: Beginning of Columbus's campaign to subdue the interior of Hispaniola.

Oct.: Investigation by Juan Aguado into Columbus's alleged misconduct as governor of Castile's New World possessions.

1496   Santo Domingo founded on Hispaniola, the first European town in the New World, though it was moved to another site following a hurricane in 1502.

5 Mar.: John Cabot (Giovanni Caboto, *c*. 1450–*c*. 1498), a Genoese-born Venetian national, together with his three sons, received letters patent from Henry VII of England to sail at their own cost to discover 'isles, countries, regions or provinces' beyond the seas.

10 Mar.: Columbus departed Hispaniola.

11 June: He arrived at Cadiz.

1497   **23 Apr.**: Columbus received 'instructions' for his third voyage from Ferdinand and Isabella.

2 May: Cabot departed Bristol in the *Mathew*.

24 June: He reached Newfoundland, explored the coastline and began his return voyage (20 July), having taken up exploration in that region where the Norsemen had left off.

July: The Portuguese Vasco da Gama (d. 1524) departed Lisbon on his first voyage to India, following Bartolomeu Dias's example, but rather than hugging the coast he sailed out into the Atlantic to catch the best winds.

6 Aug.: Cabot's return to Bristol.

25 Dec.: Vasco da Gama reached the land he named Natal.

1498 **May**: Cabot's second expedition left Bristol. One ship returned, but Cabot and four other vessels were lost. Cabot's story was later told by his son Sebastian (*c.* 1480–1557), who thereby took credit for his father's achievements while becoming a notable explorer in his own right.

20 May: Vasco da Gama landed at Calicut on India's Malabar coast.

30 May: Columbus departed from Sanlúcar de Barrameda on his third transatlantic voyage, dedicated to the Holy Trinity.

31 July: Columbus sighted Trinidad (Trinity) but did not land, preferring to continue along the coast of the South American mainland during the first half of August.

14/15 Aug.: Columbus recorded his discovery of 'a very great continent, which until today has been unknown', sensing himself close to the Earthly Paradise which medieval maps had, however, located in the East.

19 Aug.: Columbus returned to Hispaniola to discover a rebellion led by his erstwhile companion Francisco Roldán.

1499 Vasco da Gama returned to Lisbon from his epoch-making expedition to India. Spaniards Alonso de Ojeda (*c.* 1465–1515) and Juan de la Cosa (*c.* 1460–1510), veterans of Columbus's second voyage, were joined by the Florentine Amerigo Vespucci (*c.* 1451–1512), who had been agent in Seville for the Medici Bank, for a thirteen-month voyage which included exploration of the Guinea and Venezualan coasts, discovering the pearl fishery missed by Columbus.

Sept.: Conclusion of Roldán's rebellion.

28 Oct.: Azoreans Pedro Maria Barcelos and João Fernandes, a *lavrador* (husbandman), obtained letters patent from King Manoel of Portugal permitting their voyage into the North Atlantic.

1500 **Summer**: Barcelos and Fernandes reached Cape Farewell, Greenland, which they named Tiera del Lavrador, a term only later transferred to mainland Canada.

Aug.: Arrival in Hispaniola of Francisco de Bobadilla (d. 1502) to investigate further complaints about Columbus's poor leadership and maladministration.

Sept.: Arrest of Columbus, who was clearly unable to cope with his responsibilities as viceroy and governor-general.

Oct.: Columbus taken back to Spain in chains. Pedro Alvares Cabral (1460–1526) accidentally discovered Brazil for Portugal by taking a wide sweep into the Atlantic to catch good winds for a voyage to India, which he subsequently completed. Three other expeditions along the coasts of modern Brazil took place that year, led by Vincente Yáñez Pinzón, Diego de Lepe and Alonso Vélez de Mendoza. Spaniards Rodrigo Bastidas (1460–1527) and Juan de la Cosa explored the Venezualan and Colombian coasts westwards to Darién (Panama). The first North Atlantic voyage of the Portuguese Gaspar Corte-Real (c. 1450–1501) took him to Labrador. The otherwise unknown Italian Ludovico de Varthema (pre-1470–1517) began his travels in the Near East and India.

1501   Vespucci's second expedition to the New World to explore, with the Portuguese Gonçalo Coelho, the Brazilian coast south of Cape Sao Roque. Gaspar Cortes-Real's second North Atlantic voyage, in which he and his ship were lost.

1502   **Jan.**: Vespucci's party discovered Rio de Janeiro (River of January).

   14 Mar.: Ferdinand and Isabella granted permission for Columbus's fourth and final transatlantic voyage.

   15 Apr.: Bartolomé de Las Casas (1474–1566), later to be known as the Defender of, and Apostle to, the Indies, arrived at Santo Domingo.

   11 May: Columbus departed from Cadiz.

   29 June: By order of the Spanish monarchs, Columbus was refused shelter at Santo Domingo from a storm.

   30 June: Bobadilla killed in that same storm, but Columbus and his ships survived.

   20 Oct.: Columbus's discovery of Veragua on the Central American mainland. Vasco da Gama departed on his second voyage to India. Miguel Corte-Real (c. 1450–1502) sailed into the North Atlantic in search of his brother Gaspar, but also fell victim to the seas.

1503   Foundation at Seville of the Casa de Contratación to control all trade between Spain and the New World, including the collection of the *quinto real* (royal fifth), a tax on imports.

   June–Aug.: Columbus marooned on Jamaica, while Nicolás de Ovando, governor on Hispaniola, refused to lend help.

1504   **12 Sept.**: Columbus departed the Indies for Spain, where he arrived on 7 Nov., shortly before the death of Isabella of Castile. Widower Ferdinand of Aragon allowed his Aragonese subjects to emigrate to the New World, a privilege previously confined to Isabella's Castilian subjects.

1505   Francisco de Almeida (d. 1509) appointed viceroy in Portugal's Asian possessions, known as the *Estado da India*.

1506   **20 May**: Death of Columbus at Valladolid.

1507   First Portuguese landing in Ceylon. Bastidas and De la Cosa returned to areas they explored in 1500.

1508   Capture of strategically important port of Ormuz at the mouth of the Persian Gulf by the Portuguese fleet of Afonso de Albuquerque (d. 1515), who subsequently succeeded Almeida as viceroy in 1509. Spanish conquest and colonisation of Puerto Rico led by Juan Ponce de León (1460–1521) and of Jamaica by Juan de Esquivel (d. 1512). Eight-month circumnavigation of Cuba by Sebastián de Ocampo (d. 1514). Expedition along the coast of Yucatan peninsula led by Vincente Yánez Pinzón, captain of the *Niña* in 1492, and Juan Díaz de Solís (d. 1516).

1509   **Feb.**: Portuguese victory against a combined Egyptian and Gujerati fleet at the battle of Diu (Gujerat) confirmed their maritime dominance in the Indian Ocean. Diego Colón (*c.* 1480–1526) sent to Santo Domingo, capital of Hispaniola, as hereditary governor of the Indies, a post which he held until 1515. Like his father, he regarded all the islands as his personal dominion. Expeditions by Alonso de Ojeda and Juan de la Cosa to the Gulf of Urabá, off the Colombian coast.

1510   **10 Nov.**: Albuquerque's capture of Goa from the Sultan of Bijapur led to it becoming the principal Portuguese base in India.

1511   Capture of Malacca by Albuquerque's fleet. First *Audiencia* (judicial tribunal) in the New World established at Santo Domingo. Diego Colón sent Diego Velásquez (1465–1524) with 300 men to conquer Cuba, which had been explored many times by Spaniards but not subdued. Colón claimed that this was achieved 'without bloodshed' – Spanish blood, that is, for the natives died in large numbers, as Bartolomé de Las Casas witnessed.

    Dec.: Las Casas, by then a priest and shortly to become a Dominican friar, experienced a conversion which led him to devote the rest of his long life to the abolition of the *encomienda* system, by which Spaniards had lordship over large numbers of Amerindians held in a state of virtual slavery, and the betterment of conditions for native workers, in order to bring about their true conversion to Christianity. Among works he produced to draw attention to Spanish atrocities in the New World was the *Short Account of the Destruction of the Indies*, written *c.* 1541, but published 1552 to counter the racially charged arguments of Juan Ginés de Sepúlveda (1490–1573).

1512   Foundation of Baracoa, first Spanish town on Cuba.
    Mar.: Albuquerque tried and failed to take Aden.

27 Dec.: Laws of Burgos limited the exploitation of native labourers in the New World but proved exceedingly difficult to enforce. The Portuguese Antonio d'Abreu and Francisco Serrão explored eastwards from Malacca, visiting Borneo, Celebes and the Moluccas.

1513   Aden captured by the Portuguese, but lost to the Turks in 1538. The Portuguese Jorge Álvares led the first European mission to Canton. Ponce de León explored the Florida coast from east to west and gave the region the name it retains. Vasco Núñez de Balboa (*c.* 1475–1517) crossed the Isthmus of Panama, Amerindians carrying ships in sections on their backs, sighted the Pacific (25 Sept.), waded into the sea with his sword drawn and claimed it for Charles I of Spain.

1514   Pedrarias Dávila (Pedro Arias de Ávila, d. 1531), a veteran of wars in Granada and North Africa, arrived in Darién/Panama as its first governor.

1516   **Jan.**: Juan Díaz de Solís killed in Rio de la Plata while searching for a strait between the Atlantic and Pacific Oceans. Francisco Hernández de Cordoba sailed from Cuba to explore the coast of the Yucatan peninsula, returning with news of Mayan cities in the region.

1517   Sebastian Cabot, who had transferred from English to Spanish service in 1512, was appointed chief pilot of the Casa de la Contratación. The Portuguese embassy of Tomé Pires arrived at Canton. He reached Beijing by 1520 but failed to establish legitimate trade relations.

1518   Juan de Grijalva (1480–1527), whose Caribbean experiences had included the conquest of Cuba, led an exploration along the coastline of the Gulf of Mexico west from the Yucatan peninsula.

1519   Foundation of a permanent settlement at Panama after governor Pedrarias Dávila moved the seat of government from Nombre de Dios on the Caribbean side of the isthmus to the Pacific side, to continue the search for a strait between the oceans. Conflict of personalities between Pedraias Dávila and Balboa, who was arrested and executed. Hernan Cortés (1485–1547), a conquistador from Estremadura, departed from Cuba with eleven ships, *c.* 600 men and sixteen horses. They skirted the Yucatan coast and acquired a number of women at Tabasco, including the interpreter baptised as Doña Marina. The expedition's other interpreter, Jerónimo de Aguilar (1489–1531) was a conquistador who had travelled to Darién with Balboa, been shipwrecked and captured by the Maya.

28 June: Formal foundation of Vera Cruz, base camp for Cortés's expedition into the Mexican interior and where their ships were sunk to prevent desertion.

c. **8 Aug.**: Cortés left Vera Cruz with 400 Spanish infantry and 200 slaves, joined eight days later by 1,000 Amerindian allies at Zempoala, a city subject to the Aztecs, for the march to the Aztec capital Tenochtitlán.

18 Sept.: Cortés arrived at Tlaxcala, another city resentful of Aztec subjection and which proved to be a vital ally.

20 Sept.: Sent by Charles V to find a westerly route to the Indies, the Portuguese Ferdinand Magellan (Port. Fernão de Magalhaes, Sp. Fernando de Magallanes, 1480–1521) departed Seville on the voyage known as the first circumnavigation of the globe, though Magellan himself did not live to complete the journey.

Nov.: Cortés entered Tenochtitlán, later the site of Mexico City, where the 'emperor' Montezuma II (b. 1466, reigned 1502–20) was kept on as a puppet ruler. One reason the Spaniards were able to take Tenochtitlán so easily was that the Aztecs believed these strangers might be the god Quetzalcoátl and other superhuman beings.

1520   Cortés left Pedro de Alvarado (1485–1541) in command at Tenochtitlán while he returned to Vera Cruz, where Spaniards were in rebellion against him. Alvarado was unable to resist a native rebellion.

28/29 May: Cortés proved victorious in a battle with the rebels led by Pánfilo de Narváez (*c.* 1470–1528) who, in turn, was acting under orders from Diego Velásquez.

Late June: Montezuma died during the siege of Alvorado's palace in Tenochtitlán.

30 June/1 July: 1,000–1,300 of Cortés's men perished in the *noche triste*, their retreat from Tenochtitlán to the allied city of Tlaxcala, where Cortés was able to regroup.

7 July: Cortés victorious at the battle of Otumba, the turning of the tide in his campaign of conquest.

21 Oct.: Magellan reached the Strait between Patagonia and Tierra del Fuego (Land of Fire, so called from beacons lit by natives who were not themselves seen) which has since borne his name.

28 Nov.: Magellan sailed into the Pacific. The Portuguese Rodrigo de Lima and Francisco Álvares, a priest, were sent to Ethiopia, again in search of the ever-elusive Prester John, returning to Lisbon in 1527.

1521   As related in Bernal Diaz's *History of the conquest of New Spain*, Tenochtitlán was besieged and captured (13 Aug.) by Cortés. The city was then destroyed and rebuilt in Spanish style as Mexico City. Exploration of the Carolina coast by Spaniard Lucas Vásquez de Ayllón (d. 1528). Alonso de Pineda explored the north coast of the Gulf of Mexico. **27 Apr.**: Magellan reached Cebu in the Philippines, where he was killed by natives. Some of his crew, led by Juan Sebastián Elcano (1487–1526), certainly circumnavigated the globe on that voyage and it has been argued that Magellan did so in that he had experience of the Far East on previous expeditions. Antonio Pigafetta (1491–1534) of Vicenza was among the survivors and wrote an account of this expedition. From this year Spanish transatlantic voyages received military protection from pirates in the form of the Armada de la Carrera de Indias.

1522   **8 Sept.**: Elcano arrived in Lisbon. A naval expedition heading south from Panama and led by Pascual de Andegoya (1495–1548) foreshadowed the achievements of Francisco Pizarro.

1524   On his first voyage, the Italian Giovanni da Verrazzano (1485–1528), sponsored by Francis I to counter Charles V's patronage of Spanish New World exploration, explored the coast of North America from modern North Carolina, past New York Bay and the Hudson River, to Maine. He returned to France in 1525. Francisco Pizarro (1476–1541), illiterate illegitimate son of an Estremaduran *hidalgo*, entered into a partnership with Diego de Almagro (1475–1538) and Hernando L uque in Panama and undertook (1524–25) the first of his three expeditions along the Pacific coast of South America.

1525   Portuguese Estêvão Gomes commissioned by Charles V to find the North-West Passage, believed to link the Atlantic and Pacific Oceans.

1525–26   Sebastian Cabot sent by Charles V to trace the route of Magellan's circumnavigation and to find a more convenient westerly route to the Pacific. He had reached Rio de la Plata by 1527 and returned to Spain by 1529.

1526   New Guinea discovered for Portugal by Jorge de Meneses (d. 1537).

1526–27   Pizarro's second Pacific voyage included a visit to the city of Tumbres, where he was impressed by the level of civilisation and heard of a great inland empire on a par with that of the Aztecs.

1527   Spaniards began the exploration of the Pacific coast of Mexico and, led by Álvaro de Saavedra Cerón (d. 1529), pioneered a trans-Pacific route from Mexico to the Moluccas.

1528   Pizarro returned to Spain with specimens of Peruvian gold and silver work. In traditional fashion, Charles V appointed him governor of a South American province yet to be conquered. According to the literary evidence, Giovanni da Verrazzano, with his brother Girolamo, undertook a second voyage to the West Indies. At Guadaloupe, Giovanni allegedly waded ashore and was killed by man-eating Caribs while Girolamo looked on helplessly. Narváez landed in Florida, where he was responsible for some of the atrocities condemned by Las Casas. Alvar Nuñez Cabeza de Vaca and three companions were shipwrecked on the Gulf coast of Texas and spent the next eight years walking to the Pacific coast and then to Mexico City.

1529   By the treaty of Zaragoza, Spain acknowledged Portuguese possession of the Moluccas and another longitudinal line was drawn through the ocean defining their hemispheres of influence. Expedition to Quito by Sebastián de Benalcázar (1480–1551).

1530   **Jan.**: Armed with capitulations granted by Charles V in 1529, Pizarro left Spain for Panama.

1531   **Jan.**: Pizarro's departure from Panama with three ships, *c.* 180 men and twenty-seven horses, on his third and most significant expedition down the Pacific coast of South America. Apart from the horses, the numbers were smaller than those of Cortés in Mexico, but Pizarro had the advantage of being able to copy Cortes's tactics since the Peruvian Indians were unaware of the existence, let alone the fate, of the Aztecs.

1532   Beginning of Portuguese settlement in Brazil.

24 Sept.: Pizarro began the march inland to where he understood the Inca Atahualpa (*c.* 1500–33) was based. Atahualpa was the younger son of the Inca Huayna Capec (d. 1525) and had been fighting a civil war with his elder brother Huascar since 1530.

16 Nov.: Atahualpa captured at Cajamarca after Pizarro's men massacred the Inca's defenceless entourage in the enclosed town square. There followed Atahualpa's famous offer to fill a room with gold in exchange for his own freedom. Huascar was killed by order of the captive Atahualpa.

1533   **16 July**: Death of Atahualpa. Pizarro's own assassination occurred in 1541, part of the civil war then raging among the lawless conquistadors.

15 Nov.: Spanish capture of the Inca's capital at Cuzco.

1534   Sponsored by Francis I, Jacques Cartier (1491–1557) of Saint-Malo undertook his first voyage to North America, exploring

Newfoundland and the Labrador coast after an Atlantic crossing of twenty days.

1535   Cartier's second voyage to North America, during which he explored the St Lawrence river and reached the sites of the future cities of Quebec and Montreal. A third expedition followed in 1536. The foundation of Lima in Peru, which became the principal centre of Spanish settlement in the New World, marked the end of Spanish conquest and the beginning of colonisation. Portuguese capture of the Gujerati port of Diu.

1536   Foundation of Buenos Aires by Pedro de Mendoza.

1537   Foundation of Asunción (Paraguay) by Juan de Salazar.

23.2   Discovery: a literary chronology

1406   The Florentine Giacomo Angeli de Scarperia conveyed from Constantinople to Italy a Greek manuscript of the major geographical work surviving from Antiquity, the *Geography* (written *c*. AD150) of Claudius Ptolemy of Alexandria. Angeli completed his translation of the *Geography* into Latin in 1410. This discovery was a major spur to Renaissance interest in geographical matters and the text became as influential as the *Historia naturalis* (AD73) of the Elder Pliny, the classical authority on zoology, botany and other facets of the natural world.

c. 1410   Cardinal Pierre d'Ailly (d. 1420), *Imago mundi*, a geographical text based on classical and biblical sources: consulted by Columbus.

c. 1414   Pierre d'Ailly, *Compendium cosmographiae*: the development of his geographical ideas in the light of reading Ptolemy.

1418   Cardinal Guillaume Fillastre (d. 1428) commissioned a translation of Ptolemy's *Geography* into Latin.

1423   Text of Strabo's *Geography* (AD17–23) arrived in Italy from Byzantium.

1440s   Alleged date of the Vinland Map, published in 1965 and supposedly demonstrating detailed knowledge of Greenland and North America, but since exposed as a twentieth-century forgery.

1448   Poggio Bracciolini, *Historia de varietate fortunae*, containing an account of the Venetian Nicolò de' Conti's travels in India.

c. 1450   Enea Silvio Piccolomini (the future Pius II), *Historia rerum ubique gestarum*: a geographical work heavily based on Pliny.

1457   Fra Mauro (d. 1459) of Venice commissioned by Afonso V of Portugal to produce a world map; this was completed by other hands in 1460 and is now housed in the Biblioteca Nazionale Marciana, Venice.

1458 Guarino da Verona completed his translation into Latin of Strabo's *Geography*.

1469 First printed edition of Strabo's *Geography*.

1475 First printed edition of Ptolemy's *Geography*, Vicenza.

1477 Ptolemy's *Geography* printed with maps, Bologna: the maps illustrate Ptolomy's miscalculation of the Eurasian land mass as occupying 180° of longitude. This had a great impact on Columbus, who also knew of Marinus of Tyre, who calculated the same land mass as 225° from east to west, thereby creating an even narrower Atlantic.

1478 First Roman edition of Ptolemy, with maps.

1480–83 First printed edition of Pierre d'Ailly's *Imago mundi*, Louvain.

1492 First known terrestrial globe, made by Martin Behaim of Nuremberg.

1496 Richard Pynson's edition of the *Travels* of 'Sir John Mandeville', improbable tales of marvellous men inhabiting distant islands; this popular piece of travel literature provided further inspiration for Columbus and remained in print until long after its contents had been discredited as total fiction.

1500 Juan de la Cosa, a member of Columbus's second transtlantic expedition, produced the first map of the New World.

1504 Although much travel literature was printed, the pamphlet *Mundus novus*, attributed to Amerigo Vespucci, caught the European imagination. Vespucci's contribution to publicity about the New World was of greater significance than his seamanship.

1507 Vespucci's *Quattuor navigationes* built on his earlier success. His printer, Martin Waldseemüller of Saint-Dié, Alsace, suggested that the hitherto unknown continent be named after Vespucci, though both men expressed doubts about the discoveries forming a continent and were prepared to accept them as outlying parts of Asia.

1510 Ludovico de Varthema's *Itinerary*, a relation of his travels in Arabia, India and elsewhere.

1511 Publication of *De orbo novo*, vol. I by Pietro Martire d'Anghiera (1459–1526), an account of Spanish explorations in the New World; divided into *decades* in the classical style, the second and third volumes followed in 1516 and 1530 respectively.

1513 Strasbourg edition of Ptolemy's *Geography* notable for naming Columbus as the discoverer of the New World. Juan López de Palacios Rubios (d. 1525) published a *Requerimiento* which provided official justification for Spanish overlordship of Amerindians.

1516   Thomas More's *Utopia*, written in Latin, tells of how a fictional explorer, Raphael Hythlodaeus, travelled with Vespucci to South America but insisted on being left behind. His own explorations then took him into the South Pacific, where he found an island, Utopia (lit. 'nowhere'), inhabited by rational, civilised men whose crime-free society contrasted with that of More's England.

1535   Gonzálo Fernández de Oviedo, *Historia general y natural de las Indias*.

24 Maps and city plans

24.1 Europe's natural resources and patterns of trade

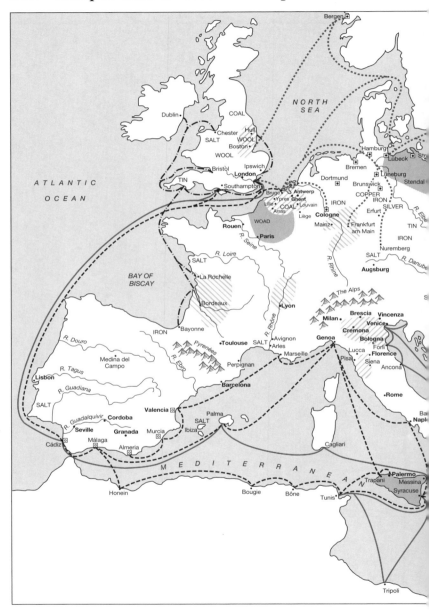

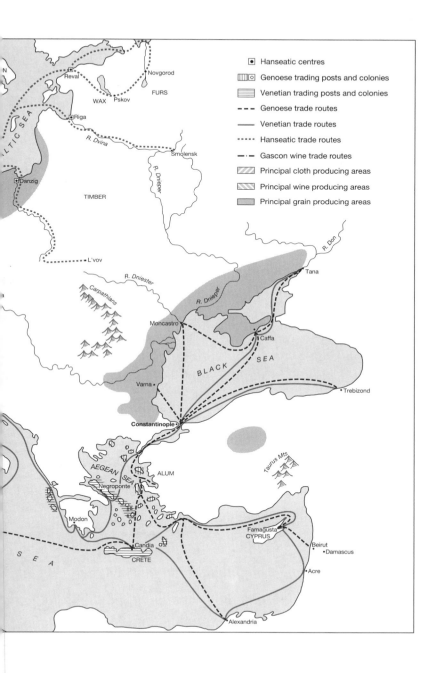

Novgorod

Reval

FURS

WAX Pskov

BALTIC SEA

Riga

R. Dvina

Smolensk

R. Dnieper

Danzig

TIMBER

L'vov

R. Dniester

Carpathians

R. Dnieper

R. Don

Tana

Moncastro

Caffa

BLACK   SEA

Varna

Trebizond

Constantinople

AEGEAN SEA   ALUM

Taurus Mts

Negroponte

Modon

Famagusta
CYPRUS

Beirut

Candia

Damascus

CRETE

Acre

SEA

Alexandria

	Hanseatic centres
	Genoese trading posts and colonies
	Venetian trading posts and colonies
- - -	Genoese trade routes
——	Venetian trade routes
·····	Hanseatic trade routes
—·—	Gascon wine trade routes
	Principal cloth producing areas
	Principal wine producing areas
	Principal grain producing areas

24.2 Europe's political divisions

- - - - Boundary of the Holy Roman Empire

SCOTLAND

Edinburgh

IRELAND

NORTH SEA

WALES

ENGLAND

London

ATLANTIC OCEAN

Rotterdam   HOLLAND
ZEELAND
Bruges
FLANDERS   Antwerp
Ghent   BRABANT
Calais   ARTOIS   Cologne
HAINAULT

Caen   Rouen
Reims   LUXEMBOURG   Trier
Rennes   Paris
BRITTANY
R. Seine

Nantes   Orléans   LORRAINE   Nancy
R. Loire

Bourges

FRANCE

BURGUNDY   Basel
SWISS CONFEDER
Lyon   DU
SAVOY   MI
M
Genoa

Bordeaux

Burgos
R. Duero   Valladolid   NAVARRE
Coimbra   Salamanca   Saragossa   Toulouse
PORTUGAL   R. Tagus   Toledo   ROUSSILLON
Lisbon   CASTILE
R. Guadiana
R.Ebro
R. Guadalquivir   ARAGON
GRANADA   Granada   Valencia

Avignon
Marseille   REPUPBLIC OF GENOA

Barcelona   CORSICA (Genoese)

BALEARIC IS.   SARDINIA (Aragonese)

Tangier   Ceuta

MEDITERRANEAN

Oran   Algiers

MOROCCO

WAY

SWEDEN

Moscow

ENMARK

TEUTONIC ORDER

BALTIC SEA

TEUTONIC
ORDER
Marienburg

LITHUANIA

POMERANIA

BRANDENBURG

SILESIA

R. Vistula

SAXONY

POLAND

UKRAINE

RE

BOHEMIA

uremberg   Prague •

MORAVIA

Cracow

ensburg

BAVARIA

Vienna

R. Danube

sburg Munich

AUSTRIA

MOLDAVIA

OL

STYRIA

Buda

CARINTHIA

na

CARNIOLA

Venice •

HUNGARY

Ferrara •

WALLACHIA

Florence •

BOSNIA

CE •   • Urbino

Ancona

SERBIA

PAPAL
STATES

ADRIATIC SEA

MONTENEGRO

BLACK SEA

Rome •

RUMELIA

OTTOMAN

Constantinople •

KINGDOM
OF NAPLES

Salonika

EMPIRE

Naples

*AEGEAN
SEA*

Otranto

Palermo •

Messina

SICILY

E A

24.3   Renaissance Florence

Quarters and gonfaloni

The city of Florence was divided into four Quarters, with each Quarter subdivided into *gonfaloni*. Two of the Quarters took their names from the churches of S. Croce (Franciscan) and S. Maria Novella (Dominican), with that of S. Giovanni occupying the central area between them. That part of the city on the opposite side of the Arno (Oltrarno) formed the Quarter of S. Spirito. They were divided into *gonfaloni* as follows:

Quarter	Gonfaloni	Quarter	Gonfaloni
S. Croce	Bue	S. Maria Novella	Lion Bianco
	Carro		Lion Rosso
	Lion Nero		Unicorno
	Ruote		Vipera
S. Giovanni	Chiavi	S. Spirito (Oltrarno)	Drago Verde
	Drago S. Giovanni		Ferza
	Lion Doro		Nicchio
	Vaio		Scala

The map is designed to highlight buildings constructed or decorated during the fifteenth and early sixteenth centuries, or those associated with significant figures of the period.

Notes to Plan 24.3

1. Duomo: cathedral, with Giotto's campanile beside it
2. Baptistery of S. Giovanni: notable for doors by Ghiberti
3. Palazzo della Signoria (Palazzo Vecchio): seat of government
4. Bargello: then the Palazzo del Podestà, now an art gallery
5. Palazzo Guicciardini: family home of Francesco Guicciardini, opposite which stood in the house of Niccolò Machiavelli
6. Palazzo Medici-Riccardi: built for Cosimo de' Medici
7. Palazzo Pitti: built for Luca Pitti
8. Palazzo Rucellai: built for Giovanni Rucellai
9. Palazzo Strozzi: built for Filippo Strozzi
10. Ponte Vecchio: lined with shops; the raised corridor over these shops which links the Uffizi with the Palazzo Pitti was created by Vasari in the later sixteenth century
11. Orsanmichele: notable for statues around the exterior (see 22.2)
12. Ospedale degli Innocenti: foundling hospital designed by Brunelleschi

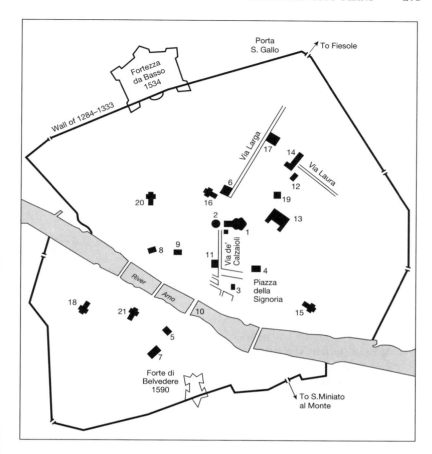

13. Ospedale S. Maria Nuova: city's principal hospital
14. SS. Annunziata: Servite church
15. S. Croce: principal Franciscan church; includes Pazzi Chapel
16. S. Lorenzo: with Biblioteca Laurenziana
17. S. Marco: Dominican house of which Savonarola was Prior in the 1490s
18. S. Maria del Carmine: Carmelite church, includes Brancacci Chapel decorated by Masolino and Masaccio
19. S. Maria degli Angeli: circular church designed by Brunelleschi
20. S. Maria Novella: principal Dominican church; includes important frescoes
21. S. Spirito: by Brunelleschi

24.4 Paris *c.* 1500

Paris was divided into three parts: *Cité*, *Ville* and *Université*. The first consisted of the Ile de la Cité, the island in the Siene. Most buildings of civic importance, together with many noble residences, were to be found on the right (north) bank of the river. The left (south) bank was, as it remains, the university district.

Notes to Plan 24.4

1. Bastille: fortress
2. Cemetery of the Innocents
3. Grand Châtelet: seat of *prévot* of Paris
4. Collège de Montaigu: one of the more notable colleges of the Renaissance period
5. Collège de Navarre
6. Collège de Sainte-Barbe
7. Halles: markets
8. Hôtel de Bourgogne: little-used residence of the dukes of Burgundy
9. Hôtel-Dieu: Paris's principal hospital
10. Hôtel d'Orléans: residence of the dukes of Orléans
11. Hôtel de Saint-Pol: king's residence
12. Hôtel des Tournelles: king's residence
13. Louvre: fortress around which many noble residences were grouped
14. Maison aux Piliers: seat of municipal government
15. Notre-Dame: cathedral
16. Palais: seat of Parlement of Paris, France's highest court of law; formerly the royal palace
17. Place de Grève: port and one of the city's few open spaces
18. Sainte-Chapelle: Gothic masterpiece built by St Louis
19. Sorbonne: theology faculty of University of Paris

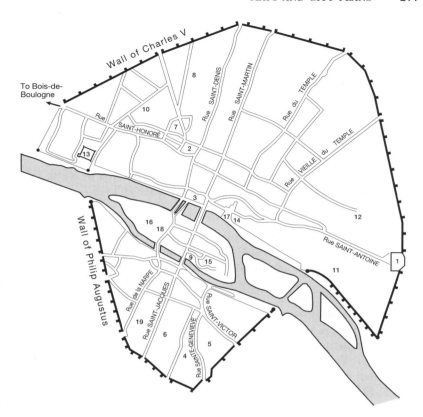

Wall of Charles V

To Bois-de-Boulogne

8

Rue SAINT-DENIS

Rue SAINT-MARTIN

Rue du TEMPLE

Rue VIEILLE du TEMPLE

Rue

10

SAINT-HONORÉ

7

2

13

3

16

18

17 14

12

Rue SAINT-ANTOINE

Wall of Philip Augustus

9 15

Rue de la HARPE

Rue SAINT-JACQUES

19

6

Rue SAINTE-GENEVIÈVE

Rue SAINT-VICTOR

4

5

11

1

24.5   Renaissance Rome

This map is designed to highlight buildings constructed or decorated during the fifteenth and early sixteenth centuries, or those associated with significant figures of the period. A selection of Rome's ancient monuments has been included and the names of hills are in italic. The city of Rome was divided into thirteen districts, called *rioni*.

Notes to Plan 24.5

1. Castel Sant'Angelo: originally Emperor Hadrian's mausoleum
2. Ospedale di S. Spirito in Sassia: hospital re-founded by Sixtus IV
3. Ponte Sisto: built by Sixtus IV for the Jubilee of 1475
4. SS. Apostoli
5. S. Clemente
6. S. Croce in Gerusalemme: pilgrimage church
7. S. Giovanni dei Fiorentini: focus of Rome's Florentine community
8. S. Giovanni in Laterano, with Lateran palace: pilgrimage church
9. S. Marco: with *palazzo*, now the Palazzo Venezia
10. S. Maria dell'Anima: focus of Rome's German community
11. S. Maria Maggiore: pilgrimage church
12. S. Maria sopra Minerva: Dominican church on the site of an ancient temple
13. S. Maria del Popolo: includes tombs of members of the Della Rovere family; located at Porta Flaminia, where most official parties entered the city
14. S. Maria in Trastevere
15. S. Paolo fuori le Mura: pilgrimage church
16. S. Pietro in Vaticano (St Peter's): pilgrimage church
17. S. Pietro in Montorio: with Bramante's Tempietto
18. S. Pietro in Vincoli: includes Julius II's tomb by Michelangelo
19. Palazzo della Cancelleria
20. Palazzo Colonna, at SS. Apostoli: urban headquarters of the Colonna family, traditional rivals of the Orsini. The power of these Roman nobles came from their dominance over the country around Rome.
21. Palazzo Farnese: by Antonio da Sangallo
22. Palazzo Massimo delle Colonne: by Peruzzi
23. Palazzo Orsini, Monte Giordano: urban headquarters of the Orsini family, traditional rivals of the Colonna.
24. Theatre of Marcellus: home of the Savelli family, allies of the Colonna
25. Vatican palace (see 24.6)
26. Villa of Cardinal Bessarion: suburban houses were traditionally located within a day's journey of a city, but not all were as close as this
27. Villa Farnesina: built for Agostino Chigi

S. Lorenzo fuori le Mura was also one of the main pilgrimage churches of Rome.

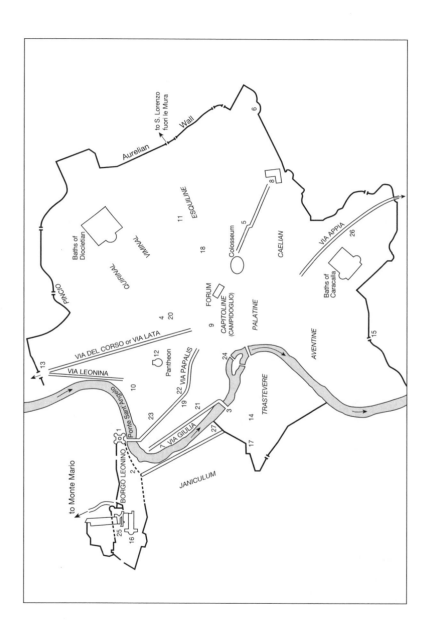

to S. Lorenzo
fuori le Mura

Aurelian Wall

6

Baths of
Diocletian

ESQUILINE

11

VIMINAL

18

Colosseum

5

8

QUIRINAL

CAELIAN

PINCIO

FORUM

9

CAPITOLINE
(CAMPIDOGLIO)

VIA APPIA

26

Baths of
Caracalla

4
20

VIA DEL CORSO or VIA LATA

PALATINE

13

VIA LEONINA

12

Pantheon

22

VIA PAPALIS

AVENTINE

15

10

23

19

21

24

3

TRASTEVERE

1

Ponte Sant'Angelo

VIA GIULIA

27

14

to Monte Mario

BORGO LEONINO

2

17

JANICULUM

25

16

24.6   The Vatican in the early sixteenth century

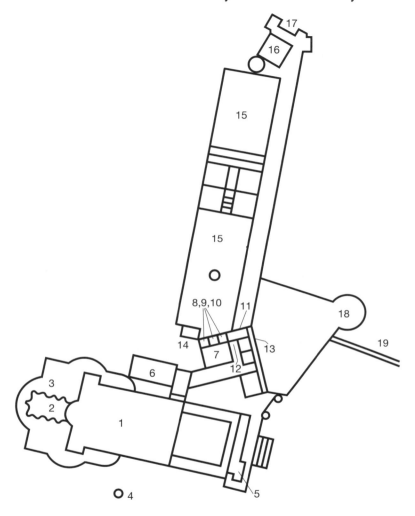

Notes to Plan 24.6

1. Old St Peter's basilica (Constantinian)
2. Tribune of Nicholas V
3. New St Peter's basilica
4. Vatican obelisk: now in Piazza S. Pietro
5. Benediction loggia
6. Sistine Chapel

7. Cortile del Pappagallo
8. Stanza dell'Incendio ⎫
9. Stanza della Segnatura ⎬ 'Raphael Stanze', from the frescoes by
10. Stanza d'Eliodoro ⎭ that master
11. Sala di Costantino
12. Chapel of Nicholas V: frescoed by Fra Angelico
13. Logge di S. Damaso: frescoed by Raphael
14. Torre Borgia: built and decorated for Alexander VI
15. Cortile del Belvedere: created by Bramante to link the Belvedere with the Vatican Palace
16. Statue court
17. Belvedere of Innocent VIII: decorated by Mantegna
18. Tower of Nicholas V
19. Corridor of Alexander VI: leading to Castel Sant'Angelo and along which Clement VII fled in 1527 prior to the Sack of Rome

24.7   Renaissance Venice

Venice is divided into six districts, called *sestieri*. Although the governmental heart of the city was at S. Marco, its banking and market area was at Rialto, linked to the Piazza S. Marco by means of the Merceria, the main shopping street. Prior to the nineteenth century, the only bridge across the Grand Canal was also at Rialto.

The map overleaf features buildings of artistic or other significance in the period up to *c*. 1530, listed by *sestiere*.

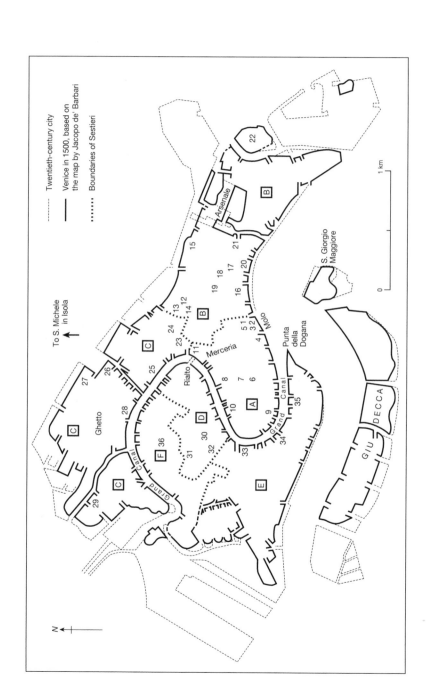

N←

To S. Michele
in Isola →

Twentieth-century city

Venice in 1500, based on
the map by Jacopo de' Barbari

Boundaries of Sestieri

1 km

0

Arsenale

S. Giorgio
Maggiore

B

22

B

15

21

20

17

18

19

16

51
32

Molo

4

Punta
della
Dogana

13 12
14

11
Merceria

23

Rialto

24

C

25

26

27

Ghetto

28

C

29

C

B

7
8

6

10

A

9

D

36

F

31

30

32

33

34

35

Grand Canal

Canal
Grand

E

GIU
DECCA

Notes to Plan 24.7

A   S. Marco

1. Basilica of S. Marco: doge's chapel
2. Palazzo Ducale (Doge's Palace): seat of government
3. Biblioteca Marciana: library of St Mark, based around the library of Cardinal Bessarion, donated to the Republic in 1468; between this building and the Palazzo Ducale is the Piazzetta where stand the pillars between which criminals were executed.
4. Piazza S. Marco, with the Campanile at its eastern end, Procuratorie Vecchie along its north side and Procuratorie Nuove to the south, these two blocks being government offices
5. Torre dell'Orologio: clock tower
6. S. Fantin: early sixteenth-century, probably by Scarpagnino
7. Palazzo Contarini del Bovolo: notable for its external spiral staircase of c. 1499
8. House of the printer Aldus Manutius
9. Ca' del Duca: a massive *palazzo* for Francesco Sforza, duke of Milan, on which building did not progress far
10. Palazzo Corner-Spinelli: by Codussi
11. Fondaco dei Tedeschi: headquarters of the German merchant community

B   Castello

12. SS. Giovanni e Paolo: principal Dominican church
13. Scuola Grande di S. Marco
14. Verrocchio's statue of Bartolomeo Colleoni
15. S. Francesco della Vigna
16. S. Zaccaria
17. Scuola di S. Giorgio degli Schiavoni
18. Palazzo Grimani, at S. Maria Formosa: home of the family of Cardinal Domenico Grimani
19. S. Maria Formosa
20. S. Giovanni in Bragora
21. Porta dell'Arsenale: official entrance to the state ship-building yard, Venice's largest employer
22. S. Pietro: cathedral of Venice, where the Patriarch had his throne; its physical distance from the governmental heart of Venice reflects the suspicion with which the Church was regarded by the Venetian authorities.

C   Cannaregio

23. S. Giovanni Crisostomo
24. S. Maria dei Miracoli

25. Ca' d'Oro: literally the 'house of gold', built for Marino Contarini
26. Abbazia and Scuola della Misericordia
27. Madonna dell'Orto
28. Palazzo Vendramin-Calergi: by Codussi
29. S. Giobbe

D   S. Polo
30. S. Maria Gloriosa dei Frari: principal Franciscan house
31. Scuola Grande di S. Giovanni Evangelista
32. Scuola Grande di S. Rocco

E   Dorsoduro
33. Ca' Foscari: built for Doge Francesco Foscari
34. Scuola Grande di S. Maria della Carità: now the Accademia delle Belle Arti
35. Palazzo Dario: built for Giovanni Dario

F   S. Croce
36. S. Giacomo dell'Orio

25 Bibliography

25.1 Historiographical note

The French historian Jules Michelet (1798–1874) was conscious of a general revival of learning in late medieval and early modern France, a revival to which he applied the term 'renaissance', in the appropriate volume of his *Histoire de France* (1855). Not until the Swiss scholar Jacob Burckhardt (1818–97) published *Die Kultur der Renaissance in Italien* (*The Civilisation of the Renaissance in Italy*, 1860) was 'renaissance' specifically applied to Italian history and culture. Burckhardt's work, which covers the period 1300–1600, is divided into six parts:

- The state as a work of art
- The development of the individual
- The revival of antiquity
- The discovery of the world and of man
- Society and festivals
- Morality and religion

For generations these categories profoundly influenced perceptions of the Renaissance period and, by extension, of 'Renaissance man', determining the topics chosen for investigation by historians, art historians and literary scholars. Various English translations of *The Civilisation of the Renaissance in Italy* are available.

The practice of viewing fifteenth- and sixteenth-century Europe, particularly Italy, through its literary and visual culture became entrenched, though recent decades have witnessed the publication of a wealth of social and political histories of the period, many of them by British and American scholars. The Renaissance period has now generated so vast a quantity of academic publications that this bibliography must, necessarily, be highly selective. The divisions are artificial, although it is hoped that they do not distort the interdisciplinarity which has become such a feature of Renaissance studies. Works in languages other than English have been kept to a mimimum.

Although this bibliography concentrates on monographs, the student of Renaissance Europe ought to consult a variety of learned journals, such as *Renaissance Studies, Renaissance and Reformation* and *Renaissance Quarterly*, all of which publish articles on history, art history, literature and philosophy, and *The Burlington Magazine* for art history.

Many of the fifteenth- and sixteenth-century histories, treatises and works of fiction mentioned throughout this volume are available in recent English translations.

25.2   General studies

C. Allmand, ed., *The New Cambridge Medieval History*, vol. VII: *c. 1415– c. 1500* (Cambridge, 1998)

R. Bonney, *The European Dynastic States 1494–1660* (Oxford, 1991)

T.A. Brady, H.A. Oberman and J.D. Tracy, eds, *Handbook of European History 1400–1600*, 2 vols (Leiden, 1994)

P. Burke, *Popular Culture in Early Modern Europe* (London, 1978)

J.R. Hale, *The Civilization of Europe in the Renaissance* (London, 1993)

D. Hay, *Europe in the Fourteenth and Fifteenth Centuries*, 2nd edn (London, 1989)

D. Hay and J. Law, *Italy in the Age of the Renaissance 1380–1530* (London, 1989)

H.G. Koenigsberger, G.L. Mosse and G.Q. Bowler, *Europe in the Sixteenth Century*, revised edn (London, 1989)

J. Larner, *Culture and Society in Italy 1290–1420* (London, 1971)

R. Mackenney, *Sixteenth-century Europe: Expansion and Conflict* (Basingstoke, 1993)

L. Martines, *Power and Imagination: City-states in Renaissance Italy* (London, 1979)

G. Mattingly, *Renaissance Diplomacy* (London, 1955)

25.3 Germany and the Holy Roman Empire, including the Swiss Confederation

G. Benecke, *Maximilian I (1459–1519): an Analytical Biography* (English trans., London, 1982)

F.L. Borchardt, *German Antiquity in Renaissance Myth* (Baltimore, MD, and London, 1971)

T.A. Brady, *Turning Swiss: Cities and Empire 1450–1550* (Cambridge, 1985)

H.J. Cohn, *The Government of the Rhine Palatinate in the Fifteenth Century* (Oxford, 1965)

P. Dollinger, *The German Hansa* (London, 1970)

F.R.H. Du Boulay, *Germany in the Later Middle Ages* (London, 1983)

M. Fernández Alvarez, *Charles V: Elected Emperor and Hereditary Ruler* (London, 1975)

B. Scribner, *Germany: a New Social and Economic History*, vol. I (London, 1995)

G. Strauss, ed., *Pre-Reformation Germany* (Basingstoke, 1972)

25.4 Bohemia, the Hussite state

R.R. Betts, *Studies in Czech History* (London, 1964)

F.G. Heymann, *George of Bohemia, King of Heretics* (Princeton, NJ, 1965)

H. Kaminsky, *A History of the Hussite Revolution* (Berkeley, CA, 1967)

J. Klassen, *The Nobility and the Making of the Hussite Revolution* (New York, 1978)

Odlozilík, *The Hussite King: Bohemia in European Affairs 1440–71* (New Brunswick, NJ, 1965)

25.5 Venice: republican society, culture and wealth creation

D.S. Chambers, *The Imperial Age of Venice 1380–1580* (London, 1970)

D.S. Chambers and B. Pullan, with J. Fletcher, eds, *Venice: a Documentary History 1450–1630* (Oxford, 1992)

R. Finlay, *Politics in Renaissance Venice* (London, 1980)

F. Gilbert, *The Pope, His Banker and Venice* (Cambridge, MA, and London, 1980)

J. Grubb, *Firstborn of Venice: Vicenza in the Early Renaissance State* (Baltimore, MD, and London, 1988)

J.R. Hale, ed., *Renaissance Venice* (London, 1973)

M.L. King, *Venetian Humanism in an Age of Patrician Dominance* (Princeton, NJ, 1986)

P. Labalme, *Bernardo Giustinian, a Venetian of the Quattrocento* (Rome, 1969)

F.C. Lane, *Venice and History: the Collected Papers of Frederic C. Lane* (Baltimore, MD, 1966)

F.C. Lane, *Venice, a Maritime Republic* (Baltimore, MD, and London, 1973)

F.C. Lane, *Studies in Venetian Social and Economic History*, ed. B.C. Kohl and R.C. Mueller (London, 1987)

F.C. Lane and R.C. Mueller, *Money and Banking in Medieval and Renaissance Venice*, 2 vols (Baltimore, MD, and London, 1985 and 1997)

O. Logan, *Culture and Society in Venice 1470–1790* (London, 1972)

M.E. Mallett and J.R. Hale, *The Military Organisation of a Renaissance State: Venice, c. 1400 to 1617* (Cambridge, 1984)

E. Muir, *Civic Ritual in Renaissance Venice* (Princeton, NJ, 1981)

B. Pullan, *Rich and Poor in Renaissance Venice: the Social Institutions of a Catholic State, to 1620* (Oxford, 1971)

D. Queller, *The Venetian Patriciate: Reality versus Myth* (Chicago, 1986)

D. Romano, *Patricians and Popolani: the Social Foundations of the Venetian Renaissance State* (Baltimore, MD, and London, 1987)

D. Romano, *Housecraft and Statecraft: Domestic Service in Renaissance Venice, 1400–1600* (Baltimore, MD, and London, 1996)

G. Ruggiero, *The Boundaries of Eros: Sex Crime and Sexuality in Renaissance Venice* (New York and London, 1985)

M. Tafuri, *Venice and the Renaissance* (Cambridge, MA, 1989)

25.6   Florence: the Medici in context

F. Ames-Lewis, ed., *Cosimo 'il Vecchio' de' Medici, 1389–1464* (Oxford, 1992)

A. Brown, *Bartolomeo Scala, Chancellor of Florence* (Princeton, NJ, 1979)

A. Brown, *The Medici in Florence: the Exercise of Language and Power* (Florence, 1992)

G.A. Brucker, *Renaissance Florence* (New York, 1969)

G.A. Brucker, *The Civic World of Early Renaissance Florence* (Princeton, NJ, 1977)

M.M. Bullard, *Lorenzo il Magnifico: Image and Anxiety, Politics and Finance* (Florence, 1994)

H.C. Butters, *Governors and Government in Early Sixteenth-century Florence* (Oxford, 1985)

R. De Roover, *The Rise and Decline of the Medici Bank* (Cambridge, MA, 1963)

F. Gilbert, *Machiavelli and Guicciardini: Politics and History in Sixteenth-century Florence* (Princeton, NJ, 1965)

R.A. Goldthwaite, *Private Wealth in Renaissance Florence: a Study of Four Families* (Princeton, NJ, 1968)

R.A. Goldthwaite, *The Building of Renaissance Florence* (Baltimore, MD, and London, 1980)

J.R. Hale, *Florence and the Medici: the Pattern of Control* (London, 1977)

D. Herlihy and C. Klapisch, *Tuscans and their Families: a Study of the Florentine Catasto of 1427* (English trans., New Haven, CT, and London, 1985)

G. Holmes, *The Florentine Enlightenment 1400–50* (London, 1969)

J. Hook, *Lorenzo de' Medici* (London, 1984)

D. Kent, *The Rise of the Medici: Faction in Florence 1426–34* (Oxford, 1978)

F.W. Kent, *Household and Lineage in Renaissance Florence: the Family Life of the Capponi, Ginori and Rucellai* (Princeton, NJ, 1977)

T. Kuehn, *Law, Family and Women in Renaissance Florence: Toward a Legal Anthropology of Renaissance Italy* (Chicago and London, 1991)

L. Martines, *The Social World of the Florentine Humanists* (London, 1963)

A. Molho, *Marriage Alliance in Late Medieval Florence* (Cambridge, MA, and London, 1994)

M. Phillips, *The Memoir of Marco Parenti: a Life in Medici Florence* (Princeton, NJ, 1987)

M. Rocke, *Forbidden Friendships: Homosexuality and Male Culture in Renaissance Florence* (New York and Oxford, 1996)

N. Rubinstein, ed., *Florentine Studies* (London, 1968)

N. Rubinstein, *The Palazzo Vecchio 1298–1532* (Oxford, 1995)

N. Rubinstein, *The Government of Florence under the Medici (1434–1494)*, 2nd edn (Oxford, 1997)

J.N. Stephens, *The Fall of the Florentine Republic, 1512–30* (Oxford, 1983)

R. Trexler, *Public Life in Renaissance Florence* (New York and London, 1980)

25.7   Papal States: the popes as princes

C.M. Ady, *The Bentivoglio of Bologna* (Oxford, 1937)

E. Breisach, *Caterina Sforza: A Renaissance Virago* (Chicago and London, 1967)

C.H. Clough, *The Duchy of Urbino in the Renaissance* (London, 1981)

D. Hay, *The Church in Italy in the Fifteenth Century* (Cambridge, 1977)

J. Hook, *The Sack of Rome* (London, 1972)

P.J. Jones, *The Malatesta of Rimini and the Papal State* (Cambridge, 1974)

J.E. Law, *The Lords of Renaissance Italy* (London, 1981)

M. Mallett, *The Borgias: the Rise and Fall of a Renaissance Dynasty* (London, 1969)

R.J. Palermino, 'The Roman Academy', *Archivium historiae pontificiae*, 18 (1980), pp. 117–56

P. Partner, *The Papal State under Martin V* (London, 1958)

P. Partner, 'The "budget" of the Roman Church in the Renaissance period', in E.F. Jacob, ed., *Italian Renaissance Studies* (London, 1960), pp. 256–78

P. Partner, *The Lands of St Peter: the Papal State in the Middle Ages and the Early Renaissance* (London, 1972)

P. Partner, *Renaissance Rome 1500–59: a Portrait of a Society* (Berkeley, CA, and London, 1976)

P. Partner, *The Pope's Men: the Papal Civil Service in the Renaissance* (Oxford, 1990)

P. Prodi, *Papal Prince – One Body and Two Souls: the Papal Monarchy in the Early Modern Period* (Cambridge, 1988)

C. Shaw, *Julius II: the Warrior Pope* (Oxford, 1993)

J.A.F. Thomson, *Popes and Princes 1417–1517: Politics and Polity in the Late Medieval Church* (London, 1980)

25.8   Naples: the southern kingdom

D. Abulafia, ed., *The French Descent into Italy, 1494–95: Antecedents and Effects* (Aldershot, 1995)

J.H. Bentley, *Politics and Culture in Renaissance Naples* (Princeton, NJ, 1987)

E. Pontieri, *Ferrante d'Aragona re di Napoli* (Naples, 1969)

A.J. Ryder, *The Kingdom of Naples under Alfonso the Magnanimous* (Oxford, 1976)

A.J. Ryder, *Alfonso the Magnanimous, King of Aragon, Naples and Sicily, 1396–1458* (Oxford, 1990)

25.9   Other Italian states, republican and princely

M.E. Bratchel, *Lucca 1430–94: the Reconstruction of an Italian City-republic* (Oxford, 1995)

A. Cole, *Art of the Italian Renaissance Courts* (London, 1995)

T. Dean, *Land and Power in Late Medieval Ferrara: the Rule of the Este 1350–1450* (Cambridge, 1988)

S.A. Epstein, *Genoa and the Genoese 958–1528* (Chapel Hill, NC, 1996)

W.L. Gundersheimer, *Ferrara: the Style of a Renaissance Despotism* (Princeton, NJ, 1973)

J.E. Law, *The Lords of Renaissance Italy* (London, 1981)

G. Lubkin, *A Renaissance Court: Milan under Galeazzo Maria Sforza* (Berkeley, CA, and London, 1994)

L. Martines, *Power and Imagination: City-states in Renaissance Italy* (London, 1979)

C. Meek, *Lucca, 1369–1400: Politics and Society in an Early Renaissance City-state* (Oxford, 1978)

T. Tuohy, *Herculean Ferrara: Ercole d'Este (1471–1505) and the Invention of a Ducal Capital* (Cambridge, 1996)

D. Waley, *The Italian City Republics*, 3rd edn (London, 1988)

E.S. Welch, *Art and Authority in Renaissance Milan* (New Haven, CT, and London, 1995)

25.10   Iberia: on the threshold of empire

J. Edwards, *The Spain of the Catholic Monarchs 1474–1520* (Oxford, 1998)

J.H. Elliott, *Imperial Spain 1469–1716* (London, 1963)

J.H. Elliott, *Spain and its World 1500–1700* (New Haven, CT, and London, 1989)

F. Fernández-Armesto, *Ferdinand and Isabella* (New York, 1975)

S. Haliczer, *The Comuneros of Castile* (Madison, WI, and London, 1981)

J.N. Hillgarth, *The Spanish Kingdoms 1250–1516*, 2 vols (Oxford, 1978)

H. Kamen, *The Spanish Inquisition* (London, 1965)

P. Liss, *Isabel the Queen* (New York and Oxford, 1992)

H.V. Livermore, *A New History of Portugal* (Cambridge, 1976)

A. MacKay, *Spain in the Middle Ages* (London, 1977)

A. MacKay, *Spain: Centuries of Crisis 1300–1474* (Oxford, 1997)

H. Nader, *The Mendoza Family in the Spanish Renaissance* (New Brunswick, NJ, 1979)

A.J. Ryder, *Alfonso the Magnanimous, King of Aragon, Naples and Sicily, 1396–1458* (Oxford, 1990)

25.11   France

D. Abulafia, ed., *The French Descent into Renaissance Italy, 1494–95: Antecedents and Effects* (Aldershot, 1995)

C.T. Allmand, *Lancastrian Normandy 1415–50: the History of a Medieval Occupation* (Oxford, 1983)

C. Allmand, ed., *Power, Culture and Religion in France, c. 1350–c. 1550* (Cambridge, 1989)

C.A.J. Armstrong, *England, France and Burgundy in the Fifteenth Century* (London, 1983)

F. Autrand, *Charles VI* (Paris, 1986)

F.J. Baumgartner, *Louis XII* (Stroud, 1994)

N.Z. Davis, *Society and Culture in Early Modern France* (London, 1975)

G. Duby, *France in the Middle Ages, 987–1460* (English trans., Oxford, 1991)

M. Jones, *The Creation of Brittany: a Late Medieval State* (London, 1988)

P.M. Kendall, *Louis XI* (London, 1971)

R.J. Knecht, *Francis I* (Cambridge, 1982)

R.J. Knecht, *Renaissance Warrior and Patron: the Reign of Francis I* (Cambridge, 1994)

R.J. Knecht, *The Rise and Fall of Renaissance France* (London, 1996)

P.S. Lewis, *Late Medieval France: the Polity* (London, 1968)

P.S. Lewis, ed., *The Recovery of France in the Fifteenth Century* (London and New York, 1971)

P.S. Lewis, *Essays in Later Medieval French History* (London, 1985)

J.R. Major, *Representative Government in Early Modern France* (London, 1980)

D. Potter, *A History of France 1460–1560: the Emergence of a Nation State* (Basingstoke, 1995)

M.G.A. Vale, *English Gascony, 1399–1453* (Oxford, 1970)

M.G.A. Vale, *Charles VII* (London, 1974)

25.12   Burgundy and the Low Countries

J. Calmette, *Les grands ducs de Bourgogne*, 2nd edn (Paris, 1987)

D. Nicholas, *Medieval Flanders* (London, 1992)

P. Spufford, *Monetary Problems and Policies in the Burgundian Netherlands 1433–96* (Leiden, 1970)

R. Vaughan, *Philip the Bold: the Formation of the Burgundian State* (London, 1962)

R. Vaughan, *John the Fearless: the Growth of Burgundian Power* (London, 1966)

R. Vaughan, *Philip the Good: the Apogee of the Burgundian State* (London, 1970)

R. Vaughan, *Charles the Bold: the Last Valois Duke of Burgundy* (London, 1973)

R. Vaughan, *Valois Burgundy* (London, 1975)

M. Weightman, *Margaret of York, Duchess of Burgundy, 1446–1503* (Gloucester, 1989)

25.13   British Isles

C.T. Allmand, *Henry V*, revised edn (New Haven, CT, and London, 1997)

S. Anglo, *Spectacle, Pageantry and Early Tudor Policy* (Oxford, 1969)

A.D. Carr, *Medieval Wales* (London, 1995)

S.B. Chrimes, *Henry VII* (London, 1972)

S.B. Chrimes, C.D. Ross and R.A. Griffiths, eds, *Fifteenth-century England, 1399–1509* (Manchester, 1972)

A. Cosgrove, *Late Medieval Ireland, 1370–1541* (Dublin, 1981)

R.R. Davies, *The Revolt of Owain Glyn Dŵr* (Oxford, 1995)

R.A. Griffiths, *The Reign of King Henry the Sixth* (London, 1981)

S.J. Gunn, *Early Tudor Government, 1485–1588* (Basingstoke, 1994)

S.J. Gunn and P.G. Lindley, eds, *Cardinal Wolsey, Church, State and Art* (Cambridge, 1991)

J. Guy, *Tudor England* (Oxford, 1988)

G.L. Harriss, *Cardinal Beaufort* (Oxford, 1988)

M.K. Jones and M.G. Underwood, *The King's Mother: Lady Margaret Beaufort, Countess of Richmond and Derby* (Cambridge, 1992)

M. Keen, *English Society in the Later Middle Ages, 1348–1500* (London, 1990)

D. Loades, *The Tudor Court* (London, 1986)
C. Ross, *Edward IV* (London, 1974)
C. Ross, *Richard III* (London, 1981)
J.J. Scarisbrick, *Henry VIII* (London, 1968)
D. Starkey, ed., *The English Court from the Wars of the Roses to the Civil War* (London, 1987)
B. Webster, *Medieval Scotland: the Making of an Identity* (Basingstoke, 1997)
B. Wolffe, *Henry VI* (London, 1981)

25.14 Scandinavia

D. Kirby, *Northern Europe in the Early Modern Period: the Baltic World 1492–1772* (London and New York, 1990)
B. and P. Sawyer, *Medieval Scandinavia: from Conversion to Reformation circa 800–1500* (Minneapolis, MN, and London, 1993)

25.15 Poland and Russia

G. Alef, *Rulers and Nobles in Fifteenth-century Muscovy* (London, 1983)
N. Davies, *God's Playground: a History of Poland*, vol. I (London, 1981)
J. Martin, *Medieval Russia, 980–1584* (Cambridge, 1995)

25.16 Hungary

T. Klaniczay and J. Jankovics, eds, *Matthias Corvinus and the Humanism in Central Europe* (Budapest, 1994)
G. Perjés, *The Fall of the Medieval Kingdom of Hungary: Mohács 1526–Buda 1541* (English trans., New York, 1989)

25.17 Byzantium and the Ottoman Empire

F. Babinger, *Mehmet the Conqueror and His Time* (English trans., Princeton, NJ, 1978)
J. Gill, *Personalities of the Council of Florence* (Oxford, 1964)
H. Inalcik, *The Ottoman Empire: the Classical Age 1300–1600* (London, 1973)
D.M. Nicol, *Byzantium and Venice: a Study in Diplomatic and Cultural Relations* (Cambridge, 1988)
D.M. Nicol, *The Last Centuries of Byzantium, 1261–1453* (Cambridge, 1993)
D.M. Nicol, *The Byzantine Lady: Ten Portraits, 1250–1500* (Cambridge, 1994)
S. Runciman, *The Fall of Constantinople, 1453* (Cambridge, 1965)
S. Runciman, *Mistra: Byzantine Capital of the Peloponnese* (London, 1980)

25.18   Urban life

J.C. Brown, *In the Shadow of Florence: Provincial Society in Renaissance Pescia* (New York and Oxford, 1982)

S.K. Cohn Jr, *The Laboring Classes in Renaissance Florence* (New York, 1980)

T. Dean and C. Wickham, eds, *City and Countryside in Late Medieval and Renaissance Italy: Essays Presented to Philip Jones* (London, 1990)

J. Edwards, *Christian Cordoba: the City and its Region in the Late Middle Ages* (Cambridge, 1982)

J. Henderson, *Piety and Charity in Late Medieval Florence* (Oxford, 1994)

D. Herlihy, *Pisa in the Early Renaissance: a Study of Urban Growth* (New Haven, CT, 1958)

D. Herlihy, *Medieval and Renaissance Pistoia: the Social History of an Italian Town* (New Haven, CT, and London, 1967)

D. Herlihy, *Medieval Households* (Cambridge, MA, 1985)

R. Mackenney, *Tradesmen and Traders: the World of the Guilds in Venice and Europe c. 1250–c. 1650* (London, 1987)

L. Martines, ed., *Violence and Civil Disorder in Italian Cities* (Berkeley, CA, 1972)

M. Mollat, *The Poor in the Middle Ages: an Essay in Social History* (New Haven, CT, 1986)

E. Muir, *Civic Ritual in Renaissance Venice* (Princeton, NJ, 1981)

L.L. Otis, *Prostitution in Medieval Society: the History of an Urban Institution in the Languedoc* (Chicago, 1985)

M.C. Rady, *Medieval Buda: a Study of Municipal Government and Jurisdiction in the Kingdom of Hungary* (Boulder, CO, 1985)

P. Ramsey, *Rome in the Renaissance: the City and the Myth* (Binghamton, NY, 1982)

J. Rossiaud, *Medieval Prostitution* (English trans., London, 1985)

G. Ruggiero, *Violence in Early Renaissance Venice* (New Brunswick, NJ, 1980)

N. Terpstra, *Lay Confraternities and Civic Religion in Renaissance Bologna* (Cambridge, 1995)

R.F.E. Weissman, *Ritual Brotherhood in Renaissance Florence* (New York and London, 1982)

See also 25.5 and 25.6 for Venice and Florence respectively.

25.19   Commerce

E. Ashtor, *The Levant Trade in the Later Middle Ages* (Princeton, NJ, 1983)

R.-H. Bautier, *The Economic Development of Medieval Europe* (London, 1971)

C.M. Cipolla, ed., *Fontana Economic History of Europe*, vol. I (London, 1972)

C. Cipolla, R. Lopez and H.A. Miskimin, 'The economic depression of the Renaissance?', *Economic History Review*, 2nd series, 16 (1963–64), pp. 519–29

R. De Roover, *The Rise and Decline of the Medici Bank* (Cambridge, MA, 1963)

R. De Roover, *The Bruges Money Market around 1400* (Brussels, 1968)

P. Dollinger, *The German Hansa* (English trans., London, 1970)

R. Ehrenberg, *Capital and Finance in the Age of the Renaissance: a Study of the Fuggers and their Connections* (English trans., New York, 1963)

R.A. Goldthwaite, *Private Wealth in Renaissance Florence: a Study of Four Families* (Princeton, NJ, 1968)

R.A. Goldthwaite, *Wealth and the Demand for Art in Italy, 1300–1600* (Baltimore, MD, and London, 1993)

F.C. Lane, *Andrea Barbarigo, Merchant of Venice 1399–1449* (Baltimore, MD, 1944)

F.C. Lane and R. Mueller, *Money and Banking in Medieval and Renaissance Venice*, 2 vols (Baltimore, MD, and London, 1985 and 1997)

T.H. Lloyd, *England and the German Hanse 1157–1611: a Study of their Trade and Commercial Diplomacy* (Cambridge, 1991)

R. Lopez and H. Miskimin, 'The economic depression of the Renaissance', *Economic History Review*, 2nd series, 14 (1962), pp. 408–26

G. Luzzatto, *The Economic History of Italy, from the Fall of the Roman Empire to the Beginning of the Sixteenth Century* (London, 1961)

M.E. Mallett, *The Florentine Galleys in the Fifteenth Century* (Oxford, 1967)

H.A. Miskimin, *The Economy of Early Renaissance Europe, 1300–1460* (Cambridge, 1975)

H.A. Miskimin, *The Economy of Later Renaissance Europe, 1460–1600* (Cambridge, 1977)

A. Molho, ed., *Social and Economic Foundations of the Italian Renaissance* (New York and London, 1969)

I. Origo, *The Merchant of Prato* (London, 1957)

J.R.S. Phillips, *The Medieval Expansion of Europe* (Oxford, 1988)

M.M. Poston and E. Miller, eds, *The Cambridge Economic History of Europe*, vol. II: *Trade and Industry in the Middle Ages*, 2nd edn (Cambridge, 1987)

M.M. Poston, E.E. Rich and E. Miller, eds, *The Cambridge Economic History of Europe*, vol. III: *Economic Organization and Politics in the Middle Ages* (Cambridge, 1963)

N.J.G. Pounds, *An Economic History of Medieval Europe*, 2nd edn (London, 1994)

P. Spufford, *Money and its Use in Medieval Europe* (Cambridge, 1988)

R. Unger, *The Ship in the Medieval Economy 600–1600* (London and Montreal, 1980)

25.20   Warfare

C.T. Allmand, *The Hundred Years War: England and France at War c. 1300– c. 1450* (Cambridge, 1988)

S. Anglo, ed., *Chivalry in the Renaissance* (Woodbridge, 1990)

C.M. Cipolla, *Guns and Sail in the Early Phase of European Expansion, 1400– 1700* (London, 1965)

P. Contamine, *War in the Middle Ages* (English trans., Oxford, 1984)

A. Curry and M. Hughes, *Arms, Armies and Fortifications in the Hundred Years War* (Woodbridge and Rochester, NY, 1994)

R. Davis, *Shipbuilders of the Venetian Arsenal* (Baltimore, MD, and London, 1991)

J.F. Guilmartin, *Gunpowder and Galleys: Changing Technology and Mediterranean Warfare at Sea in the Sixteenth Century* (Cambridge, 1974)

J.R. Hale, *Renaissance War Studies* (London, 1983)

J.R. Hale, *War and Society in Renaissance Europe, 1450–1620* (London, 1985)

J.R. Hale, *Artists and Warfare in the Renaissance* (New Haven, CT, and London, 1990)

B.S. Hall, *Weapons and Warfare in Renaissance Europe* (Baltimore, MD, and London, 1997)

J. Huizinga, *The Waning of the Middle Ages* (English trans., London, 1924)

M. Keen, *Chivalry* (New Haven, CT, and London, 1984)

F.C. Lane, *Venetian Ships and Shipbuilders of the Renaissance* (Baltimore, MD, 1934)

M.E. Mallett, *The Florentine Galleys in the Fifteenth Century* (Oxford, 1967)

M.E. Mallett, *Mercenaries and their Masters: Warfare in Renaissance Italy* (London, 1974)

M.E. Mallett and J.R. Hale, *The Military Organisation of a Renaissance State: Venice c. 1400–1617* (Cambridge, 1984)

G. Parker, *The Military Revolution: Military Innovation and the Rise of the West 1500–1800* (Cambridge, 1988)

S. Pepper and N. Adams, *Firearms and Fortifications: Military Architecture and Siege Warfare in Sixteenth-century Siena* (Chicago and London, 1986)

M. Prestwich, *Armies and Warfare in the Middle Ages: the English Experience* (New Haven, CT, and London, 1996)

C.J. Rogers, ed., *The Military Revolution Debate* (Boulder, CO, and Oxford, 1995)

S. Runciman, *The Fall of Constantinople, 1453* (Cambridge, 1965)

J.G. Russell, *Peacemaking in the Renaissance* (London, 1986)

M.G.A. Vale, *War and Chivalry: Warfare and Aristocratic Culture in England, France and Burgundy at the End of the Middle Ages* (London, 1981)

25.21 The Church: authority, hierarchy and administration

J. Bossy, *Christianity and the West, 1400–1700* (Oxford, 1985)

D.S. Chambers, *Cardinal Bainbridge and the Court of Rome* (Oxford, 1965)

C.M.D. Crowder, *Unity, Heresy and Reform: the Conciliar Response to the Great Schism* (New York, 1977)

J. Gill, *The Council of Florence* (Cambridge, 1959)

D. Hay, *The Church in Italy in the Fifteenth Century* (Cambridge, 1977)

K.J.P. Lowe, *Church and Politics in Renaissance Italy: the Life and Career of Cardinal Francesco Soderini, 1453–1524* (Cambridge, 1993)

J.W. O'Malley, *Praise and Blame in Renaissance Rome: Rhetoric, Doctrine and Reform in the Sacred Orators of the Papal Court, c. 1450–1521* (Durham, NC, 1979)

J.W. O'Malley, *The First Jesuits* (Cambridge, MA, and London, 1993)

P. Partner, *The Lands of St Peter: the Papal State in the Middle Ages and the Early Renaissance* (London, 1972)

P. Partner, *The Pope's Men: the Papal Civil Service in the Renaissance* (Oxford, 1990)

L. Pastor, *The History of the Popes from the Close of the Middle Ages* (English trans., London, 1891–1910): vols I–X cover the period 1305–1534

P. Prodi, *Papal Prince – One Body and Two Souls: the Papal Monarchy in the Early Modern Period* (Cambridge, 1988)

C. Shaw, *Julius II: the Warrior Pope* (Oxford, 1993)

P. Sigmund, *Nicholas of Cusa and Medieval Political Thought* (Cambridge, MA, 1963)

J.W. Stieber, *Pope Eugenius IV, the Council of Basle, and the Secular and Ecclesiastical Authorities in the Empire: the Conflict over Supreme Authority and Power in the Church* (Leiden, 1978)

J.A.F. Thomson, *Popes and Princes, 1417–1517: Politics and Polity in the Late Medieval Church* (London, 1980)

J.A.F. Thomson, *The Western Church in the Middle Ages* (London, 1998)

25.22 Belief, vision and reform within the Church

M. Aston, *Lollards and Reformers: Images and Literacy in Late Medival Religion* (London, 1984)

E. Cameron, *The European Reformation* (Oxford, 1991)

E. Duffy, *The Stripping of the Altars: Traditional Religion in England 1400–1580* (New Haven, CT, and London, 1992)

E.G. Gleason, *Gasparo Contarini: Venice, Rome, and Reform* (Berkeley, CA, 1993)

M. Greengrass, *The French Reformation* (Oxford, 1987)

J. Kejr, *The Hussites* (Prague, 1984)

G. Leff, *Heresy in the Later Middle Ages*, 2 vols (Manchester, 1967)

J. Le Goff, *The Birth of Purgatory* (English trans., London, 1984)

A.E. McGrath, *The Intellectual Origins of the European Reformation* (Oxford, 1992)

J.C. Olin, *Catholic Reform: from Cardinal Ximenes to the Council of Trent 1495–1563* (New York, 1990)

J.W. O'Malley, *Praise and Blame in Renaissance Rome: Rhetoric, Doctrine and Reform in the Sacred Orators of the Papal Court, c. 1450–1521* (Durham, NC, 1979)

L. Polizzotto, *The Elect Nation: the Savonarolan Movement in Florence 1494–1545* (Oxford, 1994)

R. Post, *The Modern Devotion* (Leiden, 1968)

R. Ridolfi, *The Life of Girolamo Savonarola* (English trans., London, 1959)

M. Rubin, *Corpus Christi: the Eucharist in Late Medieval Culture* (Cambridge, 1992)

J.B. Russell, *Witchcraft in the Middle Ages* (Ithaca, NY, and London, 1972)

R.N. Swanson, *Religion and Devotion in Europe c. 1215–c. 1515* (Cambridge, 1995)

T. Tentler, *Sin and Confession on the Eve of the Reformation* (Princeton, NJ, 1977)

M. Warner, *Joan of Arc: the Image of Female Heroism* (London, 1981)

D. Weinstein, *Savonarola and Florence: Prophecy and Patriotism in the Renaissance* (Princeton, NJ, 1970)

25.23   Humanism and literary culture: general

H. Baron, 'Franciscan poverty and civic wealth as factors in the rise of humanist thought', *Speculum*, 13 (1938), pp. 1–37

H. Baron, *The Crisis of the Early Italian Renaissance: Civic Humanism and Republican Liberty in an Age of Classicism and Tyranny*, revised edn (Princeton, NJ, 1966)

E. Bernstein, *German Humanism* (Boston, MA, 1983)

F.L. Borchardt, *German Antiquity in Renaissance Myth* (Baltimore, MD, and London, 1971)

G. Brucker, *The Civic World of Early Renaissance Florence* (Princeton, NJ, 1977)

P. Burke, *The Renaissance Sense of the Past* (London, 1969)

E. Cochrane, *Historians and Historiography in the Italian Renaissance* (Chicago and London, 1981)

B.P. Copenhauer and C.B. Schmitt, *Renaissance Philosophy* (Oxford and New York, 1992)

J. F. D'Amico, *Renaissance Humanism in Papal Rome: Humanists and Churchmen on the Eve of the Reformation* (Baltimore, MD, and London, 1983)

M. Dowling, *Humanism in the Age of Henry VIII* (London, 1986)

W.K. Ferguson, *The Renaissance in Historical Thought: Four Centuries of Interpretation* (Cambridge, MA, 1948)

A. Field, *The Origins of the Platonic Academy of Florence* (Princeton, NJ, 1988)

E.B. Fryde, *Humanism and Renaissance Historiography* (London, 1983)

E. Garin, *Italian Humanism* (English trans., Oxford, 1965)

D.J. Geanakoplos, *Greek Scholars in Venice: Studies in the Dissemination of Greek Learning from Byzantium to Western Europe* (Cambridge, MA, 1962)

D.J. Geanakoplos, *Byzantine East and Latin West* (Oxford, 1966)

M.P. Gilmore, *The World of Humanism, 1453–1517* (New York, 1952)

A. Goodman and A. MacKay, eds, *The Impact of Humanism on Western Europe* (London, 1990)

A. Grafton, ed., *Rome Reborn: the Vatican Library and Renaissance Culture* (New Haven, CT, and London, 1993)

A. Grafton and L. Jardine, *From Humanism to the Humanities: Education and the Liberal Arts in Fifteenth- and Sixteenth-century Europe* (London, 1986)

A. Grafton and L. Jardine, eds, *The Transmission of Culture in Early Modern Europe* (Philadelphia, PA, 1990)

W.L. Gundersheimer, ed., *French Humanism 1470–1600* (London, 1969)

J. Hankins, *Plato and the Italian Renaissance*, 2 vols (Leiden and New York, 1990)

G. Holmes, *The Florentine Enlightenment 1400–1450* (London, 1969)

G. Holmes, *Florence, Rome and the Origins of the Renaissance* (Oxford, 1986)

W. Kerrigan and G. Braden, *The Idea of the Renaissance* (Baltimore, MD, and London, 1989)

M.L. King, *Venetian Humanism in an Age of Patrician Dominance* (Princeton, NJ, 1986)

M.L. King and A. Rabil, eds, *Her Immaculate Hand: Selected Works by and about the Women Humanists of Quattrocento Italy* (Binghamton, NY, 1983)

B.G. Kohl and R.G. Witt, with E.B. Weller, *The Earthly Republic: Italian Humanists on Government and Society* (Philadelphia, PA, 1978)

J. Kraye, ed., *The Cambridge Companion to Renaissance Humanism* (Cambridge, 1996)

P.O. Kristeller, *Studies in Renaissance Thought and Letters*, 3 vols (Rome, 1956)

P.O. Kristeller, *Renaissance Thought*, 2 vols (New York, 1961 and 1965)

P.O. Kristeller, *Eight Philosophers of the Italian Renaissance* (Stanford, CA, 1964)

E. Lee, *Sixtus IV and Men of Letters* (Rome, 1978)

A.H.T. Levi, ed., *Humanism in France at the End of the Middle Ages and in the Early Renaissance* (Manchester, 1970)

L. Martines, *The Social World of the Florentine Humanists* (London, 1963)

C.G. Nauert, *Humanism and the Culture of Renaissance Europe* (Cambridge, 1995)

H.A. Oberman and T.A. Brady, eds, *Itinerarium Italicum: the Profile of the Italian Renaissance in the Mirror of its European Transformations* (Leiden, 1975)

J.W. O'Malley, *Praise and Blame in Renaissance Rome: Rhetoric, Doctrine and Reform in the Sacred Orators of the Papal Court, c. 1450–1521* (Durham, NC, 1979)

R. Porter and M. Tiech, eds, *The Renaissance in National Context* (Oxford, 1992)

A. Rabil Jr, ed., *Renaissance Humanism: Foundations, Forms and Legacy*, 3 vols (Philadelphia, PA, 1988)

C.B. Schmitt, Q. Skinner and E. Kessler, eds, *The Cambridge History of Renaissance Philosophy* (Cambridge, 1988)

J.E. Siegel, *Rhetoric and Philosophy in Renaissance Humanism* (Princeton, NJ, 1968)

F. Simone, *The French Renaissance: Medieval Tradition and Italian Influence in Shaping the Renaissance in France* (London, 1969)

Q. Skinner, *The Foundations of Modern Political Thought*, vol. I: *The Renaissance*, vol. II: *Age of Reformation* (Cambridge, 1978)

B. Smalley, *Historians in the Middle Ages* (London, 1974)

L.W. Spitz, *The Religious Renaissance of the German Humanists* (Cambridge, MA, 1963)

J. Stephens, *The Italian Renaissance: the Origins of Intellectual and Artistic Change before the Reformation* (London and New York, 1990)

C.L. Stinger, *The Renaissance in Rome* (Bloomington, IN, 1985)

D. Thornton, *The Scholar in his Study: Ownership and Experience in Renaissance Italy* (New Haven, CT, and London, 1997)

C. Trinkaus, *In Our Image and Likeness: Humanity and Divinity in Italian Humanist Thought*, 2 vols (Chicago, 1970)

C. Trinkaus, *The Scope of Renaissance Humanism* (Chicago, IL, 1983)

W. Ullmann, *The Medieval Foundations of Renaissance Humanism* (London, 1977)

D.P. Walker, *The Ancient Theology: Studies in Christian Platonism from the Fifteenth to the Eighteenth Century* (London, 1972)

R. Weiss, *Humanism in England during the Fifteenth Century* (Oxford, 1957)

R. Weiss, *The Renaissance Discovery of Classical Antiquity* (Oxford, 1969)

F.A. Yates, *Giordano Bruno and the Hermetic Tradition* (London, 1964)

25.24   Men of letters (arranged in alphabetical order of subject)

R. Black, *Benedetto Accolti and the Florentine Renaissance* (Cambridge, 1985)

J. Hankins, *A Life of Leonardo Bruni* (forthcoming)

D.O. McNeil, *Guillaume Budé and Humanism in the Reign of Francis I* (Geneva, 1975)

J.B. Gleason, *John Colet* (Berkeley, CA, 1989)

R. Bainton, *Erasmus of Rotterdam* (New York, 1969)

A.G. Dickens and W.R.D Jones, *Erasmus the Reformer* (London, 1994)

L.-E. Halkin, *Erasmus: a Critical Biography* (English trans., Oxford, 1994)

L. Jardine, *Erasmus, Man of Letters* (Princeton, NJ, 1993)

J. McConica, *Erasmus* (Oxford, 1993)

R.J. Shoeck, *Erasmus of Europe*, 2 vols (Edinburgh, 1990 and 1993)

D. Robin, *Filelfo in Milan: Writings 1451–1477* (Princeton, NJ, 1991)

C.M. Woodhouse, *George Gemistos Plethon: the Last of the Hellenes* (Oxford, 1986)

M. Phillips, *Francesco Guicciardini: the Historian's Craft* (Manchester, 1977)

R. Ridolfi, *The Life of Francesco Guicciardini* (English trans., London, 1968)

S. Anglo, *Machiavelli: a Dissection* (London, 1969)

G. Bock, Q. Skinner and M. Viroli, eds, *Machiavelli and Republicanism* (Cambridge, 1990)

F. Gilbert, *Machiavelli and Guicciardini: Politics and History in Sixteenth-century Florence*, (Princeton, NJ, 1965)

R. Ridolfi, *The Life of Niccolò Machiavelli* (English trans., London, 1963)

Q. Skinner, *Machiavelli* (Oxford, 1981)

C. Kidwell, *Marullus: Soldier Poet of the Renaissance* (London, 1989)

A. Kenny, *Thomas More* (Oxford, 1983)

R. Marius, *Thomas More: a Biography* (London, 1985)

E. McLeod, *The Order of the Rose: the Life and Ideas of Christine de Pizan* (London, 1976)

L. Febvre, *The Problem of Unbelief in the Sixteenth Century: the Religion of Rabelais* (English trans., Cambridge, MA, and London, 1982)

M. Screech, *Rabelais* (London, 1979)

R.G. Witt, *Hercules at the Crossroads: the Life, Work and Thought of Coluccio Salutati* (Durham, NC, 1983)

C.L. Stinger, *Humanism and the Church Fathers: Ambrogio Traversari (1386–1439) and Christian Antiquity in the Renaissance* (Albany, NY, 1977)

D. Hay, *Polydore Vergil: Renaissance Historian and Man of Letters* (Oxford, 1952)

25.25 Education

A.B. Cobban, *Medieval Universities, their Development and Organisation* (London, 1975)

A. Grafton and L. Jardine, *From Humanism to the Humanities: Education and the Liberal Arts in Fifteenth- and Sixteenth-century Europe* (London, 1986)

P.F. Grendler, *Schooling in Renaissance Italy: Literacy and Learning 1300–1600* (Baltimore, MD, and London, 1989)

P. Kibre, *The Nations in the Medieval Universities* (Cambridge, MA, 1948)

H. de Ridder-Symoens, ed., *A History of the University in Europe*, 2 vols (Cambridge, 1992 and 1996)

25.26   Printing

E. Armstrong, *Robert Estienne, Royal Printer* (Cambridge, 1954)

W. Blades, *The Biography and Typography of William Caxton* (London, 1971)

N. Blake, *Caxton, England's First Publisher* (London, 1976)

C.F. Bühler, *The Fifteenth-century Book: the Scribes, the Printers, the Decorators* (Philadelphia, PA, and London 1960)

M. Crisman, *Lay Culture, Learned Culture* (New Haven, CT, and London, 1982)

E.L. Eisenstein 'The advent of printing and the problem of the Renaissance', *Past and Present*, 45 (1969), pp. 19–89

E.L. Eisenstein *The Printing Press as an Agent of Change: Communications and Cultural Transformations in Early-Modern Europe*, 2 vols (Cambridge, 1979)

E.L. Eisenstein, *The Printing Revolution in Early Modern Europe* (Cambridge, 1983)

L. Febvre and H.-J. Martin, *The Coming of the Book: the Impact of Printing 1450–1800* (English trans., London, 1976)

L.V. Gerulaitus, *Printing and Publishing in Fifteenth-century Venice* (Chicago and London, 1976)

L. Hellinga, *Caxton in Focus: the Beginning of Printing in England* (London, 1982)

R. Hirsch, *Printing, Selling and Reading, 1450–1550* (Wiesbaden, 1967)

A. Kapr, *Johann Gutenberg: the Man and His Invention* (English trans., Aldershot, 1996)

M. Lowry, *The World of Aldus Manutius: Business and Scholarship in Rennaissance Venice* (Oxford, 1979)

M. Lowry, *Nicholas Jenson and the Rise of Venetian Publishing in Renaissance Europe* (Oxford, 1991)

G.D. Painter, *William Caxton: a Quincentenary Biography of England's First Printer* (London, 1976)

25.27   Science

J. Arrizabalaga, J. Henderson and R. French, *The Great Pox: the French Disease in Renaissance Europe* (New Haven, CT, and London, 1997)

M. Boas, *The Scientific Renaissance 1450–1630* (London, 1962)

J.V. Field, *The Invention of Infinity: Mathematics and Art in the Renaissance* (Oxford, 1997)

D.P. Lockwood, *Ugo Benzi, Medieval Philosopher and Physician, 1376–1439* (Chicago, 1951)

V. Nutton, ed., *From Democedes to Harvey* (London, 1988)

P.L. Rose, *The Italian Renaissance of Mathematics* (Geneva, 1975)

N.G. Siraisi, *Medieval and Early Renaissance Medicine* (Chicago and London, 1990)

L. Thorndike, *History of Magic and Experimental Science*, 8 vols (New York, 1923–58)

A. Wear, R.K. French and I.M. Lonie, eds, *The Medical Renaissance of the Sixteenth Century* (Cambridge, 1985)

25.28 Music

H.M. Brown, *Music in the Renaissance* (Englewood Cliffs, NJ, 1976)

I. Fenlon, ed., *The Renaissance, Man and Music*, 2 (London, 1989)

G. Reese, *Music in the Renaissance* (New York, 1954)

R. Strohm, *The Rise of European Music, 1380–1500* (Cambridge, 1993)

25.29 Visual arts: general

S. Anglo, *Images of Tudor Kingship* (London, 1992)

M. Barasch, *Light and Colour in the Italian Renaissance Theory of Art* (New York, 1978)

M. Barasch, *Theories of Art from Plato to Winckelmann* (New York, 1985)

M. Baxandall, *Giotto and the Orators: Humanist Observers of Painting in Italy and the Discovery of Pictorial Composition* (Oxford, 1971)

A. Blunt, *Artistic Theory in Italy, 1450–1600* (Oxford, 1940)

A. Blunt, *Art and Architecture in France 1500–1700*, revised edn (New Haven, CT, and London, 1992)

P. Bober and R. Rubinstein, *Renaissance Artists and Antique Sculpture* (Oxford 1986)

P.F. Brown, *Venice and Antiquity: the Venetian Sense of the Past* (New Haven, CT, and London, 1997)

L. Campbell, *Renaissance Portraits* (New Haven, CT, and London, 1990)

S.J. Freedberg, *Painting in Italy, 1500–1600*, 3rd edn (New Haven, CT, and London, 1993)

E.H. Gombrich, *Norm and Form: Studies in the Art of the Renaissance* (London, 1966)

E.H. Gombrich, *Symbolic Images: Studies in the Art of the Renaissance* (London, 1972)

F. Hartt, *History of Italian Renaissance Art*, 2nd edn (London, 1980)

A. Hauser, *The Social History of Art*, 4 vols (London, 1962)

L.H. Heydenreich, *Architecture in Italy 1400–1500*, revised edn (New Haven, CT, and London, 1996)

G. Kubler and M. Soria, *Art and Architecture in Spain and Portugal and their American Dominions 1500–1800* (Harmondsworth, 1959)

M. Levey, *The Early Renaissance* (Harmondsworth, 1967)

W. Lotz, *Architecture in Italy 1500–1600*, revised edn (New Haven, CT, and London, 1995)

J. Martineau and C. Hope, eds, *The Genius of Venice*, exhibition catalogue (London, 1983)

T. Müller, *Sculpture in the Netherlands, Germany, France and Spain 1400–1500*, revised edn (New Haven, CT, and London, 1992)

P. and L. Murrey, *The Art of the Renaissance* (London, 1963)

E. Panofsky, *Renaissance and Renascences in Western Art* (London, 1970)

J. Seznec, *The Survival of the Pagan Gods: Mythological Tradition and its Place in Renaissance Humanism and Art* (Princeton, NJ, 1953)

C. Seymour, *Sculpture in Italy 1400–1500*, revised edn (New Haven, CT, and London, 1992)

J. Shearman, *Mannerism* (Harmondsworth, 1967)

R. Strong, *Art and Power: Renaissance Festivals 1450–1650*, 2nd edn (Woodbridge, 1984)

P. Thornton, *The Italian Renaissance Interior 1400–1600* (London, 1991)

G. van der Osten and H. Vey, *Painting and Sculpture in Germany and the Netherlands 1500–1600*, revised edn (New Haven, CT, and London, 1992)

T. Verdon and J. Henderson, eds, *Christianity and the Renaissance: Image and Religious Imagination in the Quattrocento* (Syracuse, NY, 1990)

R. Weiss, *The Renaissance Discovery of Classical Antiquity* (Oxford, 1969)

J. White, *Art and Architecture in Italy, 1250–1400*, 3rd edn (New Haven, CT, and London, 1993)

E. Wind, *Pagan Mysteries of the Renaissance* (London, 1958)

25.30   Painting, drawing and engraving

J.J.G. Alexander, ed., *The Painted Page: Italian Renaissance Book Illumination*, exhibition catalogue (London, 1994)

F. Ames-Lewis, *Drawing in Early Renaissance Italy* (London, 1981)

F. Ames-Lewis, ed., *New Interpretations of Venetian Renaissance Painting* (London, 1994)

F. Antal, *Florentine Painting and its Social Background* (London, 1947)

L. Armstrong, *Renaissance Miniature Painters and Classical Imagery* (Reading, 1994)

M. Baxandall, *Painting and Experience in Fifteenth-century Italy* (Oxford, 1972)

P.F. Brown, *Venetian Narrative Painting in the Age of Carpaccio* (New Haven, CT, and London, 1988)

L. Campbell, *Renaissance Portraits: European Portrait Painting in the 14th, 15th and 16th Centuries* (New Haven, CT, and London, 1990)

L.D. Ettlinger, *The Sistine Chapel before Michelangelo: Religious Imagery and Papal Primacy* (Oxford, 1965)

J.R. Hale, *Artists and Warfare in the Renaissance* (New Haven, CT, and London, 1990)

P. Hills, *The Light of Early Italian Painting* (New Haven, CT, and London, 1987)

P. Humfrey, *The Altarpiece in Renaissance Venice* (New Haven, CT, and London, 1993)

P. Humfrey, *Painting in Renaissance Venice* (New Haven, CT, and London, 1995)

P. Humfrey and M. Kemp, eds, *The Altarpiece in the Renaissance* (Cambridge, 1990)

D. Landau and P.W. Parshall, *The Renaissance Print 1470–1550* (New Haven, CT, and London, 1994)

C.F. Lewine, *The Sistine Chapel Walls and the Roman Liturgy* (University Park, PA, 1993)

M. Meiss, *French Painting in the Time of Jean de Berry*, 2 vols (New York, 1974)

D. Norman, ed., *Siena, Florence and Padua: Art, Society and Religion, 1280–1400*, 2 vols (New Haven, CT, and London, 1995)

J. Steer, *A Concise History of Venetian Painting* (London, 1970)

R. Turner, *The Vision of Landscape in Renaissance Italy* (Princeton, NJ, 1966)

M. Wackernagel, *The World of the Florentine Artists* (Princeton, NJ, 1981)

E.S. Welch, *Art and Authority in Renaissance Milan* (New Haven, CT, and London, 1995)

J. White, *The Birth and Rebirth of Pictorial Space* (Cambridge, MA, 1987)

J. Wilde, *Venetian Art from Bellini to Titian* (Oxford, 1974)

W. Wolters and N. Huse, *Art of Renaissance Venice: Architecture, Sculpture and Painting* (Chicago, 1990)

H. Zerner, *The School of Fontainebleau* (London, 1969)

See also 25.29

25.31 Sculpture

C. Avery, *Florentine Renaissance Sculpture* (London, 1970)

M. Baxandall, *The Limewood Sculptors of Renaissance Germany* (New Haven, CT, and London, 1980)

S. Connell, *Employment of Sculptors and Stonemasons in Venice in the Fifteenth Century* (New York, 1987)

S.B. McHam, *The Chapel of St Anthony at the Santo and the Development of Venetian Renaissance Sculpture* (Cambridge, 1994)

R.J.M. Olson, *Italian Renaissance Sculpture* (London, 1992)

J. Pope-Hennessy, *Italian Gothic Sculpture* (London, 1955)

J. Pope-Hennessy, *Italian Renaissance Sculpture* (London, 1958)

M. Weinberger, *Michelangelo the Sculptor*, 2 vols (London and New York, 1967)

See also 25.29

25.32   Architecture

J. Ackerman, *The Villa* (London, 1990)

E. Arslan, *Gothic Architecture in Venice* (London, 1972)

D. Coffin, *The Villa in the Life of Renaissance Rome* (Princeton, NJ, 1979)

R.J. Goy, *Venetian Vernacular Architecture: Traditional Housing in the Venetian Lagoon* (Cambridge, 1989)

R.J. Goy, *The House of Gold: Building a Palace in Medieval Venice* (Cambridge, 1992)

D. Howard, *The Architectural History of Venice* (London, 1980)

C. Lazzaro, *The Italian Renaissance Garden* (New Haven, CT, and London, 1990)

R. Lieberman, *Renaissance Architecture in Venice 1450–1540* (London, 1982)

C.R. Mack, *Pienza: the Creation of a Renaissance City* (Ithaca, NY, and London, 1987)

J. McAndrew, *Venetian Architecture of the Early Renaissance* (Cambridge, MA, and London, 1980)

P. Murray, *The Architecture of the Italian Renaissance*, revised edn (London, 1986)

J. Onians, *Bearers of Meaning: the Classical Orders in Antiquity, the Middle Ages, and the Renaissance* (Princeton, NJ, 1988)

E.E. Rosenthal, *The Palace of Charles V in Granada* (Princeton, NJ, 1985)

S. Thurley, *The Royal Palaces of Tudor England* (New Haven, CT, and London, 1993)

C.W. Westfall, *In this Most Perfect Paradise* (University Park, PA, and London, 1974): on Nicholas V and urban planning in Rome

R. Wittkower, *Architectural Principles in the Age of Humanism*, revised edn (London, 1962)

See also 25.29

25.33   Lives of the artists (arranged in alphabetical order of subject)

M. Horster, *Andrea del Castagno* (Oxford, 1980)

S.J. Freedberg, *Andrea del Sarto*, 2 vols (Cambridge, MA, 1963)

J. Shearman, *Andrea del Sarto*, 2 vols (Oxford, 1965)

W. Hood, *Fra Angelico at San Marco* (New Haven, CT, and London, 1993)

R. Goffen, *Giovanni Bellini* (New Haven, CT, and London, 1989)

G. Robertson, *Giovanni Bellini* (Oxford, 1986)

C. Eisler, *The Genius of Jacopo Bellini* (New York, 1989)

R. Lightbown, *Sandro Botticelli*, revised edn (London, 1989)

H. Saalman, *Filippo Brunelleschi: the Cupola of Santa Maria del Fiore* (London, 1980)

A. Châtelet, *Robert Campin, le Maître de Flémalle* (Angers, 1996)

P. Humfrey, *Cima da Conegliano* (Cambridge, 1983)
A. Bovero, *L'opera completa del Crivelli* (Milan, 1974)
J. Beck, *Jacopo della Quercia* (New York, 1991)
J. Pope-Hennessy, *Luca della Robbia* (Oxford, 1980)
H. Wohl, *The Paintings of Domenico Veneziano, 1410–1461: a Study in Florentine Art of the Early Renaissance* (Oxford, 1980)
C. Avery, *Donatello: an Introduction* (New York, 1994)
B.A. Bennett and D.G. Wilkins, *Donatello* (Oxford, 1984)
H. Janson, *The Sculpture of Donatello* (Princeton, NJ, 1957)
J.C. Hutchison, *Albrecht Dürer: a Biography* (Princeton, NJ, and Oxford, 1990)
J.H. Wöfflin, *The Art of Albrecht Dürer* (London, 1971)
K. Christiansen, *Gentile da Fabriano* (London, 1982)
R. Krautheimer and T. Krautheimer-Hess, *Lorenzo Ghiberti*, 3rd edn (Princeton, NJ, 1982)
T. Pignatti, *Giorgione* (London, 1971)
S. Settis, *Giorgione's Tempest: Interpreting the Hidden Subject* (English trans., Oxford, 1990)
M. Kemp, *Leonardo da Vinci: the Marvellous Works of Nature and Man* (London, 1981)
M. Kemp, ed., *Leonardo on Painting: Anthology of Writings by Leonardo da Vinci, with a Selection of Documents relating to His Career as an Artist* (New Haven, CT, and London, 1989)
M. Kemp and J. Roberts, with P. Steadman, *Leonardo da Vinci: Artist–Scientist–Inventor* (New Haven, CT, and London, 1989)
S. Wilk, *The Sculpture of Tullio Lombardo* (New York, 1978)
P. Humfrey, *Lorenzo Lotto* (New Haven, CT, and London, 1997)
R. Lightbown, *Andrea Mantegna* (Oxford, 1986)
J. Martineau, ed., *Andrea Mantegna*, exhibition catalogue (London and New York, 1992)
J.T. Spike, *Masaccio* (New York, 1996)
P.L. Roberts, *Masolino da Panicale* (Oxford, 1993)
D. De Vos, *Hans Memling: the Complete Works* (English trans., London, 1994)
J.S. Ackerman, *The Architecture of Michelangelo* (Harmondsworth, 1971)
G. Bull, *Michelangelo, a Biography* (London, 1995)
H. Hibbard, *Michelangelo* (London, 1975)
M. Hirst, *Michelangelo and His Drawings* (New Haven, CT, and London, 1988)
P. Rylands, *Palma il Vecchio* (Cambridge, 1991)
C. Bertelli, *Piero della Francesca* (New Haven, CT, and London, 1992)
C. Ginzburg, *The Enigma of Piero: the 'Baptism', the Arezzo Cycle, the 'Flagellation'* (London, 1985)
R. Lightbown, *Piero della Francesca* (New York, London and Paris, 1992)
J. Pope-Hennessy, *The Piero della Francesca Trail* (London, 1991)

G. Paccagnini, *Pisanello* (London, 1973)

J. Woods-Marsden, *The Gonzaga of Mantua and Pisanello's Arthurian Frescoes* (Princeton, NJ, 1988)

L.D. Ettlinger, *Antonio and Piero Pollaiuolo* (Oxford, 1978)

M. Hirst, *Sebastiano del Piombo* (Oxford, 1981)

T. Connolly, *Mourning into Joy: Music, Raphael and Saint Cecilia* (New Haven, CT, and London, 1995)

L.D. and H.S. Ettlinger, *Raphael* (Oxford, 1987)

R. Jones and N. Penny, *Raphael* (New Haven, CT, and London, 1983)

A.M. Schulz, *Antonio Rizzo, Sculptor and Architect* (Princeton, NJ, 1983)

A.M. Schulz, *The Sculpture of Bernardo Rossellino and His Workshop* (Princeton, NJ, 1977)

D. Franklin, *Rosso in Italy: the Italian Career of Rosso Fiorentino* (New Haven, CT, and London, 1994)

B. Boucher, *Sculpture of Jacopo Sansovino* (New Haven, CT, and London, 1991)

D. Howard, *Jacopo Sansovino: Architecture and Patronage in Renaissance Venice* (London 1975)

C. Hope, *Titian* (London, 1980)

O. Pächt, *Van Eyck and the Founders of Early Netherlandish Painting* (English trans., London, 1994)

L. Campbell, *Rogier van der Weyden* (London, 1979)

C. Seymour, *The Sculpture of Verrocchio* (London, 1971)

J. Steer, *Alvise Vivarini* (Cambridge, 1981)

25.34   Patronage of the visual arts

F. Ames-Lewis, ed., *Cosimo 'il Vecchio' de' Medici, 1389–1464* (Oxford, 1992)

F. Ames-Lewis, ed., *The Early Medici and their Artists* (London, 1995)

J.H. Bentley, *Politics and Culture in Renaissance Naples* (Princeton, NJ, 1987)

P. Burke, *The Italian Renaissance: Culture and Society in Italy*, revised edn (Cambridge, 1986)

D.S. Chambers, ed., *Patrons and Artists in the Italian Renaissance* (London, 1970)

D. Chambers and J. Martineau, eds, *Splendours of the Gonzaga*, exhibition catalogue (London, 1981)

A. Cole, *Art of the Italian Renaissance Courts* (London, 1995)

T. DaCosta Kaufman, *Court, Cloister and City: the Art and Culture of Central Europe, 1450–1800* (London, 1995)

C. Elam, 'Lorenzo de' Medici and the urban development of Renaissance Florence', *Art History*, I (1978), pp. 43–66

R. Goffen, *Piety and Patronage in Renaissance Venice: Bellini, Titian and the Franciscans* (New Haven, CT, and London, 1986)

R.A. Goldthwaite, *Wealth and the Demand for Art in Italy, 1300–1600* (Baltimore, MD, and London, 1993)

E.H. Gombrich, 'The early Medici as patrons of art', in *Norm and Form: Studies in the Art of the Renaissance* (London, 1966), pp. 35–57

M. Hollingsworth, *Patronage in Renaissance Italy, from 1400 to the Early Sixteenth Century* (London, 1994)

M. Hollingsworth, *Patronage in Sixteenth-century Italy* (London, 1996)

B. Kempers, *Painting, Power and Patronage: the Rise of the Professional Artist in the Italian Renaissance* (Harmondsworth, 1992)

F.W. Kent and P. Simons, with J.C. Eade, eds, *Patronage, Art and Society in Renaissance Italy* (Oxford, 1987)

G.F. Lytle and S. Orgel, *Patronage in the Renaissance* (Princeton, NJ, 1981)

C. Robertson, *Il Gran Cardinale: Alessandro Farnese, Patron of the Arts* (New Haven, CT, and London, 1992)

M. Wackernagel, *The World of the Florentine Renaissance Artist: Projects, Workshops and the Art Market* (Princeton, NJ, 1981)

E.S. Welch, *Art and Society in Italy 1350–1500* (Oxford, 1997)

25.35 Exploration and its cultural impact

R. Bartlett, *The Making of Europe: Conquest, Colonisation and Cultural Change* (London, 1993)

L. Bethell, ed., *The Cambridge History of Latin America*, vol. I (Cambridge, 1984)

C.R. Boxer, *The Portuguese Seaborne Empire, 1415–1825* (London, 1969)

B.W. Diffie and G.D. Winius, *Foundations of the Portuguese Empire, 1415–1580* (Minneapolis, MN, and Oxford, 1977)

J.H. Elliott, *The Old World and the New, 1492–1650* (Cambridge, 1992)

F. Fernández-Armesto, *Before Columbus: Exploration and Colonisation from the Mediterranean to the Atlantic, 1229–1492* (Basingstoke and Philadelphia, PA, 1987)

F. Fernández-Armesto, *Columbus* (Oxford and New York, 1991)

A. Grafton, with A. Shelford and N. Siraisi, *New Worlds, Ancient Texts: the Power of Tradition and the Shock of Discovery* (Cambridge, MA, and London, 1992)

S. Greenblatt, *Marvelous Possessions: the Wonder of the New World* (Oxford, 1988)

L.N. McAlister, *Spain and Portugal in the New World 1492–1700* (Minneapolis, MN, 1984)

S.E. Morison, *The European Discovery of America: the Northern Voyages, AD500–1600* (New York, 1971)

S.E. Morison, *The European Discovery of America: the Southern Voyages, 1492–1616* (Oxford and New York, 1974)

K. Nebenzahl, *Maps from the Age of Discovery: Columbus to Mercator* (London and New York, 1990)

A. Pagden, *Spanish Imperialism and the Political Imagination* (New Haven, CT, and London, 1990)

J.H. Parry, *The Age of Reconnaissance: Discovery, Exploration and Settlement, 1450–1650* (London, 1963)

J.R.S. Phillips, *The Medieval Expansion of Europe* (Oxford, 1988)

D.B. Quinn, *England and the Discovery of America, 1481–1620* (New York, 1974)

P.E. Russell, *Prince Henry the Navigator: the Rise and Fall of a Cultural Hero* (Oxford, 1984)

G.V. Scammell, *The World Encompassed: the First European Maritime Empires c. 800–1650* (London, 1981)

H. Thomas, *The Conquest of Mexico* (London, 1993)

Index

Entries printed in **bold** indicate the principal sources of biographical material relating to the individuals concerned.